Frommer's®

W9-BJR-396

POSTCARDS

FROM

BOSTON

Boston is rediscovering and revitalizing its waterfront. For the best skyline views, see the box in chapter 7. © Kindra Clineff Photography.

The Hancock Tower rises behind the landmark 1877 Trinity Church, exemplifying Boston's unique mix of old and new. See chapter 8 for information about free Friday lunchtime organ recitals at Trinity Church. © *James Lemass Photography.*

The 60th-floor view from the John Hancock Observatory takes in the entire city. See the box in chapter 7. © Andy Caulfield/The Image Bank.

By day, Faneuil Hall Marketplace (a.k.a. Quincy Market) bustles with shoppers, strollers, and street performers. By night (opposite), it's abuzz with diners and revelers. See chapter 7. © Kindra Clineff/The Picture Cube.

Every Fourth of July, the Boston Pops Orchestra plays a free concert at the Hatch Shell on the Esplanade. The traditional finale, Tchaikovsky's 1812 Overture, features real cannons and churchbells. On summer Fridays, there are free outdoor movies at the Hatch Shell. See chapter 10. © Kindra Clineff Photography.

The U.S.S. Constitution, a.k.a. "Old Ironsides," earned its nickname during the War of 1812, when enemy bullets bounced off its hard oak hull. See chapter 8. © James Lemass Photography.

Something is in bloom at least half the year at the Public Garden, America's first botanical garden. See chapter 7. © Robert Holmes Photography.

Kids love the "Make Way for Duck-lings" tour, which follows the path of the Mallard family from Robert McCloskey's beloved children's classic. See chapter 7. © Kindra Clineff Photography.

Warm summer afternoons draw sun worshippers to the expansive lawns at the Public Garden. See chapter 7. © James Lemass Photography.

The courtyard at the Isabella Stewart Gardner Museum, designed in the style of a 15th-century Venetian palace, is as impressive as the eclectic collection of European and American art within. See chapter 7. © James Lemass Photography.

The highly interactive Museum of Science is a hit with kids and adults alike. You can meet a dinosaur, find out how much you weigh on the moon, or catch a super-wide-screen film at the Mugar Omni Theater. See chapter 7. © Kindra Clineff Photography.

Fenway Park's Green Monster has tantalized visiting baseball teams since 1912; it's the oldest park in the major leagues, and still has a hand-operated scoreboard. For tips on how to catch the Sox in action at Fenway, see chapter 7. © Dave Bartruff Photography.

Newbury Street, in the Back Bay, is Boston's premier neighborhood for shopping, gallery hopping, cafe sitting, and people watching. © Andrea Pistolesi Photography.

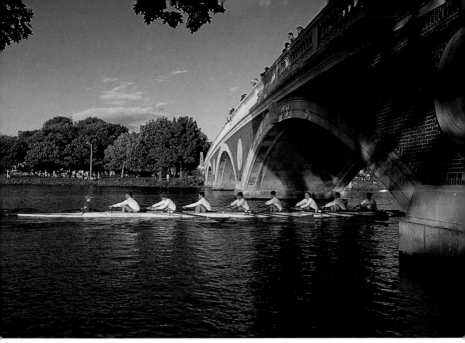

The Head of the Charles Regatta, held every October, draws preppies and rowers from every college and prep school in New England to the banks of the Charles River. See chapter 7. © James Lemass Photography.

Students lead free tours of Harvard University, across the river from Boston in Cambridge, twice a day on weekdays and once on Saturday during the school year. See chapter 7. © Andrea Pistolesi Photography.

Out-of-Town News is the unofficial center of Harvard Square in Cambridge. Just about every-body crosses paths here: students, shoppers, tourists, professors, skateboarders, subway riders, and people looking for newspapers from Argentina or Zimbabwe. © James Lemass Photography.

Mount Auburn Cemetery was the first of America's garden-style cemeteries. Oliver Wendell Holmes, Henry Wadsworth Longfellow, and Mary Baker Eddy are among the people with three names buried here. See chapter 7. © James Lemass Photography.

The serene setting that attracted Henry David Thoreau to Walden Pond in 1845 continues to draw runners, strollers, and swimmers every summer. See chapter 11. © Kindra Clineff Photography.

Lexington was the birthplace of the Revolutionary War; the "shot heard 'round the world" was fired in Minute Man National Historic Park. Actors in period costumes periodically re-enact the battle of April 18-19, 1775. See chapter 11. © James Lemass Photography.

The Mayflower II, *a full-size replica of the original that brought the first Pilgrims from England, is one of several attractions at Plymouth, 40 miles southeast of Boston. See chapter 11.* © Kindra Clineff Photography.

Frommer's® 2001

Boston

by Marie Morris

IDG Books Worldwide, Inc.
An International Data Group Company
Foster City, CA • Chicago, IL • Indianapolis, IN • New York, NY

ABOUT THE AUTHOR

Marie Morris grew up in New York and graduated from Harvard, where she studied history. She has worked for the *Boston Herald, Boston* magazine, and *The New York Times,* and she covers Boston for *Frommer's New England.* She lives in Boston, not far from Paul Revere.

IDG BOOKS WORLDWIDE, INC.

An International Data Group Company
919 E. Hillsdale Blvd.
Suite 400
Foster City, CA 94404

Find us online at **www.frommers.com**

ISBN 0-02-863743-7
ISSN 0899-322X

Editor: John Rosenthal/Dog-Eared Pages
Production Editor: Carol Sheehan
Design by Michele Laseau
Staff cartographers: John Decamillis, Elizabeth Puhl, Roberta Stockwell
Additional cartography: Ortelius Design
Page Creation by: IDG Books Indianapolis Production Department

SPECIAL SALES

For general information on IDG Books Worldwide's books in the U.S., please call our Consumer Customer Service department at 1-800-762-2974. For reseller information, including discounts, bulk sales, customized editions, and premium sales, please call our Reseller Customer Service department at 1-800-434-3422.

Manufactured in the United States of America

5 4 3 2 1

Contents

6   Dining   98

7   What to See & Do in Boston   135

8   Boston Strolls   177

List of Maps

AN INVITATION TO THE READER

In researching this book, we discovered many wonderful places—hotels, restaurants, shops, and more. We're sure you'll find others. Please tell us about them, so we can share the information with your fellow travelers in upcoming editions. If you were disappointed with a recommendation, we'd love to know that, too. Please write to:

Frommer's Boston 2001
IDG Books Worldwide, Inc.
909 Third Avenue
New York, NY 10022

AN ADDITIONAL NOTE

Please be advised that travel information is subject to change at any time—and this is especially true of prices. We therefore suggest that you write or call ahead for confirmation when making your travel plans. The authors, editors, and publisher cannot be held responsible for the experiences of readers while traveling. Your safety is important to us, however, so we encourage you to stay alert and be aware of your surroundings. Keep a close eye on cameras, purses, and wallets, all favorite targets of thieves and pickpockets.

WHAT THE SYMBOLS MEAN

✪ Frommer's Favorites

Our favorite places and experiences—outstanding for quality, value, or both.

The following abbreviations are used for credit cards:

AE	American Express	JCB	Japan Credit Bank
CB	Carte Blanche	MC	MasterCard
DC	Diners Club	V	Visa
DISC	Discover		

FIND FROMMER'S ONLINE

www.frommers.com offers up-to-the-minute listings on almost 200 cities around the globe—including the latest bargains and candid, personal articles updated daily by Arthur Frommer himself. No other Web site offers such comprehensive and timely coverage of the world of travel.

ACKNOWLEDGMENTS

Without Lisa Renaud and John Rosenthal, this book would not have been possible. Without my family, Kristin A. Goss, Betsy Buffington Bates, Betsy Block, Beth Teitell Mandl, Heather Morris, Liz First Raddock, Matthew Saal, and Cary Wyman, it would have been possible but not nearly as much fun. Many thanks to everyone.

—Marie Morris

The Best of Boston

1

Boston is hot. No, not on the thermometer—but in reputation, atmosphere, *buzz.* Tourism is up and crime is down. Real estate development is soaring and unemployment is plunging. High tech, health care, and financial services are huge, and Boston is a major player in all three. It's even in the hottest spot on the pop-culture radar—"The Sopranos." (And remember, the wiseguy who called it "Scranton, with clams" took a bullet in the head a minute later.)

Boston is also cool, and not just because there are cutting-edge college students all over the place. An unprecedented engineering marvel is unfolding along the waterfront, cleverly disguised as a giant construction site. The elevated expressway that slashes through downtown is moving underground, and Boston is preparing to show off. When the "Big Dig" highway-construction project ends (in 2004, assuming it's on schedule), it will leave behind a mecca of high technology that's also a relentlessly historic destination. The building boom may overshadow the famous 18th- and 19th-century architecture, but even rampant development can't change the colonial character of the central city.

It's not perfect, of course. Some drawbacks are large—the sickening real estate prices that go hand-in-hand with an economic boom, and the traffic headaches engendered by the Big Dig. Some are small—even a brief visit will confirm that the city's drivers have earned their terrible reputation, and the local accents are as ear-splitting as any in Brooklyn or Chicago. Although Boston is the biggest college town in the world, there isn't much of a late-night scene. And the inferiority complex that accompanies a reputation for being "like New York, but smaller" is less prevalent than it once was, but far from gone. Still, as it has for hundreds of years, Boston offers cosmopolitan sophistication on a comfortable scale, balancing celebration of the past with pursuit of the future.

Take a few days (or weeks) to get to know Boston, or use it as a gateway to the rest of New England. Plymouth's Pilgrim heritage, the historical and literary legacy of Lexington and Concord, the rugged coast and maritime tradition of the North Shore and Maine, Cape Cod's beaches, and the mountains of western Massachusetts, Vermont, and New Hampshire are all within easy driving distance and well worth exploring.

Here's hoping your experience is memorable and delightful.

Boston Orientation

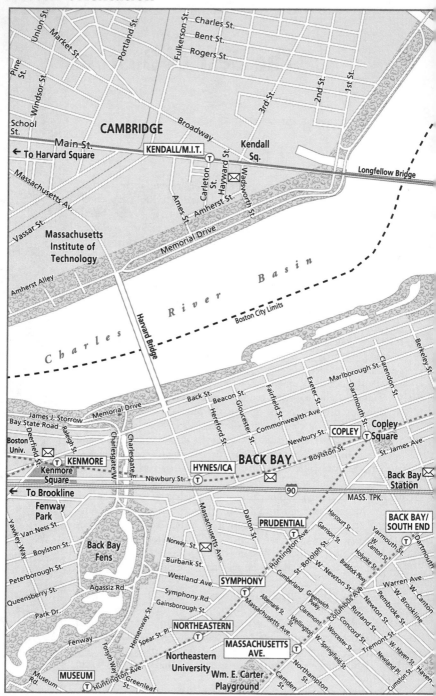

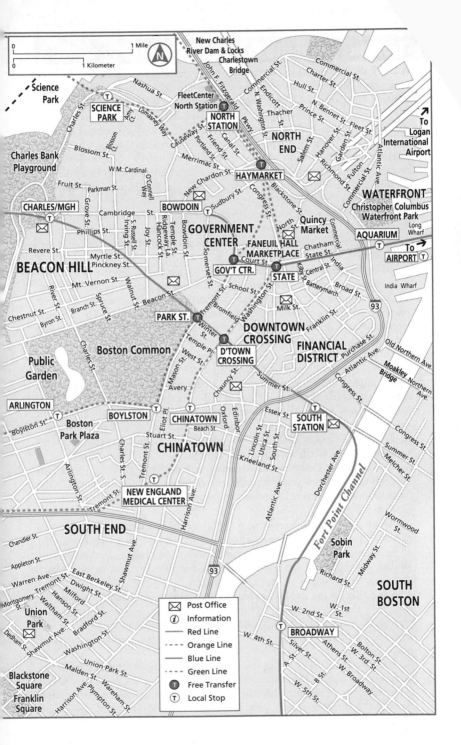

er's Favorite Boston Experiences

...rt of Fireworks. Twice during Independence Day festivities and again as the New Year begins, the firmament flashes in celebration. The Fourth of July fireworks are over the Charles River; the Harborfest display (in early July) and the First Night exhibition explode above the Inner Harbor. See chapter 2.

- **A Meal at Durgin-Park.** Dinner at this Boston institution (it opened in 1827) might start with oysters. It also might start with a waitress slinging a handful of napkins over your shoulder, dropping a handful of cutlery in front of you, and saying, "Here, give these out." The surly service usually seems to be an act, but it's so much a part of the legend that some people are disappointed when the waitresses are nice (as they often are). See chapter 6.

- **A Ride on a Duck.** A Duck Tour, that is. Board a reconditioned amphibious World War II landing craft (on Boylston Street in front of the Prudential Center) for a sightseeing ride that includes a dip in the river—for the Duck, not you. See chapter 7.

- **A "Ride" at the Museum of Science.** The Mugar Omni Theater, a five-story wraparound auditorium (or torture chamber, if you're prone to motion sickness), inundates you with sights and sounds and doesn't let go. Whether the film is on volcanoes or sharks, the larger-than-life images will draw you in. The museum proper (separate admission) is also a great place to explore, especially if you're traveling with children. See chapter 7.

- **A Bird's-Eye View.** On a clear day, you can see for at least 30 miles from the John Hancock Observatory or the Prudential Center Skywalk—not exactly forever, but an impressive view nonetheless. On a clear night, especially in winter, the cityscape looks like black velvet studded with twinkling lights. See chapter 7.

- **A Lunch Break with a Water View.** Head for the harbor or the river, perch on a park bench or a patch of grass, take off your watch, relax, and enjoy the spectacular scene. Whether it's sailboats or ocean liners, seagulls or scullers, there's always something worth watching. See chapter 7.

- **A Few Hours (at Least) at the Museum of Fine Arts.** Whether you're into Egyptian art or contemporary photography, furniture and decorative arts or the Impressionists, you're sure to find something at the MFA that tickles your interest. See chapter 7.

- **An Afternoon Red Sox Game.** Since 1912, baseball fans have made pilgrimages to Fenway Park, the "lyric little bandbox of a ball park" (in John Updike's words) off Kenmore Square. The seats are uncomfortable and too close together, the Red Sox last won the World Series in 1918, and you won't care a whit as you soak up the atmosphere and bask in the sun. See chapter 7.

- **A Spring Fling in the Public Garden.** Eight square blocks of paradise await you, filled with flowers, ornamental greenery, and flowering trees and shrubs. Pass through for a quick pick-me-up, take to the lagoon for a swan boat ride, or just enjoy the ducklings. They're on view in the flesh seasonally and in bronze year-round. See chapter 7.

- **A Vicarious Thrill.** Without so much as lacing up a sneaker, participate in the world-famous Boston Marathon. Stretch a little, so you won't cramp up. Drink plenty of fluids. Stake out a slice of sidewalk on Commonwealth Avenue and cheer as the runners thunder past. Then relax and put your feet up—you've earned it. See chapter 7.

- **A Walk Around the North End.** Boston's Little Italy (but it's *never* called that) has an old-world flavor you won't want to miss. Explore the shops on Salem Street, wander the narrow side streets, perhaps enjoy some pasta, and be sure to stop for coffee and a pastry at a Hanover Street *caffè*. See chapter 8.
- **A Newbury Street Safari.** From the genteel Arlington Street end to the cutting-edge Massachusetts Avenue end, Boston's legendary shopping destination is 8 blocks of pure temptation—galleries, boutiques, jewelry and gift shops, bookstores, and more. See chapter 9.
- **A Weekend Afternoon in Harvard Square.** It's not the bohemian hangout of days gone by, but "the Square" is packed with book and record stores, clothing and souvenir shops, restaurants, musicians, students of all ages, and so many people that it's a wonder there are any left at Faneuil Hall Marketplace. See chapter 9.
- **A Visit to Faneuil Hall Marketplace.** Specialty shops, an enormous food court, street performers, bars, restaurants, and crowds from all over the world make Faneuil Hall Marketplace (you'll also hear it called Quincy Market) Boston's most popular destination. See chapter 9.
- **A Free Friday Flick.** Families, film buffs, and impoverished culture hounds flock to the lawn in front of the Hatch Shell on the Esplanade for free movies (*The Wizard of Oz* or *Raiders of the Lost Ark,* for example) on Friday nights in the summer. Bring something to sit on, and maybe a sweater. See chapter 10.
- **A Concert Alfresco.** Summer nights swing to the beat of outdoor music by amateurs and professionals. A great spot for free jazz is Christopher Columbus Park, on the waterfront, where performances take place Fridays at 6:30pm. See chapter 10.

2 Best Hotel Bets

For details, see chapter 5.

- **Best Historic Hotel:** The **Ritz-Carlton, Boston,** 15 Arlington St. (☎ 800/241-3333), has been a landmark and a legend since it opened in 1927. A magnet for celebrities, politicians, and waterfowl (Louis, the hero of E. B. White's *The Trumpet of the Swan,* stayed here), it's a perfect place to soak up the atmosphere of a bygone age.
- **Best for Business Travelers:** In the heart of the Financial District, **Le Meridien Boston,** 250 Franklin St. (☎ 800/543-4300), has well-equipped rooms for business travelers, a full-service business center, and a great health club. You might not even need to leave the building, but in case you do, a weather report comes to your door every evening.
- **Best for a Romantic Getaway:** The intimate atmosphere and elegant furnishings make a suite at the **Eliot Hotel,** 370 Commonwealth Ave. (☎ 800/44-ELIOT), a great spot for a rendezvous. If you and your beloved need some time apart, close the French doors—you can be in separate rooms yet still maintain eye contact.
- **Best Lobby for Pretending That You're Rich:** As you walk around the ground floor of the **Boston Harbor Hotel,** 70 Rowes Wharf (☎ 800/752-7077), make believe you just tied up your yacht out front and are keeping an eye on it. Then suddenly "remember" an important meeting in the Financial District and head across the street.
- **Best for Families:** The **Doubletree Guest Suites,** 400 Soldiers Field Rd. (☎ 800/222-TREE), offers two rooms for the price of one, with two TVs and

People Are Talking About . . .

- The Big Dig: For the typical out-of-towner, the Central Artery/Third Harbor Tunnel project (its formal name) is the monstrosity that lies between you at the airport and your bed at a downtown hotel. For Bostonians who live, work, or play nearby, it's an ever-changing headache and object of fascination. For everyone, it's a great icebreaker. (To learn more, see the box on page 53).

- Fenway Park: In 1999 the Red Sox announced ambitious plans to demolish most of the current 1912 ballpark (preserving the legendary left field wall), move the playing field, and radically redesign the neighborhood. Many neighbors responded with a resounding "Oh, really?" Considering how long it took to replace Boston Garden (with the FleetCenter), this is likely to be a topic of conversation for years to come.

- Hollywood East: By the time you read this, the movie version of *The Perfect Storm* will probably be either a blockbuster or a bust. It's just one of a dozen or so film projects that have used the Boston area as a backdrop in the past few years. The best known (to date) is *Good Will Hunting*—if you have a favorite scene, by all means ask your fellow cocktail-party attendee whether it looks authentic. Also in the works: David Mamet's *State and Main*.

- The Technology Economy: The confluence of Internet innovation and venture capital makes eastern Massachusetts a hot zone. High tech touches every segment of the business community, from financial services to pharmaceuticals. The closer you are to MIT, the likelier you are to hear something that makes you say, "You can *do* that?"

- Sports, Politics, and Revenge: They're reputed to be the city's real obsessions. Throw in religion and money, and you'll have a spirited discussion on your hands in no time.

a refrigerator, and a nice pool. The location, straddling Boston and Cambridge, is especially good if you're driving from the west—you leave the turnpike before downtown traffic shatters the peace in the back of the minivan.

- **Best for Travelers with Disabilities:** The **Royal Sonesta Hotel,** 5 Cambridge Pkwy., Cambridge (☎ **800/SONESTA**), trains its staff in disability awareness and offers 11 wheelchair-accessible rooms, some of which adjoin standard units, and 16 rooms for guests with hearing impairments. A wheelchair ramp for use in conference rooms is available. Across the river, 48 fully accessible rooms at the **Westin Copley Place Boston,** 10 Huntington Ave. (☎ **800/WESTIN-1**), adjoin standard units.

- **Best Value:** The **Newbury Guest House,** 261 Newbury St. (☎ **617/ 437-7666**), would be a good deal even if it weren't ideally located in the heart of the Back Bay. Room prices even include continental breakfast.

- **Best Service:** Hands down, the **Four Seasons Hotel,** 200 Boylston St. (☎ **800/ 332-3442**). The chain's standards are sky-high, and the friendly and efficient staff here meets and exceeds them.

- **Best Pool:** The **Sheraton Boston Hotel,** 39 Dalton St. (☎ **800/225-2008**), has a great indoor-outdoor pool with a retractable dome.

- **Hidden Jewel:** The oldest hotel property in the country is one of Boston's most pleasant surprises. The recently renovated **Omni Parker House,** 60 School St. (☎ **800/THE-OMNI**), is the best-looking 145-year-old in town.
- **Best Views:** Several hotels offer impressive views of their immediate surroundings, but for a picture-postcard panorama of Boston and Cambridge, head to the upper floors of the **Westin Copley Place Boston** (see above).

3 Best Dining Bets

For details, see chapter 6.

- **Best, Period:** If you have only one meal during your visit, make it dinner at **Rialto,** in the Charles Hotel, 1 Bennett St., Cambridge (☎ **617/661-5050**).
- **Best Spot for Romance:** Soft lighting, well-spaced tables, and cushy surroundings make **Icarus,** 3 Appleton St. (☎ **617/426-1790**), the perfect place for trysting. And because it's underground, there's no view to distract you from your beloved.
- **Best Spot for a Business Lunch:** Plenty of deals go down at private clubs and formal restaurants, but that can take hours. Leave an impression with your nononsense approach and a quick but delicious meal at **Cosí Sandwich Bar,** 53 State St. (☎ **617/723-4447**), 14 Milk St. (☎ **617/426-7565**), or 133 Federal St. (☎ **617/292-2674**).
- **Best Spot for a Celebration:** Cool your heels at the bar at **Dalí,** 415 Washington St., Somerville (☎ **617/661-3254**), and toast your good news with sangria while you wait for a table. (Finally, a restaurant that makes you glad it doesn't take reservations.) The dishes on the tapas menu are perfect for sharing, and the atmosphere is lively and festive.
- **Best Decor:** The luxurious banquettes, gorgeous paintings and flowers, and picture windows overlooking the Public Garden make **Aujourd'hui,** in the Four Seasons Hotel, 200 Boylston St. (☎ **617/451-2071**), feel like an extremely elegant tree house.
- **Best View:** The dining room at the **Bay Tower,** 60 State St. (☎ **617/ 723-1666**), isn't the highest in Boston, but its view is the most impressive. From the palatial 33rd floor, everyone in the room (not just people near the windows) can see what's afoot on the harbor and at the airport. A close second is the 52nd-story panorama from **Top of the Hub,** 800 Boylston St., Prudential Center (☎ **617/536-1775**), especially at dusk.
- **Best Wine List:** Organized by characteristics (from light to rich) rather than by vintage or provenance, the excellent offerings at the **Blue Room,** 1 Kendall Sq., Cambridge (☎ **617/494-9034**), are arranged in the most user-friendly way imaginable.
- **Best Value:** At the **Midwest Grill,** 1122 Cambridge St., Cambridge (☎ **617/ 354-7536**), the hits just keep on coming. The sword-wielding waiters bring succulent grilled meats until you ask (or beg) them to stop. Arrive hungry, and you'll definitely get your money's worth.
- **Best for Kids:** The wood-fired brick ovens of the **Bertucci's** chain are magnets for little eyes, and the pizza that comes out of them is equally enthralling. Picky parents will be happy here, too. Try the locations at Faneuil Hall Marketplace (☎ **617/227-7889**), 43 Stanhope St., Back Bay (☎ **617/247-6161**), and 21 Brattle St., Harvard Square, Cambridge (☎ **617/864-4748**).

- **Best Raw Bar:** After just a few moments of gobbling fresh seafood and being hypnotized by the shuckers at **Ye Olde Union Oyster House,** 41 Union St. (☎ **617/227-2750**), you might find yourself feeling sorry for the people who wound up with the pearls instead of the oysters.

- **Best Place for a Classic Boston Experience: Durgin-Park,** 340 Faneuil Hall Marketplace (☎ **617/227-2038**), has packed 'em in since 1827. From tycoon to tourist, everyone is happy here except the famously crotchety waitresses. It's a classic, not a relic.

- **Best American Cuisine:** Chef and co-owner Bob Calderone of **Anago,** in the Lenox Hotel, 65 Exeter St. (☎ **617/266-6222**), displays a creative style that never strays into hey-look-at-me territory.

- **Best French Cuisine:** At **Maison Robert,** 45 School St. (☎ **617/227-3370**), the atmosphere is as impressive as the food. You won't find better French cuisine anywhere in the city—but you might find visiting French chefs, who make this one of their first stops in Boston.

- **Best Bistro:** A friend who knows both Paris and Boston swears by **Les Zygomates,** 129 South St. (☎ **617/542-5108**), where you can enjoy the flavor of the Left Bank in a congenial American setting.

- **Best Italian Cuisine:** "Cuisine" suggests a level of refinement, and **Mamma Maria,** 3 North Sq. (☎ **617/523-0077**), has it. In a lovely setting, it offers remarkable regional Italian fare in the red-sauce paradise of the North End.

- **Best Seafood: Legal Sea Foods,** 800 Boylston St., in the Prudential Center (☎ **617/266-6800**), and other locations, does one thing and does it exceptionally well. It's a chain for a great reason—people can't get enough of the freshest seafood in the area.

- **Best Pizza:** Considering how well pizza travels, it's surprising that the branches of **Pizzeria Regina** can't seem to get it quite right. For the real thing, head to the North End original, at 10[1/2] Thacher St. (☎ **617/227-0765**).

- **Best Investment (of Time and Money):** Dinner at **L'Espalier,** 30 Gloucester St. (☎ **617/262-3023**), is an event. As you enter, you might hear the valet-parking attendant say, "Enjoy your evening." Thanks to the grand cuisine and solicitous service, you certainly will.

- **Best Outdoor Dining:** Good food in a comfortable open-air setting sounds easy but evidently isn't, judging by the number of restaurants that can't manage both. The planets were perfectly aligned when **Upstairs at the Pudding,** 10 Holyoke St., Cambridge (☎ **617/864-1933**), opened its peaceful, verdant terrace.

- **Best Afternoon Tea:** At the **Ritz-Carlton,** 15 Arlington St. (☎ **617/536-5700**), afternoon tea is an elegant, traditional affair. You'll want to sit up and act like a lady or gentleman while you enjoy scones and Devonshire cream, among other treats.

- **Best Brunch:** The insane displays at many of the top hotels are well worth the monetary and caloric compromises. If you're looking for a delicious meal that won't destroy your budget and waistline, join the throng at the **S&S Restaurant,** 1334 Cambridge St., Cambridge (☎ **617/354-0777**).

- **Best for Pretheater Dinner:** Snappy service is the rule all over Chinatown. Start your evening at **East Ocean City,** 27 Beach St. (☎ **617/542-2504**), and you'll be both prompt and well fed.

- **Best Barbecue:** There's so much stuff on the walls of **Redbones,** 55 Chester St., Somerville (☎ **617/628-2200**)—photos, posters, T-shirts, and hand-lettered signs—that you might be distracted from your goal. Then your nose reminds you: Southern barbecue.

Planning Your Trip: The Basics

2

This chapter addresses the practical issues that arise after you select a destination. Now that you've decided to visit Boston, how do you get there? How much will it cost? When should you go? How can you learn more? You'll find answers here, along with information about the climate and the events, festivals, and parades you may want to see.

1 Visitor Information

The **Greater Boston Convention & Visitors Bureau,** 2 Copley Place, Suite 105, Boston, MA 02116-6501 (☎ **888/SEE-BOSTON** or 617/536-4100, 0171/431-3434 in the U.K.; fax 617/424-7664; www.bostonusa.com; e-mail: visitor@bostonusa.com), offers a comprehensive visitor information kit and a "Kids Love Boston" kit. Each costs $5.25 and includes a complete travel planner, guidebook, map, and coupon book with shopping, dining, attraction, and nightlife discounts. Smaller planners that concentrate on specific seasons or events often are available free. Call the main number to gain access to **"Boston By Phone,"** a service that provides information on attractions, dining, performing arts and nightlife, shopping, and travel services.

The **Massachusetts Office of Travel and Tourism,** 100 Cambridge St., 13th floor, Boston, MA 02202 (☎ **800/227-6277** or 617/727-3201; fax 617/727-6525; www.mass-vacation.com; e-mail: vacationinfo@ state.ma.us), has a great Web site that even offers a "lobster tutorial." The office's free *Getaway Guide* magazine includes information about statewide attractions and lodgings, a map, and a seasonal calendar.

For information about Cambridge, contact the **Cambridge Office for Tourism,** 18 Brattle St., Cambridge, MA 02138 (☎ **800/ 862-5678** or 617/441-2884; fax 617/441-7736; www.cambridge-usa. org; e-mail: info@cambridge-usa.org).

2 Money

Monetary descriptions and currency exchange information for foreign travelers appear in chapter 3, "For Foreign Visitors."

Boston can be an expensive destination, but if you know where to look (this book makes a good start), you'll find many money-saving opportunities.

ATMs The two most popular ATM networks are **Cirrus** (☎ **800/ 424-7787;** www.mastercard.com/atm/) and **PLUS Global ATM**

Planning Basics

What Things Cost in Boston — U.S. $

Taxi from airport to downtown or Back Bay	18.00–24.00
Water shuttle from airport to downtown	10.00
Bus from airport to downtown or Back Bay	6.00–8.00
MBTA subway token	85¢
Double at Omni Parker House hotel (expensive)	189.00–295.00
Double at Newbury Guest House (moderate)	100.00–155.00
Double at Longwood Inn (inexpensive)	65.00–109.00
Lunch for one at Ye Olde Union Oyster House (expensive)	10.00–23.00
Lunch for one at Durgin-Park (moderate)	6.00–20.00
Lunch for one at Bartley's Burger Cottage (inexpensive)	4.00–10.50
Dinner for one, without wine, at Rialto (very expensive)	23.00–50.00
Dinner for one, without wine, at Legal Sea Foods (expensive)	14.00–30.00
Dinner for one, without wine, at the Elephant Walk (moderate)	10.00–23.00
Glass of beer	2.75–5.00
Coca-Cola	75¢–1.50
Cup of coffee	1.00 and up
Roll of ASA 100 Kodacolor film, 36 exposures	6.75–8.00
Adult admission to the Museum of Fine Arts	12.00
Child (under 18) admission to the Museum of Fine Arts	free
Movie ticket	5.00–8.50
Theater ticket	30.00–90.00

Locator Service (☎ **800/843-7587;** www.visa.com/atms). Call before you leave home to check for locations. Local networks typically impose a fee ($1 to $2) for access by a customer whose account is with a different bank, and your bank at home might also charge you. At Massachusetts banks, a message should appear on the screen to warn you that you're about to be charged and offer you the chance to cancel the transaction.

CREDIT CARDS Credit cards are a safe and convenient means of payment, and they provide a record of your expenses. You can make **cash advances** on your credit cards at any bank, but consider that a last resort. Most companies impose a service fee (a percentage of the advance amount) and start charging interest on the advance the moment you receive the cash. On airline credit cards, you won't receive frequent-flyer miles for cash advances. At most banks, you don't need to go to a teller; you can get cash at an ATM if you know your personal identification number (PIN). If you don't know your PIN, call the phone number on the back of your credit card *before you leave home* and ask the bank to send it. It usually takes 5 to 7 business days. Some

The Scoop on the Web

The Internet offers abundant information about the Boston area; as with just about every other online topic, you'll find more than you can possibly use. For general and specific pointers and recommendations, turn to **Planning Your Trip: An Online Directory** on page 29.

banks will tell you your PIN over the phone if you provide your mother's maiden name or pass some other security clearance—but the middle of a long trip is a bad time to find out that your bank has tough security.

TRAVELER'S CHECKS The main advantages of traveler's checks are that they can be replaced if they're lost or stolen and can be exchanged for cash without paying a fee (although you might pay a service charge when you buy them). You do have to show identification when you cash one, and some smaller businesses, especially away from larger cities, either don't accept them or restrict the amount they will accept or cash.

You can get traveler's checks at almost any bank. Be sure to keep a list of serial numbers (*not* in the same place as the checks) in case your wallet or purse is lost or stolen. **American Express** offers denominations of $10, $20, $50, $100, $500, and $1,000. You'll pay a service charge ranging from 1% to 4%. AAA members can obtain checks without a fee at most AAA offices. You can also get American Express traveler's checks over the phone (☎ **800/ 221-7282**); by using this number, Amex gold and platinum cardholders avoid the 1% fee.

Visa (☎ **800/227-6811**) offers traveler's checks at Citibank locations nationwide and at several other banks. The service charge is 1.5% to 2%; checks come in denominations of $20, $50, $100, $500, and $1,000. **MasterCard** (☎ **800/223-9920**) also offers traveler's checks.

THEFT Almost every credit card company has an emergency toll-free number to call if your wallet or purse is stolen. The company may be able to wire you a cash advance against your credit card immediately; in many places, it can deliver a replacement card in a day or two. Call toll-free information (☎ **800/555-1212**) for your bank's number. American Express cardholders and traveler's check holders can call ☎ **800/221-7282** for all money emergencies. Visa and MasterCard strongly suggest that you contact the issuing bank, but both also have global service numbers: **Visa** customers can call ☎ **800/847-2911; MasterCard** holders should call ☎ **800/307-7309.** Citicorp Visa's U.S. emergency number is ☎ **800/336-8472.**

Odds are that if your wallet is gone, the police won't be able to recover it. However, it is still worth informing them. Your credit card company or insurer might require a police report number.

3 When to Go

Boston attracts large numbers of visitors year-round. Between April and November, there are hardly any slow times. The average annual hotel occupancy rate tops 80%, and rooms can sometimes be difficult to find. Make reservations as early as possible.

The periods around college graduation (May and early June) and the major citywide events (listed below) are especially busy. Spring and fall are extremely popular times for conventions. Families pour into the area in July and August, creating long lines at many attractions. Foliage season (mid-September to early November), when many leaf-peepers stay in the Boston area or pass through on the way to northern New England, is a huge draw. December is less busy but still a convention time—look out for weekend bargains.

The "slow" season is January through March, when many hotels offer great deals, especially on weekends. This is when the city is most likely to be socked in by snow, however, and when some suburban attractions are closed for the winter.

Boston's Average Temperatures & Rainfall

	Jan	Feb	Mar	Apr	May	June	July	Aug	Sept	Oct	Nov	Dec
Temp. (°F)	30	31	38	49	59	68	74	72	65	55	45	34
Rainfall (in.)	4.0	3.7	4.1	3.7	3.5	2.9	2.7	3.7	3.4	3.4	4.2	4.9

CLIMATE   You've probably already heard the saying about New England weather: "If you don't like it, wait 10 minutes." It's not as volatile as that, but variations from day to day can be enormous. You can roast in May and freeze in June, shiver in July and wish you'd packed shorts in March. Dressing in layers is always a good idea.

Spring and fall are the best bets for moderate temperatures, but spring (also known as mud season) is brief. It doesn't usually settle in until early May, and snow sometimes falls in late April. Summers are hot, especially in July and August, and can be uncomfortably humid. Fall is when you're most likely to catch a comfortable run of sunny days and cool nights. Winters are cold and usually snowy—bring a warm coat and sturdy boots.

In Boston, you can check the weather forecast by looking up at the short column of lights on top of the old John Hancock building in the Back Bay. (The new Hancock building is the 60-story glass tower next door.) It has its own poem: *Steady blue, clear view; flashing blue, clouds due; steady red, rain ahead; flashing red, snow instead.* During the summer, flashing red means the Red Sox game is canceled.

Boston Calendar of Events

The **Greater Boston Convention & Visitors Bureau** (☎ 800/ SEE-BOSTON or 617/536-4100; www.bostonusa.com) operates a regularly updated hotline that describes ongoing and upcoming events. The **Mayor's Office of Special Events & Tourism** (☎ 617/635-3911) can provide information about specific happenings. If something falls through or you're planning on the fly, the "Calendar" section of the Thursday *Boston Globe* and the "Scene" section of the Friday *Boston Herald* are always packed with ideas.

January

- **Martin Luther King, Jr., Birthday Celebration,** various locations. Events include speeches, musical tributes, gospel celebrations, and panel discussions. Check special listings in the Thursday *Boston Globe* "Calendar" section for specifics. Third Monday of the month.
- **U.S. Figure Skating Championships,** FleetCenter; www.boston2001. com. Tickets will sell out before you read this, but that doesn't mean you won't recognize a skater on the street—or get shut out of a hotel or restaurant reservation. Plan ahead. January 13 to 21, 2001.

- **Chinese New Year,** Chinatown. Dragon parade (which draws a big crowd no matter how cold it is), fireworks, and many raucous festivals. Special programs at the Children's Museum (☎ 617/426-8855). Depending on the Chinese lunar calendar, the holiday falls between January 21 and February 19. Late January 2001.
- **Boston Wine Festival,** Boston Harbor Hotel and other locations. Tastings, classes, lectures, receptions, and meals provide a lively liquid diversion in the dead of winter. Call the festival reservation line (☎ 888/ 660-WINE or 617/330-9355) for details. January through early April.

February

- **Black History Month,** various locations. Programs include special museum exhibits, children's activities, concerts, films, lectures, discussions, and tours of the Black Heritage Trail led by National Park Service rangers (☎ 617/742-5415; www.nps.gov/boaf). All month.
- **School Vacation Week,** various locations. The slate of activities for children includes plays, special exhibitions and programs, and tours. Contact individual attractions for information on special programs, extra open days, and extended hours. Third week of the month.

March

- **St. Patrick's Day/Evacuation Day.** Parade, South Boston. Celebration, Faneuil Hall Marketplace. The 5-mile parade salutes the city's Irish heritage and the day British troops left Boston in 1776. Head to Faneuil Hall Marketplace for music, dancing, and food. March 17.
- **New England Spring Flower Show,** Bayside Expo Center, Dorchester. This annual harbinger of spring, presented by the **Massachusetts Horticultural Society** (☎ 617/536-9280; www.masshort.org), draws huge crowds starved for a glimpse of green. Second or third week of the month.

April

- **Big Apple Circus** (www.bigapplecircus.org), near the waterfront. The New York–based "one-ring wonder" performs in a heated tent with all seating less than 50 feet from the ring. Proceeds support the Children's Museum. Visit the museum box office or contact Ticketmaster (☎ 617/ 931-ARTS; www.ticketmaster.com). Early April through early May.
- **Red Sox Opening Day,** Fenway Park. Even if your concierge is a magician, this is an extremely tough ticket. Check with the ticket office (☎ 617/267-1700; www.redsox.com) when tickets for the season go on sale in early January, or try to see the **Patriots Day** game, which begins at 11am. Middle of the month.
- **Swan Boats Return to the Public Garden.** Since their introduction in 1877, the swan boats (☎ 617/522-1966; www.swanboats.com) have been a symbol of Boston. Like real swans, they go away for the winter. Saturday before Patriots Day.
- ✪ **Patriots Day,** North End, Lexington, and Concord. The events of April 18–19, 1775, are commemorated and reenacted. Lanterns are hung in the steeple of the **Old North Church** (☎ 617/523-6676; www.oldnorth. com). Participants dressed as Paul Revere and William Dawes ride from the **Paul Revere House** (☎ 617/523-2338; www.paulreverehouse.org) in the North End to Lexington and Concord to warn the Minutemen that "the regulars are out" (not that "the British are coming"—most colonists considered themselves British). Battles are staged on the town green in Lexington and then at the Old North Bridge in Concord. Contact the

Lexington Chamber of Commerce Visitor Center, 1875 Mass. Ave., Lexington, MA 02173 (☎ 617/862-1450), or the **Concord Chamber of Commerce,** 2 Lexington Rd., Concord, MA 01742 (☎ 508/369-3120), for information on attending the battle reenactments. Third Monday of the month.

- **Boston Marathon,** Hopkinton, Massachusetts, to Boston. International stars and local amateurs join in the world's oldest and most famous marathon. The noon start means that elite runners hit Boston around 2 in the afternoon; weekend runners stagger across the Boylston Street finish line as much as 6 hours after that. Third Monday of the month.

•**Freedom Trail Week,** various locations in Boston, Cambridge, Lexington, and Concord. Another school vacation week, with plenty of crowds and diversions. Family-friendly events include tours, concerts, talks, and other programs related to Patriots Day, the Freedom Trail, and the American Revolution. Third week of the month.

May

- **Museum-Goers' Month,** various locations. Contact individual museums for details and schedules of special exhibits, lectures, and events. All month.
- **Boston Kite & Flight Festival,** Franklin Park (☎ 617/635-4505). Kites of all shapes and sizes take to the air above a celebration that includes kite-making clinics, music, and other entertainment. T: Orange Line to Forest Hills, then no. 16 bus. Middle of the month.
- **Lilac Sunday,** Arnold Arboretum, Jamaica Plain. The only day of the year that the Arboretum (☎ 617/524-1717; www.arnold.harvard.edu) allows picnicking. From sunrise to sunset, wander the grounds and enjoy the sensational spring flowers, including more than 400 varieties of lilacs in bloom. Usually the third Sunday of the month.
- **Street Performers Festival,** Faneuil Hall Marketplace. Everyone but the pigeons gets into the act as musicians, magicians, jugglers, sword swallowers, and artists strut their stuff. End of the month.

June

- **Boston Dairy Festival,** Boston Common. Cows grazed on Boston Common for its first 2 centuries; now they return once a year, accompanied by other farm animals, milking contests, and children's activities. The **"Scooper Bowl"** ice cream extravaganza takes place simultaneously on City Hall Plaza. First week of the month.
- **Dragon Boat Festival,** Charles River near Harvard Square, Cambridge (☎ 617/349-4380; www.bostondragonboat.com). Teams of paddlers synchronized by a drummer propel boats with dragon heads and tails as they race 500 meters. The winners go to the national championships; the spectators go to a celebration of Chinese culture and food on the shore. Second Sunday of the month.
- ✪ **Boston Globe Jazz & Blues Festival,** various locations, indoors and outdoors. Big names and rising stars put on lunchtime, after-work, evening, and weekend performances, some of which are free. Venues include the Hatch Shell on the Esplanade, Newbury Street, and Copley Square. Call the festival hotline (☎ 617/267-4301; www.boston.com/jazzfest) or pick up a copy of the paper for a schedule when you arrive in town. Some events require advance tickets. Late June.

July

- ✪ **Boston Harborfest,** downtown, the waterfront, and the Harbor Islands. The city puts on its Sunday best for Fourth of July, which has become a gigantic weeklong celebration of Boston's maritime history and an excuse to get out and have fun. Events surrounding **Harborfest** (☎ 617/ 227-1528; www.bostonharborfest.com) include concerts, children's activities, cruises, fireworks, the Boston Chowderfest, guided tours, talks, and the annual turnaround of USS *Constitution.* First week of the month (June 28 to July 4, 2001).

- **Boston Pops Concert and Fireworks Display,** Hatch Memorial Shell on the Esplanade. Spectators wait from dawn till dark for the music to start (overnight camping is not permitted). They also show up at the last minute—the Cambridge side of the river, near Kendall Square, is a good spot to watch the spectacular aerial show. The program includes the *1812 Overture,* with actual cannon fire. For details, check the Web site (www.july4th.org). July 4.
- **Puerto Rican Festival,** Franklin Park. The 5-day event, instituted in 1967, is part street fair, part cultural celebration, with plenty of live music. (T: Orange Line to Forest Hills, then no. 16 bus.) Late July.

August

- **Italian-American Feasts,** North End. These weekend street fairs begin in July and end before Labor Day with the two biggest, the Fishermen's Feast and the Feast of St. Anthony. The sublime (fresh seafood prepared while you wait, live music, and dancing in the street) mingles with the ridiculous (carnival games and fried-dough stands) to leave a lasting impression of fun and indigestion. Weekends, all month.
- **August Moon Festival,** Chinatown. A celebration of the harvest and the coming of autumn. Activities include the "dragon dance" through the crowded streets, and demonstrations of crafts and martial arts. Middle of the month.
- **Heritage Days,** various locations, Salem. A weeklong event with entertainment, food, and programs highlighting Salem's multicultural heritage. Contact the **Salem Office of Tourism & Cultural Affairs** (☎ 800/777-6848) for specifics. Second or third week of the month.

September

- **Cambridge River Festival** (☎ 617/349-4380; www.ci.cambridge.ma. us/CAC), Memorial Drive from John F. Kennedy Street to Western Avenue. A salute to the arts, with live music, dancing, children's activities, crafts and art exhibits, and international food on the banks of the Charles. Beginning of the month.
- **Boston Film Festival** (☎ 781/925-1373; www.bostonfilmfestival.org), various locations. Independent films continue their turn around the festival circuit or make their premiere, sometimes accompanied by a talk by an actor or a filmmaker. Most screenings are open to the public without advance tickets. Middle of the month.
- **Art Newbury Street & Fashion Walk,** Back Bay. More than 30 galleries are open, and Newbury Street from the Public Garden to Massachusetts Avenue is closed to traffic. You'll find special exhibits indoors and live entertainment outdoors. Check the Web site (www.newbury-st.com) for details. Middle of the month.

October

- **Columbus Day Parade,** downtown and the North End. Beginning with a ceremony on City Hall Plaza at 1pm, the parade, appropriately enough, winds up in the city's Italian neighborhood, following Hanover Street to the Coast Guard station on Commercial Street. Second Monday of the month.

- **Ringling Brothers and Barnum & Bailey Circus,** FleetCenter (☎ 617/624-1000; www.fleetcenter.com). The Greatest Show on Earth makes its annual 2-week visit. Middle of the month.

- ✪ **Head of the Charles Regatta,** Boston and Cambridge. High school, college, and postcollegiate rowing teams and individuals—some 4,000 in all—race in front of hordes of fans along the banks of the Charles River and on the bridges spanning it. The Head of the Charles (☎ 617/864-8415; www.hocr.org) has an uncanny tendency to coincide with the crispest, most picturesque weekend of the season. End of the month.

  Tip: The boats (called "shells") are numbered sequentially and race against the clock from a staggered start. If a higher-numbered team is ahead of one with a lower number, it's making good time.

- **Salem Haunted Happenings,** various locations. Parades, parties, a special commuter-rail ride from Boston, fortune-telling, cruises, and tours lead up to a ceremony on Halloween. Contact the **Salem Office of Tourism & Cultural Affairs** (☎ 800/777-6848) or check the Web site (www.salemhauntedhappenings.com) for specifics. Second half of the month.

November

- **An Evening with Champions,** Bright Athletic Center, Allston. World-class ice-skaters and promising local students stage three performances to benefit the Jimmy Fund, the children's fund-raising arm of the Dana–Farber Cancer Institute. Sponsored by Harvard's **Eliot House** (☎ 617/493-8172). First weekend of the month.

- **Thanksgiving Celebration,** Plymouth (☎ 800/USA-1620; www.visit-plymouth.com). The holiday that put Plymouth on the map is observed with a "stroll through the ages," showcasing 17th- and 19th-century Thanksgiving preparations in historic homes. **Plimoth Plantation,** which re-creates the colony's first years, serves a Victorian Thanksgiving feast. Reservations (☎ 800/262-9356 or 508/746-1622) are required and accepted beginning in August. Thanksgiving Day.

December

- *The Nutcracker,* Wang Center for the Performing Arts. Boston Ballet's annual holiday extravaganza is one of the country's biggest and best. This is *the* traditional way for young Bostonians (and visitors) to be exposed to culture, and the spectacular sets make it practically painless. Call **Ticketmaster** (☎ 617/931-ARTS; www.ticketmaster.com) as soon as you plan your trip, ask whether your hotel offers a *Nutcracker* package, or cross your fingers and visit the box office at 270 Tremont St. when you arrive. All month.

- **Christmas Tree Lighting** and **Newbury Street Stroll,** Back Bay. Carol singing precedes the lighting of the Prudential Center's magnificent tree on Saturday. It's an annual gift from Nova Scotia—an expression of thanks from the people of Halifax for Bostonians' speedy help in fighting a devastating fire there in 1917. On Sunday, music, holiday activities, and window-shoppers take over Newbury Street. First weekend of December.

- **Boston Tea Party Reenactment,** Tea Party Ship and Museum, Congress Street Bridge (☎ 617/338-1773). Chafing under British rule, the colonists rose up on December 16, 1773, to strike a blow where it would cause real pain—in the pocketbook. Middle of the month.

Planning Pointer

You have plane and hotel reservations, but what about restaurant reservations and tickets to that big museum show? If you've heard or read about a place or an event that you just have to check out, call ahead—a couple of minutes on the phone while you're planning everything else can be an excellent investment. And if your trip coincides (intentionally or not) with a cultural event such as the *Nutcracker* or a museum show, be sure to investigate hotel packages that include tickets. You may not save much money, but you will save time.

- **Black Nativity,** Converse Hall, Tremont Temple Baptist Church, 88 Tremont St. (☎ **617/723-3486**). Poet Langston Hughes wrote the "gospel opera," and a cast of more than 100 brings it to life. Music and dancing by soloists and choirs frame a rousing interpretation of the Gospel according to Luke. All month.
- **Christmas Revels,** Sanders Theater, Cambridge. This multicultural celebration of the winter solstice features the holiday customs of a different culture each year. Recent themes have included Renaissance Italy and the Romany Gypsies. Be ready to sing along. For information, contact the **Revels** (☎ **617/621-0505;** www.revels.org); for tickets, call the **box office** (☎ **617/496-2222**) or **Ticketmaster** (☎ **617/931-ARTS**). Last 2 weeks of the month.
- ◉ **First Night,** Back Bay and the waterfront. The original arts-oriented, no-alcohol, citywide New Year's Eve celebration is Boston's. It begins in the early afternoon and includes a parade, ice sculptures, art exhibitions, theatrical performances, and indoor and outdoor entertainment. Some attractions require tickets, but for most you just need a First Night button, available for about $15 at visitor centers and stores around the city. The carousing wraps up at midnight with a spectacular fireworks display over the harbor. For details, contact **First Night** (☎ **617/542-1399;** www. firstnight.org) or check the newspapers when you arrive. December 31.

4 Health & Insurance

STAYING HEALTHY

Here's hoping you won't need to evaluate Boston's reputation for excellent medical care. Before you leave home, be sure you are protected with adequate health insurance coverage and you understand your insurance provider's procedures for medical treatment when you're out of town. Many HMOs require that care for anything other than a life-threatening emergency be preapproved—and stringently define "life-threatening." Make sure you have your membership card and know the phone number to call.

If you have a chronic illness, consult your doctor before traveling. For conditions like epilepsy, diabetes, or heart problems, consider wearing a **Medic Alert Identification Tag** (☎ **800/825-3785;** www.medicalert.org), which will immediately inform doctors of your condition and give them access to your records through Medic Alert's 24-hour hotline. Membership is $35, plus a $15 annual fee.

For information on physician referral services and emergency rooms, see "Fast Facts: Boston" in chapter 4.

INSURANCE

There are three kinds of travel insurance: trip cancellation, medical, and lost luggage coverage. **Trip cancellation** insurance is a good idea if you have paid a large portion of your vacation expenses up front. The other two types don't make sense for most travelers. Rule number one: Check your existing policies before you buy any additional coverage.

Your existing health insurance should cover you if you get sick while on vacation (again, if you belong to an HMO, double-check its procedures). For independent travel health-insurance providers, see below. Your homeowner's insurance should cover stolen luggage. The airlines are responsible for $2,500 on domestic flights if they lose your luggage; if you plan to carry anything more valuable than that, keep it in your carry-on bag.

Some credit cards (American Express and certain gold and platinum Visa and MasterCards, for example) offer automatic flight insurance against death or dismemberment in case of an airplane crash.

If you want additional insurance, try one of the companies listed below. But don't pay for more than you need—for example, if you need only trip cancellation insurance, don't buy coverage for lost or stolen property. Trip cancellation insurance costs approximately 6% to 8% of the total value of your vacation. Among the reputable issuers of travel insurance are **Access America,** P.O. Box 90315, Richmond, VA 23286 (☎ 800/284-8300; www.accessamerica.com); **Travel Guard International,** 1145 Clark St., Stevens Point, WI 54481 (☎ 800/826-1300); **Travel Insured International, Inc.,** P.O. Box 280568, East Hartford, CT 06128 (☎ 800/243-3174); and **Travelex Insurance Services,** P.O. Box 9408, Garden City, NY 11530-9408 (☎ 800/228-9792; www.travelex-insurance.com).

CAR RENTER'S INSURANCE

For information on car renter's insurance, see "Getting Around" in chapter 4.

5 Tips for Travelers with Special Needs

FOR TRAVELERS WITH DISABILITIES

Boston, like all other U.S. cities, has taken the required steps to provide access for people with disabilities. Hotels must provide accessible rooms; museums and street curbs have ramps for wheelchairs. Some smaller accommodations, including most B&Bs, have not been retrofitted. In older neighborhoods (notably Beacon Hill and the North End), you'll find many narrow streets, cobbled thoroughfares, and brick sidewalks.

The Americans with Disabilities Act requires all forms of public transportation to provide special services to patrons with disabilities. Newer stations on the Red, Blue, and Orange lines of the MBTA **subway** are wheelchair accessible; the Green Line (which uses trolleys rather than subway cars) is in the process of being converted. Contact the **MBTA** (☎ 617/222-3200; www.mbta.com) or check a system map to see if the stations you need are accessible. All MBTA **buses** have lifts or kneelers; call ☎ 800/LIFT-BUS for more information. Some bus routes are wheelchair accessible at all times, but you may have to make a reservation as much as a day in advance for others. To learn more, call the main information number or the **Office for Transportation Access** (☎ 800/533-6282 or 617/222-5123; TDD 617/222-5415). For reduced public transportation fares, people with disabilities can apply to buy a Transportation Access Pass (TAP) from the **MBTA Access Pass Office,**

10 Boylston Place, Boston, MA 02116 (☎ **617/222-5976**). The application must be completed by a licensed health-care professional.

One taxicab company with wheelchair-accessible vehicles is **Boston Cab** (☎ **617/536-5010**); advance notice is recommended. In addition, there is an Airport Handicap Van (☎ **617/561-1769**).

An excellent source of information is **Very Special Arts Massachusetts,** 2 Boylston St., Boston, MA 02116 (☎ **617/350-7713;** fax 617/482-4298; TTY 617/350-6836; www.vsamass.org; e-mail: vsamass@accessexpressed.net). It has a comprehensive Web site, and it publishes *Access Expressed! Massachusetts: A Cultural Resource Directory* ($5), which includes general access information and specifics about more than 200 arts and entertainment facilities in the state.

GENERAL INFORMATION *A World of Options,* a 658-page book of resources, covers everything from biking trips to scuba outfitters. It costs $35 ($30 for members) and is available from **Mobility International USA,** P.O. Box 10767, Eugene, OR 97440 (☎ **541/343-1284,** voice and TDD; www.miusa.org). Annual membership is $35, which includes the quarterly newsletter, *Over the Rainbow.* **Twin Peaks Press,** P.O. Box 129, Vancouver, WA 98666 (☎ **360/694-2462**), publishes travel-related books for people with disabilities.

The Moss Rehab Hospital (☎ **215/456-9600**) has provided friendly and helpful advice and referrals to disabled travelers for years through its **Travel Information Service** (☎ **215/456-9603;** www.mossresourcenet.org).

You can join the **Society for the Advancement of Travel for the Handicapped,** 347 Fifth Ave., Suite 610, New York, NY 10016 (☎ **212/447-7284;** fax 212/725-8253; www.sath.org). Annual membership is $45, $30 for seniors and students, and gives you access to a vast network of connections in the travel industry. The society provides information sheets on travel destinations and referrals to tour operators that specialize in traveling with disabilities. The quarterly magazine, *Open World for Disability and Mature Travel,* is full of information and resources. A year's subscription is $13 ($21 outside the U.S.).

Travelers with disabilities might also want to consider joining a tour that caters specifically to them. One of the best operators is **Flying Wheels Travel,** 143 West Bridge, P.O. Box 38, Owatonna, MN 55060 (☎ **800/525-6790;** www.flyingwheels.com). It offers escorted tours and cruises, as well as private tours in minivans with lifts.

For a copy of *Air Transportation of Handicapped Persons,* write to Free Advisory Circular No. AC12032, Distribution Unit, U.S. Department of Transportation, Publications Division, M-4332, Washington, DC 20590.

Amtrak (☎ **800/USA-RAIL;** www.amtrak.com) and **Greyhound** (☎ **800/752-4841;** www.greyhound.com) offer special fares and services for people with disabilities. Call at least a week in advance of your trip for details.

Vision-impaired travelers can contact the **American Foundation for the Blind,** 11 Penn Plaza, Suite 300, New York, NY 10001 (☎ **800/232-5463**), for information on traveling with Seeing Eye dogs.

FOR GAY & LESBIAN TRAVELERS

Overall, Boston is a gay- and lesbian-friendly destination, with a live-and-let-live attitude that long ago replaced the city's legendary Puritanism.

The **Gay and Lesbian Helpline** (☎ **617/267-9001**) offers information Monday through Friday from 4 to 11pm, Saturday from 6 to 8:30pm, and Sunday from 6 to 10pm. You can also contact the **Boston Alliance of Gay and Lesbian Youth** (BAGLY) (☎ **800/422-2459;** www.bagly.org). *Bay*

Windows (☎ 617/266-6670) and *In Publications* (☎ 617/426-8246) publish weekly newspapers that concentrate on upcoming gay-related events, news, and features. The weekly *Boston Phoenix* publishes a monthly supplement, "One in 10," and has a gay-interest area in its Web site (www. bostonphoenix.com).

The *Pink Pages,* 66 Charles St., Boston, MA 02114 (☎ 800/338-6550), a guide to gay- and lesbian-owned and gay-friendly businesses, is available for $10.05; it also has a comprehensive Web site (www.pinkweb.com/boston. index.html).

GENERAL INFORMATION   Two good biannual English-language guidebooks focus on gay men and include information for lesbians. You can get the *Spartacus International Gay Guide* or *Odysseus* at most gay and lesbian bookstores, or order them from Giovanni's Room (☎ 215/923-2960) or A Different Light Bookstore (☎ 800/343-4002 or 212/989-4850). Both lesbians and gay men might want to pick up a copy of *Gay Travel A to Z* ($16).

Out and About, 8 W. 19th St. #401, New York, NY 10011 (☎ 800/929-2268 or 212/645-6922), offers guidebooks and a monthly newsletter packed with information on the global gay and lesbian scene. A year's subscription to the newsletter costs $49. *Our World,* 1104 N. Nova Rd., Suite 251, Daytona Beach, FL 32117 (☎ 904/441-5367), is a slicker monthly magazine that highlights travel bargains and opportunities. An annual subscription costs $35 ($45 outside the U.S.).

FOR SENIORS

Boston-area businesses offer many discounts to seniors with identification (a driver's license, passport, or other document that shows your date of birth). Hotels, restaurants, museums, and movie theaters offer special deals. Discounts are usually offered in restaurants and theaters only at off-peak times, but museums and other attractions offer reduced rates at all times.

Seniors can ride the MBTA **subways** for 20¢ (a 65¢ savings) and **local buses** for 15¢ (a 45¢ savings). On zoned and express buses and on the commuter rail, the senior citizen fare is half the regular fare. On the commuter rail, proof of age is a valid driver's license or passport, but for the subway and buses, you need an MBTA **senior citizen card.** It's available for a nominal fee weekdays from 8:30am to 5pm at the Back Bay MBTA station, or by mail from the Senior and Access Pass Program, 145 Dartmouth St., Boston, MA 02116-5162 (☎ 617/222-5438 or 617/222-5976).

GENERAL INFORMATION   When you first make your travel reservations, always ask about available discounts for seniors. Most of the major domestic airlines, including **American, Continental, TWA, United,** and **US Airways,** offer discount programs. **Amtrak** (☎ 800/USA-RAIL; www.amtrak.com) and **Greyhound** (☎ 800/752-4841; www.greyhound. com) offer discounts to people over 62, as do many hotel chains—but only if you ask.

The **American Association of Retired Persons,** 601 E St. NW, Washington, DC 20049 (☎ 800/424-3410; www.aarp.org), offers discounts on car rentals, accommodations, airfares, and sightseeing. It's open to anyone 50 or older, retired or not. Benefits include *Modern Maturity* magazine and a monthly newsletter.

The **National Council of Senior Citizens,** 8403 Colesville Rd., Suite 1200, Silver Spring, MD 20910 (☎ 301/578-8800), a nonprofit organization, publishes a bimonthly newsletter that's partly devoted to travel tips, and offers discounts on hotel and auto rentals. Annual dues are $13 per person or couple.

A **Golden Age Passport** ($10) gives you free lifetime admission to all recreation areas run by the federal government, including parks and monuments. It's available at any National Park Service site that charges admission.

The Mature Traveler, a monthly newsletter that covers senior citizen travel, is a valuable resource. It is available by subscription ($30 a year) from GEM Publishing Group, Box 50400, Reno, NV 89513-0400 (☎ **800/460-6676**). GEM also publishes *The Book of Deals,* which lists more than 1,000 senior discounts on airlines, lodging, tours, and attractions around the country; it costs $9.95.

Another helpful publication is *101 Tips for the Mature Traveler,* available from Grand Circle Travel, 347 Congress St., Suite 3A, Boston, MA 02210 (☎ **800/221-2610** or 617/350-7500; fax 617/350-6206; www.gct.com).

Although these two companies have Boston addresses, they run programs all over the country for people 50 and over: **Grand Circle Travel** (see above) organizes educational and adventure vacations. **SAGA International Holidays,** 222 Berkeley St., Boston, MA 02116 (☎ **800/343-0273**; www.sagaholidays.com), offers inclusive tours and cruises. SAGA also sponsors the more substantial "Road Scholar Tours" (☎ **800/621-2151**), which are fun-loving but with an educational bent.

Elderhostel, Inc., 75 Federal St., Boston, MA 02110 (☎ **617/426-8056**; www.elderhostel.org), and the University of New Hampshire's **Interhostel** program (☎ **800/733-9753**; www.learn.unh.edu) organize educational escorted tours for seniors. Seminars, lectures, and field trips fill the schedules, and academic experts lead sightseeing trips. **Elderhostel** arranges study programs for people 55 and over (and a spouse or companion of any age) in the United States and in 77 other countries. Most courses last about 3 weeks, and many packages include airfare, accommodations in student dormitories or modest inns, meals, and tuition. The free catalog lists upcoming courses and destinations. **Interhostel** takes travelers 50 and over (with companions over 40), and offers 2- and 3-week trips, mostly international. The courses in both programs are ungraded, involve no homework, and often focus on the liberal arts. They're not luxury vacations, but they're fun and fulfilling.

FOR FAMILIES

Boston is a top-notch family destination, with tons of activities that appeal to children, and relatively few that don't. Children (usually under 17, sometimes under 12) can stay free in their parents' hotel room, when using existing bedding. Most hotels charge for cots, and some charge for cribs. Many hotels have family packages that offer a suite, breakfast, and parking, plus discount coupons for museums and restaurants. Always ask whether the hotel you're considering has special offers for families.

The **Greater Boston Convention & Visitors Bureau** (☎ **888/SEE-BOSTON**; www.bostonusa.com) sells a "Kids Love Boston" kit ($5.25) with a guidebook, travel planner, map, and discount coupon book.

GENERAL INFORMATION   When you book your flight, see if your airline offers half-price tickets for children under 3 traveling in car seats. Many do, but you have to ask.

The highly regarded *Family Travel Times* newsletter is published six times a year by Travel with Your Children, or TWYCH, 40 Fifth Ave., 7th floor, New York, NY 10011 (☎ **888/822-4388** or 212/477-5524). Subscriptions are $40 a year. A free publication list and a sample issue are available on request.

Syndicated columnist Eileen Ogintz's book *Are We There Yet?: A Parent's Guide to Fun Family Vacations* (HarperCollins) is available at most bookstores.

FOR STUDENTS

Students don't actually rule Boston—it just feels that way sometimes. Many museums, theaters, concert halls, and other attractions offer discounts for college and high-school students with valid identification. Some restaurants near college campuses offer student discounts or other deals. Visiting students might want to check campus bulletin boards; many events are open to them. The weekly *Boston Phoenix* also lists activities for students.

GENERAL INFORMATION The best resource is the **Council on International Educational Exchange** (CIEE). It issues ID cards, and its travel branch, **Council Travel Service** (☎ **800/226-8624;** www.ciee.com), is the biggest student travel agency operation in the world. It has offices in Boston at 273 Newbury St., in the Back Bay (☎ **617/266-1926**), and in Cambridge at 12 Eliot St., Harvard Square (☎ **617/497-1497**), and 84 Mass. Ave., near MIT (☎ **617/225-2555**).

CIEE issues the student traveler's best friend, the $18 **International Student Identity Card** (ISIC). It's the only officially acceptable form of student identification, good for cut rates on rail passes, plane tickets, and other discounts. It also provides you with basic health and life insurance and a 24-hour help line. If you're no longer a student but are under 26, you can get a GO 25 card, which includes the insurance and some discounts, but not student admission to museums.

In Canada, **Travel CUTS,** 200 Ronson St., Suite 320, Toronto, ON M9W 5Z9 (☎ **800/667-2887** or 416/614-2887; www.travelcuts.com), offers similar services. **Campus Travel,** 52 Grosvenor Gardens, London SW1W 0AG (☎ **0171/730-3402;** www.campustravel.co.uk), opposite Victoria Station, is Britain's leading specialist in student and youth travel.

6 Getting There

BY PLANE

Most major domestic carriers serve Boston. Be prepared to show at least one form of government-issued photo identification that matches the name on your ticket (usually a driver's license or a passport) when you board.

The major airlines flying into **Logan International Airport** are **AirTran** (☎ 800/247-8726), **American** (☎ 800/433-7300), **America West** (☎ 800/235-9292), **Continental** (☎ 800/525-0280), **Delta** (☎ 800/221-1212), **Frontier** (☎ 800/432-1359), **Midway** (☎ 800/446-4392), **Northwest** (☎ 800/225-2525), **TWA** (☎ 800/221-2000), **United** (☎ 800/241-6522), and **US Airways** (☎ 800/428-4322). Many international carriers also fly into Boston; see chapter 3.

FINDING THE BEST AIRFARE

Pricing is so volatile that almost every passenger on a given aircraft may have paid a different price. Fares change constantly, varying from airline to airline and even from day to day on the same airline. Flexibility is costly—last-minute travelers pay the premium rate, or full fare—and getting a good deal usually means booking well in advance and agreeing to many restrictions. The lowest-

Make Yourself Comfortable

When you make your plane reservation, order a special meal if you have dietary restrictions. Most airlines offer a variety of special meals, including vegetarian, macrobiotic, and kosher, as well as meals for the lactose intolerant.

Let's Make a Deal

The domestic discount airline **Southwest** (☎ 800/435-9792; www.
iflyswa.com) doesn't serve Boston. But by redefining "Boston-area airport," it has helped create two magnets for budget-conscious travelers.
They're not nearly as convenient as Logan, but fares for flights to either
of these airports can be considerably cheaper than those to Boston.

T. F. Green Airport (☎ 888/268-7222; www.pvd-ri.com) is in the
Providence suburb of Warwick, R.I., about 60 miles south of Boston. It's
served by American, Continental, Delta, Southwest, United, and US Airways. **Bonanza** (☎ 800/556-3815) offers bus service between the airport and Boston's South Station daily 9am to 9pm; the fare is $16
one-way, $29 round-trip. Allow at least 90 minutes.

Manchester International Airport (☎ 603/624-6556; www.
flymanchester.com) is in southern New Hampshire, about 56 miles
north of Boston. It's served by Continental, Delta Connection, Northwest, Southwest, United, and US Airways. There's no public bus service
to Boston, but you can arrange to be picked up and dropped off by
Flight Line (☎ 800/ 245-2525). The one-way fare is $34, and 24
hours' notice is required.

priced fares are often nonrefundable, require advance purchase of 1 to 3 weeks
and a certain length of stay, and carry penalties for changing travel dates.

Try to travel on weekdays during the busy summer season and to avoid
major holiday periods, when fares go up. Staying over a Saturday night usually means a lower price. Call around, or ask your travel agent to call around, as
far in advance as possible. And be flexible if you can—shifting by a day or two
can sometimes mean great savings, but you have to ask because many airlines
won't volunteer this information.

Here are a few ways to save:

1. Check newspapers for advertised discounts, or call the airlines directly
   and ask if any **promotional rates** or special fares are available.
2. **Consolidators,** also known as bucket shops, are a good place to find low
   fares. Consolidators buy seats in bulk and sell them at prices below even
   the airlines' discounted rates. Their small ads usually run in the Sunday
   travel section at the bottom of the page. Before you pay, ask the consolidator for a confirmation number, then call the airline to confirm your
   seat—and be prepared to book your ticket with a different consolidator
   if the airline can't confirm your reservation. Also be aware that bucket
   shop tickets are usually nonrefundable or carry stiff cancellation penalties, often as high as 50% to 75% of the ticket price.

   Council Travel (☎ 800/226-8624; www.counciltravel.com) and **STA
   Travel** (☎ 800/781-4040; www.statravel.com) cater to young travelers,
   but their bargains are available to people of all ages. **Travel Bargains**
   (☎ 800/AIR-FARE; www.1800airfare.com) was formerly owned by
   TWA but now offers the deepest discounts on many other airlines, with a
   4-day advance purchase. Other reliable consolidators include **1-800-
   FLY-CHEAP** (www.1800flycheap.com) and **TFI Tours International**
   (☎ 800/ 745-8000 or 212/736-1140), which serves as a clearinghouse for
   unused seats. "Rebaters" such as **Travel Avenue** (☎ 800/333-3335 or
   312/876-1116; www.travelavenue.com) and the **Smart Traveller**

(☎ **800/448-3338** in the U.S., or 305/448-3338) rebate part of their commissions to you.

3. Surf the Web for the best deals. In addition to the Web sites for the consolidators above, check out farefinders like **Expedia** (**www.expedia.com**) or **Yahoo's Roundtrip Flight Search** (**www.yahoo.com**) which can give you the lowest available price for any itinerary, as well as suggest some even cheaper alternatives on different airlines, days, or both. See "Planning Your Trip: An Online Directory" on page 29 for details on how to make these sites work for you.

4. Book a seat on a **charter flight.** Discounted fares have pared the number available, but they can still be found. Most charter operators advertise and sell their seats through travel agents, so the local professionals are your best source. Before deciding to take a charter, check and double-check the restrictions—expect there to be many for you and few for the tour operator. Summer charters fill up quickly and are almost sure to fly, but if you decide on a charter flight at any time, seriously consider cancellation insurance. Check with the Better Business Bureau before you pay to make sure the company is reliable.

   A charter company that serves Boston from most major European cities is **Travac,** 989 Sixth Ave., New York, NY 10018 (☎ **800/872-8800** or 212/695-8101; fares-by-fax menu ☎ 888/872-8327; www.travac.com).

5. Join a travel club such as **Moment's Notice** (☎ **718/234-6295;** www. moments-notice.com) or **Sears Discount Travel Club** (☎ **800/ 433-9383,** or 800/255-1487 to join), which supply unsold tickets at discounted prices. You pay an annual membership fee to get the club's hotline number.

FLYING WITH FILM & LAPTOPS   Traveling with electronic devices and film (exposed or not) can take extra time in this age of heightened security, so plan accordingly. X-ray machines won't affect film up to ASA 400, but you might want to request an inspection by hand anyway. A visual check for computers is standard practice in most airports—you'll probably be asked to switch it on, so be sure the batteries are charged (and don't forget to turn it off). You may use your computer in flight, but not during takeoff and landing because of possible interference with cockpit controls. In many cases, airport security guards will also ask you to turn on electronic devices (including camcorders and personal stereos) to prove that they are what they appear to be. Make sure that batteries are charged and working for those items as well.

ESCORTED TOURS VS. PACKAGE TOURS

Before you start your search for the lowest airfare, you might want to consider booking your flight as part of an escorted tour or package tour. What you lose in adventure, you can gain in time and money saved when you book accommodations—and maybe even food and entertainment—with your flight.

Make Yourself Comfortable

When you check in, ask for a seat in an emergency exit row, which has extra legroom. These seats are assigned at the airport, usually on a first-come, first-served basis. You must be at least 15 and able to open the exit door and help direct traffic in an emergency. You can also request a bulkhead (first row) seat, but they're usually held back for last-minute, full-fare travelers.

In the Air, on the Web

The following major airlines serve Logan International Airport.

- **AirTran:** www.airtran.com
- **American Airlines:** www.aa.com
- **America West Airlines:** www.americawest.com
- **Continental Airlines:** www.flycontinental.com
- **Delta Airlines:** www.delta-air.com
- **Frontier Airlines:** www.frontierairlines.com
- **Northwest Airlines:** www.nwa.com
- **TWA:** www.twa.com
- **United Airlines:** www.ual.com
- **US Airways:** www.usairways.com

One unusual thing about Boston tourism is the prominent role of trolley tour companies (see "Organized Tours" in chapter 7). The sightseeing portion of a package is often a free or discounted 1-day trolley tour. A typical multiple-day bus tour spends only a day or two in Boston on the way to or from other New England destinations and activities—historic attractions, outlet shopping, skiing, and especially foliage watching. If you want the if-it's-Friday-this-must-be-Salem approach, innumerable companies offer escorted tours of New England; if you want a less superficial and more custom-tailored approach to Boston, you might be better off staying put and doing some planning on your own.

ESCORTED TOURS   This may not be the option for you if you like to navigate unfamiliar places on your own. If you like to avoid surprises, however, many package options enable you to do just that—and save money in the process.

Some people love escorted tours. They let you relax and take in the sights while a bus driver fights traffic; they spell out your costs up front; and they take you to the maximum number of sights in the minimum amount of time. Keep in mind that in a multifaceted destination such as Boston, your chances of finding a tour that covers exactly and only the things you want to see and do aren't great—it's important to have some independent time.

If you choose an escorted tour, you should ask a few questions before you buy:

1. **What is the cancellation policy?** Does the company require a deposit? Can it cancel the trip if enough people don't sign up? Do you get a refund if the company cancels? If you cancel? How late can you cancel if you are unable to go? When do you pay in full?
2. **How busy is the schedule?** How much sightseeing will you do each day? Does the timetable allow ample time for relaxing by the pool, shopping, or wandering?
3. **How big is the group?** The smaller the party, the more flexible the itinerary and the less time you'll spend waiting for people to get on and off the bus. Tour operators may be evasive about this, because they might not know the exact size until everybody has made reservations, but they should be able to give an estimate. Some tours have a minimum group size and may cancel the tour if they don't book enough people.

4. **What does the price include?** Don't assume anything. You may have to pay for transportation to and from the airport. A box lunch may be included in an excursion, but drinks may cost extra. Beer might be included, but wine might not. Can you opt out of certain activities, or does the bus leave once a day, with no exceptions? Are all your meals planned in advance? Can you choose your entree at dinner, or does everybody get the same chicken cutlet?

Note: If you choose an escorted tour, seriously consider buying travel insurance from an independent agency, especially if the tour operator asks you to pay up front. See "Health & Insurance," above. One final caveat: Because escorted tour prices are based on double occupancy, the single traveler is usually penalized.

PACKAGE TOURS   Package tours are not the same as escorted tours. They are simply a way to buy airfare and accommodations at the same time. For popular destinations like Boston, they can be a smart way to go because they save you a lot of money. In many cases, a package that includes airfare, hotel, and transportation to and from the airport costs less than the hotel alone would if you booked it yourself. That's because tour operators buy packages in bulk, and then resell them to the public at a cost that drastically undercuts standard rates.

Packages vary widely. Some offer a better class of hotels than others, or the same hotels for lower prices. Some offer flights on scheduled airlines; others book charters. In some packages, your choice of accommodations and travel days may be limited. Some packages let you choose between escorted vacations and independent vacations; others allow you to add just a few excursions or escorted day trips (also at lower prices than you could find on your own) without booking an entirely escorted tour. Each destination usually has one or two packagers that are cheaper than the rest because they buy in even greater bulk. If you spend the time to shop around, you will save in the long run.

FINDING A PACKAGE DEAL   The best place to start your search is the travel section of your local Sunday newspaper. Also check the ads in national travel magazines such as *Arthur Frommer's Budget Travel, Travel & Leisure, National Geographic Traveler,* and *Condé Nast Traveler*. **Liberty Travel** (☎ 888/ 271-1584; www.libertytravel.com), one of the biggest packagers in the Northeast, usually runs a full-page ad in Sunday papers. You won't get much in the way of service, but you will get a good deal. **American Express Vacations** (☎ 800/241-1700; http://travel.americanexpress.com) is another option.

Another good resource is the airlines themselves, which often bundle their flights with accommodations. Fly-by-night packagers are uncommon, but they do exist; when you buy your package through the airline, you can be pretty sure the company will still be in business when your departure date arrives. Among the airline packagers, good options for trips to Boston include **American Airlines Vacations** (☎ 800/321-2121), **Delta Vacations** (☎ 800/872-7786), and **US Airways Vacations** (☎ 800/455-0123). **Northwest Airlines** posts **Cyber Saver Bargain Alerts** on its Web site (www.nwa.com) every Wednesday.

One often-overlooked possibility, if you live close enough to take advantage of it, is **Amtrak Vacations** (☎ 800/250-4989; www.northeast.amtrak.com). The train definitely isn't for everyone, though. Sleepers are available, but once you're paying extra for a berth, an air package may be cheaper and certainly will be less time-consuming.

The biggest hotel chains, casinos, and resorts also offer package deals. If you already know where you want to stay, call the chain and ask if it offers land/air packages.

The Bigfoot of tour companies is **Gray Line;** its New England incarnation is **Brush Hill Tours,** 435 High St., Randolph, MA 02368 (☎ **800/343-1328** or 781/986-6100; fax 781/986-0167; www.grayline.com). It operates Beantown Trolley and offers a variety of half- and full-day escorted tours to destinations such as Plymouth, Salem, Cape Cod, and Newport, RI. The 3-night "Boston City Package" includes lodging, airport or train station transfers, and a trolley tour; prices start at about $300 per person, based on double occupancy.

Another possibility is *Yankee Magazine*'s **Best of New England Vacations** (☎ **800/996-2463;** www.bnevacations.com). Its packages include a 1-day tour and a copy of the magazine's travel guide.

BY CAR

Driving *to* Boston is not difficult, but driving *in* Boston is a nightmare. Between the cost of parking and the hassle of downtown traffic, the money you save may not be worth the annoyance. The **"Big Dig"** (formally the Central Artery/Third Harbor Tunnel project) dominates the landscape along the Central Artery, which is being moved underground without being closed. If you're thinking of driving because you want to use the car to get around town, think again.

The major highways are **I-95** (Massachusetts Route 128), which connects Boston to highways in Rhode Island, Connecticut, and New York to the south, and New Hampshire and Maine to the north; **I-90,** the Massachusetts Turnpike, an east-west toll road that links up with the New York State Thruway; **I-93/U.S. 1,** extending north to Canada and leading to the Northeast Expressway, which enters downtown Boston; and **I-93/Route 3,** the Southeast Expressway, which connects Boston with the south, including Cape Cod.

The Massachusetts Turnpike ("Mass. Pike") extends into the center of the city and connects with the Central Artery, or John F. Fitzgerald Expressway, which is linked to the Northeast Expressway. If you want to avoid Central Artery construction, exit at Cambridge/Allston or at the Prudential Center in the Back Bay.

The approach to Cambridge is either **Storrow Drive** or **Memorial Drive,** which run along each side of the Charles. Storrow Drive has a Harvard Square exit that leads you across the Anderson Bridge to John F. Kennedy Street and into the square. Memorial Drive intersects with Kennedy Street; turn away from the bridge to reach the square.

Boston is 218 miles from New York; the driving time is about 4$^{1}/_{2}$ hours. The 992-mile drive from Chicago to Boston should take around 21 hours; from Washington, D.C., it takes about 8 hours to cover the 468 miles.

The **American Automobile Association** (☎ **800/AAA-HELP;** www.aaa.com) provides its members with maps, itineraries, and other travel information, and it arranges free towing if you break down. The Mass. Pike is a privately operated road that arranges its own towing; if you break down there, wait in the car until one of the regular patrols arrives.

It's impossible to say this often enough: When you reach your hotel, leave your car in the garage and walk or use public transportation. Use the car for day trips, and before you set out, ask at the front desk for a route around or away from the construction area.

BY TRAIN

Boston has three rail centers: **South Station** on Atlantic Avenue, **Back Bay Station** on Dartmouth Street across from the Copley Place mall, and **North Station** on Causeway Street near the FleetCenter. Amtrak (☎ **800/ USA-RAIL** or 617/482-3660; www.amtrak.com) serves South Station and

In 2000, after a number of equipment-installation delays, Amtrak planned to institute **Acela** high-speed rail service from New York to Boston. Acela trains run as fast as 150 m.p.h. on their own tracks, making them (in theory) less susceptible to the delays that plague Northeast Corridor service. The new route is designed to compete with the airline shuttles in time (downtown to downtown, about 3 hr.) and undercut them in price (about $140 one-way, or two-thirds of the walk-up plane fare). Acela also replaced Metroliner service between Washington and New York, cutting the trip time on the Washington-Boston route to just under 6 hours. Call Amtrak or check the Web site (www.acela.com) for more details, schedules, and fares on the new routes.

Back Bay Station. At South Station you can take the Red Line to Cambridge or to Park Street, the hub of the MBTA **subway,** where you can make connections to the Green, Blue, and Orange lines. The Orange Line connects Back Bay Station with Downtown Crossing (where there's a walkway to Park Street station) and other points. The MBTA **commuter rail** runs to Ipswich, Rockport, and Fitchburg from North Station, and to points south of Boston, including Plymouth, from South Station.

Amtrak runs to South Station from New York and points south and in between, with stops at Route 128 and Back Bay Station. For long trips, it may be easier than you think to find an airfare that's cheaper than the train.

With the anticipated institution of high-speed rail service in 2000 (see "Planning Pointer," below), Amtrak juggled its schedules and fares. In recent years it has adopted airline-like "yield management" strategies, so plan as far ahead as possible to get the lowest fares. The non-high-speed trip from New York takes $4^{1}/_{2}$ to 5 hours or longer; round-trip fares at press time were $90 to $142. From Washington, count on $8^{1}/_{2}$ hours; round-trip fares run $136 to $172. All fares are subject to change and can fluctuate depending on the time of year. During slow times, excursion fares may be available. Discounts are not available Friday and Sunday afternoon. Always remember to ask for the discounted rate.

BY BUS

With one exception, consider long-distance bus travel a last resort. The exception is the **New York** route, which is so desirable that Greyhound and Peter Pan have drastically upgraded service. It's frequent and relatively fast (4 to $4^{1}/_{2}$ hours)—and the price is about half the regular train fare. If you can time your trip to coincide with an express bus, which makes only one stop, it's worth the extra $5 or so.

The **South Station Transportation Center** (a fancy name for the bus terminal) is on Atlantic Avenue, next to the train station. It's served by the following bus lines: **Greyhound** (☎ 800/231-2222 or 617/526-1801; www.greyhound.com), **American Eagle** (☎ 800/453-5040 or 508/993-5040), **Bonanza** (☎ 800/556-3815 or 617/720-4110), **Brush Hill** (☎ 617/986-6100), **Concord Trailways** (☎ 800/639-3317 or 617/426-8080), **Peter Pan** (☎ 800/237-8747 or 617/426-8554), **Plymouth & Brockton** (☎ 617/773-9401 or 508/746-0378; www.p-b.com), and **Vermont Transit** (☎ 800/451-3292).

Planning Your Trip: An Online Directory

Frommer's Online Directory will help you take better advantage of the travel-planning information available online. Part 1 lists general Internet resources that can make any trip easier, such as sites for obtaining the best possible prices on airline tickets. In Part 2 you'll find some top sites specifically for Boston.

This is not a comprehensive list, but a discriminating selection to get you started. Recognition is given to sites based on their content value and ease of use. Inclusion here is not paid for—unlike some Web-site rankings, which are based on payment. Finally, remember this is a press-time snapshot of leading Web sites; some undoubtedly will have evolved, changed, or moved by the time you read this.

1 Top Travel-Planning Web Sites

by Lynne Bairstow

Lynne Bairstow is the coauthor of *Frommer's Mexico*, and the managing editor of *e-com* magazine.

WHY BOOK ONLINE?

Online agencies have come a long way over the past few years, now providing tips for finding the best fare, and giving you suggested dates or times to travel that yield the lowest price if your plans are at all flexible. Other sites even allow you to establish the price you're willing to pay, and they check the airlines' willingness to accept it. However, in some cases, these sites may not always yield the best price. Unlike a travel agent, for example, they may not have access to charter flights offered by wholesalers.

Online booking sites aren't the only places to reserve airline tickets—all major airlines have their own Web sites and often offer incentives (bonus frequent-flyer miles or net-only discounts, for example) when you buy online or buy an e-ticket.

The new trend is toward conglomerated booking sites. By mid-2000, a consortium of U.S.- and European-based airlines is planning to launch an as-yet unnamed Web site that will offer fares lower than those available through travel agents. United, Delta, Northwest, and Continental have initiated this effort, based on their success at selling airline seats on their own sites.

Check Out Frommer's Site

We highly recommend **Arthur Frommer's Budget Travel Online** (**www.frommers.com**) as an excellent travel-planning resource. Of course, we're a little biased, but you'll find indispensable travel tips, reviews, monthly vacation giveaways, and online booking. Among the most popular features of this site are the regular "Ask the Expert" bulletin boards, which feature Frommer's authors answering your questions via online postings.

Subscribe to Arthur Frommer's Daily Newsletter (**www.frommers.com/ newsletters**) to receive the latest travel bargains and inside travel secrets in your e-mailbox every day. You'll read daily headlines and articles from the dean of travel himself, highlighting last-minute deals on airfares, accommodations, cruises, and package vacations.

Search our Destinations archive (**www.frommers.com/destinations**) of more than 200 domestic and international destinations for great places to stay and dine, and tips on sightseeing (including an extensive section on Boston). Once you've researched your trip, the online reservation system (**www.frommers.com/booktravelnow**) takes you to Frommer's favorite sites for booking your vacation at affordable prices.

The best of the travel planning sites are now highly personalized; they store your seating preferences, meal preferences, tentative itineraries, and credit card information, allowing you to quickly plan trips or check agendas.

In many cases, booking your trip online can be better than working with a travel agent. It gives you the widest variety of choices, control, and the 24-hour convenience of planning your trip when you choose. All you need is some time—and often a little patience—and you're likely to find the fun of online travel research will greatly enhance your trip.

WHO SHOULD BOOK ONLINE?

Online booking is best for travelers who want to know as much as possible about their travel options, for those who have flexibility in their travel dates, and for bargain hunters.

One of the biggest successes in online travel for both passengers and airlines is the offer of last-minute specials, such as American Airlines' weekend deals or other Internet-only fares that must be purchased online. Another advantage is that you can cash in on incentives for booking online, such as rebates or bonus frequent-flyer miles.

Business and other frequent travelers also have found numerous benefits in online booking, as the advances in mobile technology provide them with the ability to check flight status, change plans, or get specific directions from handheld computing devices, mobile phones, and pagers. Some sites will even e-mail or page a passenger if their flight is delayed.

Online booking is increasingly able to accommodate complex itineraries, even for international travel. The pace of evolution on the Net is rapid, so you'll probably find additional features and advancements by the time you visit these sites. The future holds ever-increasing personalization and customization for online travelers.

TRAVEL-PLANNING & -BOOKING SITES

The following sites offer domestic and international flight, hotel, and rental car bookings, plus news, destination information, and deals on cruises and vacation packages. Free (one-time) registration is required for booking.

Important Note: See "Getting There" in chapter 2 and "Getting to the United States" in chapter 3 for the Web addresses of airlines serving Boston. These sites offer schedules and flight booking, and most have pages where you can sign up for e-mail alerts for weekend deals and other late-breaking bargains.

✪ Expedia. expedia.com

Expedia is known as the fastest and most flexible online travel planner for booking flights, hotels, and rental cars. It offers several ways of obtaining the best possible fares: **Flight Price Matcher** service allows your preferred airline to match an available fare with a competitor; a comprehensive **Fare Compare** area shows the differences in fare categories and airlines; and **Fare Calendar** helps you plan your trip around the best possible fares. Its main limitation is that like many online databases, Expedia focuses on the major airlines and hotel chains, so don't expect to find too many budget airlines or one-of-a-kind B&Bs here.

Personalized features allow you to store your itineraries, and receive weekly fare reports on favorite cities. You can also check on the status of flight arrivals and departures, and through MileageMiner, track all of your frequent-flyer accounts.

Expedia also offers packages, cruises, and information on specialized travel (like casino destinations, and adventure, ski, and golf travel). There are also special features for travelers accessing information on mobile devices.

Note: In early 2000, Expedia bought travelscape.com and vacationspot.com, and incorporated these sites into expedia.com.

Travelocity (incorporates Preview Travel). www.travelocity.com; www.previewtravel.com

Travelocity uses the SABRE system to offer reservations and tickets for more than 400 airlines; you can also reserve and purchase from more than 45,000 hotels and 50 car-rental companies. An exclusive feature of the SABRE system is their **Low Fare Search Engine,** which automatically searches for the three lowest-priced itineraries based on a traveler's criteria. Last-minute deals and consolidator fares are included in the search. If you book with Travelocity, you can select specific seats for your flights with online seat maps, and also view diagrams of the most popular commercial aircraft. Their hotel finder provides street-level location maps and photos of selected hotels.

Travelocity features an inviting interface for booking trips, though the wealth of graphics involved can make the site somewhat slow to load, and any adjustment in your parameters means you'll need to completely start over.

This site also has some very cool tools. With the **Fare Watcher** e-mail feature, you can select up to five routes for which you'll receive e-mail notices when the fare changes by $25 or more. If you own an alphanumeric pager with national access that can receive e-mail, Travelocity's **Flight Paging** can alert you if your flight is delayed. You can also access real-time departure and arrival information on any flight within the SABRE system.

Note to AOL Users: You can book flights, hotels, rental cars and cruises on AOL at keyword: Travel. The booking software is provided by Travelocity/Preview Travel and is similar to the Internet site. Use the AOL "Travelers Advantage" program to earn a 5% rebate on flights, hotel rooms, and car rentals.

More people still look online than book online, partly due to fear of putting their credit card numbers out on the Net. Secure encryption, and increasing experienced buying online, has removed this fear for most travelers. In some cases, however, it's simply easier to buy from a local travel agent who can deliver your tickets to your door (especially if your travel is last-minute or if you have special requests). You can find a flight online and then book it by calling a toll-free number or contacting your travel agent, though this is somewhat less efficient. To be sure you're in secure mode when you book online, look for a little icon of a key (in Netscape) or a padlock (in Internet Explorer) at the bottom of your Web browser.

TRIP.com. www.trip.com

TRIP.com began as a site geared for business travelers, but its innovative features and highly personalized approach have broadened its appeal to leisure travelers as well. It is the leading travel site for those using mobile devices to access Internet travel information.

TRIP.com provides the average and lowest fare for the route requested, in addition to the current available fare. An on-site "newsstand" features breaking news on airfare sales and other travel specials. Among its most popular features are Flight TRACKER and intelliTRIP. **Flight TRACKER** allows users to track any commercial flight en-route to its destination anywhere in the United States, while accessing real-time FAA-based flight monitoring data. **intelliTRIP** allows you to identify the best airline, hotel, and rental-car fares in less than 90 seconds.

In addition, TRIP.com offers e-mail notification of flight delays, plus city resource guides, currency converters, and a weekly e-mail newsletter of fare updates, travel tips, and traveler forums.

Yahoo Travel. www.travel.yahoo.com

Yahoo is currently the most popular of the Internet information portals, and its travel site is a comprehensive mix of online booking, daily travel news, and destination information. Their **Best Fares** area offers what it promises, and provides feedback on refining your search if you have flexibility in travel dates or times. There is also an active section of Message Boards for discussions on travel in general, and to specific destinations.

LAST-MINUTE DEALS & OTHER ONLINE BARGAINS

There's nothing airlines hate more than flying with lots of empty seats. The Net has enabled airlines to offer last-minute bargains to entice travelers to fill those seats. Most of these are announced on Tuesday or Wednesday and are valid for travel the following weekend, but some can be booked weeks or months in advance. You can sign up for weekly e-mail alerts at the airlines' own sites (see "Getting There," in chapter 2, "Planning Your Trip: The Basics") or check sites that compile lists of these bargains, such as **Smarter Living** or **WebFlyer** (see below). To make it easier, visit a site that will round up all the deals and send them in one convenient weekly e-mail.

Cheap Tickets. www.cheaptickets.com

Cheap Tickets has exclusive deals that aren't available through more mainstream channels. One caveat about the Cheap Tickets site is that it will offer fare quotes for a route, and later show this fare is not valid for your dates of travel—most other Web sites, such as Expedia, consider your dates of travel before showing what fares are available. Despite its problems, Cheap Tickets can be worth the effort because its fares can be lower than those offered by its competitors.

✪ 1travel.com. www.1travel.com

Here you'll find deals on domestic and international flights and hotels. 1travel.com's **Saving Alert** compiles last-minute air deals so you don't have to scroll through multiple e-mail alerts. A feature called "Drive a little using low-fare airlines" helps map out strategies for using alternate airports to find lower fares. And **Farebeater** searches a database that includes published fares, consolidator bargains, and special deals exclusive to 1travel.com. *Note:* The travel agencies listed by 1travel.com have paid for placement.

Bid for Travel. www.bidfortravel.com

Bid for Travel is another of the travel auction sites, similar to Priceline.com (see below), which are growing in popularity. In addition to airfares, Internet users can place a bid for vacation packages and hotels.

LastMinuteTravel.com. www.lastminutetravel.com

Suppliers with excess inventory come to this online agency to distribute unsold airline seats, hotel rooms, cruises, and vacation packages. It's got great deals, but an excess of advertisements and slow-loading graphics.

Moment's Notice. www.moments-notice.com

As the name suggests, Moment's Notice specializes in last-minute vacation deals. You can browse for free, but if you want to purchase a trip you have to join Moment's Notice, which costs $25.

✪ Priceline.com. travel.priceline.com

Priceline lets you "name your price" for domestic and international airline tickets and hotel rooms. You select a route and dates, guarantee with a credit card, and make a bid for what you're willing to pay. If one of the airlines in Priceline's database has a fare lower than your bid, your credit card will automatically be charged for a ticket.

But you can't say when you want to fly—you have to accept any flight leaving between 6am and 10pm on the dates you selected, and you may have to make a stopover. No frequent-flyer miles are awarded, and tickets are nonrefundable and can't be exchanged for another flight. So if your plans change, you're out of luck. Priceline can be good for travelers who have to take off on short notice (and who are thus unable to qualify for advance purchase discounts). But be sure to shop around first, because if you overbid, you'll be required to purchase the ticket—and Priceline will pocket the difference between what it paid for the ticket and what you bid.

Priceline says that over 35% of all reasonable offers for domestic flights are being filled on the first try, with much higher fill rates on popular routes (New York to San Francisco, for example). They define "reasonable" as not more than 30% below the lowest generally available advance-purchase fare for the same route.

Smarter Living. www.smarterliving.com

Best known for its e-mail dispatch of weekend deals on 20 airlines, Smarter Living also keeps you posted about last-minute bargains.

SkyAuction.com. www.skyauction.com

An auction site with categories for airfare, travel deals, hotels, and much more.

Travelzoo.com. www.travelzoo.com

At this Internet portal, more than 150 travel companies post special deals. It features a Top 20 list of the best deals on the site, selected by its editorial staff

Check Your E-mail While You're on the Road

You don't have to be out of touch just because you don't carry a laptop while you travel. Web browser–based free e-mail programs make it much easier to stay in e-touch.

Just open a freemail account at a browser-based provider, such as **MSN Hotmail** (**hotmail.com**) or **Yahoo! Mail** (**mail.yahoo.com**). AOL users should check out **AOL Netmail,** and **USA.NET** (**www.usa.net**) comes highly recommended for functionality and security. You can find hints, tips and a mile-long list of freemail providers at www.emailaddresses.com.

Be sure to give your freemail address to the family members, friends, and colleagues with whom you'd like to stay in touch while you're in Boston. All you'll need to check your freemail account while you're away from home is a Web connection, easily available at net cafes, copy shops, and cash- and credit-card Internet-access machines (often available in hotel lobbies or business centers) throughout the Boston area. After logging on, just point the browser to **www.hotmail.com**, **www.yahoo.com**, or the address of any other service you're using. Enter your user name and password, and you'll have access to your mail, both for receiving and sending messages to friends and family back home, for just a few dollars an hour.

Online Directory

each Wednesday night. This list is also available via an e-mailing list, free to those who sign up.

WebFlyer. www.webflyer.com
WebFlyer is a comprehensive online resource for frequent flyers and also has an excellent listing of last-minute air deals. Click on "Deal Watch" for a roundup of weekend deals on flights, hotels, and rental cars from domestic and international suppliers.

2 The Top Web Sites for Boston

by Marie Morris

The major problem with Web sites that cover Boston (and, I'm sure, other cities) is updating—or rather, the lack thereof. If you run across a description or listing of an establishment or event that you know will make or break your trip, *always* double-check that information. In this section, I've concentrated on well-maintained sites, using criteria that won't come easily to an out-of-towner (this attraction's closed, that restaurant hasn't served brunch in over a year, and so forth). You can approximate this process by using a search engine that tells you when each site was updated—I like AltaVista for this, but there are others—and calling ahead before you block out time for an activity or destination that turns out to be closed.

ATTRACTIONS & ACTIVITIES
Also see "City Guides & Other General Resources," which are good jumping-off points for the complete novice.

✪ Metropolitan District Commission. www.magnet.state.ma.us/mdc
If it's happening on state land, you can probably find out about it here. The wide-ranging site includes descriptions of properties and activities and has a planning area to help you make the most of your time.

☻ **National Park Service. www.nps.gov**
This invaluable site provides reams of information about hundreds of places; it's especially useful in a history-rich area like eastern Massachusetts. Click on the state for site listings, which incorporate directions, nearby dining options, and loads of photos.

Society for the Preservation of New England Antiquities.
 www.spnea.org
The society operates dozens of historic buildings throughout the region, and its site often includes fascinating material on ongoing restoration and research.

CITY GUIDES & OTHER GENERAL RESOURCES

☻ **Boston.com. www.boston.com**
The Boston Globe operates this site, one of the most comprehensive in the region. Besides newspaper content, it offers access to a virtual forest of listings and links. The most helpful area for out-of-towners, the recently beefed-up arts and entertainment section, covers dining, movies, music, and the arts.

Boston Insider. www.theinsider.com/boston
Travel tips, mostly for the budget-conscious; content is staff- and user-generated. The "Survival Tip" section touches on everything from free entertainment to finding an apartment. The policy of including the date of each comment sets this site apart—you still risk running across an outdated tip, but at least you know how outdated it is.

CitySearch. boston.citysearch.com
Arts, nightlife, entertainment, and events listings, plus sassy restaurant reviews. Management is quick to disclaim any favoritism, but know that CitySearch is part of Ticketmaster Online (it absorbed Microsoft's Sidewalk service in 1999).

☻ **Excite! www.city.net/countries/united_states/massachusetts/boston**
 and **www.city.net/countries/united_states/massachusetts/cambridge**
Links galore.

Greater Boston Convention & Visitors Bureau. www.bostonusa.com
A massive database that incorporates hotels, restaurants, attractions, and nightlife destinations. This isn't the best place to start—you need some sense of where you want to go and what you want to do—but it's helpful as you move deeper into the planning process.

Massachusetts Office of Travel and Tourism. www.mass-vacation.com
Covers the whole state, so it's great if you're planning trips outside the Boston area. The ☻ **lobster tutorial** is a must-see.

Massachusetts Port Authority. www.massport.com
MassPort, which operates the airport, devotes an area of its site to helpful visitor information.

DINING

Boston Chefs. www.bostonchefs.com
Mouthwatering photos, regularly updated menus from some of the biggest names in town, and almost comically uncritical text.

☻ **Mayor's Food Court. www.mayorsfoodcourt.com**
This city-run resource is Boston's least appetizing but most informative food-oriented site. It lists the results of restaurant inspections and reinspections, with numerical scores. Search by name or by neighborhood, click on the number of

the violation—every restaurant seems to have at least one—and a pop-up window describes the relevant section of the code.

Zagat Survey. www.zagat.com
Searchable listings of brief reviews and food, dÉcor, and service scores for many (but not all) Boston-area restaurants. The survey responses that go into the reviews come from a self-selecting group of frequent diners who tend to be tough graders—a score in the high 20s really means something—but swayed by reputation.

GETTING AROUND

Logan Airport. www.massport.com/logan/default.asp
Airport map, ground transportation descriptions, traffic and parking info, and construction updates. You can also check on flight arrivals and departures. The list of airlines that serve Logan includes links to their Web sites.

✪ **Massachusetts Bay Transportation Authority. www.mbta.com**
Schedules and route maps for "T" subways, trolleys, buses, and commuter rail. You can buy visitor passports online (subject to a service charge).

GOOFING AROUND

The Big Dig. www.bigdig.com
Why would a construction project need a Web site? After you get a load of this one, you'll know why.

Massachusetts Film Office. www.state.ma.us/film
Mostly for filmmakers, this site also includes a list of movies shot in the state (not just in Boston).

Wicked Good Guide to Boston. www.boston-online.com/wicked.html
The most entertaining aspect of this site is a Boston-to-English dictionary that both mocks and celebrates local accents.

NEWSPAPERS & MAGAZINES

Boston magazine. www.bostonmagazine.com
The lifestyle-oriented monthly lists events, shopping destinations, and restaurants (advertisers and not).

✪ **Boston Globe. www.boston.com/globe**
An excellent place to bone up on local happenings as your trip approaches.

Boston Herald. www.bostonherald.com
Less content than the *Globe* site, which makes it easier to navigate but not as comprehensive. The best arts and events coverage appears on Friday.

✪ **Boston Phoenix. www.bostonphoenix.com**
The arts-oriented weekly puts its extensive entertainment listings and reviews online. Includes the area's best listings for gay, lesbian, and bisexual readers.

SIDE TRIPS FROM BOSTON
GENERAL RESOURCES

✪ **Massachusetts Office of Travel and Tourism. www.mass-vacation.com**
The best site for linking to regional visitor bureaus.

✪ **Massachusetts Bay Transportation Authority. www.mbta.com**
Invaluable if you won't have a car. Always remember to check the timing of return trips before you venture out for the day.

LEXINGTON & CONCORD

Greater Merrimack Valley Convention & Visitors Bureau.
www.lowell.org

Lexington community site. www.lexingtonweb.com

Lexington Historical Society. www.lexingtonhistory.org

Concord Chamber of Commerce. www.ultranet.com/~conchamb

Concord community site. www.concordma.com

Concord town site. www.concordnet.org

Minute Man National Historical Park. www.nps.gov/mima

✪ **Orchard House.** www.louisamayalcott.org

THE NORTH SHORE & CAPE ANN

✪ **Cape Ann.** www.cape-ann.com
This copiously illustrated site includes the Chamber of Commerce (www.
cape-ann.com/cacc), links to each Cape Ann community, and encyclopedic
listings.

Destination Salem (Office of Tourism & Cultural Affairs).
www.salem.org

Gloucester Tourism Commission. www.gloucesterma.com

Marblehead Chamber of Commerce. www.marbleheadchamber.org

North of Boston Convention & Visitors Bureau.
www.northofboston.org

Rockport Chamber of Commerce and Board of Trade.
www.rockportusa.com

Salem Chamber of Commerce. www.salem-chamber.org

✪ **Salem community site.** www.salemweb.com

Salem Maritime National Historic Site. www.nps.gov/sama

PLYMOUTH

Destination Plymouth. www.visit-plymouth.com

America's Homepage: Plymouth. pilgrims.net

Online Directory

3

For Foreign Visitors

American fads and fashions have spread across the world, making the United States seem like familiar territory long before you arrive. Perhaps you even have friends or relatives studying in the Boston area. Nevertheless, any foreign visitor will encounter many peculiarities and uniquely American situations. Be sure to consult chapter 2 for general advice, too.

1 Preparing for Your Trip

ENTRY REQUIREMENTS

Immigration laws are a hot political issue, and the following requirements may have changed somewhat by the time you plan your trip. Check at any U.S. embassy or consulate for current information and requirements. You can also check the U.S. State Department's Web site (www.state.gov).

DOCUMENTS The State Department's **Visa Waiver Pilot Program** allows citizens of some countries to enter the U.S. without a visa for stays of up to 90 days. At press time they included Andorra, Argentina, Australia, Austria, Belgium, Brunei, Denmark, Finland, France, Germany, Iceland, Ireland, Italy, Japan, Liechtenstein, Luxembourg, Monaco, the Netherlands, New Zealand, Norway, San Marino, Slovenia, Spain, Sweden, Switzerland, and the United Kingdom. Citizens of these countries need only a valid passport and a round-trip air or cruise ticket in their possession on arrival. If they first enter the United States, they may then visit Mexico, Canada, Bermuda, and the Caribbean islands and return to the United States without a visa. Further information is available from any U.S. embassy or consulate. Canadian citizens may enter the United States without visas; they need only proof of residence.

Citizens of all other countries must have a **tourist visa,** available free from any U.S. consulate, and a valid passport that expires at least 6 months after the scheduled end of the visit to the United States.

Obtaining a U.S. Visa The traveler must submit (in person or by mail) a completed application form with a $1^1/_2$-inch-square photo, and demonstrate binding ties to a residence abroad. Contact the nearest U.S. embassy or consulate for directions on applying by mail. Your travel agent or airline office may also be able to supply visa applications and instructions. Usually you can get a visa right away or within

24 hours, but it could take longer during the summer rush, from June to August. The U.S. consulate or embassy that issues your visa will determine whether you are issued a multiple- or single-entry visa and any restrictions on the length of your stay.

British subjects can call the **U.S. Embassy Visa Information Line** (☎ **0891/ 200-290**) or the **London Passport Office** (☎ **0990/210-410** for recorded information).

Driver's Licenses   Massachusetts recognizes **foreign driver's licenses,** but you might want to get an international driver's license if your home license is not written in English.

MEDICAL CONCERNS   Inoculations or vaccinations are not required unless you're arriving from an area known to be suffering from an epidemic (particularly cholera or yellow fever). If you have a disease that requires treatment with a controlled substance or syringe-administered medications, carry a valid signed prescription from your physician to allay suspicions that you might be smuggling drugs (a serious offense that carries severe penalties).

For **HIV-positive visitors,** requirements for entering the United States are somewhat vague and change frequently. The latest edition of *HIV and Immigrants: A Manual for AIDS Service Providers* states: ". . . although INS doesn't require a medical exam for everyone trying to come into the United States, INS officials may keep out people who they suspect are HIV positive. INS may stop people because they look sick or because they are carrying AIDS/HIV medicine. For this reason, temporary visitors should try not to carry their HIV medicine or literature about AIDS in their luggage when they come into the United States."

An HIV-positive person who is denied a visa can ask for a special waiver under certain circumstances. The special waiver is for people visiting the U.S. for a short time— for instance, to attend a conference, visit close relatives, or receive medical treatment. For up-to-the-minute information, contact the Centers for Disease Control's **National Center for HIV** (☎ **404/332-4559;** www.hivatis.org) or **Gay Men's Health Crisis** (☎ **212/367-1000;** www.gmhc.org).

CUSTOMS REQUIREMENTS   Every visitor over 21 years old may bring into the United States, free of duty, 1 liter of wine or hard liquor, 200 cigarettes or 100 cigars (but none from Cuba) or 3 pounds of smoking tobacco, and $100 worth of gifts. The exemptions are offered to travelers who spend at least 72 hours in the United States and who have not claimed them within the preceding 6 months. It is forbidden to bring into the country foodstuffs (particularly fruit and cooked meats) and plants (vegetables, seeds, tropical plants, and the like). Foreign tourists may bring in or take out up to $10,000 in U.S. or foreign currency with no formalities. Larger sums must be declared to customs on entering or leaving, which includes filing form CM 4790. For more specific information regarding U.S. Customs, call your nearest U.S. embassy or consulate, or the **U.S. Customs** office (☎ **202/927-1770;** www.customs.ustreas.gov).

INSURANCE

The United States has no national health system. Because the cost of medical care is extremely high, we strongly advise every traveler to secure health insurance coverage before setting out. Doctors and hospitals are expensive and in most cases require payment or proof of coverage before they provide services.

Policies can cover everything from the loss or theft of your baggage to trip cancellation to the guarantee of bail in case you're arrested. Good policies will also cover the costs of an accident, repatriation, or death. See "Health & Insurance" in chapter 2 for more information. Packages such as **Europ Assistance** in Europe are sold by automobile clubs and travel agencies at attractive rates. **Worldwide Assistance Services, Inc.** (☎ **800/ 821-2828;** www.europ-assistance.com) is the agent for Europ Assistance in the United States.

Although lack of health insurance might prevent you from being admitted to a hospital except in an emergency, don't worry about being left on a street corner to die: The American way is to fix you now and bill you (over and over, if necessary) later.

Insurance for British Travelers   Most big travel agents offer their own insurance and will probably try to sell you a package when you book a holiday. Think before you sign. **Britain's Consumers' Association** recommends that you insist on seeing the policy and reading the fine print before buying travel insurance. **The Association of British Insurers** (☎ **0171/600-3333**) gives advice by phone and publishes *Holiday Insurance,* a free guide to policy provisions and prices. You might also shop around for better deals. Try **Columbus Travel Insurance Ltd.** (☎ **020/7375-0011**) or, for students, **Campus Travel** (☎ **020/8730-2101**).

Insurance for Canadian Travelers   Check with your provincial health plan offices or call **HealthCanada** (☎ **613/957-2991**) to find out the extent of coverage and what documentation and receipts you must take home if you are treated in the U.S.

MONEY
CURRENCY   The American monetary system has a decimal base: 1 U.S. **dollar** ($1) = 100 **cents** (100¢).

Dollar bills commonly come in $1 (a "buck"), $5, $10, $20, $50, and $100 denominations. Bills larger than $20 are not welcome for small purchases and are not accepted in most taxis or fast-food restaurants. Two designs of each bill larger than $1 are or soon will be in circulation. The newer versions have larger, off-center portraits on their "faces" and are identical to old-style money in value and negotiability, with one exception: Some vending machines don't recognize the new designs and bear signs warning you not to use them. The slang term "break" (as in "Can you break a 20?") means "make change for."

There are six coin denominations: 1¢ (1 cent or a "penny"), 5¢ (5 cents or a "nickel"), 10¢ (10 cents or a "dime"), 25¢ (25 cents or a "quarter"), 50¢ (50 cents or a "half-dollar"), and $1. A new gold-colored $1 coin went into circulation in 2000. The quarter-size Susan B. Anthony coin is not in common use and is typically dispensed only by post office vending machines when you buy more than a few stamps.

CURRENCY EXCHANGE   The foreign exchange bureaus so common in Europe are rare even in airports in the United States and nonexistent outside major cities. Try to avoid changing foreign money (or traveler's checks in currency other than U.S. dollars) at small-town bank branches. In the Boston area, many banks offer currency exchange at larger, centrally located branches. For addresses, see "Currency Exchange," under "Fast Facts: For the Foreign Traveler," below.

CREDIT CARDS & ATMs   Credit cards are the most widely used form of payment in the United States. The most common are **Visa** (BarclayCard in Britain), **Master-Card** (EuroCard in Europe, Access in Britain, Chargex in Canada), **American Express, Diners Club, Discover,** and **Carte Blanche.** You need a credit card to rent a car in Massachusetts. Some stores and restaurants do not take credit cards, though, so be sure to ask in advance. Most businesses display a sticker near their entrance to let you know which cards they accept. *Note:* Some businesses require a minimum purchase, usually around $10, to use a credit card.

We strongly recommend that you bring at least one major credit card. Hotels, car-rental companies, and airlines usually require a credit-card imprint as a deposit against expenses, and in an emergency a credit card can be priceless.

You'll find **automated teller machines (ATMs)** all over Boston (and the rest of the U.S.). Some ATMs allow you to draw U.S. currency against your bank and credit cards. Check with your bank before leaving home. Remember that you will need your personal identification number (PIN) to do so, and you most likely will pay a fee. One way around these fees is to ask for cash back at grocery stores that accept ATM cards and don't charge usage fees. Of course, you'll have to purchase something first.

TRAVELER'S CHECKS   Traveler's checks are widely accepted, especially in cities, but you'll probably find credit cards cheaper and faster. Make sure your traveler's checks are denominated in U.S. dollars because foreign-currency checks are often dif-ficult to exchange. The three most widely recognized issuers are **American Express, Thomas Cook,** and **Visa.** Be sure to record the numbers of the checks and keep that information separately in case they are lost or stolen. Most businesses take traveler's checks, but you're better off cashing them in at a bank (in small amounts) and paying in cash. You need identification, such as a driver's license or passport, to change a trav-eler's check.

SAFETY

GENERAL SUGGESTIONS   Tourist areas are generally safe, but U.S. urban areas tend to be less safe than those in Europe or Japan. Visitors should always stay alert, particularly in large cities like Boston. Although the crime rate is its lowest in a gen-eration, that's no consolation if you're the victim. Ask at your hotel's front desk or at a tourist office if you plan to visit an unfamiliar area and aren't sure if it's safe.

Avoid deserted areas, especially at night. Don't go into any city park at night, even to jog or skate, unless there is an event that attracts crowds—for example, Boston's concerts and movies on the Esplanade. Generally speaking, you can feel safe in areas where there are many people and many open establishments.

Avoid carrying valuables with you on the street, and don't display expensive cam-eras or electronic equipment. Try not to stop in the middle of the sidewalk and unfurl your map—consult it inconspicuously, or ask another pedestrian for directions. Sling your pocketbook diagonally across your body and keep a hand on it, and place your wallet or billfold in an inside pocket. Make sure your wallet and other valuables are not easily accessible. If possible, keep them on your person and never, ever in the out-side pocket of a backpack. In theaters, restaurants, and other public places—especially airports and train and bus terminals—keep your possessions in sight at all times.

Remember also that hotels are open to the public, and in a large hotel security might not be able to screen everyone entering. Always lock your room door—don't assume that once inside your hotel you are automatically safe and no longer need to be on your guard.

DRIVING   If you must drive—at the risk of boring you to tears, there's no need to if you're visiting only Boston and Cambridge—the best way to protect yourself is to be aware of your surroundings. Question your rental agency about personal safety, or

Travel Tip

Keep copies of all your travel papers separate from your wallet or purse, and leave a copy with someone at home in case you need something faxed to you in an emergency.

ask for a brochure of traveler safety tips when you pick up your car. Ask for written directions, or a map with the route clearly marked, showing how to get to your destination. Some agencies will rent you a cellular phone along with the car—ask when you make your reservation. If possible, arrive and depart during daylight hours.

Park in well-lighted, well-traveled areas if possible. Always keep your car doors locked, whether the car is attended or unattended. Look around you before you get out of your car, and never leave any packages or valuables in sight. If someone attempts to rob you or steal your car, do not try to resist—report the incident to the police department immediately by dialing ☎ **911.** This is a free call, even from pay phones.

Recently more and more crime has involved cars and drivers. If you drive off a highway into a doubtful neighborhood, leave the area as quickly as possible. If you have an accident, even on the highway, stay in your car with the doors locked until you assess the situation or until the police arrive. If you are bumped from behind on the street or are involved in a minor accident with no injuries and the situation appears to be suspicious, motion to the other driver to follow you to the nearest police precinct, well-lighted service station, or all-night store. *Never* get out of your car in such situations.

If you see someone on the road who indicates a need for help, *do not* stop. Note the location, drive to a well-lighted area, and telephone the police.

2 Getting to the United States

Boston is an increasingly popular direct destination, although many itineraries from overseas still go through another American city. There's direct service on **British Airways, Delta, United,** and **Virgin Atlantic** from London; **Aer Lingus** from Dublin; **Air France, American,** and **TWA** from Paris; **Lufthansa** from Frankfurt; **Northwest/KLM** from Amsterdam; **Alitalia** from Milan; **Icelandair** from Reykjavik; and **Swissair** from Geneva and Zurich. From Canada, **Air Canada** flies directly from Halifax, Montréal, and Toronto; **Canadian Airlines/Air Atlantic** flies from Vancouver only.

AIRLINE DISCOUNTS   The idea of traveling abroad on a budget is something of an oxymoron, but travelers can reduce the price of a plane ticket by several hundred dollars if they take the time to shop around. For example, overseas visitors can take advantage of the APEX (Advance Purchase Excursion) reductions offered by all major U.S. and European carriers. For more money-saving airline advice, see "Getting There" in chapter 2. For the best rates, compare fares and be flexible with the dates and times of travel.

IMMIGRATION & CUSTOMS CLEARANCE   Visitors arriving by air, no matter what the port of entry, should cultivate a good measure of patience and resignation before setting foot on U.S. soil. Getting through immigration control might take as long as 2 hours on some days, especially on summer weekends. Add the time it takes to clear customs, and you'll see that you should allow for long delays when you plan connections between international and domestic flights—an average of 2 to 3 hours at least.

Travelers arriving by car or rail from Canada find border-crossing formalities streamlined almost to the vanishing point. Air travelers from Canada, Bermuda, and some places in the Caribbean can sometimes save time by going through customs and immigration at the point of departure.

In the Air, on the Web

The following major airlines serve Logan International Airport.

- **Aer Lingus:** www.aerlingus.ie
- **Air Canada:** www.aircanada.ca
- **Air France:** www.airfrance.com
- **Alitalia:** www.alitalia.it
- **British Airways:** www.british-airways.com
- **Canadian Airlines:** www.cdnair.ca
- **Icelandair:** www.icelandair.is
- **KLM:** www.klm.com
- **Korean Air:** www.koreanair.com
- **Lufthansa:** www.lufthansa.com
- **Olympic:** www.olympic-airways.gr
- **Qantas:** www.qantas.com.au
- **Sabena:** www.sabena-usa.com
- **Swissair:** www.swissair.com
- **TAP Air Portugal:** www.TAP-AirPortugal.pt
- **Virgin Atlantic:** www.fly.virgin.com

3 Getting Around the United States

BY PLANE   For a list of domestic carriers that serve Boston, see "Getting There" in chapter 2.

Some large American airlines (for example, Northwest and Delta) offer travelers on their transatlantic or transpacific flights special discount tickets under the name **Visit USA.** They allow mostly one-way travel between U.S. destinations at low prices. The tickets are not on sale in the U.S., and you must buy them along with your international ticket. This system is the best, easiest, and fastest way to see the United States at low cost. Get information well in advance from your travel agent or the office of the airline concerned because the conditions attached to the tickets can be changed without notice.

BY CAR   This is the best way to see the country outside the major cities, especially if you have time to explore. The major roads are excellent, and the secondary routes that branch off them can lead you to the small towns and natural wonders that help make the United States such a multifaceted destination. Renting a car just to drive around the Boston area, however, is not advisable.

National car-rental companies with offices in Boston include **Alamo** (☎ 800/ 327-9633), **Avis** (☎ 800/331-1212), **Budget** (☎ 800/527-0700), **Dollar** (☎ 800/ 800-4000), **Hertz** (☎ 800/654-3131), **National** (☎ 800/227-7368), and **Thrifty** (☎ 800/367-2277).

If you plan to rent a car in the U.S., you probably won't need the services of an additional automobile organization. If you plan to buy or borrow a car, automobile association membership is recommended. **AAA,** the **American Automobile Association**

Planning Pointer

"But New York and Boston look so close on the map," says the budget-minded international traveler. No matter how great that deal on airfare to New York is, make sure you budget enough time and money to continue to Boston. The transfer from airport to airport or to the train or bus station in the New York area can be complicated or expensive (or both).

(☎ **800/222-4357;** www.aaa.com), is the country's largest auto club and supplies its members with maps, insurance, and emergency road service. The cost of joining runs from $63 for singles to $87 for two members, but your auto club at home might have a reciprocal arrangement, entitling you to free AAA service.

BY TRAIN   International visitors can buy a **USA Railpass,** good for 15 or 30 days of unlimited travel on **Amtrak** (☎ **800/USA-RAIL;** www.amtrak.com). The pass is available through many foreign travel agents. Prices in 2000 for a 15-day pass were $295 off-peak (mid-October to late May) and $440 during peak travel periods; for a 30-day pass, $385 off-peak and $550 peak. With a foreign passport, you can also buy passes at Amtrak offices in some U.S. cities, including Boston, San Francisco, Los Angeles, Chicago, New York, Miami, and Washington. Reservations are generally required, and you should make them for each part of your trip when you buy the pass (you can change them later at no cost).

Visitors should be aware of the limitations of long-distance rail travel in the United States. With a few notable exceptions—for instance, the Northeast Corridor between Boston and Washington—service is rarely up to European standards. Delays are common, routes are limited and often infrequently served, and fares are rarely significantly lower than discount airfares.

BY BUS   This is the cheapest way to travel in the United States, but is also often slow and uncomfortable. Still, if you have the time and don't mind the conditions, it is cost-effective.

The country's nationwide bus line, **Greyhound/Trailways** (☎ **800/231-2222;** www.greyhound.com), offers an Ameripass for 7 to 60 days of unlimited travel. Prices in 2000 ranged from $169 for 7 days to $479 for 60 days.

Fast Facts: For the Foreign Traveler

Automobile Organizations   Auto clubs supply members with maps, suggested routes, guidebooks, accident and bail-bond insurance, and emergency road service. The major auto club in the United States, with offices nationwide, is the **American Automobile Association,** or AAA (☎ **800/222-4357;** www.aaa.com). If you belong to an auto club at home, inquire about AAA reciprocal arrangements before you leave. AAA can provide you with an International Driving Permit validating your foreign license, and you may be able to join the association even if you are not a member of a reciprocal club. In addition, some automobile-rental agencies now provide the same services; inquire about their availability when you reserve your car.

Business Hours   Banks are open weekdays from 8:30 or 9am to 3 or 4pm, and sometimes Saturday morning; most offer 24-hour access to automated teller machines (ATMs). Business offices generally are open weekdays from 9am to

5 or 6pm. Stores and other businesses are open 6 days a week, and most open on Sunday as well; department stores usually stay open until 9pm at least 1 night a week.

Climate   See "When to Go" in chapter 2.

Currency Exchange   BankBoston (☎ 800/2-BOSTON; www.bankboston. com) offers currency exchange at many locations, including Logan Airport, Terminal C (☎ 617/569-1172) and Terminal E (☎ 617/567-2313), and 1414 Mass. Ave., Harvard Square, Cambridge (☎ 617/556-6050). Other reliable choices are Thomas Cook Currency Services, Inc., 160 Franklin St. (☎ 800/ 287-7362); the Boston Bank of Commerce, 133 Federal St. (☎ 617/ 457-4400); and Ruesch International, 45 Milk St. (☎ 617/482-8600). Many hotels offer currency exchange; check when you make your reservation.

Drinking Laws   The legal drinking age in Massachusetts is 21; be ready to show proof of age when you buy or consume alcohol. In many bars, particularly near college campuses, you may be asked for identification if you appear to be under 30 or so. Beer, wine, and liquor are sold only in liquor stores and in the liquor sections of supermarkets, which by law are closed on Sundays. Bars, taverns, and restaurants may serve alcohol any day of the week.

Electricity   Like Canada, the United States uses 110–120 volts, 60 cycles, compared with 220–240 volts, 50 cycles, in most of Europe, Australia, and New Zealand. Besides a 100-volt converter, small appliances of non-American manufacture, such as hair dryers or shavers, require a plug adapter with two flat, parallel pins. Downward converters that change 220–240 volts to 110–120 volts are difficult to find in the United States, so bring one with you.

Embassies & Consulates   Embassies are in the national capital, Washington, D.C. Some consulates are in Boston.

Listed here are the embassies and Boston consulates of Australia, Canada, Ireland, New Zealand, and Britain. If you are from another country, call Washington, DC, directory assistance (☎ 202/555-1212) to get your embassy's number.

The embassy of **Australia** is at 1601 Mass. Ave. NW, Washington, DC 20036 (☎ 202/797-3000; www.austemb.org). The honorary **consulate in Boston** is at 20 Park Plaza, Suite 457, Boston, MA 02116 (☎ 617/542-8655). There are also consulates in New York, Honolulu, Houston, Los Angeles, and San Francisco.

The embassy of **Canada** is at 501 Pennsylvania Ave. NW, Washington, DC 20001 (☎ 202/682-1740). The **consulate in Boston** is at 3 Copley Place, Suite 400, Boston, MA 02116 (☎ 617/262-3760; www.cdnemb-washdc.org). Other Canadian consulates are in Buffalo, N.Y.; Detroit; Los Angeles; New York; and Seattle.

The embassy of the **Republic of Ireland** is at 2234 Mass. Ave. NW, Washington, DC 20008 (☎ 202/462-3939). The **consulate in Boston** is at 535 Boylston St., 3rd floor, Boston, MA 02116 (☎ 617/267-9330). Other consulates are in Chicago, New York, and San Francisco.

The embassy of **Japan** is at 2520 Mass. Ave. NW, Washington, DC 20008 (☎ 202/238-6700; www.embjapan.org). Japanese consulates are in Atlanta, Kansas City, San Francisco, and Washington.

The embassy of **New Zealand** is at 37 Observatory Circle NW, Washington, DC 20008 (☎ 202/328-4848; www.emb.com/nzemb). There is no consulate in Boston.

The embassy of the **United Kingdom** is at 3100 Mass. Ave. NW, Washington, DC 20008 (☎ **202/462-1340**). The **consulate in Boston** is at Federal Reserve Plaza, 600 Atlantic Ave., 25th floor, Boston, MA 02210 (☎ **617/ 248-9555**). Other consulates are in Atlanta, Chicago, Cleveland, Houston, Los Angeles, New York, San Francisco, and Seattle.

Emergencies   Call ☎ **911** for fire, police, and ambulance. This is a free call from public phones. If you encounter such travelers' problems as sickness, an accident, or lost or stolen baggage, call the Travelers Aid Society, 17 East St., Boston, MA 02111 (☎ **617/542-7286**). The nonprofit international agency, which specializes in helping travelers in distress, also has a branch at Logan Airport's Terminal E (☎ **617/567-5385**).

Gasoline (Petrol)   Most service stations sell several grades of gasoline or "gas." Posted prices include tax. They fluctuate widely and can be as low as half what you would pay in Europe. Each company has a different name for the various levels of octane; most rental cars take the least expensive, regular unleaded. One U.S. gallon equals 3.8 liters or .85 Imperial gallon.

Holidays   All banks, government offices, and post offices close on the following national holidays. Some stores and restaurants and many museums also close. The holidays are **New Year's Day** (January 1), **Martin Luther King, Jr., Day** (third Monday in January), **Presidents' Day** (third Monday in February), **Memorial Day** (last Monday in May), **Independence Day** (July 4), **Labor Day** (first Monday in September), **Columbus Day** (second Monday in October), **Veterans Day** (November 11), **Thanksgiving** (fourth Thursday in November), and **Christmas** (December 25). The Tuesday following the first Monday in November is **Election Day** and is a legal holiday in presidential election years (2000 and 2004).

In Massachusetts, state offices close for **Patriots Day** on the third Monday in April, and Suffolk County offices (including Boston City Hall) close on March 17 for **Evacuation Day.**

Legal Aid   The well-meaning foreign tourist will probably never become involved with the American legal system. However, you should know a few things just in case. If you are "pulled over" or stopped by the police for a minor infraction (for example, of the highway code, such as speeding), *never* attempt to pay the fine directly to a police officer. You may wind up arrested on the much more serious charge of attempted bribery. Pay fines by mail, or directly to the clerk of the court. If accused of a more serious offense, you have the right to remain silent—say and do nothing before consulting a lawyer. Under U.S. law, an arrested person is allowed one telephone call to a party of his or her choice. Call your embassy or consulate.

Mail   Post offices are scattered throughout the city; they're keyed on the map in chapter 1. Postcard stamps cost 20¢ for delivery in the United States, 35¢ for Mexico, 40¢ for Canada, and 50¢ for other international addresses. Letter stamps for up to 1 ounce in the United States are 33¢, 40¢ for half-ounce letters to Mexico, 46¢ to Canada, and 60¢ to other international addresses. A preprinted postal aerogramme costs 50¢.

If you want your mail to follow you on your vacation and you aren't sure of your address, it can be sent to you, in your name, c/o General Delivery, Fort Point Station, Boston, MA 02205 (☎ **617/654-5325**). The station is at 25 Dorchester Ave., behind South Station. If you plan to travel elsewhere, call

☎ 800/275-8777 for information on the nearest post office. The addressee must pick up the mail in person and produce proof of identity (a driver's license or passport, for example).

Medical Emergencies If you become ill, consult your hotel desk staff or concierge for referral to a physician. For an ambulance, dial ☎ 911. Also see "Doctors" in the "Fast Facts: Boston" section in chapter 4.

Newspapers/Magazines National newspapers include the *New York Times, USA Today,* and the *Wall Street Journal.* National newsweeklies include *Newsweek, Time,* and *U.S. News & World Report.* The major newspapers in Boston are the *Boston Globe,* the *Boston Herald,* and the weekly *Boston Phoenix.*

Newsstands with good selections of international periodicals include Out of Town News, Zero Harvard Square, Cambridge (☎ 617/354-7777); Nini's Corner, across the street at 1394 Mass. Ave. (☎ 617/547-3558); and the outdoor newsstand at the corner of Boylston and Dartmouth streets at the Copley T stop on the Green Line.

Radio/Television Nationally, there are six commercial over-the-air television networks—ABC, CBS, NBC, Fox, UPN, and WB—along with the Public Broadcasting System (PBS) and the cable news network CNN. In big cities, viewers have a choice of dozens of channels (including basic cable), most of which transmit 24 hours a day. Most hotels have at least basic cable, and many offer access to "premium" movie channels that show uncut theatrical releases. For the major radio and television stations in Boston, see "Fast Facts: Boston" in chapter 4.

Safety See "Safety" in "Preparing for Your Trip," above.

Taxes In the United States there is no VAT (value-added tax) or other indirect national tax. Every state, county, and city is allowed to levy its own tax on all purchases, including hotel and restaurant checks, airline tickets, and so on. Massachusetts's 5% sales tax is not levied on food, prescription drugs, newspapers, or clothing costing less than $175, but there seems to be a tax on everything else. The meal tax (which also applies to takeout food) is 5%. The lodging tax in Boston and Cambridge is 12.45%.

Telephone, Telegraph, Telex & Fax Private corporations run the U.S. telephone system. Rates, especially for long-distance service and operator-assisted calls, can vary widely, even on calls made from public telephones. Local calls in the Boston area usually cost 35¢. If you expect to make a lot of phone calls, prepaid calling cards are convenient if not particularly economical. They're available at visitor information centers and many stores, usually in multiples of $5. Many public phones at airports now accept American Express, MasterCard, and Visa credit cards.

Generally, hotel surcharges on long-distance and local calls are astronomical. You are usually better off using public pay telephones, which are clearly marked in most public buildings, in many private establishments, and on the street. Outside metropolitan areas, public telephones are more difficult to find. Stores, gas stations, and bars are your best bet.

Most long-distance and international calls can be dialed directly from any phone. For calls to other parts of the United States and to Canada, dial 1 followed by the area code and the seven-digit number. For other international calls, dial 011 followed by the country code, city code, and telephone number.

For reversed-charge or **collect** calls, and for person-to-person calls, dial 0 (zero, not the letter *O*) followed by the area code and number; an operator will come on the line, and you should specify that you are calling collect, or person to person, or both. If your operator-assisted call is international, ask for the overseas operator.

Calls to area codes **800, 888,** and **877** are toll-free. However, calls to numbers in area codes 700 and 900 (chat lines, bulletin boards, "dating" services, and so on) can be very expensive—usually 95¢ to $3 or more per minute, and they sometimes have minimum charges that can run as high as $15 or more.

For directory assistance ("information"), dial ☎ **411.**

Private corporations such Western Union provide telegraph and telex services. You can bring your telegram to a Western Union office (there are hundreds across the country) or dictate it over the phone (☎ **800/325-6000**). You can also telegraph money, or have it telegraphed to you, over the Western Union system, but the service can cost as much as 15% to 20% of the amount sent.

Most hotels have fax machines available for guests' use (be sure to ask if there's a charge to use it), and some hotel rooms have their own fax machines. It may be less expensive to send and receive faxes at a photocopy shop or a store such as Mail Boxes Etc., a national chain of packing service shops (look in the yellow pages directory under "Packaging Services").

Telephone Directories   Two kinds of telephone directories are available. Many hotels provide a set for each room, and they are usually available at the front desk, too.

The general directory is the **white pages,** which list private households and businesses (separately) in alphabetical order. The inside front cover lists emergency numbers for police, fire, and ambulance, and other vital numbers (the Coast Guard, poison-control center, crime victims' hotline, and so on). The first few pages contain a guide to long-distance and international calling, complete with country codes and area codes. Government numbers are usually printed on blue paper within the white pages.

The **yellow pages** directory, printed on yellow paper, lists local services, businesses, and industries by type of activity, with an index at the back. The listings also cover drugstores (pharmacies) and restaurants by geographical location. The directory also includes a condensed city guide, postal ZIP codes, and maps of public transportation routes.

Time   Noon in Boston or New York City (eastern time) is 6pm in Cape Town, 5pm in London, 11am in Chicago (central time), 10am in Denver (mountain time), 9am in Vancouver or Los Angeles (Pacific time), 8am in Anchorage (Alaska time), 7am in Honolulu (Hawaii time), and—1 day ahead—5am in Auckland and 3am in Sydney.

Daylight saving time is in effect from the first Sunday in April through the last Saturday in October (starting at 2am), except in Arizona, Hawaii, part of Indiana, and Puerto Rico. Daylight saving time moves the clock 1 hour ahead of standard time.

Tipping   This is part of the American way of life. Many service employees—waiters and waitresses in particular—rely on tips for the bulk of their earnings. Here are some guidelines. If you receive extraordinary service, consider tipping a bit more.

In hotels, tip bellhops at least $1 per piece, $5 or more for a lot of baggage, and housekeeping $1 to $2 a day. Tip the doorman or concierge only if he or she has provided you with a service (for example, calling a cab or obtaining difficult-to-get theater tickets). Tip valet parking attendants $1 or $2 each time they get your car.

In restaurants, bars, and nightclubs, tip service staff 15% to 20% of the check, bartenders 10% to 15%, checkroom attendants $1 per garment, and valet-parking attendants $1 to $2 per vehicle. Tipping is not expected in cafeterias and fast-food restaurants.

Tip cab drivers 15% to 20% of the fare. Tip skycaps at airports and redcaps at train stations at least $1 per bag ($5 or so if you have a lot of luggage), and hair-dressers and barbers 15% to 20%.

Tipping ushers at movies and theaters, and gas-station attendants, is not expected.

Toilets   Foreign visitors often complain that public toilets are hard to find in the United States. True, there are none on the streets, but you can usually find one in a visitor information center, shopping center, bar, restaurant, hotel, museum, or department store—and it will probably be clean. The cleanliness of toilets at railroad and bus stations and at gasoline service stations varies widely. Some restaurants and bars, including those in Boston's tourist areas, display a sign saying toilets are for the use of patrons only. Paying for a cup of coffee or a soft drink qualifies you as a patron. Many branches of fast-food restaurants or coffee bars have reliably clean rest rooms.

4 Getting to Know Boston

Boston bills itself as "America's Walking City," and walking is by far the easiest way to get around. Legend has it that the street pattern originated as a network of cow paths, but the layout owes more to 17th-century London and to Boston's original shoreline. To orient yourself, it helps to look at the big picture.

This chapter tells you how to get into town and provides an overview of the city's layout and neighborhoods. It also lists information and resources you might need while you're away from home. As you familiarize yourself with Boston's geography, it might help to identify the various neighborhoods and landmarks on the free map provided with this guide.

1 Orientation

ARRIVING

BY PLANE **Logan International Airport** (usually just called "Logan") is in East Boston at the end of the Sumner, Callahan, and Ted Williams tunnels, 3 miles across the harbor from downtown. All five terminals have ATMs, Internet kiosks, pay phones with data ports, and fax machines. Terminals A, B, C, and E have information booths; C and E have bank branches that handle currency exchange; and A and C have children's play spaces. The airport is in the throes of a massive overhaul partly related to the Big Dig (see "It's a Big, Big, Big, Big Dig" box, below). If you're returning a rental car, allow extra time to negotiate the often-confusing layout.

The Massachusetts Port Authority or MassPort (☎ **800/23-LOGAN;** www.massport.com) coordinates airport transportation. The toll-free line provides information about getting to the city and to many nearby suburbs. It's available 24 hours a day and staffed weekdays 8am to 7pm.

The ride into town takes 10 to 45 minutes, depending on traffic, your destination, and the time of day. Except at off hours, such as early on weekend mornings, driving is the slowest way to get into central Boston. Because of the Big Dig, it's also the mode of transportation most likely to leave you stranded in a mysterious traffic tie-up. If you must travel during rush hours or on Sunday afternoon, allow plenty of extra time, or plan to take the subway or water shuttle (and pack accordingly).

You can get into town by subway (the "T"), cab, bus, or boat. The **subway** is fast and cheap—Government Center is just 10 minutes away, and a token (good for one ride) costs only 85¢. Free **shuttle buses** run from each terminal to the Airport station on the Blue Line of the T from 5:30am to 1am every day, year-round. The Blue Line stops at the Aquarium (for the waterfront) and at State Street and Government Center, downtown points where you can exit or transfer to the other lines.

A **cab** from the airport to downtown or the Back Bay costs about $18 to $24. Depending on traffic, the driver may use the Ted Williams Tunnel for destinations outside downtown, such as the Back Bay. On a map, this doesn't look like the fastest route, but often it is. (See "Getting Around," below, for more information on taxis.) You can also try the **Share-A-Cab booths** at each terminal and save up to half the fare.

Some hotels have their own **limousines** or **shuttle vans;** ask about them when you make your reservations. To arrange private limo service, call ahead for a reservation, especially at busy times. Your hotel can recommend a company, or try **Carey Limousine Boston** (☎ 800/336-4646 or 617/623-8700) or **Commonwealth Limousine Service** (☎ 800/558-LIMO outside Massachusetts, or 617/787-5575).

MassPort (see above) coordinates **bus service** between the airport and Gate 25 at South Station. The one-way fare is $6, free for children under 12. Buses leave every 15 to 30 minutes from 7:15am (with an extra run on weekends and holidays at 6:25am) to 10:15pm. The last bus leaves Logan at 11:15pm. For more information about South Station, see "By Train & Bus," below.

The trip to the downtown waterfront in a weather-protected **boat** takes 7 minutes, dock to dock. The free no. 66 shuttle bus connects the airport terminals to the Logan ferry dock. The **Airport Water Shuttle** (☎ 617/330-8680) runs to Rowes Wharf every 15 minutes from 6am to 8pm on weekdays. It runs every 30 minutes on Friday from 8am to 11pm, Saturday from 10am to 11pm, and Sunday and national holidays (except January 1, July 4, Thanksgiving, and December 25) from 10am to 8pm. The one-way fare is $10 for adults and children 12 and up, $5 for seniors, free for children under 12.

Harbor Express (☎ 617/376-8417; www.harborexpress.com) runs between the airport and Long Wharf 24 times a day on weekdays between 5:30am and 9pm (Friday until 11pm), less frequently on weekends. There's no service on Thanksgiving and December 25. The one-way fare is $10.

For information on renting a car, see "Getting Around," below. Unless you need it right away, seriously consider waiting to pick up your rental car until you're starting a day trip or other excursion.

BY TRAIN & BUS   South Station is on Atlantic Avenue at Summer Street, near the Waterfront and the Financial District. It serves Amtrak and the commuter rail, and it's in the same complex as the bus station. South Station is a stop on the Red Line subway, which runs to Cambridge. At the Park Street stop on the Red Line you can make free connections to the Orange Line and Green Line. From Park Street, take the Green Line one stop to Government Center) to transfer to the Blue Line.

For Your Information

The information booth at Logan Airport's Terminal C is now a Visitor Service Center. Staff members, who have gone through concierge training, can help make hotel and restaurant reservations, plan tours, provide convention information, and buy theater and sports tickets.

Back Bay Station is on Dartmouth Street between Huntington and Columbus avenues, straddling the Back Bay and the South End. It serves Amtrak, the commuter rail, and the MBTA Orange Line. The Orange Line connects Back Bay Station with Downtown Crossing (where there's a walkway to Park Street station) and other points.

VISITOR INFORMATION

You'll probably want to begin exploring at a **visitor information center.** The staff members are knowledgeable and helpful, and you can pick up free maps, brochures, listings of special exhibits, and other materials.

The **Boston National Historic Park Visitor Center,** 15 State St. (☎ 617/ 242-5642; www.nps.gov/bost), across the street from the Old State House and the State Street T station, is a good place to start your excursion. National Park Service rangers staff the center, dispense information, and lead free tours of the Freedom Trail. The audiovisual show about the trail provides basic information on 16 historic sites. The center is accessible by stairs and ramps and has rest rooms and comfortable chairs. Open daily 9am to 5pm except January 1, Thanksgiving Day, and December 25.

The Freedom Trail, a line of red paint or painted brick on or in the sidewalk, begins at the **Boston Common Information Center,** 146 Tremont St., on the Common. The center is open Monday through Saturday 8:30am to 5pm, Sunday 9am to 5pm. The **Prudential Information Center,** on the main level of the Prudential Center, is open Monday through Saturday 9am to 8pm, Sunday 11am to 6pm. The **Greater Boston Convention & Visitors Bureau** (☎ 888/SEE-BOSTON or 617/536-4100) operates both centers.

There's a small information booth at **Faneuil Hall Marketplace** between Quincy Market and the South Market Building. It's outdoors and staffed in the spring, summer, and fall Monday through Saturday 10am to 6pm, Sunday noon to 6pm.

In Cambridge, there's an information kiosk (☎ 617/497-1630) in the heart of **Harvard Square,** near the T entrance at the intersection of Massachusetts Avenue, John F. Kennedy Street, and Brattle Street. It's open Monday through Saturday 9am to 5pm, Sunday 1 to 5pm.

PUBLICATIONS   The city's newspapers offer the most up-to-date information about events in the area. The "Calendar" section of the Thursday *Boston Globe* lists festivals, concerts, dance and theater performances, street fairs, films, and speeches. The Friday *Boston Herald* has a similar, smaller insert called "Scene." Both papers briefly list events in their weekend editions. The arts-oriented *Boston Phoenix,* published on Thursday, has extensive entertainment and restaurant listings.

Where, a monthly magazine available free at most hotels throughout the city, lists information about shopping, nightlife, attractions, and current shows at museums and galleries. Newspaper boxes around both cities dispense free copies of the weekly *Tab,* which lists neighborhood-specific event information; *Stuff@Night,* a *Phoenix* offshoot with selective listings and extensive arts coverage; and the *Improper Bostonian,* with extensive event and restaurant listings. Available on newsstands, *Boston* magazine is a lifestyle-oriented monthly with cultural and restaurant listings.

It's a Big, Big, Big, Big Dig

In a city with glorious water views, historic architecture, and gorgeous parks, the most prominent physical feature is a giant highway-construction project. The Central Artery/Third Harbor Tunnel Project, better known as the "Big Dig," is an $12.2 billion undertaking that will move Interstate 93 underground—without closing the road—and connect the Massachusetts Turnpike (I-90) directly to the airport. It encompasses a new bridge over the Charles River (north of North Station), reconfigured Mass. Pike access (south of South Station), and a giant construction site in between.

The Big Dig is scheduled to be completed in 2004; meanwhile, it's causing countless traffic nightmares, fulfilling millions of Tonka truck fantasies, and making engineering history. Many of the construction techniques are so unusual that professionals are coming from all over the world just to see them in action. To learn more, visit www.bigdig.com—or just go for a walk downtown. Completed and ongoing work near the surface is often visible from the street, causing pedestrian and automotive gridlock. Now do you see why I want you to leave the car at home?

CITY LAYOUT

When Boston was established, in 1630, it was one-third the size it is now. Much of the city reflects that original layout, a seemingly haphazard plan that leaves even long-time residents tearing their hair. Old Boston abounds with alleys, dead ends, one-way streets, streets that change names, and streets named after extinct geographical features. On the plus side, every "wrong" turn **downtown,** in the **North End,** or on **Beacon Hill** is a chance to see something interesting you might otherwise have missed.

The landfill projects of the 19th century transformed much of the city's landscape, altering the shoreline and creating the **Back Bay,** where the streets proceed in orderly parallel lines. After you've spent some frustrating time in the older part of the city, that simple plan will seem ingenious. The streets even go in alphabetical order, starting at the Public Garden with Arlington, then Berkeley, Clarendon, Dartmouth, Exeter, Fairfield, Gloucester, and Hereford (and then Massachusetts).

MAIN ARTERIES & STREETS   The most "main" street downtown is **Washington Street.** As a tribute to the first president, streets (except Mass. Ave.) change their names when they cross Washington Street: Bromfield becomes Franklin, Winter becomes Summer, Stuart becomes Kneeland.

The most prominent feature of downtown Boston is **Boston Common,** whether in person, on a map, or from atop the John Hancock Tower or the Prudential Center. Its borders are **Park Street,** which is 1 block long (but looms large in the geography of the T), and four important thoroughfares. **Tremont Street** originates at Government Center and runs through the Theater District into the South End and Roxbury. **Beacon Street** branches off Tremont at School Street and curves around, passing the golden dome of the State House at the apex of Beacon Hill and the Public Garden at the foot, and slicing through the Back Bay and Kenmore Square on its way into Brookline. At the foot of the hill, Beacon crosses **Charles Street,** the fourth side of the Common and the main street of Beacon Hill. Near Massachusetts General Hospital, Charles crosses **Cambridge Street,** which loops around to Government Center and merges with Tremont Street.

On the far side of Government Center, I-93 (also known as the Fitzgerald Expressway) separates the North End from the rest of the city. **Hanover Street** is the main street of the North End; at the harbor it intersects with **Commercial Street,** which runs along the waterfront from the North Washington Street bridge (the route to Charlestown, also known as the Charlestown Bridge) until it gives way to **Atlantic Avenue** at Fleet Street. Atlantic Avenue completes the loop around the North End and runs more or less along the waterfront past South Station.

Boylston Street is the fifth side of the Common. It runs next to the Public Garden, through Copley Square and the Back Bay, and on into the Fenway. To get there it has to cross **Massachusetts Avenue,** or "Mass. Ave.," as it's almost always called (you might as well get into the habit now). Mass. Ave. is 9 miles long, extending as far as Lexington, and cuts through Arlington and Cambridge before hitting Boston at Storrow Drive, then Beacon Street, Marlborough Street, and Commonwealth Avenue. "Comm. Ave." starts at the Public Garden and runs through Kenmore Square, past Boston University, and into the western suburbs. Farther along Mass. Ave., Symphony Hall is at the corner of **Huntington Avenue.** Huntington begins at Copley Square and passes Symphony Hall, Northeastern University, and the Museum of Fine Arts before crossing into Brookline.

FINDING AN ADDRESS   There's no rhyme or reason to the street pattern, compass directions are virtually useless, and there aren't enough street signs. The best way to find an address is to call ahead and ask for directions, including landmarks, or leave extra time for wandering around. If the directions involve a T stop, be sure to ask which exit to use—most stations have more than one.

STREET MAPS   In addition to the map provided with this guide, free maps of downtown Boston and the rapid transit lines are available at visitor information centers around the city. *Where* magazine, available free at most hotels, contains maps of central Boston and the T.

Streetwise Boston ($5.95) and *Artwise Boston* ($5.95) are sturdy, laminated maps available at most bookstores. Less detailed but more fun is MapEasy's *GuideMap to Boston* ($5.95), a hand-drawn map of the central areas and major attractions.

Neighborhoods in Brief

These are the areas visitors are most likely to frequent. When Bostonians say **"downtown,"** they usually mean the first six neighborhoods defined here; there's no "midtown" or "uptown." The numerous residential neighborhoods outside central Boston include the Fenway, South Boston, Dorchester, Roxbury, West Roxbury, and Jamaica Plain. With a couple of exceptions (noted below), Boston is generally safe, but you should still take the precautions you would in any large city, especially at night and when you're out alone.

The Waterfront   This narrow area runs along the Inner Harbor, on Atlantic Avenue and Commercial Street from the North Washington Street bridge to South Station. Once filled with wharves and warehouses, today it abounds with luxury condos, marinas, restaurants, offices, and hotels. Also here are the New England Aquarium and embarkation points for harbor cruises and whale-watching expeditions.

The North End   Crossing under I-93 from downtown on the way to the Inner Harbor brings you to one of the city's oldest neighborhoods. Home to waves of immigrants in the course of its history, it was predominantly Italian for most of the 20th century. It's now about half Italian-American and half newcomers, many of them young professionals who walk to work in the Financial District. Nevertheless, you'll hear Italian spoken in the streets and find a wealth of Italian restaurants, *caffès,* and shops. Nearby, and technically part of the North End, is the **North Station** area. With the opening of the FleetCenter, the nightspots and restaurants closer to Beacon Hill really started jumping. But despite the increased traffic, this area isn't a good place to wander around alone at night.

Faneuil Hall Marketplace & Haymarket   Employees aside, Boston residents tend to be scarce at Faneuil Hall Marketplace (also called Quincy Market, after the central building). An irresistible draw for out-of-towners and suburbanites, this cluster of restored market buildings—bounded by Government Center, State Street, the Waterfront, and the North Station area—is the city's most popular attraction. You'll find restaurants, bars, a food court, specialty shops, and Faneuil Hall itself. **Haymarket,** just off the Central Artery, is home to an open-air produce and fish market on Fridays and Saturdays.

Government Center   Love it or hate it, Government Center introduced modern design into the redbrick facade of traditional Boston architecture. Flanked by Beacon Hill, Downtown Crossing, and Faneuil Hall Marketplace, it is home to state and federal office towers and City Hall.

Financial District   Bounded loosely by State Street, Downtown Crossing, Summer Street, and Atlantic Avenue, the Financial District is the banking, insurance, and legal center of the city. Outside of some popular after-work spots, it's quiet at night.

Downtown Crossing   The intersection that gives Downtown Crossing its name is at Washington Street where Winter Street becomes Summer Street. The Freedom Trail runs through this shopping and business district between the Common, the Theater District, the Financial District, and Government Center. It hops during the day and slows down in the evening.

Beacon Hill   Narrow tree-lined streets and architectural showpieces, mostly in Federal style, make up this residential area in the shadow of the State House. Louisburg (say "Lewis-burg") Square and Mount Vernon Street, two of the loveliest and most exclusive spots in Boston, are on Beacon Hill. Bounded by Government Center, Boston Common, and the river, it's also home to Massachusetts General Hospital, on the nominally less tony north side of the neighborhood.

Charlestown   One of the oldest areas of Boston is where you'll see the Bunker Hill Monument and USS *Constitution* ("Old Ironsides"), as well as one of the city's best restaurants, Olives. Yuppification has brought some diversity to what was once an almost entirely white residential neighborhood, but pockets remain that have earned their reputation for insularity.

South Boston Waterfront (Seaport District)   The city's newest neighborhood needs a name—any suggestions? On the other side of the Fort Point Channel from the Waterfront neighborhood, it's home to the World Trade Center, Seaport Hotel, Fish Pier, federal courthouse, Museum Wharf, and a lot of construction.

Getting Your Bearings

To locate the neighborhoods, see the "Boston Orientation" map in chapter 1, pages 2–3.

Chinatown   The fourth-largest Chinese community in the country is a small but growing area jammed with Asian restaurants, groceries, and gift shops. As the "Combat Zone," or red-light district, has nearly disappeared under pressure from the business community, Chinatown has expanded to fill the area between Downtown Crossing and the Mass. Pike extension. The tiny **Theater District** extends about 1½ blocks from the intersection of Tremont and Stuart streets in each direction; be careful there at night after the crowds thin out.

South End   Cross Stuart Street or Huntington Avenue heading south and you'll soon find yourself in a landmark district packed with Victorian rowhouses and little parks. Known for its ethnic, economic, and cultural diversity, the South End has a large gay community and some of the best restaurants in the city. With the gentrification of the 1980s, Tremont Street (particularly the end closest to downtown) gained a cachet it hadn't known for almost a century. *Note:* Don't confuse the South End with South Boston, an insular, predominantly Irish-American residential neighborhood.

Back Bay   Fashionable since its creation out of landfill over a century ago, the Back Bay overflows with gorgeous architecture and chic shops. It is bounded by the Public Garden, Kenmore Square, the river, and to the south by either Huntington Avenue or St. Botolph Street, depending on who's describing it. Students dominate the area near Mass. Ave. but grow scarce as property values rise toward the Public Garden. Commonwealth Avenue is largely residential, Newbury Street largely commercial; both are excellent places to walk around.

Huntington Avenue   The honorary "Avenue of the Arts" (or, with a Boston accent, "Otts") is home to a number of landmarks. Not a formal neighborhood, Huntington Avenue is where you'll find the Christian Science Center, Symphony Hall (at the corner of Mass. Ave.), Northeastern University, and the Museum of Fine Arts. It touches on the Back Bay, the Fenway, and the Longwood Medical Area before heading southwest into the suburbs. Parts of Huntington can sometimes be a little risky, so if you're leaving the museum at night, stick to the car, a cab, or the Green Line, and travel in a group.

Kenmore Square   The white-and-red Citgo sign that dominates the skyline above the intersection of Commonwealth Avenue, Beacon Street, and Brookline Avenue tells you you're approaching Kenmore Square. Its shops, bars, restaurants, and clubs attract students from adjacent Boston University. The college-town atmosphere goes out the window when the Red Sox are in town and baseball fans pour into the area on the way to historic Fenway Park, 3 blocks away.

Cambridge   Boston's neighbor across the Charles River is a separate city; the areas you're likely to visit are along the MBTA Red Line. **Harvard Square** is a magnet for students, sightseers, and well-heeled shoppers. It's an easy walk along Mass. Ave. southeast to **Central Square,** a rapidly gentrifying area dotted with ethnic restaurants and clubs. North along Mass. Ave. is **Porter Square,** a mostly residential neighborhood with some quirky shops like those that once characterized Harvard Square. Around **Kendall Square** you'll find MIT and many technology-oriented businesses.

2 Getting Around

ON FOOT

If you can manage a fair amount of walking, this is the way to go. Being a pedestrian offers both a positive and the absence of a negative: Boston is best appreciated at street level, and walking the narrow, picturesque streets takes you through an awful lot of stalled cars.

Even more than in a typical large city, be alert. Look both ways before crossing, even on one-way streets, where many bicyclists and some drivers blithely go against the flow. The "walk" cycle of many downtown traffic signals lasts only 7 seconds, and a small but significant part of the driving population considers red lights optional anyway. Keep a close eye on the kids, especially in crosswalks.

BY PUBLIC TRANSPORTATION

The **Massachusetts Bay Transportation Authority,** or MBTA (☎ 617/222-3200; www.mbta.com), is known as the "T," and its logo is the letter in a circle. It runs subways, trolleys, buses, and ferries in Boston and many suburbs, as well as the commuter rail, which extends as far as Providence, R.I.

Newer stations on the Red, Blue, and Orange lines are wheelchair accessible; the Green Line is in the process of being converted. Call ahead or check a system map to see if the stations you need are accessible. All MBTA buses have lifts or kneelers; call ☎ 800/LIFT-BUS for more information. Some bus routes are wheelchair accessible at all times; you might have to make a reservation as much as a day in advance for others. To learn more, call the **Office for Transportation Access** (☎ 800/533-6282 or 617/222-5123; TDD 617/222-5415).

BY SUBWAY   Subways and trolleys take you around Boston faster than any other mode of transportation except walking. The oldest system in the country, the T dates to 1897, and recent and ongoing improvements have made it generally reliable. The trolleys on the ancient Green Line are the most unpredictable—leave extra time if you're taking it to a vital appointment. The system is generally safe, but always watch out for pickpockets, especially around the holidays. And remember, downtown stops are so close together that it's often faster to walk.

The subways are color-coded and are called the Red, Green, Blue, and Orange lines. (The commuter rail to the suburbs is purple on system maps, and sometimes called the Purple Line.) The local fare is 85¢—you'll need a token—and can be as much as $2.25 for some surface line extensions on the Green and Red lines. Transfers are free. Route and fare information and timetables are available at Park Street station (under the Common), which is the center of the system. Signs reading INBOUND and OUTBOUND refer to the direction of trains in relation to Park Street.

Service begins at around 5:15am and shuts down around 12:30am. The only exception is New Year's Eve, or First Night, when closing time is 2am and service is free after 8pm.

BY BUS   The MBTA runs buses and "trackless trolleys" (identifiable by their electric antennae, but otherwise indistinguishable from buses) that provide service around town and to and around the suburbs. The local routes you're likeliest to need are **no. 1,** along Mass. Ave. from Dudley Square in Roxbury through the Back Bay and Cambridge to Harvard Square; **no. 92** and **no. 93,** which run between Haymarket and Charlestown; and **no. 77,** along Mass. Ave. north of Harvard Square to Porter Square, North Cambridge, and Arlington.

The local bus fare is **60¢;** express bus fares are $1.50 and up. Exact change is required. You can use a token, but you won't get change back.

BY FERRY   Two popular and useful routes (both included in the MBTA visitor passport) run on the Inner Harbor. The first connects **Long Wharf** (near the Aquarium T stop), the **Charlestown Navy Yard**—it's a good way to get back downtown from "Old Ironsides" and the Bunker Hill Monument—and **Lovejoy Wharf,** off

Causeway Street behind North Station and the FleetCenter. The other serves **Lovejoy Wharf** and the **World Trade Center,** on Northern Avenue in South Boston near the Fish Pier and the Seaport Hotel. The fare is $1. Call ☎ **617/227-4321** for more information. Service between **Lovejoy Wharf** and **Russia Wharf,** near South Station, is scheduled to begin in 2001; call the MBTA for details.

BY WATER TAXI   From April to mid-October, there's on-call service in small boats that connect 11 stops on the Inner Harbor, including the airport. The flat fare at press time was $10. Call ☎ **617/422-0392.**

BY TAXI

Taxis are expensive and not always easy to find—seek out a cab stand or call a dispatcher. Always ask for a receipt in case you lose something and need to call the company.

Cab stands are usually near hotels. There are also busy ones at Faneuil Hall Marketplace (on North Street), South Station, Back Bay Station, and on either side of Mass. Ave. in Harvard Square, near the Coop and Au Bon Pain.

To call ahead for a cab, try the **Independent Taxi Operators Association,** or ITOA (☎ 617/426-8700), **Boston Cab** (☎ 617/536-5010), **Town Taxi** (☎ 617/ 536-5000), or **Checker Taxi** (☎ 617/536-7000). In Cambridge, call **Ambassador Brattle** (☎ 617/492-1100) or **Yellow Cab** (☎ 617/547-3000). Boston Cab will dispatch a wheelchair-accessible vehicle; advance notice is recommended.

The fare structure: The first quarter-mile (when the flag drops) costs $1.50, and each additional eighth of a mile is 25¢. Wait time is extra, and the passenger pays all tolls, as well as the $1.50 airport fee (on trips leaving Logan only). Charging a flat rate is not allowed within the city; the Police Department publishes a list of distances to the suburbs that establishes the flat rate for those trips. If you want to report a problem or have lost something in a cab, call the Police Department's **Hackney Hotline** (☎ **617/536-8294**).

BY CAR

If you plan to visit only Boston and Cambridge, there's absolutely no reason to have a car. Between the Big Dig and the narrow, one-way streets, Boston in particular is a motorist's nightmare. If you arrive by car, park at the hotel and use the car for day trips. Drive to Cambridge only if you're feeling flush—you'll probably have to pay

---

Planning Pointer

The ✪ **MBTA visitor passport** (☎ 877/927-7277 or 617/222-5218; www.mbta. com) is one of the best deals in town. You get unlimited travel on subway lines and local buses, in commuter rail zones 1A and 1B, and on two ferries, plus discounts on attractions. The cost is $5 for 1 day (so tokens are cheaper for fewer than six trips), $9 for 3 consecutive days, and $18 for 7 consecutive days. You can order passes in advance over the phone or the Web (there's a fee for shipping), or buy them when you arrive at the Airport T stop, South Station, Back Bay Station, or North Station. They're also for sale at the Government Center and Harvard T stations; the Boston Common, Prudential Center, and Faneuil Hall Marketplace information centers; and some hotels. Wait to use your passport until you're ready to start sightseeing (at the airport or front desk, if you plan to plunge in immediately). This will allow you to coordinate trips to businesses that offer discounts with the days you're eligible.

Boston Transit

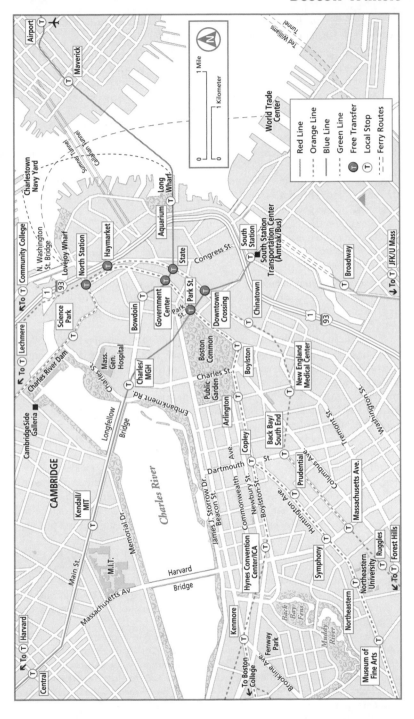

59

to park there, too. If you're not motoring and you decide to take a day trip (see chapter 11), you'll probably want to rent a car. Here's the scoop.

RENTALS   The major car-rental firms have offices at Logan Airport and in Boston, and some have other area branches. Seriously consider waiting to pick up the car until you need it, to save yourself the hassle of driving and parking. Rentals that originate in Boston carry a **$10 convention center surcharge**—you can get around it by picking up your car in Cambridge, Brookline, or another suburb.

If you're traveling at a busy time, especially during foliage season, reserve a car well in advance. Most companies set aside cars for nonsmokers, but you have to ask.

Companies with offices at the airport include **Alamo** (☎ 800/327-9633), **Avis** (☎ 800/831-2847), **Budget** (☎ 800/527-0700), **Dollar** (☎ 800/800-4000), **Hertz** (☎ 800/654-3131), and **National** (☎ 800/227-7368). **Enterprise** (☎ 800/ 325-8007) and **Thrifty** (☎ 800/367-2277) are nearby but not on the grounds, so leave time for the shuttle bus ride.

To rent from the major national chains, you must be at least 25 years old and have a valid driver's license and credit card. If you don't have a credit card, make alternative arrangements well in advance; some companies require that you meet strict eligibility requirements.

Demystifying Rental Insurance   Before you drive off, be sure you're insured. Hasty assumptions about your personal auto insurance or a rental agency's additional coverage could end up costing you thousands of dollars, even if you are involved in an accident that was clearly another driver's fault.

If you already hold a **private auto insurance** policy, you are most likely covered in the United States for loss of or damage to a rental car, and liability in case of injury to any other party involved in an accident. Be sure to find out whether you are covered in the area you are visiting, whether your policy extends to everyone who will be driving the rental car, how much liability is covered in case an outside party is injured in an accident, and whether the type of vehicle you are renting is included under your contract. (Rental trucks, sports utility vehicles, and luxury vehicles may not be covered.)

Most **major credit cards** provide some degree of coverage, but you must use the appropriate card to pay for the rental. Terms vary widely, so be sure to call your credit card company directly. If you are **uninsured,** your credit card provides primary coverage as long as you decline the rental agency's insurance. That means the credit card will cover damage to or theft of a rental car for the full cost of the vehicle. (In a few states, however, theft is not covered; ask specifically about state law where you will be renting and driving.) If you already have insurance, your credit card will provide secondary coverage—which basically covers your deductible.

Credit cards **will not cover liability,** or the cost of injury to an outside party and damage to an outside party's vehicle. If you do not hold an insurance policy, you may seriously want to consider buying additional liability insurance from your rental company. Be sure to check the terms, however: Some rental agencies cover liability only if the renter is not at fault; even then, the rental company's obligation varies from state to state.

Each credit card company has its own peculiarities. Most American Express Optima cards, for instance, do not provide any insurance. American Express does not cover vehicles valued at more than $50,000 when new, luxury vehicles, or vehicles built on a truck chassis. MasterCard does not provide coverage for loss, theft, or fire damage and covers collision only if the rental period does not exceed 15 days. Call your credit card company for details.

Boston Drivers: Beware

Everything you've heard is true. Boston drivers deserve their notoriety, and even though the truly reckless are a tiny minority, it pays to be careful. Never assume that another driver will behave as you might expect, especially when it comes to the rarely used turn signal. Watch out for cars that leave the curb and change lanes without signaling, double- and triple-park in the most inconvenient places imaginable, and travel the wrong way down one-way streets.

The basic insurance coverage offered by most car rental companies, known as the **Loss/Damage Waiver (LDW)** or **Collision Damage Waiver (CDW),** can cost as much as $20 a day. It usually covers the full value of the vehicle with no deductible if an outside party causes an accident or other damage to the rental car. In all states but California, you will probably be covered in case of theft as well. Liability coverage varies according to company policy and state law, but the minimum is usually at least $15,000. If you are at fault in an accident, you will be covered for the full replacement value of the car but not for liability. Some states allow you to buy additional liability coverage for such cases. Most rental companies require a police report to process any claims you file, but your private insurer will not be notified of the accident.

Package Deals   Many packages include airfare, accommodations, and a rental car with unlimited mileage. Compare these prices with the cost of booking airline tickets and renting a car separately. And don't forget to add the price of parking.

Arranging Car Rentals Online   Internet resources can make comparison shopping easier. **Microsoft Expedia** (www.expedia.com) and **Travelocity** (www.travelocity.com) can compare prices, locate bargains, and even make your reservation.

PARKING   It's difficult to find your way around Boston and practically impossible to find parking in some areas. Most spaces on the street are metered (and patrolled until 6pm on the dot every day except Sunday) and are open to nonresidents for hours or less between 8am and 6pm. The penalty is a $25 ticket. Read the sign or meter carefully. In some areas parking is allowed only at certain hours. Rates vary in different sections of the city (usually $1 an hour downtown); bring plenty of quarters. Time limits range from 15 minutes to 2 hours.

If you blunder into a tow-away zone, retrieving the car will cost you at least $100 and a lot of running around. The city tow lot (☎ 617/635-3900) is at 200 Frontage Rd. in South Boston. Take a taxi, or ride the Red Line to Andrew and flag a cab there (the driver can probably guess where you're going).

It's usually best to leave the car in a parking lot or garage and walk. A full day at most lots costs no more than $25 (in other words, cheaper than a parking ticket), and there's often a lower flat rate if you enter and exit before certain times or if you park in the evening. Some restaurants offer reduced rates at nearby garages; ask when you call for reservations.

The reasonably priced city-run garage under **Boston Common** (☎ 617/954-2096) accepts vehicles less than 6 feet, 3 inches tall. Enter from Charles Street between Boylston and Beacon streets. The **Prudential Center** garage (☎ 617/267-1002) has entrances on Boylston Street, Huntington Avenue, and Exeter Street, and at the Sheraton Boston Hotel. Parking is discounted if you buy something at the Shops at Prudential Center and have your ticket validated. The garage at **Copley Place** (☎ 617/375-4488), off Huntington Avenue, offers a similar deal.

Impressions

I have just returned from Boston. It is the only thing to do if you find yourself up there.
—Fred Allen, letter to Groucho Marx, 1953

Never go to Boston. Boston is a singularly horrific city, full of surly weirdos with scraggly beards and terrible manners.
—Cynthia Heimel, *Sex Tips for Girls*, 1983

Good-size garages downtown are at **Government Center** off Congress Street (☎ 617/227-0385), at **Sudbury Street** off Congress Street (☎ 617/973-6954), at the **New England Aquarium** (☎ 617/723-1731), at **75 State St.** (☎ 617/742-7275), and at **Zero Post Office Square** in the Financial District (☎ 617/423-1430). In the Back Bay, there's a large facility near the Hynes Convention Center on **Dalton Street** (☎ 617/247-8006).

SPECIAL DRIVING RULES   When traffic permits, drivers are allowed to make a right turn at a red light after stopping, unless a sign is posted saying otherwise (as it often is downtown). Seat belts are mandatory for adults and children, and infants and children under 5 must be strapped into car seats in the backseat. You can't be stopped just for having an unbelted adult in the car, but a youngster on the loose is reason enough to pull you over.

Two state laws to be aware of, if only because they're broken so frequently it'll take your breath away: Pedestrians in the crosswalk have the right of way, and vehicles already in a rotary (traffic circle or roundabout) have the right of way.

BY BICYCLE

This is not a good option unless you're a real pro or plan to visit Cambridge, which has bike lanes. The streets of Boston proper, with their bloodthirsty drivers and oblivious pedestrians, are notoriously inhospitable to two-wheelers.

For information about renting a bike and about recreational biking, see "Biking" in chapter 7. If you bring or rent a bike, be sure to lock it securely when leaving it unattended, even for a short time.

Fast Facts: Boston

Airport   See "Getting There" in chapter 2 and "Arriving," above.

American Express   The main local office is at 1 State St. (☎ 617/723-8400), opposite the Old State House. It's open weekdays 8:30am to 5:30pm. The Back Bay office, 222 Berkeley St. (☎ 617/236-1334), is open weekdays 9am to 5:30pm. The Cambridge office, just off Harvard Square at 39 John F. Kennedy St. (☎ 617/868-2600), is open weekdays from 8:30am to 7:30pm, Saturday 11am to 5:30pm, Sunday noon to 5pm.

Baby-sitters   Many hotels maintain lists of reliable sitters; check at the front desk or with the concierge. In an emergency, try Parents in a Pinch, 45 Bartlett Circle, Brookline, MA 02446 (☎ 617/739-KIDS), weekdays from 8am to 5pm. It screens child-care providers and will share references with parents who request them. The referral fee of $30 for an evening or half day, or $40 for a full day, is charged to your credit card (AE, MC, V). You pay the provider fee—$8 per hour for one child, plus 50¢ for each additional child (with a 4-hour minimum)—as well as transportation and authorized expenses, in cash or by check directly to the provider.

Camera Repair   Try Bromfield Camera & Video, 10 Bromfield St. (☎ **800/ 723-2628** or 617/426-5230), or the Camera Center, 107 State St. (☎ **800/ 924-6899** or 617/227-7255).

Car Rentals   See "Getting Around," earlier in this chapter.

Climate   See "When to Go" in chapter 2.

Convention Centers   **Hynes Convention Center,** 900 Boylston St. (☎ **617/ 954-2000** or 617/424-8585 for show info; www.jbhynes.com); **World Trade Center,** 164 Northern Ave. (☎ **800/367-9822** or 617/385-5000, or 617/385-5044 for show info; www.wtcb.com); **Bayside Expo Center,** 200 Mt. Vernon St., Dorchester (☎ **617/474-6000;** www.baysideexpo.com).

Dentists   The desk staff or concierge at your hotel might be able to provide the name of a dentist. The Massachusetts Dental Society (☎ **800/342-8747** or 508/651-7511; www.massdental.org/consumers/findadentist.cfm) can point you toward a member.

Doctors   The desk staff or concierge at your hotel should be able to direct you to a doctor, but you can also try one of the many area hospital referral services. Among them are Beth Israel Deaconess Physician Referral (☎ **800/667-5356**), Brigham and Women's Hospital Physician Referral Service (☎ **800/294-9999**), Massachusetts General Hospital Physician Referral Service (☎ **800/ 711-4MGH**), and New England Medical Center Physician Referral Line (☎ **617/636-9700**). The **Boston Evening Medical Center,** 388 Commonwealth Ave. (☎ **617/267-7171**), offers walk-in service, honors most insurance plans, and accepts credit cards.

Driving Rules   See "Getting Around," earlier in this chapter.

Drugstores   See "Pharmacies," below.

Embassies & Consulates   See "Fast Facts: For the Foreign Traveler" in chapter 3.

Emergencies   Call ☎ **911** for fire, ambulance, or the Boston, Brookline, or Cambridge police. This is a free call from pay phones. For the state police, call ☎ **617/523-1212.**

Eyeglass Repair   Cambridge Eye Doctors has offices in downtown Boston at 100 State St. (☎ **617/742-2076**) and 300 Washington St. (☎ **617/426-5536**). For Eyes Optical has branches in the Back Bay at 330 Newbury St. (☎ **617/ 536-4896**) and in Cambridge at 56 John F. Kennedy St. (☎ **617/876-6031**).

Hospitals   Massachusetts General Hospital, 55 Fruit St. (☎ **617/726-2000,** or 617/726-4100 for children's emergency services), and New England Medical Center, 750 Washington St. (☎ **617/636-5000,** or 617/636-5566 for emergency services), are closest to downtown. At the Harvard Medical Area on the Boston–Brookline border are Beth Israel Deaconess Medical Center, 330 Brookline Ave. (☎ **617/667-7000**); Brigham and Women's Hospital, 75 Francis St. (☎ **617/732-5500**); and Children's Hospital, 300 Longwood Ave. (☎ **617/ 355-6000,** or 617/355-6611 for emergency services). In Cambridge are Mount Auburn Hospital, 330 Mount Auburn St. (☎ **617/492-3500,** or 617/ 499-5025 for emergency services), and Cambridge Hospital, 1493 Cambridge St. (☎ **617/498-1000**).

Hotlines   AIDS Hotline (☎ **800/235-2331** or 617/536-7733), Poison Control Center (☎ **617/232-2120**), Rape Crisis (☎ **617/492-7273**), Samaritans Suicide Prevention (☎ **617/247-0220**), Samariteens (☎ **800/252-8336** or 617/247-8050).

Information   See "Visitor Information," earlier in this chapter. For telephone directory assistance, dial ☎ **411.**

Internet Access   Your hotel may have a terminal for guests' use. The ubiquitous **Kinko's** charges 10¢ to 20¢ a minute. Locations include 2 Center Plaza, Government Center (☎ **617/973-9000**); 10 Post Office Sq., Financial District (☎ **617/482-4400**); 187 Dartmouth St., Back Bay (☎ **617/262-6188**); and 1 Mifflin Place, off Mount Auburn Street near Eliot Street, Harvard Square (☎ **617/497-0125**).

Liquor Laws   The legal drinking age is 21. In many bars, particularly near college campuses, you may be asked to show identification if you appear to be under 30 or so. At sporting events, everyone buying alcohol must show ID. Liquor stores and a few supermarkets and convenience stores sell alcohol. Liquor stores (and the liquor sections of other stores) are closed on Sundays, but alcohol may be served in restaurants and bars. Most restaurants have full liquor licenses, but some are restricted to beer, wine, and cordials. Some suburban towns, notably Rockport, are "dry."

Luggage Storage & Lockers   The desk staff or concierge at your hotel might be able to arrange storage for you. Lockers are available at the airport; you can check your luggage during the day at South Station, but not at all at Back Bay Station.

Maps   See "City Layout," earlier in this chapter.

Newspapers/Magazines   The *Boston Globe* and *Boston Herald* are published daily. See "Publications" under "Visitor Information," above, for more information.

Pharmacies   Downtown Boston has no 24-hour pharmacy. The pharmacy at the CVS in the Porter Square Shopping Center, off Mass. Ave. in Cambridge (☎ **617/876-5519**), is open 24 hours, 7 days a week. The pharmacy at the CVS at 155–157 Charles St. in Boston (☎ **617/523-1028**), next to the Charles T stop, is open until midnight. Some emergency rooms can fill your prescription at the hospital's pharmacy.

Police   Call ☎ **911** for emergencies.

Post Office   The main post office at 25 Dorchester Ave. (☎ **617/654-5326**), behind South Station, is open 24 hours, 7 days a week. Other post offices throughout the city are keyed on the map in chapter 1.

Radio   AM stations include **680** (WRKO: talk, sports, and Celtics games); **850** (WEEI: sports, Red Sox games); **1030** (WBZ: news, Bruins games); and **1090** (WILD: urban contemporary, soul). FM stations include **89.7** (WGBH: public radio, classical, jazz); **90.9** (WBUR: public radio, classical); **92.9** (WBOS: album rock); **94.5** (WJMN: dance, urban contemporary); **96.9** (WTKK: talk); **98.5** (WBMX: adult contemporary); **99.5** (WKLB: country); **100.7** (WZLX: classic rock); **101.7** (WFNX: progressive rock); **102.5** (WCRB: classical); **103.3** (WODS: oldies); **104.1** (WBCN: rock, Patriots games); **106.7** (WMJX: pop, adult contemporary); and **107.3** (WAAF: album rock).

Rest Rooms   The visitor center at 15 State St. has a public rest room, as do most tourist attractions, hotels, department stores, and public buildings. There are rest rooms at the CambridgeSide Galleria, Copley Place, Prudential Center, and Quincy Market shopping areas. One of the few public rest rooms in Harvard Square is in the Harvard Coop. Most Starbucks outlets have reliably clean rest rooms.

Safety   On the whole, Boston is a safe city for walking. As in any large city, stay out of parks (including the Esplanade) at night unless you're in a crowd. In general, trust your instincts—a dark, deserted street is probably deserted for a reason. Specific areas to avoid at night include Boylston Street between Tremont and Washington streets, and Tremont Street from Stuart to Boylston streets. Try not to walk alone late at night in the Theater District and around North Station. Public transportation in the areas you're likely to visit is busy and safe, but service stops between 12:30 and 1am.

Taxes   The 5% sales tax is not levied on food, prescription drugs, newspapers, or clothing that costs less than $175. The lodging tax is 12.45% in Boston and Cambridge; the meal tax (which also applies to takeout food) is 5%.

Taxis   See "Getting Around," earlier in this chapter.

Television   Stations include **Channel 2** (WGBH), public television; **Channel 4** (WBZ), CBS; **Channel 5** (WCVB), ABC; **Channel 7** (WHDH), NBC; **Channel 25** (WFXT), Fox; **Channel 38** (WSBK), UPN; and **Channel 56** (WLVI), WB. Cable TV is available throughout Boston and the suburbs.

Time Zone   Boston is in the Eastern time zone. Daylight saving time begins on the first Sunday in April and ends on the last Sunday in October.

Transit Info   Call ☎ **617/222-3200** for the MBTA (subways, local buses, commuter rail) and ☎ **800/23-LOGAN** for the Massachusetts Port Authority (airport transportation).

Weather   Call ☎ **617/936-1234.**

5 Accommodations

Boston has one of the busiest hotel markets in the country, with some of the highest prices. Because of the thriving economy, occupancy rates are soaring, and renovations and new construction are going on all over the area. Almost every large property in town has undergone a significant refurbishment or renovation in the past 5 years. That doesn't mean you need to pay through the nose for comfort or stay in a windowless cell for affordability, but you do need to do some planning.

As you go through this chapter, keep Boston's relatively small size in mind, and check a map before you rule out a particular location. The listings in this chapter match the neighborhood descriptions in chapter 4, "Getting to Know Boston"; especially downtown, the areas are so small and close together that the borders are somewhat arbitrary. The division to consider is **downtown vs. the Back Bay vs. Cambridge,** and not, say, the Waterfront vs. the Financial District.

With enough notice and flexibility, you probably won't have much difficulty finding a suitable place to stay in or near the city, but it's always a good idea to make a reservation. Try to book ahead between April and November, when spring conventions, college graduations, summer vacation, foliage season, and fall conventions follow one after the other and overlap.

These listings cover Boston, Cambridge, Brookline, and a few other convenient suburbs. (If you plan to visit a suburban town and want to stay overnight, see chapter 11, "Side Trips from Boston," for suggestions.)

Rates are for a double room; if you're traveling alone, single rates are almost always lower. The rates given here **do not include the 5.7% state hotel tax.** In Boston and Cambridge there's a **2.75% convention center tax** on top of the **4% city tax,** bringing the **total tax to 12.45%.** Not all suburbs have a local tax, so some towns charge only the 5.7% state tax.

MONEY-SAVING TIPS The "rack rate" is the maximum price a hotel charges for a room. It's the rate you'd get if you walked in off the street and asked for a room for the night. Hardly anybody pays those prices, however, and there are many ways around them. The key is to ask a lot of questions (or pay someone to ask them for you).

- **Don't be afraid to bargain.** Most rack rates include commissions of 10% to 25% or more for travel agents, which many hotels will cut if you make your own reservation and haggle a bit. Always ask politely whether a less expensive room is available and whether any special rates apply to you. You may qualify for corporate, student, military, senior, or other discounts (for example, for members of AAA, AARP, frequent-flyer programs, or trade unions), but they generally won't be offered unless you ask.

- **Call the Hotel Hot Line** (☎ **800/777-6001**). A service of the **Greater Boston Convention and Visitors Bureau** (☎ **888/SEE-BOSTON** or 617/536-4100; www.bostonusa.com), it can help make reservations even during the busiest times. It's staffed weekdays until 8pm, weekends until 4pm.
- **Dial direct.** When booking a room in a chain hotel, call the local line *and* the toll-free number, and compare. A hotel makes nothing on an empty room. The clerk on the scene is more likely to know about vacancies and will often grant deep discounts to fill rooms.
- **Rely on a qualified professional.** Certain hotels give travel agents discounts in exchange for steering business their way, so if you're shy about bargaining, an agent may be better equipped to negotiate discounts.
- **Remember the law of supply and demand.** Downtown business hotels are busiest and most expensive during the week; expect discounts and package deals over the weekend. Hotels that court leisure travelers are most crowded on weekends; discounts are usually available for midweek stays.
- **Visit in the winter.** Boston-bound bargain hunters who don't mind cold and the possibility of snow (sometimes *lots* of snow) will want to aim for **January through March,** when you can find great deals, especially on weekends. Many hotels participate in the Convention and Visitors Bureau's "Boston Overnight! Just for the Fun of It" winter-weekend program—it targets suburbanites, but out-of-towners benefit, too.
- **Be flexible.** As with travel plans, be ready to shift a little in selecting dates—a hotel that's full of conventioneers one week might be courting business a few days later. Avoid high-season stays whenever you can; planning your vacation just a week before or after official peak season can mean big savings.
- **Look into group or long-term discounts.** If you come as part of a large group, you should be able to negotiate a bargain. Likewise, when you're planning a long stay (usually 5 to 7 days), you'll qualify for a discount.
- **Avoid excess charges.** When you book a room, ask whether the hotel charges for parking—almost every hotel in Boston and Cambridge does. Hotels that own their own garages might include free parking when business is slow, but you have to ask. See "Getting Around" in chapter 4 for help in deciding whether you'll need a car at all. Find out before you dial whether your hotel imposes a surcharge on local or long-distance phone calls. A pay phone, however inconvenient, could save you money. And if you don't need extra perks such as a pool, a health club, or room service, consider less luxurious (and less expensive) lodgings.
- **Watch for coupons and advertised discounts.** Scan ads in your local Sunday travel section, an excellent source for up-to-the-minute hotel deals. If you have a favorite hotel chain, monitor its Web site for last-minute bargains and other specials. Also check the offers enclosed with your credit card and frequent-flyer statements.
- **Consider a suite.** If you're traveling with your family or another couple, you can pack more people into a suite (which usually comes with a sofa bed), and reduce your per-person rate. Remember that most places charge for extra guests.
- **Book a room with a refrigerator or kitchenette.** Eating some meals in is a great way to save money on food, especially if you're traveling with children (those $3 bowls of cereal can really add up).

Where There's Smoke . . .

Accommodations reserved for nonsmokers—often in blocks as large as several floors—are so common that we no longer single out hotels that offer them. However, nonsmokers should not assume that they'll get a smoke-free room without specifically requesting one. As hotels squeeze smokers into fewer and fewer rooms, the ones they are allowed to use become saturated with the smell of smoke, even in lodgings that are otherwise antiseptic. To avoid this disagreeable situation, be sure that everyone who handles your reservation knows you need a smoke-free room.

- **Investigate reservation services.** These outfits usually work as consolidators, buying up or reserving rooms in bulk and then dealing them out to customers at a profit. They do offer deals that range from 10% to 50% off, but remember, the discounts apply to rack rates—inflated prices that people rarely end up paying. You're probably better off dealing directly with a hotel, but if you don't like bargaining, this is certainly a viable option. Most of them offer online reservation services as well. Here are a few reputable providers: **Accommodations Express** (☎ 800/950-4685; www.accommodationsxpress.com); **Hotel Reservations Network** (☎ 800/96-HOTEL; www.180096HOTEL.com); **Quikbook** (☎ 800/789-9887, includes fax-on-demand service; www.quikbook.com); **Room Exchange** (☎ 800/846-7000 in the U.S., 800/486-7000 in Canada); and **Boston & New England Reservation Service** (☎ 800/754-7470).

    Online, try booking your hotel through **Arthur Frommer's Budget Travel** (www.frommers.com) and save up to 50% on the cost of your room. **Microsoft Expedia** (www.expedia.com) features a "Travel Agent" that can also direct you to affordable lodgings.
- If you're driving from the west, stop at the **Massachusetts Turnpike's Natick rest area** and try the reservation service at the visitor information center. If you arrive at Logan Airport without a room reservation (you daredevil, you), ask the staff at the **Visitor Service Center** in Terminal C for help.

GETTING WHAT YOU WANT   Someone has to get the best room in the house, and it might as well be you. Always ask for a corner room. They're usually larger, brighter, and quieter, but they sometimes cost more. Ask for a room on a high floor. This is often the "club" level or some other designation that costs extra. If you don't want to pay for the extra amenities (usually business features), ask for the highest standard floor.

If you have allergies or special requests—for a bed board, a foam pillow, a room that faces a particular direction, special amenities for female travelers, or accommodations for your pet—make arrangements in advance. When you reserve and again when you check in, ask if the hotel is renovating; if it is, request a room away from the construction. Inquire, too, about the location of restaurants and bars, which can be a source of noise. If you aren't happy with your room when you arrive, talk to the front desk. If they have another room, the staff should be happy to accommodate you, within reason.

BED-AND-BREAKFASTS   Whether you're uncomfortable with big, impersonal chain hotels or just can't afford them, a B&B can be a good option. Home accommodations are usually less expensive than hotels and often more comfortable; most are near public transportation. As downtown hotel prices soar, B&Bs are becoming even more popular. Because most are so small, they fill quickly; using an agency can save you a lot of calling around. Reserve as soon as you start planning your trip, especially if you'll be visiting during foliage season.

Expect to pay at least $65 a night for a double in the summer and fall, and more during special events. The room rate usually includes breakfast. Many lodgings require a minimum stay of at least 2 nights, and most offer winter specials—discounts or third-night-free deals. The following organizations can help match you with a suitable B&B in Boston, Cambridge, or the Greater Boston area:

- **Bed and Breakfast Agency of Boston,** 47 Commercial Wharf, Boston, MA 02110 (☎ **800/CITY-BNB** or 617/720-3540; from the U.K., 0800/89-5128; fax 617/523-5761; www.boston-bnbagency.com).
- **Bed and Breakfast Associates Bay Colony Ltd.,** P.O. Box 57166, Babson Park Branch, Boston, MA 02457 (☎ **800/347-5088** or 781/449-5302; fax 781/449-5958; www.bnbboston.com; e-mail: info@bnbboston.com).
- **Bed & Breakfast Reservations North Shore/Greater Boston/Cape Cod,** P.O. Box 590264, Greater Boston Branch, MA 02459-0264 (☎ **800/832-2632** outside MA, or 617/964-1606; fax 617/332-8572; www.bbreserve.com; e-mail: info@bbreserve.com).
- **Host Homes of Boston,** P.O. Box 117, Waban Branch, Boston, MA 02468 (☎ **800/600-1308** or 617/244-1308; fax 617/244-5156).
- **New England Bed and Breakfast,** P.O. Box 1426, Waltham, MA 02454 (☎ **617/244-2112**).

1 Downtown

The downtown area includes most of the **Freedom Trail** and the neighborhoods defined in chapter 4 as the **Waterfront, Faneuil Hall Marketplace,** the **Financial District,** and **Downtown Crossing.** (The North End and Government Center are here, too, but they don't have hotels.) Accommodations in the moderate and inexpensive price categories are mostly bed-and-breakfasts. Consult the agencies listed above.

THE WATERFRONT & FANEUIL HALL MARKETPLACE

At all hotels in these neighborhoods, **ask for a room on a high floor**—you'll want to be as far as possible from the noise and disarray of the Big Dig.

VERY EXPENSIVE

○ **Boston Harbor Hotel.** 70 Rowes Wharf (entrance on Atlantic Ave.), Boston, MA 02110. ☎ **800/752-7077** or 617/439-7000. Fax 617/330-9450. www.bhh.com. 230 units. A/C MINIBAR TV TEL. $255–$510 double; from $365 suite. Extra person $50. Children under 18 free in parents' room. Weekend packages available. AE, CB, DC, DISC, MC, V. Valet parking $28 weekdays, $20 weekends; self-parking $24 weekdays, $15 weekends. T: Blue Line to Aquarium, or Red Line to South Station. Pets accepted.

The Boston Harbor Hotel is one of the finest in town, and certainly the prettiest, whether you approach its landmark arch from land or sea (the Airport Water Shuttle stops here). The 16-story brick building is within walking distance of downtown and the waterfront attractions, and it prides itself on offering top-notch service to travelers pursuing both business and pleasure.

The plush guest rooms, which were renovated in 1998 and 1999, look out on the harbor or the skyline (rooms with city views are less expensive). Each unit is a luxurious bedroom–living room combination, with mahogany furnishings that include an armoire, a desk, and comfortable chairs. Standard guest-room features include three telephones, data ports, hair dryers, robes, slippers, umbrellas, and windows that open.

Boston Accommodations

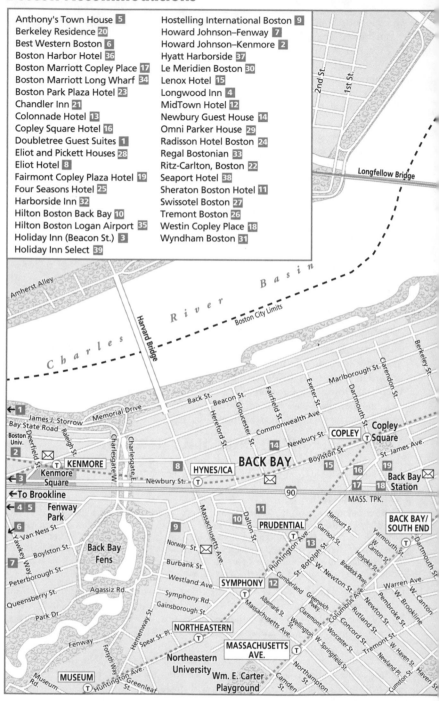

Anthony's Town House **5**
Berkeley Residence **20**
Best Western Boston **6**
Boston Harbor Hotel **36**
Boston Marriott Copley Place **17**
Boston Marriott Long Wharf **34**
Boston Park Plaza Hotel **23**
Chandler Inn **21**
Colonnade Hotel **13**
Copley Square Hotel **16**
Doubletree Guest Suites **1**
Eliot and Pickett Houses **28**
Eliot Hotel **8**
Fairmont Copley Plaza Hotel **19**
Four Seasons Hotel **25**
Harborside Inn **32**
Hilton Boston Back Bay **10**
Hilton Boston Logan Airport **35**
Holiday Inn (Beacon St.) **3**
Holiday Inn Select **39**

Hostelling International Boston **9**
Howard Johnson–Fenway **7**
Howard Johnson–Kenmore **2**
Hyatt Harborside **37**
Le Meridien Boston **30**
Lenox Hotel **15**
Longwood Inn **4**
MidTown Hotel **12**
Newbury Guest House **14**
Omni Parker House **29**
Radisson Hotel Boston **24**
Regal Bostonian **33**
Ritz-Carlton, Boston **22**
Seaport Hotel **38**
Sheraton Boston Hotel **11**
Swissotel Boston **27**
Tremont Boston **26**
Westin Copley Place **18**
Wyndham Boston **31**

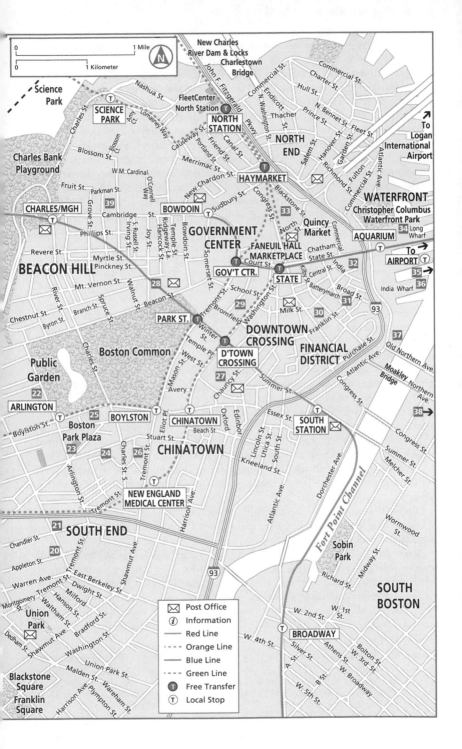

Some suites have private terraces. A museum-quality collection of paintings, drawings, prints, and nautical charts enhances the grand public spaces.

Dining/Diversions: The excellent **Rowes Wharf Restaurant** overlooks the harbor, as does **Intrigue,** the ground-floor cafe. The latter opens at 5:30am for breakfast (take-out or sit-down); serves lunch, dinner, and afternoon tea; and has seasonal outdoor seating. The **Rowes Wharf Bar** serves cocktails and light fare.

Amenities: Health club and spa with 60-foot lap pool; whirlpool; sauna, steam, and exercise rooms; salon for facials, massage, manicures, pedicures, and spa treatments. State-of-the-art business center with professional staff; conference rooms; concierge; 24-hour room service; dry cleaning and laundry; video rentals; newspaper delivery; in-room massage; twice-daily maid service; baby-sitting available; express checkout; valet parking; courtesy car; complimentary shoeshine. Rooms for travelers with disabilities are available.

✪ **Bostonian Hotel.** At Faneuil Hall Marketplace, 40 North St., Boston, MA 02109. ☎ **800/343-0922** or 617/523-3600. Fax 617/523-2454. www.regal-hotels.com/boston. 201 units. A/C MINIBAR TV TEL. $245–$420 double; $265–$450 deluxe double; $500–$775 suite. Extra person $20. Children under 18 free in parents' room. Weekend and other packages available. AE, DC, DISC, JCB, MC, V. Parking $30. T: Green or Blue Line to Government Center, or Orange Line to State.

The relatively small Bostonian offers excellent service and features that make it competitive with larger hotels. Although it doesn't offer wall-to-wall business features, its boutique feel makes it popular with travelers who want a break from more convention-oriented rivals. The recently redecorated, traditionally appointed guest rooms vary in size. All boast top-of-the-line furnishings and amenities, including on-command video, safes, terry robes, irons and ironing boards, and two-line phones with data ports. The bathrooms have hair dryers, heat lamps, and both overhead and European-style handheld shower sprays. Half of the units have French doors that open onto small private balconies, and some suites have working fireplaces or Jacuzzis.

Three brick 19th-century buildings make up the hotel; the 38 units in the new wing, added in 1999, include a suite and four rooms on the glass-enclosed top floor. Soundproofing throughout the hotel means you can watch the scene at Faneuil Hall Marketplace or Haymarket (or the Big Dig, from some rooms) without hearing all the noise.

Dining/Diversions: On the fourth-floor rooftop is the glass-enclosed **Seasons** restaurant. The **Atrium** lounge in the glass-walled lobby affords a great view of the scene at the marketplace.

Amenities: 24-hour room service; conference rooms; concierge; dry cleaning and laundry; newspaper delivery; in-room massage; twice-daily maid service; secretarial services available; express checkout; valet parking; complimentary morning limousine service. Complimentary health-club and swimming-pool privileges at the excellent Sky Club, 4 blocks away; small fitness room; in-room exercise equipment delivery on request. Rooms for people with disabilities; rooms with special amenities for female travelers.

Boston Marriott Long Wharf. 296 State St., Boston, MA 02109. ☎ **800/228-9290** or 617/227-0800. Fax 617/227-2867. www.marriott.com/marriott/BOSLW. 400 units. A/C TV TEL. Apr–Nov $285–$375 double; Dec–Mar $199–$285 double; $450–$490 suite year-round. Weekend packages from $155 per night. AE, DC, DISC, JCB, MC, V. Parking $30. T: Blue Line to Aquarium.

The terraced brick exterior of this seven-story hotel looks nothing like the ocean liner it supposedly resembles, but it is one of the most recognizable sights on the harbor.

The chief appeal of this otherwise ordinary Marriott is its location, a stone's throw from the New England Aquarium, convenient to downtown and waterfront attractions, and just two subway stops from the airport.

Rooms are large and decor varies; each has either one king-size or two double beds, two phones, a coffeemaker, a hair dryer, and a table and chairs in front of the window. The Big Dig construction is directly under the windows of the rooms near the street. Ask to be as close to the water as possible, and you'll have good views of the wharves and waterfront without all the noise. The seventh floor is the Concierge Level, with complimentary continental breakfast, cocktails, and hors d'oeuvres served in a private lounge, and private exercise facilities.

Dining/Diversions: Oceana Restaurant, with a 180-degree expanse of glass wall fronting the harbor; cafe and lounge; bar and grill.

Amenities: Indoor pool with outdoor terrace; exercise room; whirlpools; saunas; game room. Business center; conference rooms; concierge; room service (until 2am); dry cleaning and laundry; newspaper delivery; twice-daily maid service; express checkout; valet parking; baby-sitting available.

MODERATE

۞ Harborside Inn. 185 State St. (between I-93 and the Custom House Tower), Boston, MA 02109. ☎ **617/723-7500.** Fax 617/670-2010. www.hagopianhotels.com. 54 units. A/C TV TEL. $155–$200 double; $210–$295 suite. Extra person $15. Rates include continental breakfast. Rates may be higher during special events. AE, DC, DISC, MC, V. Parking $24–$30 at nearby public garages. T: Blue Line to Aquarium.

Under the same management as the Newbury Guest House in the Back Bay, the Harborside Inn offers a similar combination of value and location. The renovated 1858 warehouse is across the street from Faneuil Hall Marketplace and the harbor, a short walk from the Financial District, and near ground zero of the Big Dig. The nicely appointed guest rooms have queen-size beds, hair dryers, hardwood floors, Oriental rugs, and Victorian-style furniture. They surround a skylit atrium; those with city views are more expensive but noisier. Interior rooms have windows that open only to the atrium. Rooms on the top floors of the eight-story building have lower ceilings but better views. The hotel has some features you'd expect at pricier lodgings, including room service (until 10pm), free local phone calls, and voicemail. The hotel is wheelchair accessible, and accessories for hearing-impaired guests are available. On the ground floor are a small exercise room and the Mermaid Restaurant, which serves lunch and dinner.

FINANCIAL DISTRICT & DOWNTOWN CROSSING

Besides being great for corporate travelers, the hotels in this area can be even more convenient than those nearer the water—they're that much closer to the major shopping areas and the start of the Freedom Trail. Especially in the winter, all offer sensational weekend packages.

VERY EXPENSIVE

۞ Le Meridien Boston. 250 Franklin St. (at Post Office Sq.), Boston, MA 02110. ☎ **800/543-4300** or 617/451-1900. Fax 617/423-2844. www.lemeridienboston.com. 326 units. A/C MINIBAR TV TEL. $295–$415 double; $475–$1,330 suite. Extra person $30. Weekend rates from $209. AE, CB, DC, DISC, MC, V. Valet parking $29, $13 Fri–Sat; self-parking $28, $8 Fri–Sat. T: Red Line to Downtown Crossing or South Station, or Blue or Orange Line to State. Small pets accepted.

This is the city's premier business hotel. If you don't need to leave the Financial District, you might not even need to leave the premises—ask for a Business Traveler room (with a fax machine, oversized desk, coffeemaker, and halogen lighting) and arrange a power lunch in the elegant Julien restaurant. Vacationing visitors are near the waterfront and downtown attractions but not all that close to public transportation. Whatever your purpose, you'll find the service by the multilingual staff superb.

Guest rooms have 153 configurations, including loft suites with two bathrooms. All rooms have two telephones (one in the bathroom) and hair dryers. The glass mansard roof surrounds the top three stories, where a number of rooms have large sloped windows and extraordinary views. The imposing nine-story building, designed by R. Clipston Sturgis in 1922 in the style of a 16th-century Roman palace, originally housed the Federal Reserve Bank. The bank's original grand marble staircase now leads to the dining areas, and two murals by N. C. Wyeth grace the walls of the bar.

Dining/Diversions: Julien serves lunch and dinner; the bar features live piano music 6 nights a week. The less formal **Café Fleuri** serves three meals daily, the Saturday "Chocolate Bar Buffet" (September through May), and Sunday jazz brunch. **La Terrasse** is the seasonal outdoor cafe.

Amenities: 40-foot indoor pool; well-equipped health club with whirlpool and sauna; staffed business center with library; conference rooms; concierge; 24-hour room service; dry cleaning and laundry; newspaper delivery; twice-daily maid service; express checkout; valet parking; weekend courtesy car to Newbury Street; daily weather report. Two rooms on each floor for people with disabilities.

Swissôtel Boston. 1 Avenue de Lafayette, Boston, MA 02111. ☎ **888/73-SWISS** or 617/451-2600. Fax 617/451-0054. www.swissotel.com. 501 units. A/C MINIBAR TV TEL. $329–$379 double; $399–$449 deluxe double; $499–$699 suite or Swiss Butler Executive Level; $2,500 Presidential Suite. Extra person $25. Children under 12 free in parents' room. Weekend packages from $139 per night. AE, CB, DC, DISC, JCB, MC, V. Valet parking $30; self-parking $26. T: Red Line to Downtown Crossing, or Green Line to Boylston. If you're driving, call for directions to avoid construction traffic. Small pets accepted.

This centrally located 22-story hotel lives two lives. It's a busy convention and business destination during the week, and the excellent weekend packages make it popular with sightseers. The plain exterior contrasts with the luxurious second-floor lobby, where elegant European style takes over. Guest rooms cluster around four atriums with semiprivate lobbies, creating the effect of several small hotels in one. Rooms have sitting areas with a desk and settee, and king or European twin beds. All rooms have three telephones with data ports, fax machines, and coffeemakers. On the Executive Level, a Swiss butler performs traditional valet functions, acts as a private concierge, and even runs errands.

Dining/Diversions: Café Suisse serves three meals daily and Sunday brunch. The lounge in the atrium offers cocktails, vintage wines by the glass, and light meals.

Amenities: 52-foot indoor pool; health club; exercise room; saunas; sun terrace; high-tech business center; conference rooms; 24-hour room service; dry cleaning; valet service; nightly turndown.

Wyndham Boston. 89 Broad St., Boston, MA 02110. ☎ **800/WYNDHAM** or 617/556-0006. Fax 617/556-0053. www.wyndham.com. 362 units. A/C MINIBAR TV TEL. $295–$535 double; $335–$560 suite. Children under 13 free in parents' room. Weekend, holiday, and other packages available. AE, CB, DC, DISC, JCB, MC, V. Valet parking $30 weekdays, $16 weekends. T: Blue or Orange Line to State, or Red Line to South Station.

Boston's newest luxury hotel is contemporary yet conservative—21st-century technology in an art deco package. The meticulously designed hotel (a complete rehab of the 1928 Batterymarch Building) opened in 1999. The 14-story building is near Faneuil Hall Marketplace and the Waterfront, but not all that close (by downtown standards) to the T. The spacious guest rooms have 9^1/$_2$-foot ceilings, high-speed Internet access, triple-glazed windows that open, individual climate control, hair dryers, coffeemakers, terry robes, umbrellas, irons, and ironing boards. Units on the upper floors have great views of the harbor and downtown, and soundproofing throughout makes the whole building—even the halls—exceptionally quiet. The Wyndham's closest competitor (literally and figuratively) is Le Meridien, which is less convenient to public transit but has a swimming pool.

Dining: Caliterra Bar & Grille serves California- and Italian-inspired cuisine at breakfast, lunch, and dinner.

Amenities: Concierge; 24-hour room service; business center (staffed 7am to 7pm); 24-hour fitness center; saunas; state-of-the-art conference rooms; dry cleaning and laundry; weekday newspaper delivery; baby-sitting; valet parking. Rooms with special amenities for female travelers and travelers with disabilities.

EXPENSIVE

✪ Omni Parker House. 60 School St., Boston, MA 02108. ☎ **800/THE-OMNI** or 617/227-8600. Fax 617/742-5729. www.omnihotels.com. 552 units (some with shower only). A/C MINIBAR TV TEL. $189–$295 double; $249–$375 superior double; $279–$435 1-bedroom suite. Children under 18 free in parents' room. Weekend packages available. AE, CB, DC, DISC, MC, V. Valet parking $27; self-parking $20. T: Green or Blue Line to Government Center, or Red Line to Park St.

The Parker House offers a great combination of nearly 150 years of history and extensive renovations. It has operated continuously longer than any other hotel in America—since 1855—and a massive overhaul completed in 1998 upgraded it throughout and added a business center and an exercise facility. Guest rooms have two-line phones, modem hookups, hair dryers, and irons and ironing boards. They're not huge, but they are thoughtfully laid out and nicely appointed; many have views of Old City Hall or Government Center. The pattern on the bedspreads—so gaudy that it's elegant—is a reproduction of the original, and the lobby of the 14-story hotel boasts its original American oak paneling.

Over the years, the Parker House has entertained many famous guests and even had some famous employees—Malcolm X and Ho Chi Minh both worked here. The room that's now Parker's Bar hosted the best-known group of guests: Henry Wadsworth Longfellow, Oliver Wendell Holmes, Ralph Waldo Emerson, Nathaniel Hawthorne, and sometimes even Charles Dickens, who made up a literary salon called the Saturday Club.

Dining/Diversions: Parker's Restaurant serves three meals daily. There are two bars: **The Last Hurrah,** off the lobby, is a hopping after-work destination; **Parker's Bar** has live piano music Monday through Saturday nights.

Amenities: Health club; staffed business center; conference rooms; concierge; 24-hour room service; dry cleaning and laundry; newspaper delivery; in-room massage; express checkout; valet parking. Rooms for people with disabilities are available.

Food for Thought

Yes, this is the Parker House of Parker House roll fame. They were invented (if food is "invented") here, as was Boston cream pie.

2 Beacon Hill

Less expensive lodgings in this neighborhood are mostly B&Bs. Check with the agencies listed in the chapter introduction, or try the moderately priced **Eliot and Pickett Houses,** 6 Mount Vernon Place, Boston, MA 02108 (☎ **617/248-8707;** fax 617/742-1364; www.uua.org/ep). The Unitarian Universalist Association runs the B&B, whose 20 guest rooms are extremely popular, especially in the high season.

EXPENSIVE

Holiday Inn Select Boston Government Center. 5 Blossom St., Boston, MA 02114. ☎ **800/HOLIDAY** or 617/742-7630. Fax 617/742-4192. www.bristolhotels.com. 303 units. A/C TV TEL. From $200 double. Extra person $20. Rollaway $20. Children under 18 free in parents' room. Weekend and corporate packages and 10% AARP discount available. AE, DC, DISC, JCB, MC, V. Parking $25. T: Red Line to Charles/MGH.

At the base of Beacon Hill, near Massachusetts General Hospital, this utilitarian hotel rises 15 stories above a retail plaza with a supermarket, shops, and restaurants. It's scheduled for renovations, so be sure to ask for a room that's away from the work area. This location was one of the chain's leaders in its battle for the business traveler— rooms, which are furnished in contemporary style, have fax machines, data ports, coffeemakers, hair dryers, and irons and ironing boards. Each unit has a picture-window view of the city or the State House (or the parking lot—ask to be as high up as possible). Executive rooms, on the 12th and 14th floors, have two phones, terry robes, turndown service, and minifridges; rates there include continental breakfast and access to a private lounge.

Dining: Foster's Bar & Grille serves three meals daily.

Amenities: Outdoor heated pool; small exercise room; sundeck; business center; conference rooms; coin laundry; concierge; room service until 11pm; dry cleaning and laundry; newspaper delivery; express checkout; currency exchange. Rooms for people with disabilities are available.

3 South Boston Waterfront (Seaport District)

VERY EXPENSIVE

Seaport Hotel. At the World Trade Center, 1 Seaport Lane, Boston, MA 02210. ☎ **877/ SEAPORT** or 617/385-4000. Fax 617/385-5090. www.seaporthotel.com. 426 units. A/C MINIBAR TV TEL. $299 double; $329 concierge level; $349–$1,700 suite. Service charge $3 per room per night. Children under 17 free in parents' room. Weekend packages available. AE, CB, DC, DISC, JCB, MC, V. Valet parking $24; self-parking $20. T: Red Line to South Station, then take free shuttle bus (or walk 20 min.). Pets under 50 lbs. accepted.

The independent Seaport Hotel rises out of the Big Dig like the Emerald City, and it has an air of fantasy about it. The hotel was built with every feature the pampered, techno-savvy business traveler might dream of. It's across Northern Avenue from the World Trade Center, about the same distance from the airport as from the Financial District (10 min. by cab), but a long walk from the subway.

The decent-sized rooms are exceptionally well appointed. They have high-speed Internet access, Logan Airport flight information (and Nintendo) on the TV, oversized towels, hair dryers, coffeemakers, individual climate control, safes, and three phones, including a speakerphone with Caller ID. Rooms have excellent views of the city or harbor, especially from the higher floors. T-1 lines throughout the building, shuttle service to downtown, and great weekend packages—among other appealing features—make it no surprise that the hotel has been busy since it opened in May 1998.

Dining/Diversions: The lobby restaurant, **Aura** (☎ 617/385-4300), serves three meals a day and Sunday brunch, often to nonguests drawn by chef Ed Doyle's growing reputation. There's a lounge and a cafe that serves quick meals and snacks to eat in or take out.

Amenities: 24-hour business center with professional staff (7am to 8pm) and meeting space; conference rooms; 24-hour room service; concierge; excellent health club with 50-foot indoor pool, sauna, spa treatments; dry cleaning and laundry; newspaper delivery; twice-daily maid service; baby-sitting available; express check-in and checkout; valet parking; gift shop; florist; shuttle to downtown.

4 Chinatown/Theater District

EXPENSIVE

Radisson Hotel Boston. 200 Stuart St. (at Charles St. S.), Boston, MA 02116. ☎ 800/333-3333 or 617/482-1800. Fax 617/451-2750. www.radisson.com. 356 units. A/C TV TEL. $160–$359 double. Extra person $20. Cot $20. Cribs free. Children under 18 free in parents' room. Weekend, theater, and other packages available. AE, DC, DISC, JCB, MC, V. Parking $19. T: Green Line to Boylston, or Orange Line to New England Medical Center.

A top-to-bottom renovation completed in 1997 left the centrally located Radisson in great shape. The 24-story hotel was already quite agreeable, and a recent push to attract business travelers has made it even more so. The tastefully decorated guest rooms are among the largest in the city. Each has a private balcony (with great views from the higher floors), sitting area, king or two queen-size beds, hair dryer, coffeemaker, iron and ironing board, and two phones. Business-traveler rooms on the top four floors come with upgraded amenities and access to a private lounge.

Dining/Diversions: The **57 Steakhouse** is a traditional à la carte restaurant; the **Theatre Café** is more casual. The **57 Theatre** (☎ 800/233-3123) is an intimate venue that often books one-person shows.

Amenities: Heated indoor pool with sundeck and exercise room; staffed business center; conference rooms; concierge; room service until 11pm; dry cleaning and laundry; newspaper delivery; express checkout; valet parking.

The Tremont Boston. 275 Tremont St., Boston, MA 02116. ☎ 800/331-9998 or 617/426-1400. Fax 617/482-6730. www.wyndham.com. 322 units (most with shower only). A/C TV TEL. $159–$412 double; $399–$599 suite. Extra person $20. Children under 17 free in parents' room. Weekend packages and 10% AAA discount available. AE, DC, DISC, MC, V. Valet parking $24; self-parking $15 in nearby garage. T: Orange Line to New England Medical Center or Green Line to Boylston.

This hotel, a Wyndham Grand Heritage property, is as close to Boston's theaters as you can be without actually attending a show. It's also convenient to downtown and the Back Bay. The neighborhood is improving, and a recently completed $15 million renovation expanded some units and spruced up all of them. An overhaul of the public areas, which will gain a fitness facility and business center, was scheduled at press time. The good-size guest rooms have modern furnishings, coffeemakers, and hair dryers. The 15-story brick building captures the style that prevailed when the hotel was built in 1924. The original gold-leaf decorations and crafted ceilings in the huge lobby and ballrooms have been restored and the original marble walls and columns refurbished.

Dining/Diversions: Caprice restaurant serves food until 1am (for the post-theater crowd); the **Roxy** nightclub features dancing, live music, and occasional concerts.

Amenities: Conference rooms; secretarial services; dry cleaning and laundry; newspaper delivery; concierge; room service until 10pm; express checkout; valet parking. Rooms for people with disabilities are available.

If your trip involves a cultural event—a big show at a museum, Boston Ballet's *The Nutcracker*—seek out a hotel package that includes tickets. Usually offered on weekends, these deals always save time and often save money.

5 The South End

Berkeley Street runs from the Back Bay across the Mass. Pike to the most convenient corner of the sprawling South End, where you'll find these two lodgings.

MODERATE

Chandler Inn Hotel. 26 Chandler St. (at Berkeley St.), Boston, MA 02116. ☎ **800/842-3450** or 617/482-3450. Fax 617/542-3428. www.chandlerinn.com. 56 units. A/C TV TEL. Apr–Dec $145–$155 double; Jan–Mar $125–$135 double. Rates include continental breakfast. Children under 12 free in parents' room. AE, CB, DC, DISC, MC, V. No parking available. T: Orange Line to Back Bay.

The Chandler Inn underwent a transformation in early 2000, with the completion of $1 million in renovations. Even with the accompanying price hike, the comfortable, unpretentious hotel is an excellent deal. The guest rooms, revamped from the walls out, have individual climate control and tasteful contemporary-style furniture, including desks, small wardrobes, and TV armoires. Each holds either a queen or double bed or two twin beds, without enough room to squeeze in a cot. Bathrooms are tiny but contain hair dryers. The one elevator in the eight-story inn can be slow. But the staff is friendly and helpful, and the Back Bay is 2 blocks away. This is a gay-friendly hotel—Fritz, the bar next to the lobby, is a neighborhood hangout—that often books up early. Plan ahead.

INEXPENSIVE

Berkeley Residence YWCA. 40 Berkeley St., Boston, MA 02116. ☎ **617/482-8850.** Fax 617/482-9692. www.ywcaboston.org. 200 units (none with bathroom). $60 single; $100 double; $120 triple. Rates include breakfast. Long-term rates available (5-week minimum). JCB, MC, V. Parking $16 in public lot 1 block away. T: Orange Line to Back Bay or Green Line to Arlington.

This pleasant, convenient hotel/residence for women offers a dining room, a patio garden, pianos, a library, and laundry facilities. The guest rooms are basic, containing little more than beds, but are well maintained and comfortable—definitely not luxurious, but not cells either. That description might not seem to justify the prices, but check around a little before you turn up your nose. The public areas were renovated in 1997. Guests have access to the pool and exercise room at the YWCA 3 blocks away.

6 Back Bay

BOSTON COMMON/PUBLIC GARDEN
VERY EXPENSIVE

✪ **Four Seasons Hotel.** 200 Boylston St., Boston, MA 02116. ☎ **800/332-3442** or 617/338-4400. Fax 617/423-0154. www.fourseasons.com. 288 units. A/C MINIBAR TV TEL. $465–$695 double; $1,950 1-bedroom suite; $2,300 2-bedroom suite. Weekend packages available. AE, CB, DC, DISC, JCB, MC, V. Valet parking $27. T: Green Line to Arlington. Pets accepted.

Many hotels offer exquisite service, a beautiful location, elegant guest rooms and public areas, a terrific health club, and wonderful restaurants. No other hotel in Boston—indeed, in New England—combines every element of a luxury hotel as seamlessly as the Four Seasons. If I were traveling with someone else's credit cards, I'd head straight here.

Overlooking the Public Garden, the 16-story brick-and-glass building (the hotel occupies eight stories) incorporates the traditional and the contemporary. Each spacious room is elegantly appointed and has a striking view. All rooms have bay windows that open, climate control, three two-line phones with computer and fax capability, hair dryers, terry robes, and a safe. Children receive bedtime snacks and toys, and can ask at the concierge desk for duck food to take to the Public Garden. Small pets even enjoy a special menu and amenities. Larger accommodations range from Executive Suites, with enlarged alcove areas for meetings or entertaining, to luxurious one-, two-, and three-bedroom deluxe suites.

Dining/Diversions: Aujourd'hui, one of Boston's best restaurants, serves contemporary American cuisine. The **Bristol Lounge** is open for lunch, afternoon tea, dinner, and Sunday breakfast, and features live entertainment nightly.

Amenities: In general, if you want it, you'll get it. VCRs; free video rentals; indoor heated 51-foot pool and whirlpool with a view of the Public Garden; excellent spa with fitness equipment, private masseuse, Jacuzzi, and sauna (residents of the condominiums on the upper floors of the hotel share the pool and spa); excellent business center; conference rooms; concierge; 24-hour room service; dry cleaning and laundry; newspaper delivery; in-room massage; twice-daily maid service; baby-sitting available; express checkout; valet parking; complimentary shoeshine; complimentary limousine service to downtown Boston addresses. Rooms for people with disabilities are available.

✪ **The Ritz-Carlton, Boston.** 15 Arlington St., Boston, MA 02117. ☎ **800/241-3333** or 617/536-5700. Fax 617/536-1335. www.ritzcarlton.com. 278 units. A/C MINIBAR TV TEL. $330–$495 double; $545–$2,500 1-bedroom suite; $645–$2,825 2-bedroom suite. Ritz-Carlton Club $645–$825 1-bedroom suite; $1,140–$1,320 2-bedroom suite. Extra person $20. Weekend packages available. AE, CB, DC, DISC, JCB, MC, V. Valet parking $26. T: Green Line to Arlington. Small pets accepted.

This legendary hotel overlooking the Public Garden has attracted both the "proper Bostonian" and the celebrated visitor since 1927. It has the highest staff-to-guest ratio in the city, including white-gloved elevator operators. Although the pricier Four Seasons has better amenities, notably the on-premises pool, the status-conscious consider the Ritz—well, ritzier.

Guest rooms have French provincial furnishings, crystal chandeliers, two telephones (one in the bathroom), safes, closets that lock, and climate control; some have windows that open. Bathrooms, finished in Vermont marble, have hair dryers and terry robes. You'll pay more for rooms with a view. Fresh flowers grace the suites, many of which have wood-burning fireplaces. Guests in Club Level rooms have access to a private lounge, which has its own concierge and serves complimentary food six times a day (including a caviar and champagne hour).

Dining/Diversions: The Dining Room and **Bar at the Ritz** are as legendary for their clientele as for their food and drink. **The Café,** although rather cramped, is famous for breakfast. **The Lounge** serves the city's best afternoon tea, then cognac, cordials, caviar, and desserts. On weekend evenings, there's dancing to live jazz. **The Roof Restaurant,** open seasonally, offers dinner and dancing to the Ritz-Carlton Orchestra 17 stories up.

Amenities: Well-equipped fitness center with massage room; use of pool at the nearby Candela of Boston spa; 24-hour room service; concierge; dry cleaning and laundry; newspaper delivery; twice-daily maid service; beauty salon; gift shop; baby-sitting available; business center; conference rooms; complimentary shoeshine; complimentary limousine service (limited hours).

EXPENSIVE

Boston Park Plaza Hotel. 64 Arlington St., Boston, MA 02116. ☎ **800/225-2008** or 617/426-2000. Fax 617/423-1708. www.bostonparkplaza.com. 960 units (some with shower only). A/C TV TEL. $175–$265 double; $375–$2,000 suite. Extra person $20. Children under 18 free in parents' room. Senior discount and weekend and family packages available. AE, CB, DC, DISC, MC, V. Valet parking $23; self-parking $19. T: Green Line to Arlington.

A Boston mainstay—it was built as the Statler Hilton in 1927—the Park Plaza Hotel does a hopping convention and function business. It's the antithesis of generic, with an old-fashioned atmosphere and a cavernous, ornate lobby, yet it offers the full range of modern comforts. Room size and decor vary greatly, and some rooms are quite small. All have hair dryers, and many have two phones and a coffeemaker. The lobby of the 15-story hotel is a little commercial hub, with a travel agency, a currency exchange, Amtrak and airline ticket offices, and a pharmacy.

Dining/Diversions: On the ground floor are two restaurants, **Finale** and the **Arlington Street Grille,** and two lounges, **Swans Court** and the cozy **Captain's Bar.**

Amenities: Health club; business center; conference rooms; beauty salon; concierge; room service until 11pm; dry cleaning and laundry; express checkout; valet parking.

COPLEY SQUARE/HYNES CONVENTION CENTER
VERY EXPENSIVE

The Colonnade Hotel. 120 Huntington Ave., Boston, MA 02116. ☎ **800/962-3030** or 617/424-7000. Fax 617/424-1717. www.colonnadehotel.com. 285 units. A/C MINIBAR TV TEL. $315–$395 double; $450–$1,400 suite. Children under 12 free in parents' room. Weekend packages available. AE, CB, DC, DISC, MC, V. Parking $24. T: Green Line E to Prudential. Pets accepted.

The swimming pool and "rooftop resort" are probably this hotel's best-known features, with excellent service a close runner-up. Adjacent to Copley Place and the Prudential Center, the independently owned Colonnade is a slice of Europe in the all-American shopping mecca of the Back Bay. You might hear a dozen languages spoken by the guests and employees of the 11-story concrete-and-glass hotel, whose friendly, professional staff is known for personalized service.

The elegance of the quiet, high-ceilinged public spaces carries over to the large guest rooms, which have contemporary oak or mahogany furnishings, marble bathrooms, two phones (one in the bathroom), robes, on-demand movies, hair dryers, and windows that open. Suites have dining rooms and sitting areas, and the "author's suite" contains autographed copies of the work of celebrated (or at least published) literary guests.

Dining: The authentically sassy waitstaff at **Brasserie Jo** serves French-Alsatian cuisine until 1am.

Amenities: Seasonal "rooftop resort" with heated outdoor pool and sundeck; well-equipped fitness center; business center; conference rooms; concierge; 24-hour room service; dry cleaning and laundry; newspaper delivery; children's programs; baby-sitting available; express checkout; car-rental desk; currency exchange. Rooms for people with disabilities are available.

○ **Eliot Hotel.** 370 Commonwealth Ave. (at Mass. Ave.), Boston, MA 02215. ☎ **800/ 44-ELIOT** or 617/267-1607. Fax 617/536-9114. www.eliothotel.com. 95 units. A/C MINIBAR TV TEL. $315–$415 1-bedroom suite for 2; $570–$740 2-bedroom suite. Extra person $20. Children under 18 free in parents' room. AE, DC, MC, V. Valet parking $24. T: Green Line B, C, or D to Hynes/ICA. Small pets accepted.

This exquisite hotel combines the flavor of Yankee Boston with European-style service and amenities. It feels more like a classy apartment building than a hotel, with features that attract tycoons as well as honeymooners. The spacious suites have antique furnishings, traditional English-style chintz fabrics, and authentic botanical prints. French doors separate the living rooms and bedrooms, and bathrooms are outfitted in Italian marble. Standard features include dual-line telephones with data ports, high-speed Internet access, a personal fax-copier-printer, and two TVs. Many suites also have a pantry with a microwave. The hotel is near Boston University and MIT (across the river), and the location on tree-lined Commonwealth Avenue contrasts pleasantly with the bustle of Newbury Street, a block away.

Dining: Breakfast is served in the elegant restaurant, **Clio.** At dinner, Clio specializes in contemporary French and American cuisine.

Amenities: VCRs; safe-deposit boxes; concierge; room service until midnight; dry cleaning and laundry; newspaper delivery; twice-daily maid service; baby-sitting and secretarial services available; express checkout; valet parking. Rooms for people with disabilities are available.

○ **The Fairmont Copley Plaza Hotel.** 138 St. James Ave., Boston, MA 02116. ☎ **800/ 527-4727** or 617/267-5300. Fax 617/247-6681. www.fairmont.com. 379 units. A/C MINI-BAR TV TEL. From $249 double; from $429 suite. Extra person $30. Weekend and other packages available. AE, CB, DC, JCB, MC, V. Valet parking $30. T: Green Line to Copley, or Orange Line to Back Bay. Small pets accepted.

The Fairmont Hotel Group acquired the grande dame of Boston hotels in 1996 and upgraded it into a true "grand hotel," in line with the chain's most famous property, New York's Plaza. Extensive renovations, plush accommodations, and superb service indicate a job well done. Built in 1912, the six-story Renaissance-revival building faces Copley Square, with Trinity Church and the Boston Public Library on either side. The large guest rooms underwent renovation and restoration from 1996 to 1998. Furnished with reproduction Edwardian antiques, they reflect the elegance of the opulent public spaces. In-room features include oversized desks, climate control, coffeemakers, phones with data ports, and irons and ironing boards. Bathrooms have hair dryers, terry robes, and oversize towels.

Dining/Diversions: There are two restaurants—the **Oak Room,** a traditional steak house, and **Copley's Grand Café**—and two lounges, the clubby **Oak Bar** and **Copley's Bar.**

Amenities: Concierge; 24-hour room service; VCRs; fitness center; well-equipped business center; conference rooms; dry cleaning and laundry; newspaper delivery. In-room massage; twice-daily maid service; baby-sitting; express checkout; valet parking; currency exchange; complimentary shoeshine; beauty salon; gift shop. Guests have access to the nearby coed YWCA, which has a swimming pool. Rooms for people with disabilities are available.

○ **The Lenox Hotel.** 710 Boylston St., Boston, MA 02116. ☎ **800/225-7676** or 617/536-5300. Fax 617/236-0351. www.lenoxhotel.com. 212 units. A/C TV TEL. From $308 double; $398 executive corner room with fireplace; $498 fireplace suit. Extra person $20. Cots $20. Cribs free. Children under 18 free in parents' room. Corporate and weekend packages available. AE, CB, DC, DISC, JCB, MC, V. Valet and self-parking $28. T: Green Line to Copley.

The Lenox was the latest thing when it opened in 1900, and in its second century, it echoes that *fin-de-siècle* splendor everywhere from the ornate lobby to the spacious, luxurious rooms. Building on its great location, the 11-story hotel courts business travelers with in-room fax machines, two-line speakerphones, data ports, function space, and an accommodating staff. The high-ceilinged guest rooms have sitting areas with custom-designed wood furnishings, marble bathrooms, terry robes, hair dryers, umbrellas, and irons and ironing boards. Twelve corner rooms have wood-burning fireplaces, and rooms on the top two floors have excellent views.

　Dining: The excellent restaurant **Anago** serves dinner and Sunday brunch and provides the hotel's food services. **The Upstairs Grille** serves breakfast; the congenial **Samuel Adams Brew House** serves lunch and dinner and has a dozen brews on tap.

　Amenities: Small exercise room; conference rooms; concierge; room service until midnight; dry cleaning and laundry; newspaper delivery; express checkout; nightly turndown; secretarial services available; barbershop; car-rental desk; valet parking. Children's TV channel; baby-sitting available. Rooms for people with disabilities and wheelchair lift to the lobby are available.

❂ **The Westin Copley Place Boston.** 10 Huntington Ave., Boston, MA 02116. ☎ **800/ WESTIN-1** or 617/262-9600. Fax 617/424-7483. www.westin.com. 800 units. A/C MINIBAR TV TEL. $229–$499 double; $269–$2,200 suite. Extra person $25; $20 Guest Office; $40 junior suites and Executive Club Level. Weekend packages available. AE, CB, DC, DISC, JCB, MC, V. Valet parking $28. T: Green Line to Copley, or Orange Line to Back Bay. Pets under 20 lbs. accepted.

Towering 36 stories in the air above Copley Square, the Westin attracts convention-goers, sightseers, and dedicated shoppers. Skybridges link the hotel to Copley Place and the Prudential Center complex, and Copley Square is across the street from the pedestrian entrance. The multilingual staff emphasizes quick check-in.

　The spacious guest rooms—all on the eighth floor or higher—have traditional oak and mahogany furniture, coffeemakers, two phones, data ports, hair dryers, safes, and windows that open. They're scheduled to be spruced up and outfitted with even more comfortable beds by early 2001. You might not notice any of that at first, because you'll be captivated by the view. Qualms you might have had about choosing a huge chain hotel will fade as you survey downtown Boston, the airport and harbor, or the Charles River and Cambridge. Executive Club Level guests have private check-in and a lounge that serves complimentary continental breakfast and hors d'oeuvres.

　Dining/Diversions: The Palm, a branch of the famous New York–based chain, serves lunch and dinner—steak, chops, and jumbo lobsters. The excellent seafood restaurant **Turner Fisheries** features live jazz Thursday through Saturday after 8pm. **Bar 10** serves drinks and Mediterranean food in a posh space off the lobby.

　Amenities: Indoor pool; health club with Nautilus equipment and saunas; concierge; 24-hour room service; business center with computer rentals and secretarial services; conference rooms; car-rental desk; tour desk; barbershop; dry cleaning and laundry; newspaper delivery; twice-daily maid service; express checkout; valet parking. Forty-eight guest rooms for people with disabilities adjoin standard rooms.

EXPENSIVE

Boston Marriott Copley Place. 110 Huntington Ave., Boston, MA 02116. ☎ **800/ 228-9290** or 617/236-5800. Fax 617/236-5885. www.marriott.com/marriott/BOSCO. 1,147 units. A/C TV TEL. $199–$344 double; $450–$1,050 suite. Children free in parents' room. Weekend and other packages available. AE, DC, DISC, JCB, MC, V. Valet parking $24; self-parking $22. T: Orange Line to Back Bay, or Green Line E to Prudential.

ℹ️ Family-Friendly Hotels

Almost every hotel in the Boston area regularly plays host to children, and many offer special family packages. Moderately priced chains have the most experience with young guests—you can't go wrong with a Howard Johnson's or a Holiday Inn—but their higher-end competitors put on a good show.

Units at the **Doubletree Guest Suites** (see p. 86) have two rooms in which to spread out, and they cost far less than adjoining rooms at any other hotel this nice. You can use the in-room coffeemaker and refrigerator to prepare your own breakfast, then splurge on lunch and dinner.

In the Back Bay, the **Colonnade Hotel** (see p. 80) offers a family weekend package that includes parking; breakfast for two adults; up to four passes (two adult, two children) to an attraction of your choice; and a fanny pack for younger guests that holds sunglasses, a pad and pen, a yo-yo, and a toy duck.

The **Seaport Hotel** (see p. 76), near Museum Wharf, offers excellent weekend deals, splendid views of the Big Dig and the airport, underwater music piped into the swimming pool, and even a grandparent-grandchild package.

In Cambridge, the **Royal Sonesta Hotel** (see p. 92) fills the vacation months with Summerfest, which includes complimentary use of bicycles, the health club and indoor/outdoor pool, free ice cream every day, and boat rides along the Charles River. And it's right around the corner from the Museum of Science.

Another riverfront hotel, the **Hyatt Regency Cambridge** (see p. 92), courts families with its pool, bicycle rentals, easy access to the banks of the Charles, and discounted rates (subject to availability) on a separate room for the kids.

At Cambridge's **Charles Hotel** (see p. 89), the adjoining WellBridge Health and Fitness Center sets aside time for family swimming. The Harvard Square scavenger hunt is fun, as is the room service menu, which includes pepperoni pizza. Phone the "Children's Storyline" to hear four bedtime tales for guests under 7.

Yes, 1,147 units. This 38-story tower feels generic, but it does offer something for everyone—namely, complete business facilities and easy access to Boston's shopping wonderland. The guest rooms have Queen Anne–style mahogany furniture and are large enough to hold a desk and table and either two armchairs or an armchair and an ottoman. Other features include hair dryers, coffeemakers, full-length mirrors, irons, ironing boards, and phones with data ports. Ultrasuites feature individual whirlpool bathtubs. The Concierge Level has a private lounge that serves complimentary continental breakfast, cocktails, and hors d'oeuvres. This is New England's biggest convention hotel (the Sheraton is larger but attracts more vacationers), so if you're not part of a group, you may feel a bit lost.

Dining/Diversions: The sports bar **Champions** is a fun place to watch TV and eat bar food and burgers. There are two restaurants, a sushi bar, and a lounge that offers live entertainment 5 nights a week.

Amenities: Heated indoor pool; well-equipped health club with exercise room, whirlpools, saunas; full-service business center; conference rooms with Internet access; car-rental desk; tour desk; concierge; 24-hour room service; dry cleaning and laundry; valet parking. Rooms for people with disabilities are available.

Copley Square Hotel. 47 Huntington Ave., Boston, MA 02116. ☎ **800/225-7062** or 617/536-9000. Fax 617/236-0351. www.copleysquarehotel.com. 143 units. A/C TV TEL. $225–$285 double; $385 suite. Children under 17 free in parents' room. Packages and senior discounts available. AE, CB, DC, DISC, JCB, MC, V. Parking in adjacent garage $25. T: Green Line to Copley, or Orange Line to Back Bay.

The Copley Square Hotel offers a great location along with the advantages and drawbacks of its relatively small size. Built in 1891, the seven-story hotel extends attentive service that's hard to find at the nearby megahotels, without those giants' abundant amenities. If you don't need to engineer a corporate takeover from your room, it's a fine choice, but a larger competitor might offer more features for the same price. Each attractively decorated unit has a queen- or king-size bed or two double beds; some rooms are on the small side. All have hair dryers, coffeemakers, safes, and phones with modem hookups and guest voicemail.

Dining/Diversions: Afternoon tea is served in the lobby. **Speeder & Earl's** serves breakfast. **Café Budapest** (Hungarian and Continental cuisine) and the **Original Sports Saloon** (barbecue) serve lunch and dinner.

Amenities: Concierge; room service until 11pm; dry cleaning; 24-hour currency exchange.

Hilton Boston Back Bay. 40 Dalton St., Boston, MA 02115. ☎ **800/874-0663**, 800/HILTONS, or 617/236-1100. Fax 617/867-6104. www.bostonbackbay.hilton.com. 385 units (some with shower only). A/C TV TEL. $179–$295 double; $450 minisuite; $650 1-bedroom suite; $850 2-bedroom suite. Packages and AAA discount available. Extra person $20. Rollaway $20. Children free in parents' room. AE, CB, DC, DISC, MC, V. Valet parking $24; self-parking $17. T: Green Line B, C, or D to Hynes/ICA. Small pets accepted.

Across the street from the Prudential Center complex, this 26-story tower is primarily a business hotel, but vacationing families also find it convenient and comfortable. Rooms are large and soundproofed; 44 are executive units added in 1998. All have modern furnishings, with either one king-size or two double beds, windows that open, coffeemakers, hair dryers, irons, and ironing boards. Rates for executive rooms include continental breakfast and upgraded amenities.

Dining/Diversions: Boodles Restaurant draws businesspeople for grilled steaks and seafood, and **Boodles Bar** offers nearly 100 American microbrews. There is a lounge and a nightclub, **Club Nicole,** which attracts a young crowd.

Amenities: Heated indoor pool; sundeck; well-equipped 24-hour fitness center; business center; conference rooms; concierge; room service until 1am; dry cleaning and laundry; newspaper delivery; express checkout; currency exchange. Rooms for people with disabilities are available.

✪ **Sheraton Boston Hotel.** 39 Dalton St., Boston, MA 02199. ☎ **800/325-3535** or 617/236-2000. Fax 617/236-1702. www.sheraton.com. 1,181 units. A/C TV TEL. $149–$369 double; suites from $400. Children under 17 free in parents' room. Weekend packages available. 25% discount for students, faculty, and retired persons with ID, depending on availability. AE, CB, DC, DISC, JCB, MC, V. Valet or self-parking $28. T: Green Line E to Prudential, or B, C, or D to Hynes/ICA. Small pets accepted.

Its central location, range of accommodations, lavish convention facilities, and huge pool make this 29-story hotel one of the most popular in the city. It offers direct access to the Hynes Convention Center and the Prudential Center complex, and recent and ongoing renovations have left it in remarkably good shape.

A $73 million overhaul upgraded the bathrooms, installed individual climate control and new windows, and reconfigured the convention space and lobby. The fairly large guest rooms are being redecorated in sleek contemporary style and outfitted with "pillow top" beds. They also boast coffeemakers, hair dryers, irons, and ironing boards.

Many suites have a wet bar and a refrigerator. Club Level guests get free local calls, no access charges on long-distance calls, personal printer-fax-copiers, safes, and admission to a lounge that serves complimentary continental breakfast and hors d'oeuvres.

Dining/Diversions: The lobby restaurant, **Apropos,** serves three meals daily; the **Turning Point Lounge** offers picture-window views of the neighborhood. The clubby **Punch Bar** serves after-dinner drinks, cordials, and a breathtaking selection of cigars.

Amenities: Heated indoor/outdoor pool with retractable dome, pavilion, Jacuzzi, and sauna; large, well-equipped health club; recently expanded and reconfigured conference and function space. Concierge; 24-hour room service; dry cleaning and laundry; car-rental desk; newspaper delivery; in-room massage; express checkout; valet parking; courtesy car. Rooms for people with disabilities are available.

MODERATE

The MidTown Hotel. 220 Huntington Ave., Boston, MA 02115. ☎ **800/343-1177** or 617/262-1000. Fax 617/262-8739. www.midtownhotel.com. 159 units. A/C TV TEL. Apr–Aug $149–$209 double; Sept to mid-Dec $189–$249 double; mid-Dec to Mar $99–$169 double. Extra person $15. Children under 18 free in parents' room. 10% AARP discount available; government employees' discount, subject to availability. AE, CB, DC, DISC, MC, V. Free parking. T: Green Line E to Prudential, or Orange Line to Mass. Ave.

Even without free parking and a pool (open seasonally), this centrally located two-story hotel would be a good deal for families and budget-conscious businesspeople. It's on a busy street within easy walking distance of Symphony Hall, the Museum of Fine Arts, and the Back Bay attractions. The recently renovated rooms are large, bright, and attractively outfitted, although bathrooms are on the small side. All units have coffeemakers and hair dryers, and some have connecting doors that allow families to spread out. For business travelers, many rooms have two-line phones; photocopying and fax services are available at the front desk. Dry cleaning and video rentals are available, and baby-sitting can be arranged. The heated outdoor pool is open from Memorial Day through Labor Day. The on-premises restaurant serves breakfast from 7 to 11am.

○ **Newbury Guest House.** 261 Newbury St. (between Fairfield and Gloucester sts.), Boston, MA 02116. ☎ **617/437-7666.** Fax 617/262-4243. www.hagopianhotels.com. 32 units (some with shower only). A/C TV TEL. $110–$155 double; winter $100–$145 double. Extra person $15. Rates include continental breakfast. Rates may be higher during special events. Minimum 2 nights on weekends. AE, CB, DC, DISC, MC, V. Parking $15 (reservation required). T: Green Line B, C, or D to Hynes/ICA.

After just a little shopping in the Back Bay, you'll appreciate what a find this cozy inn is—a bargain on Newbury Street. It's a pair of brick townhouses built in the 1880s and combined into a refined guesthouse. It offers comfortable furnishings, a pleasant staff, nifty architectural details, and—*such* a deal—a buffet breakfast served in the ground-level dining room, which adjoins a brick patio. Rooms are modest in size but nicely appointed and well maintained. The Hagopian family opened the B&B in 1991, and it operates near capacity all year, drawing business travelers during the week and sightseers on weekends. A room for travelers with disabilities is available. At these prices in this location, there's only one caveat: Reserve early.

INEXPENSIVE

Hostelling International–Boston. 12 Hemenway St., Boston, MA 02115. ☎ **888/ HOST222** or 617/536-9455. Fax 617/424-6558. www.bostonhostel.org. 205 beds. Members $24 per bed; nonmembers $27 per bed. JCB, MC, V. T: Green Line B, C, or D to Hynes/ICA.

This hostel near the Berklee College of Music and Symphony Hall caters to students, youth groups, and other travelers in search of comfortable, no-frills lodging. It has two full dine-in kitchens, 19 bathrooms, a coin laundry, and a large common room. The recently remodeled public areas contain meeting and workshop space. Accommodations are dorm-style, with three to six beds per room.

The hostel provides a "sheet sleeping sack," or you can bring your own; sleeping bags are not permitted. The enthusiastic staff organizes free and inexpensive cultural, educational, and recreational programs on the premises and throughout the Boston area. The first-floor rooms and bathrooms are wheelchair accessible, and there's a wheelchair lift at the entrance to the building.

Note: To get a bed during the summer, you must be a member of Hostelling International–American Youth Hostels. For information and an application, contact HI-AYH, P.O. Box 37613, Washington, DC 20013 (☎ **202/783-6161;** www.hiayh.org). If you are not a U.S. citizen, apply to your home country's hostelling association.

7 Outskirts & Brookline

What Bostonians consider "outskirts" would be centrally located in many larger cities. Lodgings in this area are close to Fenway Park, the hospitals at the Longwood Medical Area, and several colleges and museums. Brookline starts about 3 blocks beyond Boston's Kenmore Square.

EXPENSIVE

✪ **Doubletree Guest Suites.** 400 Soldiers Field Rd., Boston, MA 02134. ☎ **800/ 222-TREE** or 617/783-0090. Fax 617/783-0897. www.doubletreehotels.com. 308 units. A/C MINIBAR TV TEL. $139–$259 double. Extra person $20. Children under 18 free in parents' room. Weekend packages $154–$264. AARP and AAA discounts available. AE, CB, DC, DISC, JCB, MC, V. Parking $15–$18.

This hotel is one of the best deals in town—every unit is a two-room suite with a living room, bedroom, and bathroom. Business travelers can entertain in their rooms, and families can spread out, making this a good choice for both. Overlooking the Charles River at the Allston/Cambridge exit of the Mass. Pike, the hotel is near Cambridge and the bike and jogging path that runs along the river, although not in an actual neighborhood. There's complimentary van service to and from attractions and business areas in Boston and Cambridge, making the somewhat inconvenient location easier to handle.

The suites surround a 15-story atrium. Rooms are large and attractively furnished, and most bedrooms have king-size beds and a writing desk. Each living room contains a full-size sofa bed, a dining table, and a good-size refrigerator. Each suite has a coffeemaker, two TVs, and three telephones (one in the bathroom).

Dining/Diversions: Scullers Grille and **Scullers Lounge** serve meals from 6:30am to 11pm. The celebrated **Scullers Jazz Club** schedules two nightly shows.

Amenities: Heated indoor pool; exercise room; whirlpool; sauna; 24-hour room service; 24-hour business center; conference rooms; concierge; newspaper delivery;

Hotels from Mass. Ave. to Brookline

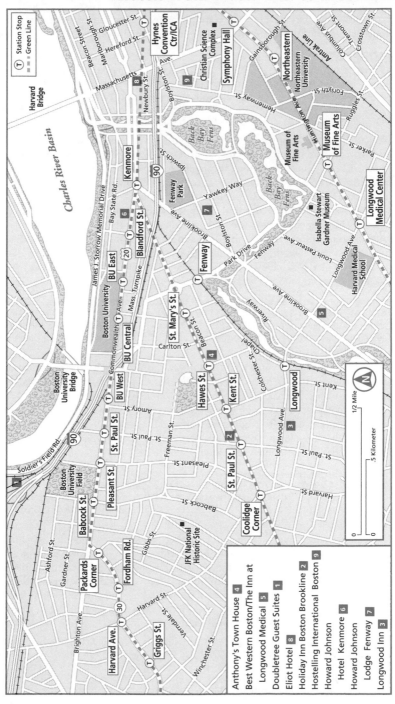

Station Stop
Green Line

Harvard Bridge

Charles River Basin

Hynes Convention Ctr/ICA

Christian Science Complex

Symphony Hall

Northeastern University

Museum of Fine Arts

Museum of Fine Arts

Beacon Street
Gloucester St.
Marlborough St.
Hereford St.
Massachusetts Ave.
Newbury St.
Boylston St.
Commonwealth Ave.
Gainsborough St.
Hemenway St.
Forsyth St.
Amtrak Line
Columbus Ave.
Tremont St.
Crosstown St.
Ruggles St.

Kenmore

Back Bay Fens

Fenway Park

Yawkey Way

Isabella Stewart Gardner Museum

Longwood Medical Center

Bay State Rd.
James J. Storrow Memorial Drive
Ipswich St.
Blandford St.
Brookline Ave.
Boylston St.
Park Drive
Fenway
Louis Pasteur Ave.
Longwood Ave.
Harvard Medical School

BU East
BU Central
BU West
St. Paul St.
Pleasant St.
Babcock St.
Packards Corner
Fordham Rd.

Boston University
Boston University Bridge
Boston University Field

Mass. Turnpike
Comm Ave.
Amory St.
St. Paul St.
Freeman St.
Pleasant St.
Babcock St.
Gibbs St.

St. Mary's St.
Carlton St.
Beacon St.
Hawes St.
Kent St.
Longwood
Chapel St.
Colchester St.
Chapel St.
Riverway
Brookline Ave.
Kent St.
Longwood Ave.
St. Paul St.
Harvard St.

Fenway

Coolidge Corner

Harvard Ave.
Griggs St.
Ashford St.
Gardner St.
Brighton Ave.
Vendale Ave.
Harvard St.
Winchester St.

JFK National Historic Site

Soldier's Field Rd.

1/2 Mile
.5 Kilometer

Anthony's Town House 4
Best Western Boston/The Inn at Longwood Medical 5
Doubletree Guest Suites 1
Eliot Hotel 8
Holiday Inn Boston Brookline 2
Hostelling International Boston 9
Howard Johnson Hotel Kenmore 6
Howard Johnson Lodge Fenway 7
Longwood Inn 3

87

express checkout. Dry cleaning and laundry; laundry room; game room; baby-sitting available; car-rental desk; van service. Suites for people with disabilities on each floor.

MODERATE

Best Western Boston/The Inn at Longwood Medical. 342 Longwood Ave., Boston, MA 02115. ☎ **800/528-1234** or 617/731-4700. TDD 617/731-9088. Fax 617/731-6273. E-mail: innlwm@erols.com. 158 units (14 with kitchenette). A/C TV TEL. $139–$209 double; $219–$259 suite. Extra person $15. Children under 18 free in parents' room. AE, CB, DC, DISC, MC, V. Parking $14. T: Green Line D or E to Longwood.

Next to Children's Hospital in the Longwood Medical Area (Beth Israel Deaconess and Brigham and Women's hospitals, the Dana–Farber Cancer Institute, and the Joslin Diabetes Center are nearby), this eight-story hotel is a good base for those with business at the hospitals. Near museums, colleges, and Fenway Park, it's about 15 minutes from downtown Boston by public transportation.

Guest rooms are quite large and equipped with hair dryers, irons, and ironing boards. There's room service until 11pm. Hotel facilities include a restaurant, a lounge, meeting rooms, dry-cleaning and laundry service, and a laundry room. Rooms for travelers with disabilities are available. The hotel abuts the Longwood Galleria business complex, which has a food court, retail stores, and a fitness center that's available to hotel guests for $8 to $10 a day.

Holiday Inn Boston Brookline. 1200 Beacon St., Brookline, MA 02446. ☎ **800/ HOLIDAY** or 617/277-1200. Fax 617/734-6991. www.holiday-inn.com/brookline. 225 units (some with shower only). A/C TV TEL. $139–$199 double; $199–$300 suite. Extra person $10. Children under 18 free in parents' room. AE, DC, DISC, JCB, MC, V. Parking $10. T: Green Line C to St. Paul St.

Just 15 minutes from downtown on the subway, this sparkling hotel is more than just another Holiday Inn. It offers recently redecorated rooms that are large and well appointed, with coffeemakers, hair dryers, and irons and ironing boards. The lobby surrounds a colorful atrium with a small indoor pool, whirlpool, and exercise room. Dry cleaning is available. Ten rooms are equipped for guests with disabilities. The six-story hotel has a restaurant, lounge, and coffee shop. The bustling Coolidge Corner neighborhood is a 10-minute walk away.

Howard Johnson Hotel Kenmore. 575 Commonwealth Ave., Boston, MA 02215. ☎ **800/654-2000** or 617/267-3100. Fax 617/424-1045. www.hojo.com. 179 units. A/C TV TEL. $125–$225 double. Extra person $10. Children under 18 free in parents' room. Senior and AAA discounts available. AE, CB, DC, DISC, JCB, MC, V. Free parking. T: Green Line B to Blandford St. Pets accepted.

If the location doesn't get you, the pool and free parking might. The Boston University campus surrounds this eight-story hotel, with the T to downtown out front and Kenmore Square and Fenway Park nearby. The recently refurbished rooms are standard-issue Howard Johnson's—comfortable, but still nothing fancy—and some are small. The hotel has a glass-enclosed elevator, which runs to the rooftop lounge and provides a good view of the area. The indoor swimming pool and skylit sundeck on the roof are open year-round from 11am to 9pm.

Howard Johnson Lodge Fenway. 1271 Boylston St., Boston, MA 02215. ☎ **800/ 654-2000** or 617/267-8300. Fax 617/267-2763. www.hojo.com. 94 units. A/C TV TEL. $115–$185 double. Extra person $10. Children under 18 free in parents' room. Family packages and senior and AAA discounts available. AE, CB, DC, DISC, JCB, MC, V. Free parking. T: Green Line B, C, or D to Kenmore; 10-min. walk. Pets accepted.

This is as close to Fenway Park as you can get without buying a ticket. The outdoor pool and free parking make the motel particularly attractive to vacationing families. If you're not visiting during baseball season, the busy street in a commercial-residential neighborhood is convenient to the Back Bay, the Museum of Fine Arts, and the Isabella Stewart Gardner Museum. When the Red Sox are playing, guests contend with crowded sidewalks and raucous fans who flood the area. The decent-sized rooms contain coffeemakers, and some have microwaves and refrigerators. Laundry service is available. There's an outdoor pool, open from 9am to 7pm in the summer. On the premises are a steak house and a popular lounge that has live jazz entertainment.

INEXPENSIVE

Anthony's Town House. 1085 Beacon St., Brookline, MA 02446. ☎ **617/566-3972.** Fax 617/232-1085. 12 units (none with private bathroom). A/C TV. $65–$95 double. Extra person $10. Weekly rates and winter discounts available. No credit cards. Free parking. T: Green Line C to Hawes St.

The Anthony family has operated this four-story brownstone guesthouse since 1944, and a stay here is very much like tagging along with a friend who's spending the night at Grandma's place. Each floor has three high-ceilinged rooms furnished in rather ornate Queen Anne or Victorian style, and a shared bathroom with enclosed shower. Smaller rooms (one per floor) have twin beds, and the large front rooms have bay windows. Guests have the use of two refrigerators. The guesthouse is 1 mile from Boston's Kenmore Square, about 15 minutes from downtown by subway, and 2 blocks from a busy commercial strip. The turn-of-the-20th-century building is listed on the National Register of Historic Places.

Longwood Inn. 123 Longwood Ave., Brookline, MA 02446. ☎ **617/566-8615.** Fax 617/738-1070. http://go.boston.com/longwoodinn. 22 units, 17 with bathroom (some with shower only). A/C TEL. Apr–Nov $79–$109 double; Dec–Mar $65–$89 double. 1-bedroom apt (sleeps 4-plus) $89–$119. Weekly rates available. No credit cards. Free parking. T: Green Line D to Longwood, or C to Coolidge Corner.

In a residential area 3 blocks from the Boston–Brookline border, this three-story Victorian guesthouse offers comfortable accommodations at modest rates. Guests have the use of a fully equipped kitchen and common dining room, coin laundry, and TV lounge. The apartment has a private bathroom, kitchen, and balcony. Tennis courts, a running track, and a playground at the school next door are open to the public. Public transportation is easily accessible, and the Longwood Medical Area and busy Coolidge Corner neighborhood are within walking distance.

8 Cambridge

A city so close to Boston that they're usually thought of as a unit, Cambridge has its own attractions and excellent hotels. College graduation season (May and early June) is especially busy, but campus events can cause high demand at unexpected times, so plan ahead.

VERY EXPENSIVE

✪ **The Charles Hotel.** 1 Bennett St., Cambridge, MA 02138. ☎ **800/882-1818** outside Mass., or 617/864-1200. Fax 617/864-5715. www.charleshotel.com. 293 units. A/C MINIBAR TV TEL. $349–$429 double; $489–$3,000 suite. Extra person $20. Children under 18 free in parents' room. Weekend packages available. AE, CB, DC, JCB, MC, V. Valet and self-parking $18. T: Red Line to Harvard. Pets accepted.

The Charles Hotel is a phenomenon—an instant classic. The nine-story brick hotel a block from Harvard Square has been *the* place for business and leisure travelers to Cambridge since it opened in 1985. Much of its fame derives from its excellent restaurants, jazz bar, and day spa, and the service is, if anything, equally exalted. In the posh

Cambridge Accommodations

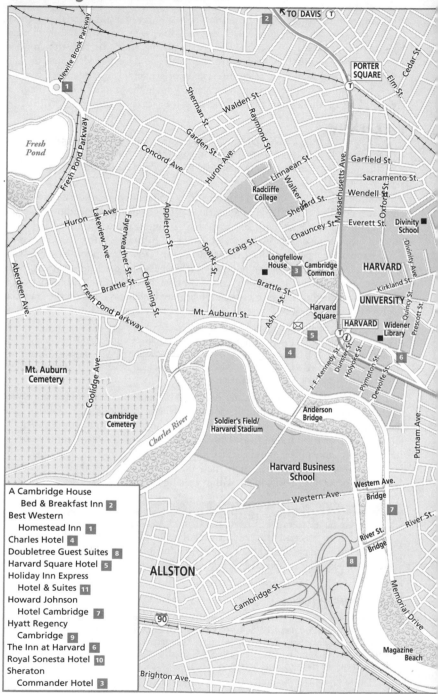

A Cambridge House
  Bed & Breakfast Inn **2**
Best Western
  Homestead Inn **1**
Charles Hotel **4**
Doubletree Guest Suites **8**
Harvard Square Hotel **5**
Holiday Inn Express
  Hotel & Suites **11**
Howard Johnson
  Hotel Cambridge **7**
Hyatt Regency
  Cambridge **9**
The Inn at Harvard **6**
Royal Sonesta Hotel **10**
Sheraton
  Commander Hotel **3**

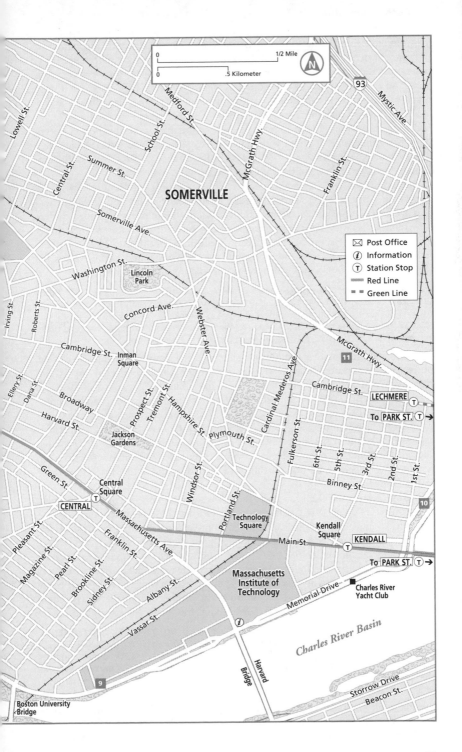

guest rooms, the style is contemporary country, with custom-designed adaptations of Early American Shaker furniture and down quilts. Bathrooms have telephones, TVs, hair dryers, and scales. All rooms have large windows that open, three phones, data ports, and state-of-the-art Bose Wave radios. And it wouldn't be Cambridge if your intellectual needs went unfulfilled—you can order books over the phone, and a Charles staffer will pick them up at WordsWorth Books and bill your room.

Dining/Diversions: Rialto, one of the best restaurants in Greater Boston, serves Mediterranean cuisine by award-winning chef Jody Adams. **Henrietta's Table** offers New England country cooking. The renowned **Regattabar** features live jazz Tuesday through Saturday nights, and the **Tini Bar** specializes in martinis.

Amenities: Concierge; 24-hour room service; dry cleaning and laundry; newspaper delivery; in-room massage; twice-daily maid service. Baby-sitting and secretarial services available; express checkout; video rentals; valet parking; newly expanded conference rooms; facilities for teleconferencing; car-rental desk. Glass-enclosed pool, Jacuzzi, and exercise room at the adjacent WellBridge Health and Fitness Center; beauty treatments available at the European-style Le Pli Spa and Salon. Rooms for people with disabilities; rooms with special amenities for female travelers.

The Hyatt Regency Cambridge. 575 Memorial Dr., Cambridge, MA 02139. ☎ **800/ 233-1234** or 617/492-1234. Fax 617/491-6906. www.cambridge.hyatt.com. 469 units. A/C TV TEL. $239–$399 double weekdays, $149–$234 weekend; $265–$394 Regency Club; $450–$750 suite. Extra person $25. Children under 18 free in parents' room. Weekend packages available. AE, DC, DISC, JCB, MC, V. Valet parking $17; self-parking $15.

This dramatic brick hotel, a prominent feature of the Cambridge skyline, makes up for its not-exactly-central location with its appointments and architecture. Across the street from the Charles River and not far from the Allston/Brighton exit of the turnpike, it encloses a 16-story atrium with glass elevators, fountains, trees, and balconies. The spacious guest rooms were renovated in 1997. All have coffeemakers and hair dryers, and some have breathtaking views of Boston and the river. Families are especially welcome, with special two-room rates (subject to availability), and bicycles for rent. The hotel is about 10 minutes from downtown Boston by car and convenient for those visiting colleges—it's between Harvard and MIT and across the bridge from Boston University.

Dining/Diversions: On the rooftop, the revolving, glass-enclosed **Spinnaker Italia** restaurant serves dinner and Sunday brunch, and it has a lounge where there's dancing on Friday and Saturday nights. A new restaurant and lounge, overlooking the river, serves three meals daily and specializes in wood-grilled cuisine.

Amenities: 75-foot indoor lap pool; health club with whirlpool, sauna, and steam room; sundeck; business center; conference rooms; car-rental desk; concierge; room service until late evening; dry cleaning and laundry; baby-sitting referrals; valet parking; ATM and currency exchange. Complimentary scheduled shuttle service to Cambridge and Boston destinations. Twenty-four rooms for people with disabilities.

✪ **Royal Sonesta Hotel.** 5 Cambridge Pkwy., Cambridge, MA 02142. ☎ **800/SONESTA** or 617/806-4200. Fax 617/806-4232. www.sonesta.com. 400 units. A/C MINIBAR TV TEL. $239–$279 standard double, $259–$299 superior double, $279–$319 deluxe double; $329–$950 suite. Extra person $25. Children under 18 free in parents' room. Weekend and other packages available. AE, CB, DC, DISC, JCB, MC, V. Parking $16. T: Green Line to Lechmere; 10-min. walk.

This luxurious hotel is in a curious location—it's close to only a few things but convenient to everything, making it a good choice for both businesspeople and families. The CambridgeSide Galleria mall is across the street, and the Museum of Science is around the corner on the bridge to Boston, which is closer than Harvard Square. In the other direction, MIT is a 10-minute walk. Most of the spacious rooms have a lovely view of the river or the city (higher prices are for better views), and all have two phones plus hair dryers. Everything is custom designed and renovated regularly—every unit has been completely revamped in the past 4 years. Original contemporary artwork, including pieces by Andy Warhol and Frank Stella, hangs throughout the public spaces and guest rooms.

Dining/Diversions: Davio's, a branch of the Newbury Street favorite, serves three meals daily and has an outdoor patio overlooking the Charles River. The casual **Gallery Café** also has a patio. Both restaurants offer live music on summer evenings (schedules vary).

Amenities: Heated indoor/outdoor pool with retractable roof; well-equipped health club; Jacuzzi; sauna; spa services, including massage. Business center; conference rooms; concierge; room service until 1am (2am on weekends); dry cleaning and laundry; baby-sitting available; express checkout; valet parking. Eleven wheelchair-accessible rooms, sixteen for those with hearing impairments; staff trained in disability awareness.

Sheraton Commander Hotel. 16 Garden St., Cambridge, MA 02138. ☎ **800/325-3535** or 617/547-4800. Fax 617/868-8322. www.sheratoncommander.com. 175 units. A/C TV TEL. $195–$345 double; $330–$550 suite. Extra person $20. Children under 18 free in parents' room. Weekend packages and AAA and AARP discounts available. AE, CB, DC, DISC, JCB, MC, V. Free parking. T: Red Line to Harvard.

This six-story hotel in the heart of Cambridge's historic district opened in 1927, and it's exactly what you'd expect of a traditional hostelry within sight of the Harvard campus. It doesn't have the cachet of the Charles, but free parking in Harvard Square is worth a barrel of cachet. The Colonial-style decor begins in the elegant lobby and extends to the decent-sized guest rooms, which are attractively furnished and well maintained. Rooms have two phones with data ports, coffeemakers, hair dryers, irons and ironing boards, and nightlights. The Club Level offers additional amenities, including in-room fax machines, free local phone calls, and a private lounge that serves complimentary continental breakfast and afternoon hors d'oeuvres on weekdays. Suites have two TVs, and some have wet bars, refrigerators, and whirlpools.

Dining: The restaurant serves three meals daily and Sunday brunch. The cafe serves lighter fare in the afternoon and evening.

Amenities: Small fitness center; sundeck; conference rooms; laundry room; concierge; room service until 11pm; dry cleaning and laundry; newspaper delivery; baby-sitting available; express checkout; valet parking.

EXPENSIVE

The Inn at Harvard. 1201 Mass. Ave. (at Quincy St.), Cambridge, MA 02138. ☎ **800/ 458-5886** or 617/491-2222. Fax 617/491-6520. www.theinnatharvard.com. 109 units (some with shower only). A/C TV TEL. $169–$309 double; $500 presidential suite. Extra person $10. Children under 19 free in parents' room. Packages and senior, AAA, and AARP discounts available. AE, CB, DC, DISC, MC, V. Valet parking $25. T: Red Line to Harvard.

At first glance, the red-brick Inn at Harvard looks almost like a college dorm—it's adjacent to Harvard Yard, and its Georgian-style architecture would fit nicely on campus. Inside, there's no mistaking it for anything other than an elegant hotel, popular with business travelers and university visitors. The four-story skylit atrium holds the "living room," a well-appointed guest lounge. The elegantly decorated guest rooms have cherry furniture, and each has a lounge chair or two armchairs around a table, a work area, windows that open, and an original painting from the Fogg Art Museum.

Each room has two phones, one with a modem hookup. Some rooms have dormer windows and window seats.

Dining: The Atrium Dining Room serves seasonal New England fare at breakfast, lunch, dinner, and afternoon tea. Guests have dining privileges at the Harvard Faculty Club, a half-block away.

Amenities: Conference rooms; safe-deposit boxes; room service; dry cleaning and laundry; newspaper delivery; secretarial services available; express checkout; valet parking. Six wheelchair-accessible rooms.

MODERATE

The **Holiday Inn Express Hotel and Suites,** 250 Msgr. O'Brien Hwy., Cambridge, MA 02141 (☎ **888/887-7690** or 617/577-7600; fax 617/354-1313; www. bristolhotels.com), is a limited-services lodging on a busy street a 5-minute walk from Lechmere station on the Green Line. The neighborhood is busy and noisy, but the hotel is convenient. Rates for a standard double run $119 to $199.

Best Western Homestead Inn. 220 Alewife Brook Pkwy., Cambridge, MA 02138. ☎ **800/ 491-4914** or 617/491-8000. Fax 617/491-4932. www.bwhomestead.com. 69 units. A/C TV TEL. Mid-Mar to Oct $119–$229 double; Nov to mid-Mar $99–$199 double. Extra person $10. Rates include continental breakfast. Rates may be higher during special events. Children under 16 free in parents' room. AE, CB, DC, MC, V. Free parking. T: Red Line to Alewife, 10-min. walk.

The busy commercial neighborhood is nothing to write home about, but this four-story motel is comfortable and convenient for motorists. Guest rooms are spacious, with contemporary or reproduction colonial furnishings, and are at least one floor up from the busy street. All have hair dryers, coffeemakers, irons, and ironing boards. There's an indoor pool with a Jacuzzi, and a $2^1/_2$-mile jogging trail around Fresh Pond is across the street. A renovation project was scheduled at press time; a health club, business center, and accommodations for travelers with disabilities should be available by the time you read this. Laundry service (weekdays only), meeting facilities for up to 45 people, and rental-car pickup and drop-off are available. There's a restaurant next door, and a shopping center with a 10-screen movie theater nearby. Boston is about a 15-minute drive or a 30-minute T ride away; Lexington and Concord are less than 30 minutes away by car.

A Cambridge House Bed & Breakfast Inn. 2218 Mass. Ave., Cambridge, MA 02140. ☎ **800/232-9989** or 617/491-6300; 800/96-2079 in the U.K. Fax 617/868-2848. www.acambridgehouse.com. 15 units (some with shower only). A/C TV TEL. $139–$275 double. Extra person $35. Rates include buffet breakfast. AE, DISC, MC, V. Free parking. T: Red Line to Porter.

A Cambridge House is a beautifully restored 1892 Victorian that's listed on the National Register of Historic Places. The three-story building feels almost like a country inn, but is on a busy stretch of Cambridge's main street (Mass. Ave.), set back from the sidewalk by a lawn. Rooms vary widely in size; all contain hair dryers. They're warmly decorated with Waverly–Schumacher fabrics and period antiques, and most have fireplaces and four-poster canopy beds with down comforters. The inn serves a generous breakfast and afternoon refreshments. Rooms for travelers with disabilities are available.

Harvard Square Hotel. 110 Mount Auburn St., Cambridge, MA 02138. ☎ **800/ 458-5886** or 617/864-5200. Fax 617/864-2409. www.doubletreehotels.com. 73 units. A/C TV TEL. $129–$209 double. Extra person $10. Children under 17 free in parents' room. Corporate rates and AAA and AARP discounts available. AE, DC, DISC, MC, V. Parking $20. T: Red Line to Harvard.

Smack in the middle of Harvard Square, this six-story brick hotel is a favorite with visiting parents and budget-conscious business travelers. The unpretentious guest rooms were renovated in early 2000 and outfitted with new furniture and carpeting. They're relatively small, but comfortable and neatly decorated in contemporary style. All have data ports, voicemail, hair dryers, irons, and ironing boards; some overlook Harvard Square. The front desk handles fax and copy services and distributes complimentary newspapers (weekdays only). Dry-cleaning and laundry service are available. There are four wheelchair-accessible rooms. Guests have dining privileges at the Inn at Harvard—like the Harvard Square Hotel, managed by Doubletree—and the Harvard Faculty Club.

Howard Johnson Hotel Cambridge. 777 Memorial Dr., Cambridge, MA 02139. ☎ **800/ 654-2000** or 617/492-7777. Fax 617/492-6038. www.hojo.com. 205 units. A/C TV TEL. $119–$235 double. Extra person $10. Cribs free. Children under 18 free in parents' room. AARP and AAA discounts available. AE, CB, DC, DISC, JCB, MC, V. Free parking. Pets accepted.

An attractive, modern hotel with an indoor swimming pool and sundeck, this 16-story tower is across the street from the Charles River. It's near the major college campuses and the Massachusetts Turnpike and a 10-minute drive from downtown Boston. Each room has a picture window, giving guests who are up high enough a panoramic view of the Boston skyline. Rooms have modern furnishings, and some have a private balcony. Prices vary with the size of the room, the floor, and the view. Room service, laundry service, conference rooms, and rooms for people with disabilities are available.

Also at the hotel is the **Bisuteki Japanese Steak House,** where dinners are prepared at the table in the hibachi style of "firebowl" cooking.

9 Dorchester

Best known as a residential neighborhood, Dorchester has a busy commercial area that's home to these two establishments. They're accessible from the Southeast Expressway (Exit 12 southbound, Exit 13 northbound) and close to the Kennedy Library.

MODERATE

Susse Chalet Boston Hotel. 800 Morrissey Blvd., Boston, MA 02122. ☎ **800/5-CHALET** or 617/287-9100. Fax 617/265-9287. www.bostonhotel.com. 175 units. A/C TV TEL. $81–$120 double. Extra person $5. Rates include continental breakfast. AE, CB, DC, DISC, MC, V. Free parking. T: Red Line to JFK/UMass, then take free shuttle bus.

This three-story motor lodge offers utilitarian lodgings at reasonable prices. Here, too, ask to face away from traffic. The recently redecorated rooms have hair dryers and data ports. An outdoor swimming pool is open in the warmer months. Guests have the use of the facilities in the adjacent Susse Chalet Boston Inn (see below).

Susse Chalet Boston Inn. 900 Morrissey Blvd., Boston, MA 02122. ☎ **800/886-0056** or 617/287-9200. Fax 617/282-2365. www.bostonhotel.com. 172 units. A/C TV TEL. $91–$150 double; $125 suite. Extra person $5. Rates include continental breakfast. AE, CB, DC, DISC, MC, V. Free parking. T: Red Line to JFK/UMass, then take free shuttle bus.

The Susse Chalet Boston properties (see the Hotel listing, above) are inexpensive but not cheap—they have high standards and low prices. The Inn is a five-story building with large guest rooms, including rooms for people with disabilities. The newest rooms are on the fifth floor, which was added in 1998. Ask—beg if you have to—to be on the side of the building that faces away from the interstate. Rooms have a full, double, or king-size bed, and all have hair dryers, data ports, and access to free local calls. There are coin-operated washers and dryers, dry-cleaning and laundry service, and a seasonal outdoor swimming pool.

10 At the Airport

✪ Hilton Boston Logan Airport. 85 Terminal Rd., Logan International Airport, Boston, MA 02128. ☎ **800/HILTONS** or 617/568-6700. Fax 617/568-6800. www. bostonloganairport.hilton.com. 599 units. A/C MINIBAR TV TEL. $149–$259 double; from $500 suite. Children under 19 free in parents' room. Weekend and other packages from $159 per night. AE, CB, DC, DISC, MC, V. Valet parking $25; self-parking $18. T: Blue Line to Airport, then take shuttle bus.

This spanking-new hotel in the middle of the airport draws most of its guests from meetings, conventions, and recently canceled flights. Opened in 1999, it's accessible through walkways from Terminals A (close) and E (distant), and by shuttle bus from all over the airport. It's convenient and well equipped for business travelers, and an excellent fall-back for vacationers in search of a deal. Guest rooms are large and tastefully furnished; they have two two-line speakerphones, wireless Internet access through the TV, coffeemakers, hair dryers, irons, and ironing boards. There's high-speed Internet access throughout the 10-story building and great views from the higher floors. Guests on the concierge level (10th floor) have access to a staffed private lounge that serves continental breakfast, snacks, and hors d'oeuvres.

The big concern with a hotel this close to the runways is noise, but the picture-window views of approaching aircraft—and some lingering construction—look like TV with the sound off. The Hyatt Harborside is the closest competition (see below); it's at the edge of the airport, on the water, which means less commotion outside but less convenient access to the T.

Dining/Diversions: Off the lobby, **Berkshire's** serves breakfast (continental, buffet, and à la carte), lunch, and dinner; **Kitty O'Shea's Irish Pub** (lunch and dinner) is open until 1:30am. There's a gourmet coffee counter in the lobby.

Amenities: Health club with large exercise room, indoor lap pool, whirlpool, saunas, massage, and tanning bed; well-equipped business center; conference rooms with Internet access; 24-hour room service; dry-cleaning and laundry service; weekday newspaper delivery; gift shop; 24-hour shuttle bus service to airport destinations, including car-rental offices and ferry dock; on-bus electronic check-in.

Hyatt Harborside. 101 Harborside Dr., Boston, MA 02128. ☎ **800/233-1234** or 617/568-1234. Fax 617/567-8856. www.boston.hyatt.com. 270 units. A/C TV TEL. From $169 double. Children under 12 free in parents' room. AE, CB, DC, DISC, JCB, MC, V. Parking $15. T: Blue Line to Airport, then take shuttle bus. By car, follow signs to Logan Airport and take Harborside Dr. past car-rental area and tunnel entrance.

This striking 14-story waterfront hotel offers unobstructed views of the harbor and city skyline. It caters to the convention and business trade; sightseers whose budget for transportation doesn't include a fair amount of time (on the shuttle bus and subway) or money (on ferries, parking, or cabs) will be better off closer to downtown. Water shuttles to the waterfront leave from the hotel's rear entrance.

The good-sized guest rooms have all the features you'd expect at a deluxe hotel, plus such extras as hair dryers, coffeemakers, irons and ironing boards, luxury bathrooms, and fine wood furnishings. Particularly from the higher floors, the views are dramatic. And there's an interesting architectural quirk: The building's tower is a lighthouse (the airport control tower manages the beacon so that it doesn't interfere with runway lights).

Dining/Diversions: The restaurant serves three meals daily and has floor-to-ceiling windows that offer spectacular views. The lounge offers live music on Friday and Saturday nights.

Amenities: Indoor heated pool; health club with sauna and whirlpool; business center; room service until midnight; conference rooms; concierge; dry cleaning and laundry; express checkout; valet parking; 24-hour airport shuttle service. Ferries to Rowes Wharf and Long Wharf dock outside. Rooms for people with disabilities are available.

6 Dining

A friend once laughed and said, "From 1940 to 1970, you could have used the same dining guide every year—now you could probably do a new one every 6 months or so." That was 5 years ago, and it's even truer today. Boston's restaurant scene is one of the most dynamic in the country, and likely to remain that way for as long as the economy can support it. Hot spots open and former hot spots close almost as often as blockbuster movies, and top chefs and their protégés turn up everywhere.

At press time, two big names were on the move: Stan Frankenthaler of Salamander was relocating his restaurant from Cambridge's Kendall Square to Boston's Back Bay, and legendary seafood chef Jasper White reportedly had plans to return to the stove, possibly in Cambridge. Ask at your hotel if you're a chef groupie (or would like to be one).

Seafood is a good specialty in Boston, where you'll find it on the menu at almost every restaurant—trendy or classic, expensive or cheap, typical American (whatever that is) or ethnic. Ipswich and Essex clams, Atlantic lobsters, Wellfleet oysters, mussels, and all kinds of fish are available in every imaginable form. Chowder fans who have never had fresh clams are in for a treat.

Almost every menu in every price range includes vegetarian offerings. Like the rest of the country, Boston has embraced the return of meat (not that it ever really went away). Another trend is the rise of hotel restaurants, which have shed their colorless reputation; some of the most imaginative dining rooms in the area are in hotels. Female chefs and co-owners are now so common as to be almost unremarkable. And as in any college community, there are many little restaurants that serve ethnic cuisine from around the world.

The guiding thought for this chapter, without regard to price, was, "If this were your only meal in Boston, would you be delighted with it?" At the restaurants in this chapter, the answer, for one reason or another, is yes.

1 Restaurants by Cuisine

AFGHAN
The Helmand, Cambridge (*M*)

AMERICAN
Anago, Back Bay (*VE*)
Aujourd'hui, Back Bay (*VE*)
Bartley's Burger Cottage,
   Cambridge (*I*)
The Bay Tower, Faneuil Hall (*VE*)
Grill 23 & Bar, Back Bay (*VE*)
Jacob Wirth Company, Theater
   District (*M*)
Locke-Ober, Downtown
   Crossing (*VE*)
Milk Street Café kiosk, Financial
   District (*I*)
Tea-Tray in the Sky, Cambridge (*I*)
Top of the Hub, Back Bay (*VE*)
Zaftigs Delicatessen, Brookline (*M*)

ASIAN
Billy Tse Restaurant, Waterfront (*M*)
Jae's, Theater District (*E*)

BARBECUE
East Coast Grill, Cambridge (*E*)
Redbones, Cambridge (*M*)

BRAZILIAN
Midwest Grill, Cambridge (*M*)

CAJUN
Bob the Chef's Jazz Cafe,
   South End (*M*)
Border Café, Cambridge (*M*)

CAMBODIAN
The Elephant Walk, Kenmore Square
   to Brookline (*M*)

CANTONESE
Chau Chow, Chinatown (*I*)
East Ocean City, Chinatown (*M*)
Grand Chau Chow, Chinatown (*M*)

CARIBBEAN
Green Street Grill, Cambridge (*M*)

CHINESE
Billy Tse Restaurant, Waterfront (*M*)
Chau Chow, Chinatown (*M*)
East Ocean City, Chinatown (*M*)
Grand Chau Chow, Chinatown (*M*)

CONTINENTAL
Locke-Ober, Downtown
   Crossing (*VE*)
Upstairs at the Pudding,
   Cambridge (*VE*)

CUBAN
Chez Henri, Cambridge (*E*)

DELI
S&S Restaurant, Cambridge (*I*)
Zaftigs Delicatessen, Brookline (*M*)

ECLECTIC
The Blue Room, Cambridge (*E*)
Cosí Sandwich Bar, Financial
   District (*I*)
Hamersley's Bistro, South End (*VE*)
Icarus, South End (*VE*)
Les Zygomates, Financial District (*E*)
Olives, Charlestown (*VE*)

ETHIOPIAN
Addis Red Sea, South End (*M*)

FRENCH
Chez Henri, Cambridge (*E*)
The Elephant Walk, Kenmore Square
   to Brookline (*M*)
Julien, Financial District (*VE*)
Le Gamin Café, South End (*I*)
L'Espalier, Back Bay (*VE*)
Les Zygomates, Financial District (*E*)
Maison Robert, Faneuil Hall/
   Financial District (*VE*)

GERMAN
Jacob Wirth Company, Theater
   District (*M*)

INDIAN
Bombay Club, Cambridge (*M*)

Key to Abbreviations: *VE* = Very Expensive   *E* = Expensive   *M* = Moderate   *I* = Inexpensive

ITALIAN

Artú, North End (*M*)
Cosí Sandwich Bar, Financial
District (*I*)
Daily Catch, South Boston
Waterfront (*M*)
Davio's, Back Bay (*E*)
Galleria Umberto, North End (*I*)
Giacomo's, North End (*E*)
La Groceria Ristorante Italiano,
Cambridge (*M*)
La Summa, North End (*M*)
Mamma Maria, North End (*VE*)
Piccola Venezia, North End (*M*)
Pizzeria Regina, North End (*I*)
Upstairs at the Pudding,
Cambridge (*VE*)

JAPANESE

Ginza Japanese Restaurant,
Chinatown (*E*)
Tatsukichi-Boston, Faneuil Hall (*M*)

KOREAN

Jae's, Theater District (*E*)

MEDITERRANEAN

Casablanca, Cambridge (*E*)
Julien, Financial District (*VE*)
Rialto, Cambridge (*VE*)

MEXICAN

Casa Romero, Back Bay (*E*)

MIDDLE EASTERN

Café Jaffa, Back Bay (*I*)

NEW ENGLAND

Durgin-Park, Faneuil Hall (*M*)
L'Espalier, Back Bay (*VE*)
No. 9 Park, Beacon Hill (*VE*)
Rowes Wharf Restaurant,
Waterfront (*VE*)
Ye Olde Union Oyster House,
Faneuil Hall (*E*)

SEAFOOD

Daily Catch, South Boston
Waterfront (*M*)
East Coast Grill, Cambridge (*E*)
East Ocean City, Chinatown (*M*)
Giacomo's, North End (*E*)
Green Street Grill, Cambridge (*M*)
Grillfish, South End (*M*)
Jimbo's Fish Shanty, South Boston
Waterfront (*I*)
Jimmy's Harborside Restaurant,
South Boston Waterfront (*E*)
Legal Sea Foods, Back Bay (*E*)
Turner Fisheries of Boston,
Back Bay (*E*)
Ye Olde Union Oyster House,
Faneuil Hall (*E*)

SOUTHERN

Bob the Chef's Jazz Cafe,
South End (*M*)

SPANISH

Dalí, Cambridge (*E*)
Tapéo, Back Bay (*E*)

SUSHI

Billy Tse Restaurant, Waterfront (*M*)
Ginza Japanese Restaurant,
Chinatown (*E*)
Jae's, Theater District (*E*)
Tatsukichi-Boston, Faneuil Hall (*M*)

TEX-MEX

Border Café, Cambridge (*M*)
Fajitas & 'Ritas, Downtown
Crossing (*I*)

THAI

Bangkok Cuisine, Back Bay (*M*)

TURKISH

Istanbul Café, Beacon Hill (*M*)

VIETNAMESE/VEGETARIAN

Buddha's Delight, Chinatown (*I*)

2 The Waterfront

VERY EXPENSIVE

Rowes Wharf Restaurant. In the Boston Harbor Hotel, 70 Rowes Wharf (entrance on Atlantic Ave.). ☎ **617/439-3995.** www.bhh.com. Reservations recommended. Main courses

Time Is Money

Lunch is an excellent, economical way to check out a fancy restaurant without breaking the bank. At restaurants that take reservations, it's always a good idea to make them, particularly for dinner. Boston restaurants are far less busy early in the week than they are from Thursday through Sunday. If you're flexible about when you indulge in fine cuisine and when you go for pizza and a movie, choose the low-budget option on the weekend and pamper yourself on a weeknight.

$11.25–$18.50 at lunch; $28–$38 at dinner. Wine pairing menu varies. Breakfast $9–$14.50. Sun buffet brunch $47. AE, CB, DC, DISC, MC, V. Mon–Fri 6:30–11am and 11:30am–2:30pm; Sun brunch 10:30am–2pm; daily 5:30–10pm. Valet parking available. T: Blue Line to Aquarium or Red Line to South Station. NEW ENGLAND.

Tucked away on the second floor of the Boston Harbor Hotel, the wood-paneled Rowes Wharf Restaurant feels almost like a private club—one with breathtaking picture-window views of the water. It's not a trendy destination, but regularly appears on lists of the city's best restaurants because the food and wine are consistently excellent. Chef Daniel Bruce uses local ingredients prepared in deceptively simple ways that accent natural flavors without overwhelming them.

The signature appetizer is luscious Maine lobster meat seasoned and formed into a sausage, grilled, sliced, and served in a light cream sauce with lobster claw meat and lemon pasta. Or try polenta topped with flavorful wild mushrooms. Entrees might include herb- and mustard-rubbed grilled filet mignon, lobster with chorizo and sweet corn pudding, and pan-seared turbot over couscous with carrot-lime sauce. Desserts vary with the inspiration of the chef—there's usually an excellent sorbet sampler. Symbols on the menu indicate items low in fat, sodium, and calories.

EXPENSIVE
Legal Sea Foods (see "Back Bay," below) has a branch at 255 State St. (☎ 617/227-3115) opposite the Aquarium.

MODERATE
Billy Tse Restaurant. 240 Commercial St. ☎ **617/227-9990.** Reservations recommended at dinner on weekends. Main courses $5–$20; lunch specials $5.50–$7.50. AE, DC, DISC, MC, V. Mon–Thurs 11:30am–11:30pm; Fri–Sat 11:30am–midnight; Sun 11:30am–11pm. T: Blue Line to Aquarium or Green or Orange Line to Haymarket. CHINESE/PAN-ASIAN/SUSHI.

A pan-Asian restaurant on the edge of the Italian North End might seem incongruous, but this casual, economical spot is no ordinary Chinese restaurant. It serves excellent renditions of the usual dishes, and the kitchen also has a flair for fresh seafood. The pan-Asian selections and sushi are just as enjoyable. Start with wonderful soup, sinfully good crab rangoon, or fried calamari with garlic and pepper. Main dishes range from seven kinds of fried rice to scallops with garlic sauce to the house special fried noodles, topped with shrimp, calamari, and scallops in a scrumptious sauce.

Be sure to ask about the daily specials—bitter Chinese broccoli, when it's available, is deftly prepared. Lunch specials, served until 4pm, include vegetable fried rice or vegetable lo mein. You can eat in the comfortable main dining room or near the bar, which has French doors that open to the street. Although it's opposite a trolley stop, Billy Tse doesn't have an especially touristy clientele—the neighborhood patrons obviously welcome a break from pizza and pasta.

Boston Dining

Addis Red Sea **24**
Anago **9**
Artu (Beacon Hill) **58**
Artú (North End) **77**
Aujourd'hui **32**
Bangkok Cuisine **5**
The Bay Tower **65**
Bertucci's (Back Bay) **26**
Bertucci's (Faneuil Hall) **62**
Billy Tse Restaurant **71**
Bob the Chef's Jazz Café **19**
Bristol Lounge **32**
Buddha's Delight **38**
Café Jaffa **11**
Café Fleuri **51**
Caffe dello Sport **81**
Caffè Graffiti **75**
Caffè Vittoria **82**
California Pizza Kitchen
   (Prudential) **8**
California Pizza Kitchen
   (Theater District) **35**
Casa Romero **12**
Chau Chow **41**
Chau Chow City **46**
China Pearl **42**
Cosí Sandwich Bar (Federal St.) **51**
Cosí Sandwich Bar (Milk St.) **50**
Cosí Sandwich Bar (State St.) **60**
Daily Catch (Brookline) **2**
Daily Catch (North End) **74**

Daily Catch (Waterfront) **68**
Davio's **15**
Durgin-Park **63**
Dynasty Restaurant **45**
East Ocean City **40**
The Elephant Walk **1**
Empire Garden Restaurant **37**
Fajitas & 'Ritas **48**
Figs **56**
Galleria Umberto **80**
Giacomo's **78**
Ginza Japanese Restaurant **44**
Ginza Japanese Restaurant
   (Brookline) **3**
Golden Palace Restaurant **43**
Grand Chau Chow **39**
Grill 23 & Bar **27**
Grillfish **28**
Ground Round **6**
Hamersley's Bistro **22**
Hard Rock Cafe **18**
Icarus **25**
Intrigue **67**
Istanbul Café **59**
Jacob Wirth Company **36**
Jae's (South End) **20**
Jae's (Theater District) **34**
Jimbo's Fish Shanty **69**
Jimmy's Harborside Restaurant **70**
Julien **52**
La Summa **72**

Le Gamin Cafe **23**
Legal Sea Foods (Copley) **7**
Legal Sea Foods (Park Square) **33**
Legal Sea Foods (Prudential) **10**
Legal Sea Foods (Waterfront) **66**
Les Zygomates **47**
L'Espalier **13**
Locke-Ober **49**
Maison Robert **54**
Mamma Maria **76**
Mike's Pastry **79**
Milk Street Café **53**
Modern Pastry **73**
No. 9 Park **55**
Olives **85**
Parish Cafe and Bar **29**
Piccola Venezia **83**
Pizzeria Regina **84**
The Ritz-Carlton Dining Room **30**
Rowes Wharf Restaurant **67**
Savenor's Supermarket **57**
Swans Court **31**
Tapéo **14**
Tatsukichi-Boston **61**
TGI Friday's **16**
Top of the Hub **6**
Tremont 647 **21**
Turner Fisheries **17**
Ye Olde Union Oyster House **64**
Zaftig's Delicatessen **4**

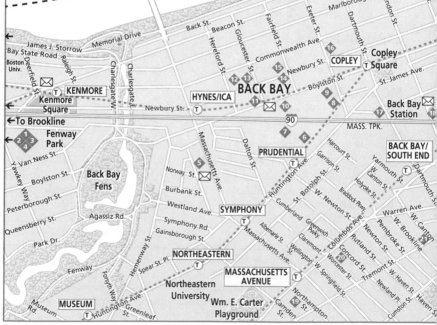

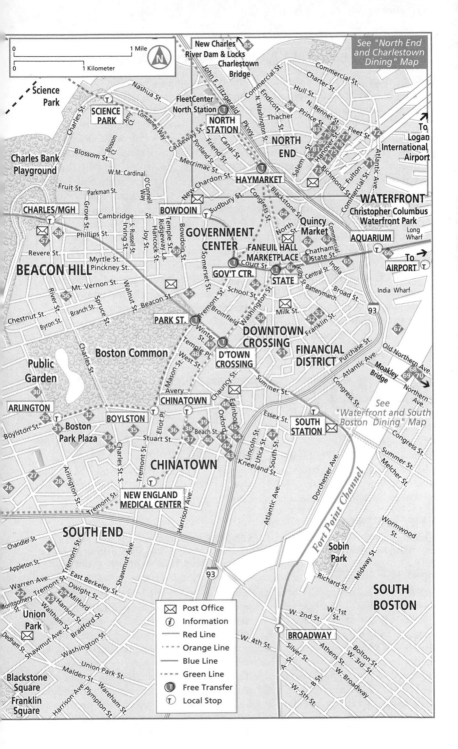

The Great Outdoors: Alfresco Dining

Cambridge is a better destination for outdoor dining than Boston, which only recently made it legal to place tables on public property—namely, sidewalks—but both cities offer agreeable destinations for lounging under the sun or stars.

You'll feel suspended in midair on the idyllic patio outside **Upstairs at the Pudding** (see p. 128), in Harvard Square. Nearby, **Shay's Pub & Wine Bar,** 58 John F. Kennedy St. (☎ 617/864-9161), has a small brick seating area and such a casual atmosphere that you can even bring your dog (or pet someone else's). Across the street from the Charles River near Kendall Square, the **Sail Loft,** 1 Memorial Dr. (☎ 617/225-2222), opens onto a leafy plaza that usually picks up a breeze from the water. Both restaurant patios at the **Royal Sonesta Hotel,** 5 Cambridge Pkwy. (☎ 617/491-3600), have great views. The Gallery Café is casual, Davio's (see p. 121) a bit fancier.

On the other side of the river, try the hideaway garden at **Casa Romero** (see p. 121). The airy terrace at **Intrigue,** in the Boston Harbor Hotel, 70 Rowes Wharf (☎ 617/439-7000), overlooks the harbor and the airport. Most bars and restaurants in Faneuil Hall Marketplace offer outdoor seating and great people watching. A popular shopping stop and after-work hangout in the Back Bay is the **Parish Café and Bar,** 361 Boylston St. (☎ 617/247-4777), where the sandwich menu is a "greatest hits" roster of top local chefs' creations.

3 The North End

Boston's Italian-American enclave has dozens of restaurants; many are tiny and don't serve dessert and coffee. Hit the *caffès* for coffee and fresh pastry in an atmosphere where lingering is welcome—as is smoking. Favorites include **Caffè dello Sport,** 308 Hanover St. (☎ 617/523-5063), **Caffè Graffiti,** 307 Hanover St. (☎ 617/367-3016), and **Caffè Vittoria,** 296 Hanover St. (☎ 617/227-7606). There's also table service at **Mike's Pastry,** 300 Hanover St. (☎ 617/742-3050), a bakery that's famous for its bustling take-out business and its cannoli.

VERY EXPENSIVE

✪ **Mamma Maria.** 3 North Sq. ☎ **617/523-0077.** www.mammamaria.com. Reservations recommended. Main courses $19–$35. AE, DC, DISC, MC, V. Sun–Thurs 5–9:30pm; Fri–Sat 5–10:30pm. Closed 1 week in Jan. Valet parking available. T: Green or Orange Line to Haymarket. REGIONAL ITALIAN.

In a townhouse overlooking North Square and the Paul Revere House, this traditional-looking restaurant offers innovative cuisine and a level of sophistication far removed from the North End's familiar "Hey, whaddaya want?" service. The menu changes seasonally; you can usually start with excellent *pasta e fagioli* (bean-and-pasta soup) or risotto, and the daily pasta special is always a great choice. The excellent entrees are unlike anything else in this neighborhood, except in size—portions are more than generous. The fork-tender osso buco is almost enough for two, but you'll want it all for yourself. You can't go wrong with any of the pastas on the menu either, and the fresh seafood specials are uniformly marvelous. The pasta, bread, and desserts are homemade, and the shadowy, whitewashed rooms make this a popular spot for getting engaged—we have to assume the kitchen staff regularly fields offers.

North End & Charlestown Dining

Artú ⟨10⟩
Billy Tse Restaurant ⟨8⟩
Caffè dello Sport ⟨5⟩
Caffè Graffiti ⟨12⟩
Caffè Vittoria ⟨3⟩
Daily Catch ⟨11⟩
Galleria Umberto ⟨13⟩
Giacomo's ⟨6⟩
Lo Summa ⟨7⟩
Mamma Maria ⟨9⟩
Mike's Pastry ⟨4⟩
Modern Pastry ⟨15⟩
Olives ⟨1⟩
Piccola Venezia ⟨14⟩
Pizzeria Regina ⟨2⟩

EXPENSIVE

Giacomo's. 355 Hanover St. ☎ **617/523-9026.** Reservations not accepted. Main courses $15–$25. No credit cards. Mon–Thurs 5–10pm; Fri–Sat 5–10:30pm; Sun 4–10pm. T: Green or Orange Line to Haymarket. ITALIAN/SEAFOOD.

Fans of Giacomo's seem to have adopted the Postal Service's motto: They brave snow, sleet, rain, and gloom of night. The line forms early, especially on weekends. No reservations, cash only, a tiny dining room with an open kitchen—what's the secret? Well, the food is terrific, there's plenty of it, and the we're-all-in-this-together atmosphere certainly helps.

The fried calamari appetizer, served with marinara sauce, is light and crisp. You can take the chef's advice or put together your own main dish from the list of daily ingredients on a board on the wall. Salmon in pesto cream sauce with fettuccine is a keeper, as is any dish with shrimp. Nonseafood offerings such as butternut squash ravioli in mascarpone cheese sauce are equally memorable. Service is friendly but incredibly swift, and lingering is not encouraged—but unless you have a heart of stone, you won't want to take up a table when people are standing outside in 90° heat or an ice storm waiting for your seat.

MODERATE

The **Daily Catch**—see "South Boston Waterfront (Seaport District)," below—has a branch at 323 Hanover St. (☎ **617/523-8567**).

Artú. 6 Prince St. ☎ **617/742-4336.** Reservations not accepted. Main courses $9–$18; sandwiches $5.50–$9. MC, V. Daily 11am–10pm. T: Green or Orange Line to Haymarket. ITALIAN.

Plates of roasted vegetables draw your eye to the front window at Artú, and the accompanying aromas will draw the rest of you. Don't resist—this is a neighborhood favorite for a reason. The best appetizer consists of those gorgeous veggies. Trust the chef to choose for you, or ask to have something included (excellent carrots) or left out (licorice-tasting fennel isn't for everyone). The helpful waitstaff can offer advice. Move on to superb roasted meats or bounteous home-style pasta dishes. Roast lamb, ziti with sausage and broccoli rabe, and chicken stuffed with ham and cheese are all terrific. The *panini* (sandwiches) are big in size and flavor—prosciutto, mozzarella, and tomato is sublime, and chicken parmigiana is tender and filling. This isn't a great place for quiet conversation, especially during dinner in the noisy main room, but do you really want to talk with your mouth full?

There's another Artú on **Beacon Hill** at 89 Charles St. (☎ **617/227-9023**). It opens at 4pm on Sunday and Monday and stays open nightly until 11.

La Summa. 30 Fleet St. ☎ **617/523-9503.** Reservations recommended. Main courses $11–$17. AE, CB, DC, DISC, MC, V. Daily 4:30–10:30pm. T: Green or Orange Line to Haymarket. ITALIAN.

Because La Summa isn't on the restaurant rows of Hanover and Salem streets, it maintains a cozy neighborhood atmosphere. Unlike some neighborhood places, it's friendly to outsiders—you'll feel welcome even if you're not greeted by name. La Summa is worth seeking out just for the wonderful homemade pasta and desserts, and most of the more elaborate entrees are scrumptious, too. You might start with ravioli or superb soup (our waitress one night didn't know exactly what was in the butternut-squash soup because, and I quote, "My mother made it"). Or stick to the salad that's included with each meal, and save room for sweets.

Try any seafood special, lobster ravioli, *pappardelle e melanzane* (strips of eggplant tossed with ethereal fresh pasta in light marinara sauce), or the aptly named "house special"—veal, chicken, sausage, shrimp, artichokes, pepperoncini, olives, and mushrooms in white-wine sauce. Desserts, especially tiramisú, are terrific.

Piccola Venezia. 263 Hanover St. ☎ **617/523-3888.** Reservations recommended at dinner. Main courses $10–$20; lunch specialties $5–$8. AE, DISC, MC, V. Daily 11am–10pm; lunch menu Mon–Fri 11am–4pm. T: Green or Orange Line to Haymarket. ITALIAN.

The glass front wall of Piccola Venezia ("little Venice") shows off the exposed-brick dining room, decorated with prints and photos and filled with happy patrons. Portions are large, and the homey food tends to be heavy on red sauce, although more sophisticated dishes are available. The delicious sautéed mushroom appetizer is solidly in the latter category; a more traditional starter is the tasty *pasta e fagioli* (bean-and-pasta soup). Then dig into spaghetti and meatballs, chicken parmigiana, eggplant rolatini, or pasta puttanesca. This is a good place to try traditional Italian-American favorites such as polenta (home-style, not the yuppie croutons available at so many other places), *baccala* (reconstituted salt cod), or the house specialty, tripe.

Go to the Source

The tiramisú on the menu at many North End restaurants comes from **Modern Pastry,** 257 Hanover St. (☎ **617/523-3783**). The surreally good concoction ($3.50 a slice at the shop) makes an excellent picnic dessert on a summer night—the waterfront is 4 blocks away, at the foot of Richmond Street.

INEXPENSIVE

Galleria Umberto. 289 Hanover St. ☎ **617/227-5709.** All items less than $3. No credit cards. Mon–Sat 11am–2pm. Closed 3 weeks in July. T: Green or Orange Line to Haymarket. ITALIAN.

The long, fast-moving line of businesspeople and tourists tips you off to the fact that this cafeteria-style spot is a real bargain. The food is good, too. You can fill up on a couple of slices of pizza, but if you're feeling adventurous, try *arancini* (a rice ball filled with ground beef, peas, and cheese). The calzones—ham and cheese, spinach, spinach and cheese, or spinach and sausage—and potato croquettes are tasty, too. Study the cases while you wait and be ready to order at once when you reach the head of the line. Have a quick lunch and get on with your sightseeing.

✪ **Pizzeria Regina.** 10½ Thacher St. ☎ **617/227-0765.** www.pizzeriaregina.com. Reservations not accepted. Pizza $9–$16. No credit cards. Mon–Thurs 11am–11:30pm; Fri–Sat 11am–midnight; Sun noon–11pm. T: Green or Orange Line to Haymarket. PIZZA.

Regina's looks almost like a movie set, but look a little closer—this is the place the movie sets are trying to re-create. Busy waitresses who call everyone "dear" weave through the boisterous dining room—sorry, no slices here—delivering peerless pizza steaming hot out of the brick oven. Let it cool a little before you dig in. Nouveau ingredients like sun-dried tomatoes appear on the list of toppings, but that's not authentic. House-made sausage, maybe some pepperoni, and a couple of beers—now, *that's* authentic.

4 Faneuil Hall Marketplace & Financial District

This is expense-account country, where standards, service, and prices are sky-high (as is one of the restaurants). You'll also find excellent places that cater to office workers on a budget.

VERY EXPENSIVE

✪ **The Bay Tower.** 60 State St. ☎ **617/723-1666.** www.baytower.com. Reservations recommended. Jacket requested for men in dining room. Main courses $22–$36. AE, CB, DC, JCB, MC, V. Mon–Thurs 5:30–10pm; Fri 5:30–11pm; Sat 5–11pm. Validated parking available. T: Blue or Orange Line to State or Green Line to Government Center. CREATIVE AMERICAN.

Let's cut to the chase: Would you pay this much at a restaurant with a view of a brick wall or a street corner? Of course not. Is it worth it? Absolutely. One of the most beautiful dining rooms in Boston, the 33rd-floor Bay Tower has enormous glass walls facing a glorious panorama of Faneuil Hall Marketplace, the harbor, and the airport. The terraced table area is arranged so that every seat has a view, and the shiny (polished, not mirrored) surfaces lend a casinolike air to the romantic, candlelit room.

The menu, an intriguing variety of traditional and contemporary dishes, changes seasonally. You might start with lobster bisque, shrimp cocktail, or beef carpaccio. Entrees include the usual meat, chicken, and seafood, often with a twist. Roast chicken is served with herb risotto, smoked-shrimp mousse, and red-pepper cream; for more traditional palates, Dover sole is filleted at the table. There's always at least one vegetarian entree. Many people come just for sweets, drinks, and dancing in the lounge, so desserts are wonderful, with an emphasis on chocolate.

Julien. In Le Meridien Boston, 250 Franklin St. ☎ **617/451-1900.** Reservations recommended. Main courses $14.50–$18.75 at lunch; $29–$34 at dinner. Business lunch $28. AE, CB, DC, MC, V. Tues–Fri noon–2pm; Mon–Thurs 6–10pm; Fri–Sat 6–10:30pm. T: Blue or Orange Line to State or Red Line to Downtown Crossing. FRENCH/MEDITERRANEAN.

Sunday Brunch

Several top hotels (see below) serve Sunday brunch buffets of monstrous propor-
tions. In the past few years, these outrageous spreads have become outrageously
expensive. They're worth the investment for a special occasion, but you can have
a less incapacitating experience for considerably less money.

The best à la carte brunch in town is at Cambridge's **S&S Restaurant**
(☎ 617/354-0777; see p. 134). It doesn't take reservations, but the wait for a table
is part of the experience. You'll need a reservation for brunch at the **House of Blues**
(☎ 617/491-2583; see p. 229), which serves a buffet of Southern specialties to the
strains of a gospel choir. It's $26 for adults, $13 for children. (Walk-ins pay just
$13.95 but have to watch the show on TV monitors.) In Boston's South End,
Tremont 647, 647 Tremont St. (☎ 617/266-4600), serves New American cuisine
in a fantastically casual atmosphere—the staff wears pajamas, and you can, too.

If you have your heart set on a fancy brunch at a hotel, make reservations (especially on holidays) but do *not* make elaborate dinner plans. The top choices are
Aujourd'hui, in the Four Seasons Hotel, 200 Boylston St. (☎ 617/451-2071;
$55 adult, $26 child); **Café Fleuri,** in Le Meridien Boston, 250 Franklin St.
(☎ 617/451-1900; $39 to $49 adult, $16.50 child); the **Ritz-Carlton, Boston,**
15 Arlington St. (☎ 617/536-5700; $47 adult, $26 child); and the **Rowes
Wharf Restaurant,** in the Boston Harbor Hotel, 70 Rowes Wharf (☎ 617/
439-3995; $47 adult, $21 child).

Julien is in one of the most beautiful rooms in the city, under a vaulted, gilt-edged ceiling and five crystal chandeliers. Listen closely and you can almost hear the business
deals going down, especially at lunch. The seasonal menus emphasize fresh regional
products. Specialty starters include terrine of fresh homemade foie gras with truffles,
and Maine lobster salad on a bed of diced vegetables. Sautéed tuna steak with bro-
chette of asparagus and wild mushrooms is an excellent choice, as is rack of lamb with
artichoke ragout and fresh asparagus. The desserts are among the best in town. The
wine list offers selections from top French, American, German, and Italian wineries.
The business lunch includes a soup or salad, a choice of entrees, and coffee or tea.

Café Fleuri, Le Meridien's atrium-style informal dining room, serves lunch on
weekdays and Sunday brunch ($39 to $49 adult, $16.50 child) at 11 and 11:30am
and 1 and 1:30pm. On Saturday afternoons from September through May, the
"Chocolate Bar Buffet" takes over.

✪ Maison Robert. 45 School St. ☎ **617/227-3370.** www.maisonrobert.com. Reservations recommended. Main courses $12–$24 at lunch; $19–$32 at dinner. Le Café fixed-price
menu $18 or $25; à la carte main courses $13–$28. AE, CB, DC, MC, V. Mon–Fri
11:30am–2:30pm; Mon–Sat 5:30–10pm. Valet parking available at dinner. T: Red Line to Park
Street or Green Line to Government Center. CLASSIC AND INNOVATIVE FRENCH.

This world-class French restaurant has been a legend in Boston since it opened in
Old City Hall in 1971. Like many excellent restaurants, it's family-owned and
-operated—proprietors Lucien and Ann Robert are executive chef Andrée Robert's
parents, and nephew Jacky Robert took over in the kitchen in 1996 after many years
as a top chef in San Francisco (including 10 years at Ernie's).

The formal dining room is spectacular, with majestic crystal chandeliers and tall
windows. The food equals the setting, classic but dramatic, with unexpected but

welcome twists. You might start with a tender, airy cheese soufflé or smoked lobster cream soup. Entrees include options you would expect and pleasant surprises—filet mignon is a meat-lover's delight, Dover sole is served *à la meunière,* and ostrich fillet is marinated in pomegranate juice. The impressive desserts range from excellent soufflés to heart-stopping chocolate concoctions to upside-down apple tart, served warm with cinnamon sabayon.

The ground-floor **Café** is more casual and less expensive than the upstairs room, but also thoroughly French. In the summer, cafe seating spills onto the lovely terrace next to the landmark statue of Benjamin Franklin.

EXPENSIVE

✪ **Les Zygomates.** 129 South St. ☎ **617/542-5108.** www.winebar.com. Reservations recommended. Main courses $15–$25; prix-fixe $11 at lunch, $19 at dinner (Mon–Thurs). AE, CB, DC, DISC, MC, V. Mon–Fri 11:30am–1am (lunch until 2pm, dinner until 10:30pm); Sat 6pm–1am (dinner until 11:30pm). Valet parking available at dinner. T: Red Line to South Station. FRENCH/ECLECTIC.

You have to negotiate the construction wasteland near South Station to reach this delightful bistro and wine bar, but it's worth the trouble. The bar in the high-ceilinged, brick-walled space serves a great selection of wine, available by the bottle, the glass, and the 2-ounce "taste."

The efficient staff will guide you to a good accompaniment for chef and co-owner Ian Just's delicious food. Salads are excellent, lightly dressed and garden-fresh, and main courses are hearty and filling but not heavy. Roasted salmon fillet with French lentils and celery-root purée is toothsome, and meat-lovers will find flank steak with garlic mashed potatoes and sautéed vegetables succulent. For dessert, try not to fight over the lemon mousse, a cloud of citrus and air. Tuesday through Saturday night, you can linger over a glass of wine and listen to live jazz.

✪ **Ye Olde Union Oyster House.** 41 Union St. (between North and Hanover sts.). ☎ **617/227-2750.** www.unionoysterhouse.com. Reservations recommended. Main courses $9.50–$20 at lunch; $15–$31 at dinner. Children's menu $5–$10. AE, CB, DC, DISC, MC, V. Sun–Thurs 11am–9:30pm (lunch menu until 5pm); Fri–Sat 11am–10pm (lunch until 6pm). Union Bar daily 11am–midnight (lunch until 3pm, late-supper fare until 11pm). Closed Thanksgiving, Dec 25. Valet and validated parking available. T: Green or Orange Line to Haymarket. NEW ENGLAND/SEAFOOD.

America's oldest restaurant in continuous service, the Union Oyster House opened in 1826, and the booths and oyster bar haven't moved since. The food is tasty, traditional New England fare, popular with tourists on the adjacent Freedom Trail (the subject of a new mural by folk artist Thomas Lynch) and savvy locals. At the crescent-shaped bar on the lower level of the cramped, low-ceilinged building, "where Daniel Webster drank many a toddy in his day," try the cold seafood sampler of oysters, clams, and shrimp to start. Follow with a broiled or grilled dish such as scrod or salmon, or perhaps shrimp scampi, fried seafood, or grilled pork loin. A "shore dinner" of chowder, steamers or mussels, lobster, corn, potatoes, and dessert is an excellent introduction to local favorites. For dessert, try gingerbread with whipped cream. Ask to be seated at John F. Kennedy's favorite booth (no. 18), which is marked with a plaque.

MODERATE

✪ **Durgin-Park.** 340 Faneuil Hall Marketplace. ☎ **617/227-2038.** Reservations not accepted. Main courses $5–$18; specials $16–$25. AE, DC, DISC, MC, V. Daily 11:30am–2:30pm; Mon–Thurs 2:30–10pm; Fri–Sat 2:30–10:30pm; Sun 2:30–9pm. T: Green or Blue Line to Government Center or Orange Line to Haymarket. NEW ENGLAND.

For huge portions of delicious food, a rowdy atmosphere where CEOs share tables with students, and famously cranky waitresses who can't seem to bear the sight of any of it, people have poured into Durgin-Park since 1827. It's everything it's cracked up to be—a tourist magnet that attracts hordes of locals, where everyone's disappointed when the waitresses are nice (they often are). Approximately 2,000 people a day find their way to the line that stretches down a flight of stairs to the first floor of Faneuil Hall Marketplace's North Market building. The queue moves quickly, and you'll probably wind up seated at a long table with other people (smaller tables are available).

The food is wonderful, and there's plenty of it—prime rib the size of a hubcap, giant lamb chops, piles of fried seafood, roast turkey that might fill you up till Thanksgiving. Steaks and chops are broiled on an open fire over wood charcoal. Fresh seafood arrives twice daily, and fish dinners are broiled to order. Vegetables come à la carte; if you want to try Boston baked beans, now's the time. For dessert, the strawberry shortcake is justly celebrated, and molasses lovers (this is not a dish for dabblers) will want to try Indian pudding: molasses and cornmeal baked for hours and served with ice cream.

If you're having "dinner" (otherwise known as lunch; the evening meal is "supper"), beat the crowd by arriving when the restaurant opens. Or start out at the ground-floor Gaslight Pub, which has a private staircase that leads upstairs.

Tatsukichi-Boston. 189 State St. ☎ **617/720-2468.** Reservations recommended at dinner. Main courses $11–$22; sushi $2.50–$7.50 per order; lunch specials from $6.75. AE, DC, DISC, JCB, MC, V. Mon–Fri 11:30am–2:30pm; Sun–Thurs 5–10pm; Fri–Sat 5–11pm. Validated parking available. T: Blue Line to Aquarium. JAPANESE/SUSHI.

A block from Faneuil Hall Marketplace, this award-winning restaurant with an excellent sushi bar is a favorite with the Japanese community and other fans of the cuisine. At half of the tables, patrons sit on chairs; at the rest, they kneel on an elevated platform. Non-sushi offerings include an extensive array of authentic Japanese dishes, such as *shabu shabu* (beef and vegetables cooked in seasoned boiling water) and *kushiage* (meat, seafood, and vegetables on skewers, lightly battered and fried, served with dipping sauces). At lunch, the *unagi-don* (grilled eel) is as tasty as it is scary-sounding.

Downstairs is the more casual, less expensive **Goemon** (☎ **617/367-8670**). It serves all kinds of noodles—excellent for a quick lunch—and Japanese tapas (how's that for multicultural?). The little plates ($3.50 to $7.25), available at dinner only, are great for a group that wants some culinary adventure, They range from endive salad with Japanese plum vinaigrette to soy-flavored duck confit.

INEXPENSIVE
✪ **Cosí Sandwich Bar.** 53 State St. (at Congress St.). ☎ **617/723-4447.** Sandwiches $5.75–$8.25; soups and salads $2.95–$6.50. AE, DC, MC, V. Mon–Thurs 7am–6pm; Fri 7am–5pm. T: Orange or Blue Line to State. ITALIAN/ECLECTIC.

Flavorful fillings on delectable bread make Cosí the newest lunch hot spot downtown—times three. This location, right on the Freedom Trail, makes a fantastic refueling stop. Italian flatbread baked fresh all day—so tasty that it's even good plain—gets split open and filled with your choice of meat, fish, vegetables, cheese, and spreads. The more fillings you choose, the more you pay. Tandoori chicken with caramelized onions is sensational, as is smoked salmon with spinach-artichoke spread. The lunch crowds are more manageable in the summer, when seating extends outdoors. Other branches are at 14 Milk St. (☎ 617/426-7565), near Downtown Crossing, and at 133 Federal St. (☎ 617/292-2674). Open hours probably will have expanded by the time you visit—in 1999 the New York–based chain merged with Xando Coffee and Bar, a company known for serving java at all hours and drinks (including "coffee cocktails") into the night.

5 Downtown Crossing

VERY EXPENSIVE

Locke-Ober. 3–4 Winter Place. ☎ **617/542-1340.** Reservations required. Main courses $8–$24.50 at lunch; $17–$40 at dinner. AE, CB, DC, DISC, MC, V. Mon–Fri 11:30am–2:30pm; Mon–Fri 5:30–10pm; Sat 5:30–10:30pm. Valet parking available after 6pm. T: Red or Orange Line to Downtown Crossing. AMERICAN/CONTINENTAL.

"Locke's" is *the* traditional Boston restaurant, a power-broker favorite since 1875. At press time, rumors about a change of ownership were swirling, but the old-time atmosphere was unruffled. In a tiny alley off the Winter Street pedestrian mall, the dark, wood-paneled restaurant feels like a men's club, with exquisite service, stained-glass windows, and crystal chandeliers. The long, mirrored downstairs bar dates from 1880. Women won't feel unwelcome, but this is definitely not a "girls' night out" place; for one thing, anyone on a diet will be sorely tempted.

The food is definitely old-fashioned—famous Jonah crab cakes or steak tartare to start, then superb grilled salmon with horseradish sauce, Wiener schnitzel à la Hol-stein, or excellent veal chop. The signature dish is lobster Savannah, a sinful concoc-tion that calls for the meat of a 3-pound lobster diced with pepper and mushrooms, bound with cheese and sherry sauce, stuffed into the shell, and baked. The dessert menu lists about two dozen items, and as you might expect, the chocolate mousse is a dish for the ages.

INEXPENSIVE

There's a **Cosí Sandwich Bar** (see "Faneuil Hall Marketplace & Financial District," above) at 14 Milk St. (☎ **617/426-7565**).

Fajitas & 'Ritas. 25 West St. (between Washington and Tremont sts.). ☎ **617/426-1222.** Most dishes under $9. AE, DC, DISC, MC, V. Mon–Tues 11:30am–9pm; Wed–Thurs 11:30am–10pm; Fri–Sat 11:30am–11pm. T: Red or Green Line to Park St. or Orange Line to Downtown Crossing. TEX-MEX.

This entertaining restaurant isn't the most authentic in town, but it's one of the most fun. You order by filling out a slip, checking off your choices of fillings and garnishes to go with your nachos, quesadillas, burritos, or, of course, fajitas. There's nothing exotic, just the usual beef, chicken, shrimp, beans, and so forth. You can also try bar-becue items, such as smoked brisket or pulled pork. A member of the somewhat har-ried staff relays your order to the kitchen and returns with big portions of fresh food—this place is too busy for anything to be sitting around for very long. As the name indicates, 'ritas (margaritas, ordered from a list of about a dozen options using the same check-off system as the food) are a house specialty.

6 Beacon Hill

VERY EXPENSIVE

No. 9 Park. 9 Park St. ☎ **617/742-9991.** Reservations recommended. Main courses $21–$35. AE, DC, MC, V. Mon–Fri 11:30am–2:30pm; Mon–Sat 5:30–10:30pm. Valet parking available at dinner. T: Green or Red Line to Park St. CREATIVE NEW ENGLAND.

One of Boston's most acclaimed new restaurants sits in the shadow of the State House, an area better known for politicians' pubs than for fine dining. No. 9 Park is fine indeed, thanks to chef-owner Barbara Lynch's flair for strong flavors and superb pasta. To start, try beet salad—an upright cylinder of shredded vegetables atop blue cheese, surrounded by greens—or oysters on the half shell with unusually tasty cocktail sauce. Move on to succulent roast chicken served with outrageously buttery mashed potatoes,

Impressions

Their hotels are bad. Their pumpkin pies are delicious. Their poetry is not so good.
—Edgar Allan Poe, *Broadway Journal,* 1845

retro but luscious beef Wellington, braised lamb shank with baby flageolet beans, or a sampler of those famous pastas. For dessert, the profiteroles (a chocolate version served with coconut ice cream) are worth every calorie. One caveat: The austere but comfortable space can get a bit too loud.

MODERATE

Artú (see "The North End," above) has a branch at 89 Charles St. (☎ 617/227-9023).

Istanbul Café. 37 Bowdoin St. ☎ **617/227-3434.** Main courses $7–$16.50; sandwiches $5–$6.50. MC, V. Mon–Wed 11am–10pm; Thurs–Sat 11am–11pm; Sun noon–10pm. T: Red or Green Line to Park St. or Blue Line to Bowdoin. TURKISH.

Hidden away behind the State House, the Istanbul Café is worth seeking out. It's a small, crowded room, four steps down from the street, where the scent of Middle Eastern spices hits you as soon as you open the door. This is a great place to go if you want to linger, because the always-helpful service sometimes grinds to a halt. But that's not a complaint—I go there to catch up with friends and tarry over the food, which ranges from familiar and unusually good to just unusual (and also good).

The appetizer sampler makes a great introduction to the cuisine. *Adana kebab* appears several times in main dishes; the elongated meatballs of spiced ground lamb, threaded onto skewers and grilled, are a must if you like lamb. Cheese lovers at the table will monopolize the plainest version of Turkish pizza, an odd but delicious dish. But unless you can't get enough okra, steer clear of the *etli bamya,* which is more vegetable than meat. The baklava is a lovely rendition of the traditional dessert, crunchy and not too sweet, perfect with a Turkish coffee.

7 Charlestown

VERY EXPENSIVE

🟢 **Olives.** 10 City Sq. ☎ **617/242-1999.** Reservations accepted only for parties of 6 or more. Main courses $19–$32. AE, DC, MC, V. Mon–Fri 5:30–10pm; Sat 5–10:30pm. Valet parking available. T: Orange or Green Line to North Station; 15-min. walk. ECLECTIC.

This informal bistro near the Charlestown Navy Yard just keeps getting more popular. Patrons often line up shortly after 5pm—befriending five strangers and calling for a reservation won't sound so crazy after a couple of hours waiting for a table. If you don't arrive by 5:45pm, expect to spend at least 2 hours, at the bar if there's room. Once you're seated, perhaps on a cushy banquette, you'll find the noise level high (thanks partly to the open kitchen), the service uneven, and the ravenous customers festive.

Happily, the food is worth the wait. Celebrity chef Todd English, co-owner with his wife, Olivia, is a culinary genius. The regularly changing menu includes "Olives Classics"—perhaps a delicious tart of olives, caramelized onions, and anchovies, or spit-roasted chicken flavored with herbs and garlic, oozing succulent juices into old-fashioned mashed potatoes. Grilling is a favorite technique, and with reason—yellowfin tuna, atop parsley mashed potatoes and accented with perfect mussels, holds up beautifully, and any lamb dish is sure to please. When you order your entree, you'll be asked if you want falling chocolate cake for dessert. Say yes.

Waterfront & South Boston Dining

Daily Catch (Waterfront) **5**
Intrigue **2**
Jimbo's Fish Shanty **4**
Jimmy's Harborside Restaurant **3**
Legal Sea Foods (Waterfront) **1**
Rowes Wharf Restaurant **2**

8 South Boston Waterfront (Seaport District)

EXPENSIVE

Jimmy's Harborside Restaurant. 242 Northern Ave. ☎ **617/423-1000.** Reservations recommended at dinner. Main courses $15–$32. AE, CB, DC, DISC, JCB, MC, V. Mon–Sat noon–4pm; daily 4–9:30pm. Closed Dec 25. Valet parking available. T: Red Line to South Station; 25-min. walk. SEAFOOD.

This Boston landmark—the sign out front reads HOME OF THE CHOWDER KING— offers tasty seafood and fine views of the harbor to businesspeople at lunch and tourists at dinner. In the summer, seating extends outside onto the new harborfront deck. You might start with the Chowder King's fish chowder, with generous chunks of whitefish, or excellent Maine crab cakes. Entrees include simple seafood preparations (grilled, broiled, blackened, or fried) and more ambitious specialties—Jimmy's famous *finnan haddie* (smoked haddock in cream sauce) is famous for good reason. If you don't like fish, wait till Friday or Saturday night and come for prime rib. There's a children's menu, and the lounge serves cheese and crackers while you wait for your table. Meter parking is available on Atlantic Avenue; getting a cab is usually not difficult.

MODERATE

✪ **Daily Catch.** 261 Northern Ave. ☎ **617/338-3093.** Reservations accepted only for parties of 8 or more. Main courses $10–$18. AE. Sun–Thurs 11:30am–10:30pm; Fri–Sat 11:30am–11pm. T: Red Line to South Station; 25-min. walk. SOUTHERN ITALIAN/SEAFOOD.

After a meal at this Fish Pier institution, you're going to emanate garlic for at least a day—bring your fellow travelers, because you might as well have someone to share it with. The Daily Catch is a basic storefront, where the staff sometimes seems overwhelmed and it can take forever to get a table, but the food is terrific. The menu includes Sicilian-style calamari (squid stuffed with bread crumbs, raisins, pine nuts, parsley, and tons of garlic), freshly shucked clams, mussels in garlic-flavored sauce, broiled and fried fish, and shellfish. Calamari comes at least eight ways—even the garlic-and-oil pasta sauce has ground-up squid in it. Fried calamari makes an excellent appetizer. Squid ink pasta puttanesca is unusual and delicious. All food is prepared to order, and some dishes are served in the frying pans in which they were cooked.

This is the only Daily Catch that accepts credit cards and reservations. The original Daily Catch, in the **North End** at 323 Hanover St. (☎ **617/523-8567**), keeps the same hours as the Fish Pier location. The **Brookline** restaurant, at 441 Harvard St. (☎ **617/734-5696**), opens at 5pm nightly.

INEXPENSIVE

Jimbo's Fish Shanty. 245 Northern Ave. ☎ **617/542-5600.** Main courses $7–$17. AE, DC, DISC, MC, V. Mon–Thurs 11:30am–9pm; Fri–Sat 11:30am–10pm; Sun noon–8pm. T: Red Line to South Station; 25-min. walk. SEAFOOD.

Bring your sense of humor to this jam-packed restaurant, where model trains run overhead on tracks suspended from the low ceiling, road signs hang everywhere, and the staff is incredibly informal. Under the same management as Jimmy's Harborside (across the street), Jimbo's serves decent portions of fresh seafood to office workers, families, tourists, and bargain hunters. If you can't make up your mind, count on your server for a good suggestion—someone who calls you "pal" or "honey" isn't holding back. You can also order skewers threaded with fish or beef, burgers, and pasta dishes (at dinner only) with varied sauces, including a lobster cream version. The decadent desserts generally involve ice cream and chocolate—save room.

9　Chinatown/Theater District

The most entertaining and delicious introduction to Chinatown's cuisine is **dim sum** (see box). If you're eating dinner, many restaurants have a second menu for Chinese patrons (often written in Chinese). You can ask for it, or tell your waiter you want your meal Chinese style.

EXPENSIVE

There's a branch of **Legal Sea Foods** (see "Back Bay," below) at 36 Park Sq., between Columbus Avenue and Stuart Street (☎ **617/426-4444**).

Ginza Japanese Restaurant. 14 Hudson St. ☎ **617/338-2261.** Reservations accepted only for parties of 6 or more. Sushi from $3.50; main courses $11–$20. AE, DC, MC, V. Mon–Fri 11:30am–2:30pm; Sat–Sun 11:30am–4pm; Sun–Mon 5pm–2am; Tues–Sat 5pm–4am. T: Orange Line to New England Medical Center. SUSHI/JAPANESE.

Tucked away on a side street in Chinatown, you'll find one of the city's best Japanese restaurants. Track down the nondescript entrance, settle into one of the two rooms (in a booth if you're lucky), and watch as kimono-clad waitresses glide past, bearing sushi boats the size of small children. Ginza is a magnet for Japanese expatriates, sushi-lovers, and, in the wee hours, club-hoppers. It's not the only place in town where expert chefs work wonders with ocean-fresh ingredients, but it is the only place that serves "spider maki"—a soft-shelled crab fried and tucked into a *nori* (seaweed) wrapper with avocado, cucumber, and flying-fish roe. An excellent starter is the suddenly

Yum, Yum, Dim Sum

Many restaurants in Chinatown offer dim sum, the traditional midday meal featuring a variety of appetizer-style dishes. You'll see steamed buns (*bao*) filled with pork or bean paste; meat, shrimp, and vegetable dumplings; spareribs; shrimp-stuffed eggplant; sticky rice dotted with sausage and vegetables; spring rolls; sweets such as sesame balls and coconut gelatin, and more. Waitresses wheel carts laden with tempting snack-sized morsels to your table, and you order by pointing (unless you know Chinese). The waitress then stamps your check with the symbol of the dish, adding about $1 to $3 to your tab. Unless you're ravenous or you order à la carte items from the regular menu, the total usually won't be more than about $10 to $12 per person.

Dim sum varies from restaurant to restaurant and chef to chef; if something looks familiar, don't be surprised if it's different from what you're used to, and equally good. This is a great group activity, especially on weekends. The selection is wider than on weekdays, and you'll see two and three generations of families sharing dishes and calling for more. Even picky children can usually find something they enjoy. If you don't eat pork and shrimp, be aware that many, but not all, dishes include one or the other; calorie counters should be aware that many dishes (again, not all) are fried.

Empire Garden Restaurant, 690–698 Washington St., 2nd floor (☎ 617/482-8898), serves a dazzling variety of dishes in a cavernous, ornate former theater balcony. Also known as Emperor's Garden, it opened in 1998 and instantly challenged the dim sum supremacy of the **Golden Palace Restaurant,** 14 Tyler St. (☎ 617/423-4565), and **China Pearl,** 9 Tyler St., 2nd floor (☎ 617/426-4338). All three are excellent. Two other popular destinations are **Chau Chow City,** 83 Essex St. (☎ 617/338-8158), and **Dynasty Restaurant,** 33 Edinboro St. (☎ 617/350-7777).

---

fashionable *edamame*—addictive boiled and salted soybeans served in the pod (you pull the beans out with your teeth). Then let your imagination run wild, or trust the chefs to assemble something dazzling. Green tea ice cream makes an unusually satisfying dessert, but nobody will blame you for finishing up with another round of California maki.

There's another Ginza in **Brookline,** at 1002 Beacon St. (☎ 617/566-9688). It serves a similar menu, but not to night-crawlers (the late nights are Friday and Saturday, when closing time is 10:30pm).

Jae's. 212 Stuart St. ☎ **617/451-7788.** www.jaescafe.com. Reservations recommended at dinner. Main courses $8.25–$21; sushi from $3.50. AE, DC, MC, V. Mon–Sat 11:30am–4pm; Mon–Wed 5–10:30pm; Thurs–Sat 5–11pm; Sun noon–10pm. T: Green Line to Arlington or Orange Line to New England Medical Center. KOREAN/SUSHI/PAN-ASIAN.

This restaurant is a three-story food festival, with sushi on the first floor, Korean and pan-Asian dishes on the second, and a steak house on the third. Owner Jae Chung says it's his dream, and he must not get much rest if he's dreaming about a place as fun and frantic as this. It draws crowds of adventurous food fans, pretheater suburbanites, and hungry businesspeople to its dark spaces splashed with bright colors. The food is even more diverse; the encyclopedic menu ranges from traditional and "designer" sushi to bountiful noodle dishes (*rad nar*—soft, wide rice noodles—is a great choice) to traditional Korean fare. A salad spring roll appetizer is an ethereal Vietnamese-style package of crispy vegetables with a spicy dipping sauce, and (not exactly pan-Asian, but so what?) the crab cakes are divine. The service is not divine, or at least not always—during the calmer times early in the week you'll get better attention. And desserts are delicious but, curiously, European in style. That didn't stop us from inhaling the white and dark chocolate mousse cake, though.

There are other branches of Jae's in the **South End,** 520 Columbus Ave. (☎ **617/ 421-9405**), and **Cambridge's Inman Square,** 1281 Cambridge St. (☎ **617/ 497-8380**), that are smaller but equally busy.

MODERATE

✪ **East Ocean City.** 25–29 Beach St. ☎ **617/542-2504.** Reservations accepted only for parties of 6 or more. Main courses $5–$22. AE, MC, V. Sun–Thurs 11am–3am; Fri–Sat 11am–4am. T: Orange Line to Chinatown. CANTONESE/SEAFOOD.

Don't get too attached to the inhabitants of the fish tanks here—they might turn up on your plate. Tanks make up one wall of the high-ceilinged space, decorated with lots of glass and other hard surfaces that make it rather noisy. The encyclopedic menu offers a huge range of dishes, but as the name indicates, seafood is the focus. It's fresh, delicious, and carefully prepared. One specialty is clams in black-bean sauce, a spicy rendering of a messy, delectable dish. Just about anything that swims can be ordered steamed with ginger and scallions; for variety, check out the chow foon section of the menu.

Grand Chau Chow. 45 Beach St. ☎ **617/292-5166.** Reservations accepted only for parties of 10 or more. Main courses $6–$24. AE, DC, DISC, MC, V. Sun–Thurs 10am–3am; Fri–Sat 10am–4am. T: Orange Line to Chinatown. CANTONESE.

This is one of the best and busiest restaurants in Chinatown, with niceties the smaller restaurants don't offer, such as tablecloths and tuxedoed waiters. In the large fish tanks, both salt- and freshwater, you can watch your dinner swimming around (if you have the heart). Clams with black-bean sauce is a signature dish, as is gray sole with fried fins and bones. Stick to seafood and you can't go wrong. Lunch specials are a great deal, but skip the chow fun, which quickly turns gelatinous. If you're in town during Chinese New Year celebrations, phone ahead and ask that a banquet be prepared for your group. For about $25 a person, you'll get so many courses that you'll lose track. It's a great way to start any year.

Across the street, **Chau Chow,** 52 Beach St. (☎ **617/426-6266**), is Grand Chau Chow's bare-bones sibling. It's downright ugly, doesn't accept credit cards, and packs 'em in for the excellent food and reasonable prices, not the unyielding red plastic benches. The salt-and-pepper shrimp is the best around.

Jacob Wirth Company. 33–37 Stuart St. ☎ **617/338-8586.** www.jacobwirthrestaurant. com. Reservations recommended at dinner. Main courses $7–$17. AE, DC, DISC, MC, V. Mon 11:30am–8pm; Tues–Thurs 11:30am–11pm; Fri–Sat 11:30am–midnight; Sun noon–8pm. Validated parking available. T: Green Line to Boylston or Orange Line to New England Medical Center. GERMAN/AMERICAN.

In the heart of the Theater District, "Jake's" has been serving Bostonians since 1868— even before there were theaters here. The wood floor and brass accents give the room the feeling of a saloon, or perhaps a beer garden. The hearty German specialties include Wiener schnitzel, sauerbraten, mixed grills, bratwurst, and knockwurst. Daily blue-plate specials, a large selection of sandwiches and brews on tap, and more contemporary American fare—often including excellent prime rib—round out the menu.

Service at lunchtime is snappy, but if you want to be on time for the theater, the suspense might be greater in the restaurant than at the show.

INEXPENSIVE

Buddha's Delight. 5 Beach St., 2nd floor. ☎ **617/451-2395.** Main courses $6–$12. MC, V. Sun–Thurs 11am–9:30pm; Fri–Sat 11am–10:30pm. T: Orange Line to Chinatown. VEGETARIAN/VIETNAMESE.

Fresh and healthful intersect with cheap and filling at this busy restaurant. The grim stairwell is off-putting, but the glass-walled dining room and cheerful service are worth the climb. The menu lists "chicken," "shrimp," "pork," and even "lobster"—all in quotes because the kitchen doesn't use meat, poultry, fish, or dairy (some beverages have condensed milk). The chefs fry and barbecue tofu and gluten into more-than-reasonable facsimiles using techniques owner Cuong Van Tran learned from Buddhist monks in a temple outside Los Angeles. Between trying to figure out how they do it and savoring the strong, clear flavors characteristic of Vietnamese cuisine, you might not miss your usual protein. To start, try delectable spring rolls, fried or "fresh" (in paper-thin mungbean wrappers with mint leaves peeking through). Move on to "shrimp" or "pork" with rice noodles, any of the combination dishes, or excellent chow fun.

10 The South End

VERY EXPENSIVE

Hamersley's Bistro. 553 Tremont St. ☎ **617/423-2700.** www.hamersleysbistro.com. Reservations recommended. Main courses $23–$38. Menu dégustation varies. AE, DISC, MC, V. Mon–Fri 6–10pm; Sat 5:30–10pm; Sun 5:30–9:30pm. Closed 2 weeks in Jan. Valet parking available. T: Orange Line to Back Bay. ECLECTIC.

This is the place that put the South End on Boston's culinary map, a pioneering restaurant that's both classic and contemporary. The husband-and-wife team of Gordon and Fiona Hamersley presides over a long dining room with lots of soft surfaces that absorb sound, so you can see but not quite hear what's going on at the tables around you. That means you'll have to quiz one of the courteous servers about the dish that just passed by—perhaps an appetizer of tuna carpaccio over white-bean salad, or grilled mushrooms and garlic on country bread.

The menu changes seasonally and offers about a dozen carefully considered entrees (always including vegetarian dishes) noted for their emphasis on taste and texture. The signature dish is roast chicken, flavored with garlic, lemon, and parsley and served with roast potato, roast onions, and whole cloves of sweet baked garlic. Salmon au poivre with sorrel, leeks, and fingerling potatoes is delicious, as is grilled port-glazed fillet of beef. The wine list is excellent.

✪ **Icarus.** 3 Appleton St. ☎ **617/426-1790.** Reservations recommended. Main courses $19.50–$32.50. AE, CB, DC, DISC, MC, V. Mon–Thurs 6–10pm; Fri 6–10:30pm; Sat 5:30–10:30pm; Sun 5:30–10pm. Closed Sun July–Aug. Valet parking available. T: Green Line to Arlington or Orange Line to Back Bay. ECLECTIC.

This shamelessly romantic subterranean restaurant offers every element of a great dining experience. It's perfect for everything from helping a friend heal a broken heart to celebrating a milestone anniversary. Marble accents and dark-wood trim lend an elegant air to the two-level dining room, and the service is efficient but not formal. Chefowner Christopher Douglass uses choice local seafood, poultry, meats, and produce to create imaginative dishes that seem more like alchemy than cooking. The menu changes regularly—you might start with braised exotic mushrooms atop polenta, or the daily "pasta whim." Move on to soft-shell crabs on a black-rice cake, or lemony grilled chicken with garlic mashed potatoes so good you'll want to ask for a plate of them. Don't. Instead, save room for one of the unbelievable desserts. The trio of fruit sorbets is one of the best nonchocolate desserts I've ever run across.

EXPENSIVE

Jae's (see "Chinatown/Theater District," above) has a restaurant at 520 Columbus Ave. (☎ 617/421-9405).

MODERATE

Addis Red Sea. 544 Tremont St. ☎ **617/426-8727.** Main courses $9–$17. AE, MC, V. Mon–Fri 5–10:30pm; Sat noon–11pm; Sun noon–10pm. T: Orange Line to Back Bay. ETHIOPIAN.

If you're in the mood to experiment, Addis Red Sea is a good place to start. Colorful carpets and wall hangings decorate the dimly lit, subterranean space, and you sit on stools at *mesobs,* traditional Ethiopian tables. Wash your hands! Ethiopian food is served family-style on a platter, without utensils. The waitress covers the platter with a layer of *injera,* a spongy, tangy bread, and spoons the food on top of it. Tear off a piece of injera, scoop up a mouthful of food, and dig in. Ask for more injera if you need it to finish off the stewlike main courses. Many are vegetarian, and the vegetable combination makes a good introduction to this cuisine, with a choice of dishes that might include lentils, split peas, cracked wheat, onions, potatoes, beans, carrots, and greens. The spice level varies, but even the mildest dishes are flavorful and filling. There are also tasty meat dishes—*doro wat* is lemon-marinated chicken, *yebez wat* is lamb with red pepper, and *kifto* is the Ethiopian version of steak tartare.

Bob the Chef's Jazz Cafe. 604 Columbus Ave. ☎ **617/536-6204.** Main courses $9–$15; sandwiches $5–$8. AE, DC, MC, V. Tues–Wed 11:30am–10pm; Thurs–Sat 11:30am–midnight; Sun 11am–9pm (brunch until 3pm). Self-parking ($5) across the street. T: Orange Line to Mass. Ave.; 5-min. walk. SOUTHERN/CAJUN.

Bob the Chef's resembles a yuppie fern bar, but it serves generous portions of Southern specialties against a backdrop of jazz. The music is live Thursday through Saturday nights and at Sunday brunch. You'll find dishes such as fried chicken, served alone or with barbecued ribs; meat loaf; "soul fish" (in cornmeal batter); and Creole specialties like jambalaya and shrimp étoufée. Dinners come with a corn muffin and your choice of two side dishes—including black-eyed peas, macaroni and cheese, collard greens, and candied yams. Frying is done in vegetable oil, not the customary lard, and everywhere you'd expect bacon for flavoring, smoked turkey is used instead. For dessert, try the sweet-potato pie, which will instantly ruin pumpkin pie for you.

Grillfish. 162 Columbus Ave. ☎ **617/357-1620.** www.grillfish.com. Reservations accepted only for parties of 6 or more. Main courses $10–$21. AE, DISC, MC, V. Sun–Mon 5:30–10pm; Tues–Thurs 5:30–11pm; Fri–Sat 5:30–midnight. SEAFOOD.

A splash of Florida style in conservative Boston, this sassy interloper specializes in reasonably priced seafood. It's part of a small chain that's also in the Miami and Washington areas. An open-fire grill and a PG-13–rated mural over the bar dominate the high-ceilinged dining room. Grilled shrimp scampi (an unusual version, with tomatoes in the sauce) is available as an appetizer or main course. The grilled fish selections—a regular roster augmented with specials—come with your choice of sweet onion or garlic-tomato sauce. Sautéed dishes have marsala or piccata sauce, and several types of shellfish are available over pasta. Diners shout to be heard over the loud music; ask for a table near the windows or on the small patio (open seasonally) if you prefer a quieter atmosphere.

INEXPENSIVE

Le Gamin Café. 550 Tremont St. ☎ **617/654-8969.** www.legamin.com. Main courses $5–$11.50; crêpes $3–$9.50. MC, V. Daily 8am–midnight. T: Orange Line to Back Bay. FRENCH.

The waiter has a heavy French accent. The posters on the walls do, too. It's freezing out, but the salad is right-from-the-garden fresh. The signature sandwiches—with three fillings mixed and matched from a list of more than a dozen—are splendid. The crêpes are perfect, and the homemade caramel sauce on the orange-filled one is swooningly good. The tuna in the salade Niçoise is a tad dry and the room a bit noisy, but everything else is just so. This is a perfect spot for lingering over morning coffee or a mid-afternoon glass of wine. It's a recent addition to a small chain that originated in Manhattan. Oh, shoot—another thing New York got right first.

11 Back Bay

VERY EXPENSIVE

At press time, celebrity chef Stan Frankenthaler planned to move his celebrated **Salamander** (☎ **617/451-2150**) here from Cambridge in the summer of 2000. Besides elaborate Asian-influenced creations, the new Salamander will have a satay bar.

✪ **Anago.** In the Lenox Hotel, 65 Exeter St. ☎ **617/266-6222.** Reservations recommended. Main courses $18–$35. AE, DC, MC, V. Mon–Thurs 5:30–10pm; Fri–Sat 5:30–10:30pm; Sun 5–9pm; Sun brunch 11am–2:30pm. Valet parking available. T: Green Line to Copley. CREATIVE AMERICAN.

Anago opened in Boston in 1997 with a reputation for bold, inventive food (gained during its days as Anago Bistro in Cambridge) and quickly established itself as one of the city's top restaurants. You can schedule a business meeting, romantic rendezvous, or family brunch here with equal confidence. Chef Bob Calderone, co-owner with his wife, Susan Finegold, makes good use of fresh regional produce, seafood, and meats.

To start, winter-squash soup garnished with a risotto cake is impressive, as is the house antipasto (roast pear, prosciutto, mozzarella, and vegetables). Main dishes might include oven-roasted bass with warm potato salad, grilled corn, and heirloom tomato salad, and toothsome grilled sirloin with red-wine sauce and porcini baked potato. Desserts are fanciful—try "chocolate, chocolate, chocolate," when it's available, and be ready to swoon. Service is friendly but polite. Even with an open kitchen, the tall, wide room is surprisingly quiet, thanks to the soundproofed ceiling, plush upholstery, and well-spaced tables and banquettes.

✪ **Aujourd'hui.** In the Four Seasons Hotel, 200 Boylston St. ☎ **617/451-2071.** Reservations recommended (required on holidays). Main courses $19–$23.50 at lunch, $32–$45 at dinner; Sun buffet brunch $55 adult, $26 child. AE, CB, DC, DISC, MC, V. Mon–Fri 6:30–11am, Sat–Sun 7–11am; Mon–Fri 11:30am–2:30pm; Sun brunch 11:30am–2:30pm; Mon–Sat 5:30–10:30pm, Sun 6–10:30pm. Valet parking available. T: Green Line to Arlington. CONTEMPORARY AMERICAN.

On the second floor of the city's premier luxury hotel, the most beautiful restaurant in town has floor-to-ceiling windows overlooking the Public Garden. Even if it were under a pup tent, the incredible service and food would make Aujourd'hui a hit with its special-occasion and expense-account clientele. Yes, the cost is astronomical, but how often is it true that you get what you pay for? Here, you do.

The regularly changing menu encompasses basic offerings you'd expect in a hotel dining room and creations that characterize an inventive kitchen. Executive chef Edward Gannon uses regional products and the freshest ingredients available, and the

Boston Tea Party, Part 2

This is Boston, the only city that has a whole tea party named after it, and the tradition of afternoon tea at a plush hotel is alive and well. You'll need a reservation at the Ritz or the Four Seasons.

The **Ritz-Carlton, Boston,** 15 Arlington St. (☎ **617/536-5700**), serves the city's most celebrated tea ($22) in the elegant Ritz Lounge every day at 3 and 4:30pm. Harp music plays as you're served pastries, breads, delectable scones, and finger sandwiches.

Across the Public Garden, the **Bristol Lounge** at the Four Seasons Hotel, 200 Boylston St. (☎ **617/351-2053**), offers a sensational view and wonderful scones, tea sandwiches, pastries, and nut bread ($21.50, or $28.50 with a kir royale) every day from 3 to 4:30pm.

A player piano serenades tea partyers at **Swans Court,** in the lobby of the Boston Park Plaza Hotel, 64 Arlington St. (☎ **617/426-2000**), daily from 3 to 5pm. There's no view, and the finger sandwiches, strawberries and cream, and petit fours ($10.50) aren't quite as elegant as at the other hotels, but it's still fun—and a great deal.

wine list is excellent. To start, you might try a perfectly balanced seasonal soup or a huge salad. Entrees include rack of lamb served with eggplant galette, black-olive tapenade, and flageolet ragout; roasted lobster comes with pineapple compote and crabmeat wontons. "Alternative Cuisine" offerings slash calories, cholesterol, sodium, and fat, but not flavor. The dessert menu also changes but always includes picture-perfect soufflés and homemade sorbets.

✪ **Grill 23 & Bar.** 161 Berkeley St. ☎ **617/542-2255.** www.grill23.com. Reservations recommended. Main courses $20–$36. AE, CB, DC, DISC, MC, V. Mon–Thurs 5:30–10:30pm; Fri–Sat 5:30–11pm; Sun 5:30–10pm. Valet parking available. T: Green Line to Arlington. AMERICAN.

Grill 23, a wood-paneled, glass-walled room with a businesslike air, is more than just a steak house. A briefcase-toting crowd comes here for traditional slabs of beef and chops as well as bolder, more creative options. Steak au poivre and lamb chops are perfectly grilled, crusty, juicy, and tender. The inventively updated meat loaf incorporates sirloin and chorizo under tomato coulis. And if the fish dishes aren't quite as memorable as the meat offerings—hey, it's a steak house. The bountiful à la carte side dishes include creamed spinach, roasted portabellos, and out-of-this-world garlic mashed potatoes. Desserts, especially crème brûlée, are toothsome, but (this is *not* your father's steak house) they don't always include cheesecake. The service is exactly right for the setting, helpful but not familiar.

A couple of caveats: The wine list is pricey, and the noise grows louder as the evening progresses. Still, you probably won't realize you're shouting until you're outside yelling about what a good meal you had.

✪ **L'Espalier.** 30 Gloucester St. ☎ **617/262-3023.** www.lespalier.com. Reservations required. Prix-fixe (4 courses) $65; menu dégustation (7 courses; whole tables only) $82. AE, DISC, MC, V. Mon–Sat 6–10pm. Valet parking available. T: Green Line B, C, or D to Hynes/ICA. NEW ENGLAND/FRENCH.

Dinner at L'Espalier is a unique experience, very much like spending the evening at the home of a dear friend who has only your pleasure in mind—and has a dozen

You Paid What?

47,000 hotels, 700 airlines,
50 rental car companies. And a few
million ways to save money.

Travelocity.com

A Sabre Company

Go Virtually Anywhere.

AOL Keyword: Travel

Will you have enough stories to tell your grandchildren?

Yahoo! Travel

helpers in the kitchen. Owners Frank and Catherine McClelland (he's the chef) preside over three dining rooms on the second floor of an 1886 townhouse. The space is formal yet inviting, and the service is beyond excellent, in that eerie realm where it seems possible that the waiter just read your mind. The food, an exploration of the freshest and most interesting ingredients available, is magnificent.

A first course of foie gras strudel arrives with rhubarb and dried-cherry compote, and perfectly balanced fresh Cabernet grape vinaigrette dresses a salad of greens with wild rice, herbed polenta, and white asparagus. Main courses usually include a game offering, perhaps rack of venison with caramelized endive, wild-rice salad, and gooseberry *jus;* salmon in a sesame crust over noodles in a ginger-and-sesame broth is equally impressive. The breads, sorbets, ice creams, and alarmingly good desserts (many adapted from the family's heirloom cookbooks) are made on the premises. Even if you have one of the superb soufflés, which are ordered with dinner, ask to see the beautiful desserts. Or order the celebrated cheese tray, which always includes two local cheeses.

✪ The Ritz-Carlton Dining Room. 15 Arlington St. ☎ **617/536-5700.** Reservations required. Jacket and tie required for men. Prix-fixe menus $61 (3 courses), $69 (4 courses), $75 (5 courses); chef's dégustation table $87; weekly tasting menu (5 courses) $75, with wine $99. Sun buffet brunch $52 adult, $26 child. AE, CB, DC, DISC, JCB, MC, V. Tues–Sun 5:30–10pm; Sun brunch 10:45am–2:30pm. Valet parking available. T: Green Line to Arlington. CONTEMPORARY FRENCH.

This elegant room overlooking the Public Garden has traditionally been, well, traditional. In late 1999 the hotel shook up its oh-so-conservative restaurant and gave wunderkind chef Mark Allen free rein, with utterly delightful results. The big news is the menu, where stodgy favorites yielded to a dreamlike combination of French technique, California innovation, and seasonal New England ingredients. Every dish is as satisfying as a well-chosen word, appealing to all your senses (except hearing, which is well taken care of by solicitous staff members murmuring in your ear).

Langoustine and wild-mushroom profiterole with dill cream; lobster and beet risotto with white-truffle sauce; foie gras and polenta terrine wrapped in Serrano ham, with marinated vegetables and blue cheese dressing—everything tastes as good as it sounds. Beef tenderloin with shrimp, potato cake, and asparagus is a little tower of flavor; luscious peekytoe crab cake and perfect red snapper sit atop spinach and tomato relish. Desserts are ravishing, in every sense of the word. The waiters no longer wear tuxedos (they're in suits—it's still the Ritz), and the subtly reconfigured space is more intimate, still lit by elaborate chandeliers and accented by live piano music. It's a new tradition, and an exceptionally enjoyable one.

✪ Top of the Hub. In the Prudential Center, 800 Boylston St. ☎ **617/536-1775.** Reservations recommended. Jacket advised for men. Main courses $7–$16 at lunch, $18–$32 at dinner. Tasting menus $55 (5 courses), $75 (7 courses). Sun brunch $34. AE, DC, DISC, MC, V. Mon–Sat 11:30am–2:30pm, Sun brunch 10am–2:30pm; Mon–Thurs 5:30–10pm, Fri 5:30–11pm, Sat 5–11pm, Sun 5–10pm. Discounted parking available in Prudential Center garage after 4pm Mon–Fri, all day Sat–Sun. T: Green Line B, C, or D to Hynes/ICA; or E to Prudential. CREATIVE AMERICAN.

For many years, the answer to the question "How's the food at Top of the Hub?" was "The view is spectacular." The cuisine has improved dramatically—not to the point where it's a match for the 52nd-floor panorama, but that would be nearly impossible. Still, if you can't reserve a table by the window, don't bother with the restaurant; you can always have a drink in the lounge. Check the weather forecast and aim to eat here when it's clear out, taking the best advantage of the space's three glass-walled sides. And consider coming before sunset and lingering until dark for a true spectacle.

The menu emphasizes the seafood that the tourist-intensive clientele expects, with the customary simple preparations and some that show off the kitchen's creative side— soy-glazed yellowfin tuna roasted and served with quinoa salad, for example. Grilled sirloin is another good choice at dinner. Lunch offerings include pizzas and half a dozen tasty sandwiches. At either meal, the clam chowder is a standout, with more broth than cream. Salads are large and varied, but if you don't like vegetables drowning in dressing, ask for it on the side.

EXPENSIVE

Tapéo, 266 Newbury St. (☎ 617/267-4799), has the same owners as **Dalí** (see "Outside Harvard Square," in the "Cambridge" section, below).

Casa Romero. 30 Gloucester St., side entrance. ☎ **617/536-4341.** Reservations recommended. Main courses $12.50–$24. DISC, MC, V. Sun–Thurs 5–10pm; Fri–Sat 5–11pm. T: Green Line B, C, or D to Hynes/ICA. MEXICAN.

There's something about restaurants in alleys. They feel like secret clubs or speakeasies, and if they're really worth seeking out, so much the better. Casa Romero is just such a place. The tiled floor, heavy wood furnishings, dim lighting, and clay pots lend a real Mexican feel—you're definitely not at the local Tex-Mex counter. The food is excellent, both authentic and accessible, with generous portions of spicy-hot and milder dishes; the friendly staff will help you negotiate the menu. If the soup of the day is garlic, don't miss it. Main-dish specialties include several kinds of enchiladas, excellent stuffed squid in tomato-and-chipotle sauce, chicken breast in mole poblano sauce (a spicy concoction with a hint of chocolate), and terrific pork tenderloin marinated with oranges and smoked peppers. In the summer, reserve a table in the walled garden.

Davio's. 269 Newbury St. ☎ **617/262-4810.** www.davios.com. Reservations recommended downstairs. Main courses $10–$25; pizzas $7–$8.50. AE, CB, DC, DISC, MC, V. Daily 11:30am–1am (lunch until 5pm, dinner until 11pm). Valet parking available. T: Green Line to Copley. CREATIVE NORTHERN ITALIAN.

While the rest of the Boston-area culinary community plays musical chefs, owner-chef Steve DiFillippo has buckled down and turned Davio's into a local favorite. The restaurant's excellent reputation rests on its top-notch kitchen, dedicated staff, and pleasant atmosphere. In a Back Bay brownstone, you wouldn't expect to find typical Italian fare, and you won't. Start with excellent minestrone, beautifully balanced salad, or the day's homemade ravioli selection (also available as a main course). Move on to grilled veal chop in port wine sauce, salmon grilled to pink perfection, or any dish that involves homemade sausage. There are usually three special entrees daily, plus a house pâté. Desserts change regularly; try the ethereal tiramisú if it's available. Davio's has a well-edited wine selection, including some rare and expensive Italian vintages. The upstairs cafe (open 11:30am to 3pm and 5 to 11pm) offers terrace seating in good weather.

There are branches of Davio's in Providence, R.I., Philadelphia, and **Cambridge,** at the Royal Sonesta Hotel, 5 Cambridge Pkwy. (☎ **617/661-4810**). It's open the same hours, except dinner service ends at 10pm nightly.

✪ **Legal Sea Foods.** In the Prudential Center, 800 Boylston St. ☎ **617/266-6800.** www.legalseafoods.com. Reservations recommended at lunch, not accepted at dinner. Main courses $7–$13 at lunch, $14–$27 at dinner; lobster priced daily. AE, CB, DC, DISC, MC, V. Mon–Thurs 11am–10:30pm; Fri–Sat 11am–11:30pm; Sun noon–10pm. T: Green Line B, C, or D to Hynes/ICA or E to Prudential. SEAFOOD.

The food at Legal Sea Foods ("Legal's," in Bostonian parlance) isn't the fanciest, the cheapest, or the trendiest. It's the freshest, and management's commitment to that policy has produced a thriving chain. The family-owned business has an international reputation for serving only top-quality fish and shellfish, prepared in every imaginable way. The menu includes regular selections (scrod, haddock, bluefish, salmon, shrimp, calamari, and lobster, among others) plus whatever looked good at the market that morning, and it's all splendid. The clam chowder is great, the fish chowder lighter but equally good, the smoked bluefish pâté rich and creamy. Entrees run the gamut from grilled fish served plain or with Cajun spices (try the Arctic char), to seafood fra'diavolo on fresh linguine, to salmon baked in parchment with vegetables and white wine. Or go the luxurious route and order the biggest lobster you can afford (remember to lose the bib when you're done). The classic dessert is ice cream bonbons, but a recent addition, Boston cream pie, is so good that you may come back just for that.

I suggest the Prudential Center branch because it takes reservations (at lunch only), a deviation from a long tradition. Equally annoying but equally traditional is the policy of serving each dish when it's ready, instead of one table at a time. Other locations have the same blue-and-white-checked decor and menu. The first waterfront branch, at 255 State St. (☎ 617/227-3115), sits somewhat disconcertingly opposite the New England Aquarium. There are restaurants at 36 Park Sq., between Columbus Avenue and Stuart Street, opposite the Boston Park Plaza Hotel (☎ 617/426-4444); on the second level of Copley Place (☎ 617/266-7775); and in Kendall Square, 5 Cambridge Center (☎ 617/864-3400).

Turner Fisheries of Boston. In the Westin Copley Place Boston, 10 Huntington Ave. ☎ 617/424-7425. Reservations recommended. Main courses $9–$15 at lunch; $17–$28 at dinner. AE, CB, DC, DISC, MC, V. Mon–Sat 11am–10:30pm (lunch until 2pm Mon–Fri, until 3pm Sat); Sun 11am–3pm (brunch) and 5–10:30pm. Valet parking available. T: Orange Line to Back Bay, or Green Line to Copley. SEAFOOD.

This restaurant is best known for winning the Boston Harborfest Chowderfest contest so many times that its superb clam chowder was elevated to the Hall of Fame. It's also known as a place to go when you can't get into Legal Sea Foods, which does it a disservice—it also serves some of the freshest fish in town, in a calmer atmosphere than you'll usually find at Legal's. Packed with businesspeople at lunch and out-of-towners (and savvy locals who appreciate the more placid setting) at dinner, Turner Fisheries is obviously doing something right.

The menu features each day's special catch and suggested preparations—pan-fried, broiled, grilled, baked, steamed, or "spicy bronzed." Specials are more inventive, from the signature bouillabaisse to pan-seared scallops in miso broth to excellent pastas (with and without seafood). The raw bar is also a draw, and there are always a few non-seafood options. Ask for a booth if you want privacy, or a table if you want to enjoy the atriumlike ambience.

MODERATE

Bangkok Cuisine. 177A Mass. Ave. ☎ 617/262-5377. Reservations not accepted. Main courses $5–$8 at lunch; $8–$15 at dinner. AE, DISC, MC, V. Daily 11:30am–10:30pm. T: Green Line B, C, or D to Hynes/ICA. THAI.

Extremely popular with patrons of nearby Symphony Hall and the students who dominate this neighborhood, Bangkok Cuisine is a classic. The first Thai restaurant in Boston, it opened in 1979 and set (and has maintained) high standards for the many others that followed. For the unadventurous, it serves fantastic pad Thai. The rest of

ⓘ   Family-Friendly Restaurants

Like chocolate and champagne, well-behaved children are welcome almost everywhere. Most Boston-area restaurants can accommodate families, and many youngsters can be stunned into tranquillity if a place is fancy enough. If your kids can't or won't sign a good-conduct pledge, here are some suggestions.

The ✪ **Bertucci's** chain of pizzerias appeals to children and adults equally, with wood-fired brick ovens that are visible from many tables, great rolls made from pizza dough, and pizzas and pastas that range from basic to sophisticated. There are convenient branches at Faneuil Hall Marketplace (☎ **617/227-7889**); in the Back Bay at 43 Stanhope St. (☎ **617/247-6161**), around the corner from the Hard Rock Cafe; and in Cambridge at 21 Brattle St., Harvard Square (☎ **617/864-4748**).

The **Hard Rock Cafe,** 131 Clarendon St. (☎ **617/424-ROCK**), and ✪ **House of Blues,** 96 Winthrop St., Cambridge (☎ **617/491-2583**), serve up music with their food—and your kids will think you're *so* cool.

The nonstop activity and smart-mouthed service at ✪ **Durgin-Park,** 340 Faneuil Hall Marketplace (☎ **617/227-2038**), will entrance any child, and parents of picky eaters will appreciate the straightforward New England fare.

Another chain, **TGI Friday's,** 26 Exeter St., at Newbury Street (☎ **617/266-9040**), made its reputation by catering to singles. All that pairing off apparently led to children, who are courted as well. They receive a kids' package with balloons, crayons, a coloring book, peanut butter and crackers, and surprises wrapped in the chain's signature red-and-white stripes.

California Pizza Kitchen (yes, another chain) has two Boston locations, 137 Stuart St., in the Theater District (☎ **617/720-0999**), and the Prudential Center, near the Huntington Avenue entrance (☎ **617/247-0888**).

The **Bristol Lounge,** in the Four Seasons Hotel, 200 Boylston St. (☎ **617/351-2053**), looks almost too nice to have a kids' menu (with appetizers, plain main courses, desserts, and beverages). The staff is unflappable and accommodating, and high chairs and sticker fun books are available.

the menu runs the gamut from excellent basil chicken to all sorts of curry offerings, pan-fried or deep-fried whole fish, noodle soups, and hot-and-sour salads. Green curry in coconut milk and vegetables prepared with strong green Thai chili pepper are the most incendiary dishes. In this long, narrow room, there are no secrets—if the person at the next table is eating something appealing, ask what it is.

INEXPENSIVE

Café Jaffa. 48 Gloucester St. ☎ **617/536-0230.** Main courses $4.75–$12.95. AE, DC, DISC, MC, V. Mon–Thurs 11am–10:30pm; Fri–Sat 11am–11pm; Sun 1–10pm. T: Green Line B, C, or D to Hynes/ICA. MIDDLE EASTERN.

A long, narrow brick room with a glass front, Café Jaffa looks more like a snazzy pizza place than the excellent Middle Eastern restaurant it is. The reasonable prices, high quality, and large portions draw hordes of young people for traditional Middle Eastern offerings such as falafel, baba ghanoush, and hummus, as well as burgers and steak tips. Lamb, beef, and chicken kabobs come with Greek salad, rice pilaf, and pita bread. For dessert, try the baklava if it's fresh (give it a pass if not). There is a short list of beer and wine and, somewhat incongruously, many fancy coffee offerings.

12 Kenmore Square to Brookline

EXPENSIVE

Ginza Japanese Restaurant (see "Chinatown/Theater District," above) has a second location at 1002 Beacon St., Brookline (☎ **617/566-9688**).

MODERATE

There's a branch of the **Daily Catch**—see "South Boston Waterfront (Seaport District)," above—at 441 Harvard St., Brookline (☎ **617/734-5696**).

The Elephant Walk. 900 Beacon St., Boston. ☎ **617/247-1500.** Reservations recommended at dinner Sun–Thurs, not accepted Fri–Sat. Main courses $6–$18.50 at lunch; $9.50–$23.95 at dinner. AE, DC, DISC, MC, V. Mon–Sat 11:30am–2:30pm; Mon–Thurs 5–10pm; Fri 5–11pm; Sat 4:30–11pm; Sun 4:30–10pm. Valet parking available at dinner. T: Green Line C to St. Mary's St. FRENCH/CAMBODIAN.

France meets Cambodia on the menu at the Elephant Walk, 4 blocks from Kenmore Square on the Boston–Brookline border and decorated with lots of little pachyderms. This madly popular spot has a two-part menu (French on one side, Cambodian on the other), but the boundary is quite porous. Many Cambodian dishes have part-French names, such as *poulet dhomrei* (chicken with Asian basil, bamboo shoots, fresh pineapple, and kaffir lime leaves) and *curry de crevettes* (shrimp curry with picture-perfect vegetables). My mouth is still burning from *loc lac,* fork-tender beef cubes in addictively spicy sauce. On the French side, you'll find pan-seared filet mignon with *pommes frites,* and pan-seared tuna with three-peppercorn crust. Many dishes are available with tofu substituted for animal protein. The pleasant staff members will help out if you need guidance. Ask to be seated in the plant-filled front room, which is less noisy than the main dining room and has a view of the street.

There's another Elephant Walk at 2067 Mass. Ave., just north of **Cambridge's Porter Square** (☎ **617/492-6900**). It keeps the same hours as the Boston location, except it opens for dinner at 5pm on weekends, and it somehow manages to be even louder. There's free parking at the back of the building.

Zaftigs Delicatessen. 335 Harvard St., Brookline. ☎ **617/975-0075.** Reservations recommended. Main courses $8–$13; breakfast items $2.50–$9. AE, DISC, MC, V. Daily 8am–10pm. T: Green Line C to Coolidge Corner. DELI/AMERICAN.

The magical words "breakfast served all day" might be enough to lure you to this bustling restaurant, but even breakfast haters (yes, there is such an animal) will be happy at Zaftigs. The name, Yiddish for "pleasingly plump," is no joke—everything is good, and portions are more than generous. Try fluffy pancakes, challah French toast, or a terrific omelet. They share the menu with wonderful deli sandwiches as well as apparently basic entrees, which have a certain flair. Roasted chicken is juicy and flavorful, grilled salmon equally enjoyable. The usual knock on Boston-area deli food is that (well, duh) it's not New York, but the hard-core deli items here are more than acceptable. The gefilte fish is light, blintzes have a tang of citrus in the filling, and the chicken soup is excellent.

13 Cambridge

The dining scene in Cambridge, as in Boston, offers something for everyone, from penny-pinching students to the tycoons many of them aspire to become. The Red Line runs from downtown Boston to the heart of Harvard Square. Many of the restaurants listed here can easily be reached on foot from there; others (including a couple

Cambridge Dining

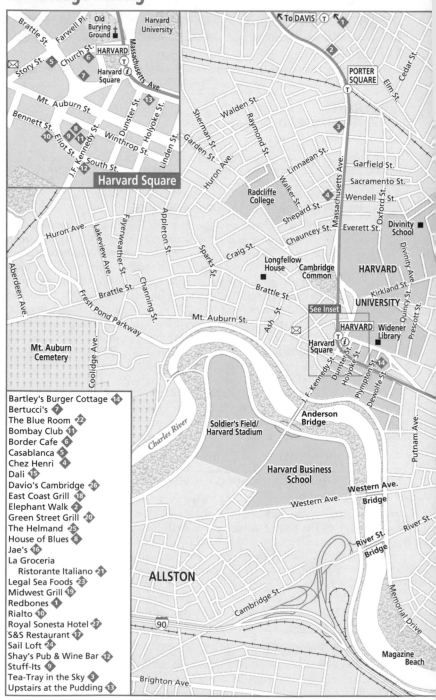

Bartley's Burger Cottage 🔞
Bertucci's 🟣7
The Blue Room 🔵22
Bombay Club 🟣11
Border Cafe 🟣6
Casablanca 🟣5
Chez Henri 🟣4
Dali 🔵15
Davio's Cambridge 🔵26
East Coast Grill 🔵18
Elephant Walk 🔵2
Green Street Grill 🔵20
The Helmand 🔵25
House of Blues 🟣8
Jae's 🔵16
La Groceria
  Ristorante Italiano 🔵21
Legal Sea Foods 🔵23
Midwest Grill 🔵19
Redbones 🔵1
Rialto 🟣10
Royal Sonesta Hotel 🔵27
S&S Restaurant 🔵17
Sail Loft 🔵24
Shay's Pub & Wine Bar 🟣12
Stuff-Its 🟣9
Tea-Tray in the Sky 🔵3
Upstairs at the Pudding 🔵13

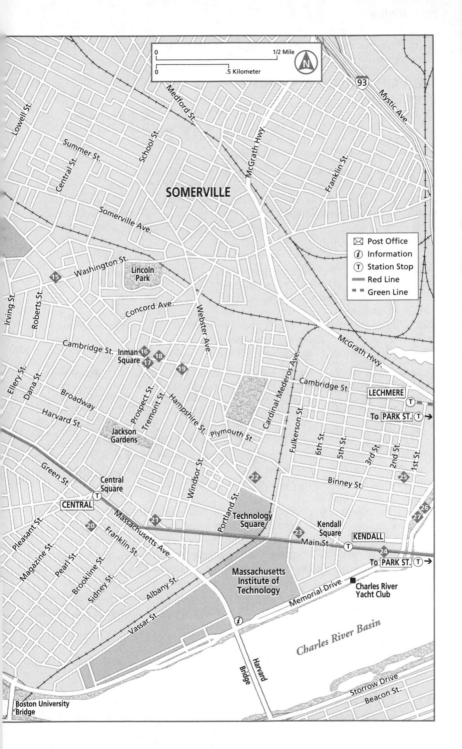

SOMERVILLE

Post Office
Information
Station Stop
Red Line
Green Line

Lowell St.
Summer St.
Central St.
School St.
Medford St.
McGrath Hwy.
Franklin St.
Mystic Ave.
93

Somerville Ave.

Washington St.
Lincoln Park
Irving St.
Roberts St.
Concord Ave.
Webster Ave.
McGrath Hwy.

Cambridge St.
Inman Square
Ellery St.
Dana St.
Broadway
Prospect St.
Tremont St.
Hampshire St.
Plymouth St.
Cardinal Medeiros Ave.
Cambridge St.
Fulkerson St.
LECHMERE
To PARK ST. →

Harvard St.
Jackson Gardens
Windsor St.
Portland St.
6th St.
5th St.
3rd St.
2nd St.
1st St.
Binney St.

Green St.
Central Square
CENTRAL
Massachusetts Ave.
Technology Square
Kendall Square
KENDALL
Main St.
To PARK ST. →

Pleasant St.
Magazine St.
Pearl St.
Brookline St.
Sidney St.
Franklin St.
Albany St.
Vassar St.
Massachusetts Institute of Technology
Memorial Drive
Charles River Yacht Club

Harvard Bridge
Boston University Bridge
Charles River Basin
Storrow Drive
Beacon St.

0   1/2 Mile
0   .5 Kilometer

127

of real finds just over the Somerville border) are listed under the heading "Outside Harvard Square."

HARVARD SQUARE & VICINITY
VERY EXPENSIVE

✪ **Rialto.** In the Charles Hotel, 1 Bennett St. ☎ **617/661-5050.** Reservations recommended. Main courses $20–$33. AE, CB, DC, MC, V. Sun–Thurs 5:30–10pm; Fri–Sat 5:30–11pm. Bar Sun–Thurs 4:30pm–midnight; Fri–Sat 5pm–1am. Valet and validated parking available. T: Red Line to Harvard. MEDITERRANEAN.

If Rialto isn't the best restaurant in the Boston area, it's close. It attracts a chic crowd, but it's not a "scene" in the sense that out-of-towners will feel left behind. Every element is carefully thought out, from the architecture to the service to chef Jody Adams's extraordinary food. It's a dramatic but comfortable room, with floor-to-ceiling windows overlooking Harvard Square, cushy banquettes, and standing lamps that cast a golden glow.

The menu changes regularly. You might start with grilled mussels with andouille sausage and garlic bread, or Provençal fisherman's soup with rouille, gruyère, and basil oil, the very essence of seafood. Main courses are so good that you might as well close your eyes and point. Seared duck breast with foie gras, squash raviolis, and quince is wonderful, and any fish is a guaranteed winner—say, seared tuna in mustard seeds with wild rice and olive vinaigrette. A plate of creamy potato slices and mushrooms is so juicy it's almost like eating meat. For dessert, seasonal sorbets are a great choice, alone or in a combination such as tarte Tatin with mulled-cider sorbet.

✪ **Upstairs at the Pudding.** 10 Holyoke St. ☎ **617/864-1933.** Reservations recommended. Main courses $9–$14 at lunch, $20–$38 at dinner, $9–$15 at brunch; tasting menu (dinner) $45. AE, CB, DC, MC, V. Mon–Sat 11:30am–2:30pm; Sun brunch 11am–2:30pm; daily 6–11pm. Validated parking available. T: Red Line to Harvard. CONTINENTAL/NORTHERN ITALIAN.

An oasis of calm above the tumult of Harvard Square, Upstairs at the Pudding is a special-occasion spot with food so good you'll want to make up a reason (and save up some money) to go there. At the top of the Hasty Pudding Club's creaky stairs, it's a high-ceilinged room with soft, romantic lighting. The menu changes daily and always features hand-rolled pasta.

To start, you might try fettuccine with truffle cream, or pizzetta with tomato confit, olives, garlic, chèvre, and Parmesan. Entrees include at least one pasta dish and a small but choice selection of meat and fish. If mashed potatoes are on the menu, you can't go wrong by ordering any main course that comes with them—perhaps peppered beef tenderloin with blue cheese and charred tomato coulis. Rack of lamb might be offered with braised artichokes, roasted onions, creamer potatoes, and rosemary-mustard *jus*. Portions are large, but try to save room for dessert—anything with chocolate is a good choice. There is a lovely terrace and herb garden off the dining room for seasonal alfresco dining.

EXPENSIVE

Casablanca. 40 Brattle St. ☎ **617/876-0999.** Reservations recommended at dinner. Main courses $7–$12 at lunch; $14–$23 at dinner. AE, MC, V. Daily 11:30am–3pm; Sun–Thurs 5:30–10pm; Fri–Sat 5:30–11pm. T: Red Line to Harvard. MEDITERRANEAN.

This old-time Harvard Square favorite has long been known more for its hopping bar scene than for its food. These days the dining room is the place where you're sure to get lucky—Casablanca remains true to its reputation for serving tasty Mediterranean cuisine. Service is erratic (it's better at lunch than at dinner), but there's plenty to look at while you wait. The walls of the long, skylit dining room and crowded, noisy bar sport murals of scenes from the movie. Humphrey Bogart looks as though he might lean down to ask for a taste of your crispy mascarpone chicken or juicy pork tenderloin over spaetzle (tell him no—you'll want them all to yourself). Appetizers—North African flatbread with bean puree and spicy eggplant spreads; hot goat cheese with garlic toast and carrot salad; Provençal chickpea fries—are so good you might want to assemble them into a meal. Just be sure to leave room for dessert. The plate of cookies is a good choice, as is gingerbread.

Chez Henri. 1 Shepard St. (at Mass. Ave.). ☎ **617/354-8980.** Reservations accepted only for parties of 6 or more. Main courses $17–$24; bar food $5–$8. AE, DC, MC, V. Mon–Thurs 6–10pm; Fri–Sat 5:30–11pm; Sun 5:30–9pm; Sun brunch 11am–2pm. Bar food Mon–Sat until midnight, Sun until 10pm. T: Red Line to Harvard. FRENCH/CUBAN.

In a dark, elegant space off Mass. Ave. near Harvard Law School, Chez Henri is an example of how good fusion cuisine can be. Academic types and foodies flock here for French bistro-style food with Cuban accents. The menu changes regularly; to start, try coconut shrimp with black-bean salad, or brioche-crusted frog's legs. (This is one of the only places in the area where you can try frog's legs—no, really, they're good.) Entrees include generous portions of meat, fish, and vegetables. You might find a wood-grilled pork chop served with roasted pears and mashed potatoes, traditional Cuban paella, or layered eggplant torte. The dessert menu is a bit short on chocolate options, but I swear you won't mind—the crème brûlée is magnificent. The food at the bar is Cuban, as are the strong specialty drinks.

MODERATE

Bombay Club. In the Galleria Mall, 57 John F. Kennedy St. ☎ **617/661-8100.** Lunch buffet $7 Mon–Fri, $9–$12 Sat–Sun; main courses $5–$9 at lunch, $9–$18 at dinner. AE, CB, DC, MC, V. Daily 11:30am–11pm. T: Red Line to Harvard. INDIAN.

This third-floor spot overlooking Harvard Square gained fame through its lunch buffet, a generous assortment of some of the best items on the menu. The buffet's reasonable price and the lively daytime scene make midday the best time to dine here. At all times, the food—a wide-ranging selection of typical dishes from across the subcontinent—is fresh and flavorful. The breads, baked to perfection in a traditional charcoal-fired clay oven, and the lamb offerings are especially tasty. The "chef's recommendations" platters of assorted meat or vegetarian dishes make good samplers if you're new to the cuisine (or indecisive). If grazing isn't your thing, *rogan josh* (lamb in garlicky tomato sauce) and fiery chicken vindaloo merit ordering full portions.

Border Café. 32 Church St. ☎ **617/864-6100.** Reservations not accepted. Main courses $7–$15. AE, MC, V. Mon–Thurs 11am–1am; Fri–Sat 11am–2am; Sun noon–11pm. T: Red Line to Harvard. TEX-MEX/CAJUN.

When you first see this restaurant, your thoughts might turn to, of all people, baseball Hall of Famer Yogi Berra. He supposedly said, "Nobody goes there anymore; it's too crowded." He was talking about a New York club, but people have been saying it about this Harvard Square hangout for over 15 years. Patrons loiter at the bar for hours, enhancing the festival atmosphere. Many are waiting to be seated for generous portions of tasty, if not completely authentic, food. The menu features Tex-Mex, Cajun, and some Caribbean specialties, and the beleaguered staff keeps the chips and salsa coming. When you shout your order over the roar of the crowd, try the excellent chorizo appetizer, enchiladas (seafood are particularly delectable), any kind of tacos, or popcorn shrimp. Fajitas for one or two, sizzling noisily in a large iron frying pan, are also a popular choice. Set aside a couple of hours, be in a party mood, and ask to be seated downstairs if you want to be able to hear your companions.

INEXPENSIVE

✪ **Bartley's Burger Cottage.** 1246 Mass. Ave. ☎ **617/354-6559.** Most items under $7. No credit cards. Mon–Wed, Sat 11am–9pm; Thurs–Fri 11am–10pm. T: Red Line to Harvard. AMERICAN.

Great burgers and the best onion rings in the world make Bartley's a perennial favorite with a cross section of Cambridge, from Harvard students to regular folks. It's not a cottage, but a high-ceilinged, crowded room plastered with signs and posters (there's also a small outdoor seating area), where the waitresses might call you "honey." Burgers bear the names of local and national celebrities; the names change, but the ingredients stay the same.

Anything you can think of to put on ground beef is available, from American cheese to béarnaise sauce. There are also some good dishes that don't involve meat, notably veggie burgers and creamy, garlicky hummus. Bartley's is one of the only places in the area where you can still get a real raspberry lime rickey (raspberry syrup, lime juice, lime wedges, and club soda—the taste of summer even in the winter).

Tea-Tray in the Sky. 1796 Mass. Ave. ☎ **617/492-8327.** Reservations not accepted. Main courses $5–$12.75. AE, DISC, MC, V. Tues–Fri 10am–10pm; Sat 10am–11pm; Sun 10am–7pm. Closed Sun in summer. T: Red Line to Porter. AMERICAN/TEAROOM.

This cozy little storefront is a perfect stop for a meal or snack on a shopping expedition north of Harvard Square. Lavishly decorated with tea-related accessories and original art (much of it for sale), the room seats just 20. The encyclopedic tea menu encompasses the familiar and the exotic (white tea, several kinds of *chai*) and accompanies an extensive food menu. The baked goods, all made in-house, are as fresh as can be—arrive early enough and you might have to wait for your sandwich until the bread cools off. Salads, soups, and sandwiches served on focaccia (including a superb tuna melt) are so delectable that you might forget to save room for the cakes, tarts, scones, and other pastries. Try anything involving chocolate, and be prepared to share. Oh, and the name? It's a tribute to *Alice's Adventures in Wonderland*—check out the mural at the front of the room.

OUTSIDE HARVARD SQUARE
EXPENSIVE

Jae's (see "Chinatown/Theater District," above) has a restaurant at 1281 Cambridge St., Inman Square (☎ 617/497-8380). There's a **Legal Sea Foods** (see "Back Bay," above) at 5 Cambridge Center, Kendall Square (☎ 617/864-3400).

✪ **The Blue Room.** 1 Kendall Sq. ☎ **617/494-9034.** www.blueroom.net. Reservations recommended. Main courses $16–$22. AE, DC, DISC, MC, V. Sun–Thurs 5:30–10pm; Fri–Sat 5:30–11pm; Sun brunch 11am–2:30pm. Validated parking available. T: Red Line to Kendall/MIT; 10-min. walk. ECLECTIC.

The Blue Room sits just below plaza level in an office-retail complex, a slice of foodie paradise in high-tech heaven. Its out-of-the-way location means it doesn't get as much publicity as it deserves, but it's one of the very best restaurants in the Boston area. The cuisine is a rousing combination of top-notch ingredients and layers of aggressive flavors, the service is excellent, and the crowded dining room is not as noisy as you might fear when you first spy it through the glass front wall. Upholstered banquettes, carpeting, and draperies help soften the din, but this is still not a place for cooing lovers—it's a place for food lovers, who savor co-owner Steve Johnson's regularly changing menu.

Appetizers range from salad with an assertive vinaigrette to seared scallops with hoisin and sesame to summer vegetables served with a lemony aïoli. Entrees tend to be roasted, grilled, or braised, with at least two vegetarian choices. The roast chicken, served with garlic mashed potatoes, is world-class. Grilled tuna appears often, and pork loin with cider glaze will make you think twice the next time you skip over pork on a menu to get to the steak. In warm weather, there's seating on the brick patio.

✪ **Dalí.** 415 Washington St., Somerville. ☎ **617/661-3254.** www.DaliRestaurant.com. Reservations not accepted. Tapas $3.50–$7.50; main courses $17–$22. AE, DC, MC, V. Daily winter 5:30–11pm; summer 6–11pm. T: Red Line to Harvard; follow Kirkland St. to intersection of Washington and Beacon sts. (20 min.). SPANISH.

Dalí casts an irresistible spell—it's noisy and crowded, it doesn't take reservations, it's not all that close to Harvard Square (but it's a short cab ride), and it still fills with people cheerfully waiting an hour or more for a table. The bar offers plenty to look at while you wait, including a clothesline festooned with lingerie. The payoff is authentic Spanish food, notably tapas, little plates of hot or cold creations that burst with flavor.

Entrees include excellent paella, but most people come in a group and cut a swath through the delectable tapas offerings—32 on the menu and 9 monthly specials, all perfect for sharing. They include *patatas ali-oli* (garlic potatoes), *albóndigas de salmón* (salmon balls with not-too-salty caper sauce), *setas al ajillo* (sautéed mushrooms), and *lomito al cabrales* (pork tenderloin with blue goat cheese and mushrooms). The helpful staff sometimes seems rushed but never fails to supply bread for sopping up juices and sangria for washing it all down. If you want to experiment and order in stages, that's fine. Finish up with excellent flan, or try the super-rich *tarta de chocolates* (order your own if you like chocolate).

The owners of Dalí also run **Tapéo** at 266 Newbury St. (☎ **617/267-4799**), between Fairfield and Dartmouth streets in Boston's **Back Bay.** It offers the same menu and similarly wacky decor in a more sedate two-level setting.

East Coast Grill. 1271 Cambridge St. ☎ **617/491-6568.** Reservations accepted only for parties of 5 or more, Sun–Thurs. Main courses $13.50–$30; sandwich plates $7.50–$8.50. AE, DISC, MC, V. Sun–Thurs 5:30–10pm; Fri–Sat 5:30–10:30pm; Sun brunch 11am–2:30pm. T: Red Line to Harvard, then no. 69 (Harvard–Lechmere) bus to Inman Sq. Or Red Line to Central, 10-min. walk on Prospect St. SEAFOOD/BARBECUE.

Funky decor, country and rock music, huge portions, and a dizzying menu make the East Coast Grill madly popular. The kitchen handles fresh seafood (an encyclopedic variety), barbecue, and grilled fish and meats with equal authority. The influence of founder Chris Schlesinger, a national expert on grilling and spicy food, is apparent in the exuberant menu descriptions—"fried, freshest available, local, underappreciated fish of the day," "grilled jerk pork cutlet from hell!" To start, check out the raw bar offerings, or try mussels steamed in coconut milk with chiles and lime. The seafood entrees are exceptional, and barbecue comes on abundant platters in three styles: Texas beef, Memphis spareribs, and North Carolina pork. Should you have room for dessert, know that a certifiable Key lime pie fiend has pledged allegiance to the great slab served here. One quibble: Service is friendly but far more casual than you'd expect— not inattentive, exactly, but less helpful as the meal wears on. Considering how full you'll be, though, you might not care.

MODERATE
The **Elephant Walk** (see "Kenmore Square to Brookline," above) has a restaurant at 2067 Mass. Ave., Porter Square (☎ **617/492-6900**).

The Great Outdoors: Picnic Food

With its acres of waterfront property, Boston is the perfect place for a meal or snack. For a classic experience, pick up takeout from the Colonnade food court at **Faneuil Hall Marketplace** and cross the street under the Expressway. Walk past the Marriott to the end of Long Wharf and eat on the plaza as you watch the boats and planes, or walk around to the left of the hotel and eat in Christopher Columbus Park overlooking the marina.

In the **Financial District**, the **Milk Street Café** operates a kiosk (☎ **617/ 350-7275**) in the park at Zero Post Office Square. Its strictly kosher offerings include salads, meat sandwiches (on bread and rolled up in pita), fish dishes, fruit, and pastries. Eat in the park, or head to the harbor.

On the Cambridge side of the river, **Harvard Square** is close enough to the water to allow a riverside repast. For many years before wraps were trendy, **Stuff-Its**, 8¹/₂ Eliot St. (☎ **617/497-2220**), was serving delectable sandwiches rolled up in pita. (Watch out for the incredibly strong onions.) Take yours to John F. Kennedy Park, on Memorial Drive and Kennedy Street, or right to the riverbank.

On the way to a concert or movie on the Esplanade (also along the river, on the Boston side), stop at the foot of **Beacon Hill** for provisions. **Savenor's Supermarket,** 160 Charles St. (☎ **617/723-6328**), carries all you need for a do-it-yourself feast. Or call ahead to **Figs**, 42 Charles St. (☎ **617/742-3447**), a minuscule pizzeria that's an offshoot of the celebrated Olives. The upscale fare isn't cheap, but avoiding that long line is worth the price—as is the delectable pizza.

✪ **Green Street Grill.** 280 Green St. ☎ **617/876-1655.** www.2nite.com/greenstreet. Reservations not accepted. Main courses $14–$19. AE, MC, V. Daily 6–10pm. T: Red Line to Central Sq. CARIBBEAN/SEAFOOD.

Out-of-towners lean in close and ask conspiratorially, "Where do people who live around here *really* go?" If the no-frills atmosphere won't put them off, I whisper this name. It's basically a bar (and not a very promising-looking one, either) where the food is among the tastiest and hottest in town. If you can take the heat, you'll be in heaven; if not, you might feel like a cartoon character with flames licking out of your ears. Some dishes have as many as five kinds of peppers. Red-wine and squid-ink fettuccine with shrimp, scallops, and squid will clear that head cold right up, and I'd walk a mile for the yellowfin tuna. Not everything is completely incendiary—the helpful staff can steer you in the right direction. Grilled seafood is also done well, and there's a wide variety of beers to help put out the fire.

✪ **The Helmand.** 143 First St. ☎ **617/492-4646.** Reservations recommended. Main courses $9–$16. AE, MC, V. Sun–Thurs 5–10pm; Fri–Sat 5–11pm. T: Green Line to Lechmere. AFGHAN.

Even in cosmopolitan Cambridge, Afghan food is a novelty, and if any competitors are setting their sights on the Helmand, they're contemplating a daunting task. The elegant setting belies the reasonable prices at this spacious spot near the Cambridge-Side Galleria mall. The courteous staff patiently answers questions about the unusual cuisine, which is distinctly Middle Eastern with Indian and Pakistani influences. Many dishes are vegetarian, and meat is often one element of a dish rather than the centerpiece. Every meal comes with delectable bread made while you watch in a wood-fired brick oven.

To start, you might try the slightly sweet baked pumpkin topped with a spicy ground meat sauce—a great contrast of flavors and textures—or *aushak*, pasta pockets filled with leeks or potatoes and buried under a sauce of split peas and carrots. Aushak, also available as a main course, can be prepared with meat sauce as well. Other entrees include several versions of what Americans would call stew, including *deygee kabob*, an excellent mélange of lamb, yellow split peas, onion, and red peppers. For dessert, don't miss the Afghan version of baklava.

La Groceria Ristorante Italiano. 853 Main St., Central Sq. ☎ **617/497-4214.** Reservations recommended at dinner. Main courses $6–$10 at lunch; $11–$18 at dinner. Pizzas $6.25–$10. Children's menu $7. AE, CB, DC, DISC, MC, V. Mon–Fri 11:30am–4pm; Mon–Thurs 4–10pm; Fri–Sat 4–11pm; Sun 1–10pm. Valet parking available on weekends. T: Red Line to Central Sq. ITALIAN.

The Mastromauro family has dished up large portions of delicious Italian food at this colorful, welcoming restaurant since 1972. You'll see business meetings at lunch, family outings at dinner, and students and bargain-hunters at all times. Cheery voices bounce off the stucco walls and tile floors, but it seldom gets terribly noisy, probably because everyone's mouth is full. You might start with the house garlic bread, lavished with chopped tomato, red onion, fennel seed, and olive oil. The antipasto platter overflows with the chef's choice of meats, cheeses, and roasted vegetables. Main dishes might include homemade pasta from the machine you see as you enter—the daily specials are always good bets. Lasagna (a vegetarian version) is an excellent choice, as are lobster ravioli and savory chicken marsala. Chicken also comes roasted, and 10 varieties of brick-oven pizza are available in individual and large sizes.

✪ Midwest Grill. 1122 Cambridge St. ☎ **617/354-7536.** Reservations recommended Mon–Thurs; accepted only for parties of 8 or more Fri–Sun. *Rodizio* $18.95; main courses $11.95–$14.95. AE, DISC, MC, V. Daily 11:30am–11:30pm. T: Red Line to Harvard, then no. 69 (Harvard–Lechmere) bus just past Inman Sq. Or Red Line to Central, 10-min. walk on Prospect St. BRAZILIAN.

As soon as you open the door of the Midwest Grill, the aroma of garlic and meat starts your mouth watering. Distractions abound: personable waiters, lively music, the salad bar–like selection of side dishes (superb potatoes, black-bean stew, salads, olives, and rice). But you can't ignore the scent of meat juices dripping onto an open fire. Finally, here come the waiters, bearing the long, swordlike skewers of meat that make up *rodizio*, or Brazilian barbecue. They slice off portions of perfectly grilled pork, lamb, or beef, as you help with salad tongs. They return with linguiça sausage, chicken, and even chicken hearts. Take a break and check out the families, students, and other carnivores around you, then flag down a circulating waiter and dig in again.

✪ Redbones. 55 Chester St. (off Elm St.), Somerville. ☎ **617/628-2200.** www.redbonesbbq.com. Reservations accepted only for parties of 11 or more, Sun–Thurs. Main courses $7–$15. No credit cards. Sun–Thurs noon–10:30pm; Fri–Sat noon–11:30pm (lunch until 4pm, late-night menu until 12:30am). T: Red Line to Davis. BARBECUE.

Geographically, this raucous restaurant is in Somerville, but it's *really* on a back road in Texas or Arkansas or someplace like that—where the sun is hot, the beer is cold, and a big slab of meat is done to a turn. Barbecued ribs (Memphis, Texas, and Arkansas style), smoked beef brisket, fried Louisiana catfish, and grilled chicken come with appropriate side dishes alone or in any combination you want. The chummy staff can help you choose sweet, hot, mild, or vinegar sauce. Portions are large, so pace yourself. You'll want to try the wonderful appetizers and sides—catfish "catfingers," buffalo shrimp served with blue cheese sauce, creamy corn pudding—and desserts, especially pecan pie. There's a huge selection of beers, and valet parking for your bicycle in warm weather. Given a choice, sit upstairs—Underbones, downstairs, is more of a bar.

INEXPENSIVE

✪ **S&S Restaurant.** 1334 Cambridge St., Inman Sq. ☎ **617/354-0777.** www.sandsrestaurant.com. Main courses $4–$13. No credit cards. Mon–Wed 7am–11pm, Thurs–Fri 7am–midnight, Sat 8am–midnight, Sun 8am–10pm; brunch Sat–Sun 8am–4pm. T: Red Line to Harvard, then no. 69 (Harvard–Lechmere) bus to Inman Sq. Or Red Line to Central, 10-min. walk on Prospect St. DELI.

Es is Yiddish for "eat," and this Cambridge classic is as straightforward as its name ("eat and eat"). Founded in 1919 by the great-grandmother of the current owners, the wildly popular brunch spot draws what seems to be half of Cambridge at busy times on weekends. It's northeast of Harvard Square, west of MIT, and worth a visit during the week, too. With huge windows and lots of light wood and plants, it looks contemporary, but the brunch offerings run to the likes of traditional pancakes, waffles, fruit salad, and fantastic omelets. After noon, you can order an excellent bloody Mary. Bagels were a tasty staple here long before they were available at every corner store, and you'll also find traditional deli items (corned beef, pastrami, tongue, potato pancakes, and blintzes), and breakfast anytime. Be early for brunch, or plan to spend a good chunk of your Saturday or Sunday standing around people watching and getting hungry.

What to See & Do in Boston

7

Whether you want to follow in the footsteps of Paul Revere or Ally McBeal, Boston offers something for everyone, and plenty of it. Throw out your preconceptions of the city as some sort of open-air history museum—although that's certainly one of the guises it can assume—and allow your interests to dictate where you go. It's possible but not advisable to take in most major attractions in 2 or 3 days if you don't linger anywhere too long. For a more enjoyable and less rushed visit, plan fewer activities and spend more time on them.

There's nothing prefab about Boston, and the most popular way to soak up the atmosphere of living history is to walk the ✪ **Freedom Trail.** For complete descriptions of the 16 destinations and the 3-mile path that links them, see chapter 8.

Travelers in 2001 can visit a new immigration museum, walk and ride along new visitor trails, and take a 200-mile hike. At press time the museum, known as the **Dreams of Freedom Center,** was scheduled to open on the Freedom Trail (see chapter 8) in the summer of 2000. Four heritage trails that complement the Freedom Trail are evolving; the first two are the **Literary Trail** (see "Specialty Tours," below) and **Boston by Sea** (see "Guided Walking Tours"). The newly configured **Bay Circuit Trail** (see "Hiking"), a beltway of conservation land through two dozen Boston suburbs, has become a reality.

Return visitors will find as many as three popular attractions missing. In 1999, the internationally renowned **Computer Museum** closed its downtown location; its collections are now part of the **Museum of Science.** And two attractions that were under renovation at press time should have reopened, but the projects are taking longer than originally expected. Be sure to call ahead before visiting the glass **Mapparium** at the world headquarters of the First Church of Christ, Scientist (see "More Museums & Attractions"), and the **Longfellow National Historic Site** (see "Historic Houses").

Suggested Itineraries

If You Have 1 Day

Sample some experiences unique to Boston—you won't have time to immerse yourself, but you can touch on several singular attractions. Follow part of the **Freedom Trail** (see chapter 8) on your own from

Let's Make a Deal

As you plan your sightseeing, remember that visitors (and residents, for that matter) have access to valuable money-saving offers. If you'll be in town for more than a day or so, you'll want an **Arts/Boston coupon book** (☎ 617/423-4454, press "3"; www.boston.com/artsboston). It offers discounts on admission to many area museums and attractions. Couples and families can take advantage of the reduced rates for—among many others—the Museum of Fine Arts, New England Aquarium, Kennedy Library, Massachusetts Bay Lines cruises, and Beantown and Old Town trolleys. It's not worth the money (currently $9) for single travelers because many of the coupons offer two-for-one deals. They're on sale at **BosTix** booths (☎ 617/423-4454; www.boston.com/artsboston) at Faneuil Hall Marketplace (on the south side of Faneuil Hall) and in Copley Square (at the corner of Boylston and Dartmouth streets).

If you plan to concentrate on the included attractions, a **CityPass** offers great savings. It's a booklet of tickets (so you can go straight to the entrance) to the Isabella Stewart Gardner Museum, Kennedy Library, John Hancock Observatory, New England Aquarium, Museum of Fine Arts, and Museum of Science. The price—at press time, adults $30.25; seniors $22.25; youths 12 to 17 $14—offers a 50% savings if you visit all six. It feels like an even better deal on a steamy day when the line at the Aquarium is long. The passes, good for 9 days from the date of purchase, are on sale at participating attractions, at the Boston Common and Prudential Center visitor information centers, through the Greater Boston Convention & Visitors Bureau (☎ 800/SEE-BOSTON), through some hotel concierge desks, and from www.citypass.net.

Even if you're visiting for only one day, the MBTA's **visitor passport** (☎ 617/222-5218; www.mbta.com) can be a good deal. See "Getting Around" in chapter 4.

Boston Common to **Faneuil Hall Marketplace.** Alternatively, National Park Service rangers lead free 90-minute tours from the Visitor Center, 15 State St. (☎ 617/242-5642; www.nps.gov/bost). They start as often as four times a day during busy periods, once daily in the winter. They cover the "heart" of the trail, from the Old South Meeting House to the Old North Church. You don't need a reservation, but call for schedules. **Boston By Foot** (☎ 617/367-2345; www.bostonbyfoot.com) also offers a "Heart of the Freedom Trail" tour at 10am Tuesday through Saturday in warm weather. Tickets are $8, and you don't need reservations. Then launch a picnic with takeout food from Faneuil Hall Marketplace or the North End. Head toward the plaza at the end of Long Wharf (pass the Marriott and keep going to the end of the wharf) or in Christopher Columbus Park (across Atlantic Avenue from the marketplace).

If you'd rather eat indoors, stay at the marketplace and have lunch at **Durgin-Park,** or go across the street to **Ye Olde Union Oyster House** (see chapter 6). In the afternoon, complete your independent Freedom Trail foray in the **North End** and take a **sightseeing cruise** from Long Wharf or Rowes Wharf. Or cruise and then explore the **New England Aquarium** or the **Children's Museum.** Or skip the afternoon sightseeing altogether and go shopping on Newbury Street or at Downtown Crossing, home to Filene's Basement. Feast in a fine restaurant in Boston or Cambridge (see chapter 6 for suggestions), then enjoy a panoramic view of Boston by night from the **John Hancock Observatory** or the **Prudential Center Skywalk** (see "On Top of the World," below).

If You Have 2 Days

On the first day, follow the suggestions for 1 day or pick and choose—you can spend more time along the Freedom Trail, on a longer harbor cruise, or at another destination. On the second day, branch out a little, again letting your preferences be your guide. Spend the morning at the **Museum of Fine Arts** and have lunch there or at the **Isabella Stewart Gardner Museum.** Start the afternoon at the Gardner Museum or, if it's a Friday during the season, at the **Boston Symphony Orchestra** (see chapter 10). If art isn't your passion, the **Museum of Science** or the **John F. Kennedy Library and Museum** might be a better choice, followed by lunch at the Prudential Center and a **Duck Tour.**

Then make a leisurely trek around the **Back Bay** (see chapter 8) or a high-intensity shopping trip to **Newbury Street** (see chapter 9). On summer weekdays, **Boston By Foot** (see above) conducts a tour of **Beacon Hill** that starts at the State House at 5:30pm. Decompress with dinner in the North End, then coffee and dessert at a caffè. The **Comedy Connection** at Faneuil Hall is nearby if you want to cap off the day with some laughs. Or dress up for dinner and enjoy dessert and dancing at the **Custom House Lounge** at the Bay Tower, or a drink and a dance in the lounge at **Top of the Hub,** on the Prudential Center's 52nd floor.

If You Have 3 Days

The options seem to expand to fill the time you have. The suggestions for the first 2 days can easily fill another day, but you'll probably want to explore farther afield. A visit to **Cambridge** is the logical next step. Ride the MBTA Red Line or the no. 1 bus to Harvard Square. Take a walking tour (see chapter 8), squeeze in some shopping, or head straight to one of the university's museum complexes. Have lunch in Harvard Square and continue exploring, or visit **Mount Auburn Cemetery** (see "Celebrity Cemetery," below). Or rent a car and range even farther from the city. You might start in Cambridge and have lunch in **Lexington** or **Concord** (see chapter 11). Spend the afternoon learning about the area's historical or literary legacy, or communing with nature at **Walden Pond.** Without wheels, you can use public transportation to reach Lexington or Concord but not to travel between them—forced to choose, history buffs opt for Lexington, literary types for Concord. Have dinner in Cambridge or Boston, then enjoy live music at the **Hatch Shell,** a jazz or rock club, or the **House of Blues.**

If You Have 4 Days or More

Now you're cooking. Having scratched the surface in the first 3 days, you'll have a better sense of what you want to explore more extensively. Check out other Boston

---

One Singular Sensation

On a 1-day visit, consider concentrating on **one or two things** you're most excited about (plus a good meal or two). If what really gets you going is the Museum of Fine Arts, the Museum of Science, the Newbury Street art galleries, or even a day trip (see chapter 11), you have a built-in excuse for not doing more—and for a return trip to Boston!

Boston Attractions

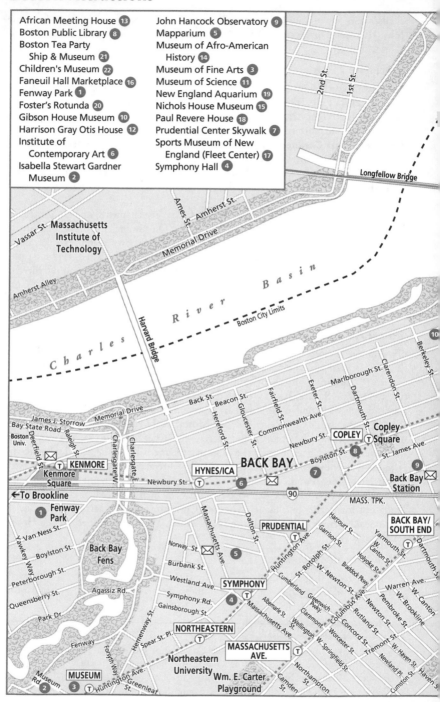

African Meeting House ⑬
Boston Public Library ⑧
Boston Tea Party
  Ship & Museum ㉑
Children's Museum ㉒
Faneuil Hall Marketplace ⑯
Fenway Park ①
Foster's Rotunda ⑳
Gibson House Museum ⑩
Harrison Gray Otis House ⑫
Institute of
  Contemporary Art ⑥
Isabella Stewart Gardner
  Museum ②
John Hancock Observatory ⑨
Mapparium ⑤
Museum of Afro-American
  History ⑭
Museum of Fine Arts ③
Museum of Science ⑪
New England Aquarium ⑲
Nichols House Museum ⑮
Paul Revere House ⑱
Prudential Center Skywalk ⑦
Sports Museum of New
  England (Fleet Center) ⑰
Symphony Hall ④

Longfellow Bridge

Vassar St.
Ames St.
Amherst St.
Amherst St.
Massachusetts Institute of Technology
Memorial Drive

2nd St.
1st St.

Charles River Basin

Memorial Drive
Harvard Bridge
Boston City Limits

Amherst Alley

James J. Storrow
Bay State Road
Memorial Drive
Boston Univ.
Deerfield St.
Raleigh St.
Back St.
Beacon St.
Gloucester St.
Hereford St.
Fairfield St.
Commonwealth Ave.
Exeter St.
Marlborough St.
Clarendon St.
Dartmouth St.
Berkeley St.

10

KENMORE
Kenmore Square
Charlesgate E.
Charlesgate W.

Newbury St.
BACK BAY
Newbury St.
Boylston St.
COPLEY Copley Square
St. James Ave.
8

HYNES/ICA
6

9
Back Bay Station

←To Brookline

① **Fenway Park**

90
MASS. TPK.

BACK BAY/ SOUTH END

Van Ness St.
Yawkey Way
Boylston St.
Peterborough St.
Queensberry St.
Park Dr.

Back Bay Fens
Agassiz Rd.
Norway St.
Burbank St.
Westland Ave.

Dalton St.
Massachusetts Ave.

PRUDENTIAL
5

Harcourt St.
Garrison St.
Huntington Ave.
Botolph St.
Cumberland St.
W. Newton St.
Greenwich Pkwy.
Columbus Ave.
Braddock Pkwy.
Holyoke St.
W. Canton St.
Yarmouth St.
W. Canton St.
Dartmouth St.

Warren Ave.
W. Canton St.
W. Brookline
Pembroke St.
Rutland St.
Concord St.

SYMPHONY
Symphony Rd.
Gainsborough St.
4
Albemarle St.
Wellington St.
Clearmont St.
W. Newton St.
Worcester St.
W. Springfield St.
W. Concord St.
Tremont St.
Newland St.
W. Haven St.
Haven St.

NORTHEASTERN
Hemenway St.
Forsyth Way
Spear St. Pl.
Fenway
Forsyth St.

MASSACHUSETTS AVE.
Northampton St.
Camden St.

Northeastern University
MUSEUM
Museum Rd.
2
3
Huntington Ave.
Greenleaf St.
Wm. E. Carter Playground
Cumston St.

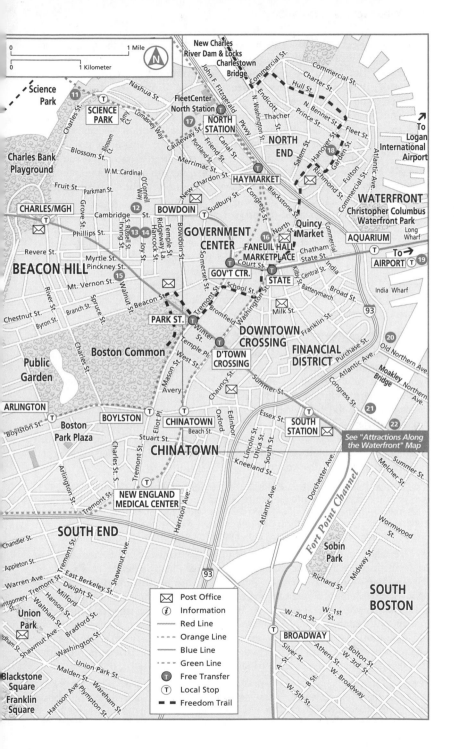

139

attractions that catch your fancy, perhaps including one or more of the historic **house museums,** and plan a full day trip—to Lexington and Concord, to **Plymouth,** to **Marblehead** and **Salem,** or to **Gloucester** and **Rockport.** Visit Museum Wharf, where you'll find the **Children's Museum** and the **Boston Tea Party Ship & Museum.** If you haven't taken a sightseeing cruise, try one that goes to Charlestown, where you can explore USS *Constitution* and **Bunker Hill.** Go on a **whale watch** or make an unstructured visit to a city **neighborhood** (see "Boston Neighborhoods to Explore," below). Take in a show at the Museum of Science, or evaluate Boston's reputation as a great **sports** town by attending a pro or college event. And if you're just plain sick of sightseeing, don't worry—you're not alone. An excellent antidote in the summer is a daylong **cruise to Provincetown,** at the tip of Cape Cod. A boat leaves Boston at 9am and arrives at noon, giving you 3¹/₂ hours in P-Town before the trip back. (There's also a high-speed option that takes an hour less and costs more than twice as much.) You'll have time for world-class people watching, strolling around the novelty shops and art galleries, lunching on seafood, and—if you're quick—a short trip to the famous beaches. You'll have to forgo the hopping gay nightlife scene unless you've planned a longer excursion, however. (For in-depth coverage of Provincetown and other Cape Cod locales, consult *Frommer's New England* or *Frommer's Cape Cod, Nantucket & Martha's Vineyard.*) You'll return to Boston at 6:30pm. Have dinner on or near the waterfront and start planning your next trip.

1 The Top Attractions

The establishments in this section are easily accessible by **public transportation;** given the difficulty and expense of parking, it's preferable to take the T everywhere. Even the Kennedy Library, which has a large free parking lot, has a free shuttle bus that connects it to the Red Line. To maximize your enjoyment, try to go to any attraction during relatively slow times. If possible, especially in the summer, try to do your sightseeing on weekdays; if you're traveling without children, aim for times when school is in session. And if you're visiting on a weekend in July or August, relax and try to convince yourself that you love crowds.

Boston Tea Party Ship & Museum. Congress Street Bridge. ☎ **617/338-1773.** www.historictours.com/boston/teaparty.htm. Admission $8 adults, $7 students, $4 children 4–12, free for children under 4. Mar–Nov daily 9am–dusk (about 6pm in summer, 5pm in spring and fall). Closed Dec–Feb. T: Red Line to South Station. Walk north on Atlantic Ave. 1 block, past the Federal Reserve Bank, turn right onto Congress St., and walk 1 block.

On December 16, 1773, a public meeting of independent-minded Bostonians led to the symbolic act of resistance commemorated here. The brig *Beaver II* is a full-size replica of one of the three merchant ships loaded with tea that stood at anchor that night. After assembling at the Old South Meeting House, colonists poorly disguised as Indians emptied the vessels' cargo into the harbor. The ship sits alongside a museum with exhibits on the "tea party." The audio and video displays (including a 15-min. film), dioramas, and information panels tell the story of the uprising. You can dump a bale of tea into Boston Harbor—a museum staffer retrieves it—and drink some complimentary tax-free tea (iced in summer, hot in winter).

✪ **Faneuil Hall Marketplace.** Between North, Congress, and State sts. and I-93. ☎ **617/ 338-2323.** Marketplace Mon–Sat 10am–9pm; Sun noon–6pm. Colonnade food court opens earlier; some restaurants open early for Sun brunch and close at 2am daily. T: Green Line to Government Center, Orange Line to State or Haymarket, or Blue Line to State or Aquarium.

Attractions Along the Waterfront

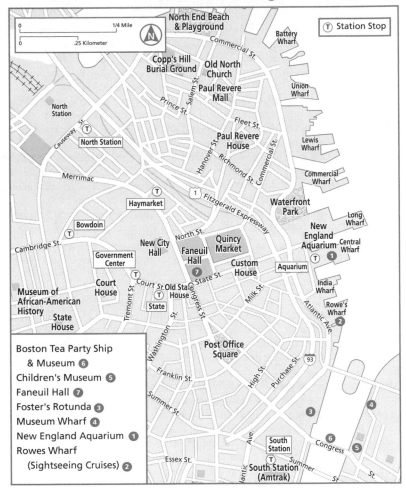

It's impossible to overstate the effect of Faneuil Hall Marketplace on Boston's economy and reputation. A daring idea when it opened in 1976, the "festival market" has been widely imitated, and each new complex of shops, food stands, restaurants, bars, and public spaces in urban centers around the country reflects its city. Faneuil Hall Marketplace, brimming with Boston flavor and regional goods and souvenirs, is no exception. Its success with tourists and suburbanites is so great, in fact, that you could be forgiven for thinking that the only Bostonians in the crowd are employees.

The marketplace includes five buildings—the central three-building complex is on the National Register of Historic Places—set on brick and stone plazas that teem with crowds shopping, eating, performing, watching performers, and just people-watching. **Quincy Market** (you'll hear the whole complex called by that name as well) is the central three-level Greek revival–style building. It reopened after extensive renovations on August 26, 1976, 150 years of hard use after Mayor Josiah Quincy opened the original market. The **South Market building** reopened on August 26, 1977, the **North Market building** on August 26, 1978.

The central corridor of Quincy Market, known as the **Colonnade,** is the food court, where you can find anything from a bagel to a full Greek dinner, a fruit smoothie to a hunk of fudge. On either side, under the glass canopies, pushcarts hold everything from crafts created by New England artisans to hokey souvenirs. In the plaza between the **South Canopy** and the South Market building is an **information kiosk,** and throughout the complex you'll find an enticing mix of chain stores and unique shops (see chapter 9). On summer evenings, the tables that spill outdoors from the restaurants and bars fill with people. One constant since the year after the market—the *original* market—opened is **Durgin-Park,** a traditional New England restaurant with traditionally crabby waitresses (see chapter 6).

✪ **Faneuil Hall** itself sometimes gets overlooked, but it's well worth a visit. Known as the "Cradle of Liberty" for its role as a center of inspirational (some might say inflammatory) speech in the years leading to the Revolutionary War, the building opened in 1742 and was expanded using a Charles Bulfinch design in 1805. National Park Service rangers give **free 20-minute talks** every half hour from 9am to 5pm in the second-floor auditorium, which, after a recent refurbishment, is in mint condition.

✪ **Isabella Stewart Gardner Museum.** 280 The Fenway. ☎ **617/566-1401.** www.boston.com/gardner. Admission $11 adults weekends, $10 adults weekdays; $7 seniors, $5 college students with valid ID, $3 college students on Wed, free for children under 18. Tues–Sun, some Mon holidays 11am–5pm. T: Green Line E to Museum.

Isabella Stewart Gardner (1840–1924) was an incorrigible individualist long before such behavior was acceptable for a woman in polite Boston society, and her iconoclasm has paid off for art lovers. "Mrs. Jack" designed her exquisite home in the style of a 15th-century Venetian palace and filled it with European, American, and Asian painting and sculpture, much chosen with the help of her friend and protégé Bernard Berenson. You'll see works by Titian, Botticelli, Raphael, Rembrandt, Matisse, and Mrs. Gardner's friends James McNeill Whistler and John Singer Sargent. Titian's magnificent *Europa,* which many scholars consider his finest work, is one of the most important Renaissance paintings in the United States.

The building, which opened to the public after Mrs. Gardner's death, holds a hodgepodge of furniture and architectural details imported from European churches and palaces. The pièce de résistance is the magnificent skylit courtyard, filled year-round with fresh flowers from the museum greenhouse. Although the terms of Mrs. Gardner's will forbid changing the arrangement of the museum's content, there has been some evolution: A special exhibition gallery, which opened in 1992, features two or three changing shows a year, often by contemporary artists in residence.

See chapter 10 for a description of the ✪ **concert series** (☎ **617/734-1359**). The cafe serves lunch and desserts, and unique items are available at the gift shop.

✪ **John F. Kennedy Library and Museum.** Columbia Point. ☎ **617/929-4523.** www.cs.umb.edu/jfklibrary. Admission $8 adults, $6 seniors and students with ID, $4 youths 13–17, free for children under 13. Daily 9am–5pm (last film begins at 3:55pm). T: Red Line to JFK/UMass, then take free shuttle bus, which runs every 20 min. By car, take Southeast Expressway (I-93/Rte. 3) south to Exit 15 (Morrissey Blvd./JFK Library), turn left onto Columbia Rd., and follow signs to free parking lot.

The Kennedy era springs to life at this dramatic library, museum, and educational research complex overlooking Dorchester Bay. It captures the 35th president's accomplishments and legacy in sound and video recordings and fascinating displays of memorabilia and photos. Far from being a static experience, it changes regularly, with temporary shows and reinterpreted displays that highlight and complement the permanent exhibits.

More JFK

For details about visiting President Kennedy's birthplace in suburban Brookline, see "Historic Houses," below.

Your visit begins with a 17-minute film narrated by John F. Kennedy—a detail that seems eerie for a moment, then perfectly natural. Through skillfully edited audio clips, he discusses his childhood, education, war experience, and early political career. Then you enter the museum to spend as much time as you like on each exhibit. Starting with the 1960 presidential campaign, you're immersed in the era. The connected galleries hold campaign souvenirs, a film of Kennedy debating Richard Nixon and delivering his inaugural address, a replica of the Oval Office, gifts from foreign dignitaries, letters, documents, and keepsakes. There's a film about the Cuban Missile Crisis, and displays on the civil rights movement, the Peace Corps, the space program, and the Kennedy family. Expanded exhibits focus on First Lady Jacqueline Bouvier Kennedy and Attorney General Robert F. Kennedy. As the tour winds down, you pass through a darkened chamber where news reports of John Kennedy's assassination and funeral play.

From the final room, the soaring glass-enclosed pavilion that is the heart of the I. M. Pei design, there's a glorious view of the water and the Boston skyline. In the summer, JFK's boyhood sailboat, *Victura,* sits on a strip of dune grass between the library and the harbor.

✪ **Museum of Fine Arts.** 465 Huntington Ave. ☎ **617/267-9300.** www.mfa.org. Adults $12 when entire museum is open, $10 when only West Wing is open. Students and seniors $10 when entire museum is open, $9 when only West Wing is open. Children 7–17 $5 on school days before 3pm, otherwise free. Voluntary contribution Wed 4–9:45pm. Surcharges may apply for special exhibitions. No admission fee to visit only the Museum Shop, library, restaurants, or auditoriums. Entire museum Mon–Tues 10am–4:45pm, Wed 10am–9:45pm, Thurs–Fri 10am–5pm, Sat–Sun 10am–5:45pm; West Wing only, Thurs–Fri 5–9:45pm. T: Green Line E to Museum, or Orange Line to Ruggles.

Not content with the MFA's reputation as the second-best art museum in the country (after New York's Metropolitan Museum of Art), the management team works nonstop to make the collections more accessible and interesting. Recent moves to raise the museum's profile have included mounting even more top-notch exhibitions, expanding educational programs, and opening new permanent galleries for the art of Africa, Oceania, and the ancient Americas.

The museum's not-so-secret weapon in its quest is a powerful one: its magnificent collections. Every installation reflects a curatorial attitude that makes even those who go in with a sense of obligation leave with a sense of discovery and wonder. The MFA is especially noted for its Impressionist paintings (including 43 Monets—the largest collection outside Paris), Asian and Old Kingdom Egyptian collections, classical art, Buddhist temple, and medieval sculpture and tapestries. It's also expanding its modern and contemporary art collections.

The works you might find more familiar are paintings and sculpture by Americans and Europeans. Some favorites: Renoir's *Dance at Bougival,* Van Gogh's *Postman Joseph Roulin,* Childe Hassam's *Boston Common at Twilight,* Gilbert Stuart's 1796 portrait of George Washington, John Singleton Copley's 1768 portrait of Paul Revere, a bronze casting of Edgar Degas's sculpture *Little Dancer,* John Singer Sargent's *The Daughters of Edward Darley Boit,* and Fitz Hugh Lane's Luminist masterpieces. There are also magnificent print and photography collections, and that's not even touching on the furnishings and decorative arts, including the finest collection of Paul Revere silver in the world.

MFA FYI

The Huntington Avenue entrance to the Museum of Fine Arts is usually much less busy than the West Wing lobby. Walk back along Huntington Avenue when you leave the T, enter from the curved driveway, and stop to take in the recently restored murals by John Singer Sargent.

I. M. Pei designed the West Wing (1981), the latest addition to the original 1909 structure. It contains the main entrance, an auditorium, and an atrium with a tree-lined "sidewalk" cafe. The excellent Museum Shop carries the full range of souvenirs and a huge selection of art books. The museum has two restaurants: the cafe and a cafeteria. Pick up a floor plan at the information desk, or take a free guided tour (weekdays except Monday holidays at 10:30am and 1:30pm, Wednesday at 6:15pm, Saturday at 10:30am and 1pm).

A special note: Visitors from November 5, 2000, to February 24, 2001, can see ***Dangerous Curves: The Art of the Guitar,*** an exhibition of more than 120 instruments from the early 17th to late 20th century. Check ahead for schedules of concerts (all around town, not just at the museum) that show off the guitar's range.

✪ **Museum of Science.** Science Park. ☎ **617/723-2500.** www.mos.org. Admission to exhibit halls $10 adults, $7 seniors and children 3–11, free for children under 3. To Mugar Omni Theater, Hayden Planetarium, or laser shows, $7.50 adults, $5.50 seniors and children 3–11, free for children under 3. Discounted tickets to 2 or 3 parts of the complex available. July 5–Labor Day Sat–Thurs 9am–7pm; Fri 9am–9pm. Day after Labor Day to July 4 Sat–Thurs 9am–5pm; Fri 9am–9pm. T: Green Line to Science Park. Or commuter rail to North Station, then 10-min. walk.

For the ultimate pain-free educational experience, head to the Museum of Science. The demonstrations, experiments, and interactive displays introduce facts and concepts so effortlessly that everyone winds up learning something. Take a couple of hours or a whole day to explore the permanent and temporary exhibits, which are dedicated to improving "science literacy."

Among the more than 600 exhibits, you might meet an iguana or a dinosaur, find out how much you'd weigh on the moon, or climb into a space module. Visitors to the activity center **Investigate!** learn to think like scientists, formulating questions, finding evidence, and drawing conclusions through activities such as strapping on a skin sensor to measure reactions to stimuli or sifting through an archaeological dig. In the **Seeing Is Deceiving** section, auditory and visual illusions challenge your belief in what is "real." The **Science in the Park** exhibit introduces the concepts of Newtonian physics—through familiar recreational tools such as playground equipment and skateboards. You can also visit the theater of electricity to see lightning manufactured indoors. And there's a **Discovery Center** especially for preschoolers.

In 1999 the museum joined forces with the **Computer Museum** and acquired the latter's fascinating interactive exhibits. The first to find a home here, the **Virtual Fish-Tank,** uses 3-D computer graphics and character-animation software to allow visitors to program their own fish and watch as they relate to other people's creations.

The separate-admission **theaters** are worth planning for. Even if you're skipping the exhibits, try to see a show. If you're making a day of it, buy all your tickets at once, not only because it's cheaper but also because shows sometimes sell out. Tickets for daytime shows must be purchased in person. Evening show tickets can be ordered over the phone using a credit card; there's a service charge for doing so.

On Top of the World

Two of Boston's top attractions are literally *top* attractions. From hundreds of feet in the air, you'll get an unbeatable look at the city and its surroundings. The nearest T stops to both are Copley on the Green Line and Back Bay on the Orange Line and commuter rail.

The ✪ **John Hancock Observatory,** 200 Clarendon St. (☎ **617/572-6429;** www.cityviewboston.com), would be a good introduction to Boston even if it didn't have a sensational 60th-floor view. The multimedia exhibits include a light-and-sound show that chronicles the events leading to the Revolutionary War and demonstrates how Boston's landmass has changed. There are an illustrated time line, an interactive computer quiz about the city, and a display that generates walking, driving, and public transportation directions to points of interest of your choosing. Powerful binoculars (bring quarters) allow long-distance views, and facsimiles of newspapers give a look at headlines from the past. Admission is $6 for adults, $4 for seniors and children 5 to 15. Hours from April to October are 9am to 11pm daily; from November to March Monday through Saturday 9am to 11pm, Sunday 9am to 6pm. The ticket office closes 1 hour before the observatory.

The ✪ **Prudential Center Skywalk,** 800 Boylston St. (☎ **617/859-0648**), offers the only 360-degree view of Boston and beyond. From the enclosed observation deck on the 50th floor of the Prudential Tower, you can see for miles, even (when it's clear) as far as the mountains of southern New Hampshire to the north and the beaches of Cape Cod to the south. The limited exhibits are less interesting than those at the John Hancock Observatory, but the view is a little better, especially at sunset. Hours are 10am to 10pm Monday to Saturday, noon to 10pm Sunday. Admission is $4 for adults, $3 for seniors and children 2 to 10. On the 52nd floor you can enjoy the view with food and drink at the Top of the Hub restaurant and lounge (see chapter 6).

The **Mugar Omni Theater,** which shows IMAX movies, is an intense experience. You're bombarded with images on a five-story domed screen and sounds from a state-of-the-art digital system. Even though you know you're not moving, the engulfing sensations and steep pitch of the seating area will have you hanging on for dear life, whether the film is about whales, Mount Everest, or hurricanes and tornadoes. Features change every 4 to 6 months.

The **Charles Hayden Planetarium** takes you into space with daily star shows and shows on special topics that change several times a year. On weekends, rock-music laser shows take over. At the entrance is a hands-on astronomy exhibit, *Welcome to the Universe.*

The museum has a terrific gift shop, where toys and games promote learning without lecturing, and the ground-floor Galaxy Cafés have spectacular views of the skyline and river. There's a parking garage on the premises, but it's on a busy street, and entering and exiting can be harrowing.

New England Aquarium. Central Wharf. ☎ **617/973-5200.** www.neaq.org. Admission summer weekends and holidays, $14 adults, $12 seniors, $7.50 children 3–11; weekdays year-round and off-season weekends, $12.50 adults, $10.50 seniors, $6.50 children 3–11. Free for children under 3 and for those visiting only the outdoor exhibits, cafe, and gift shop.

July–Labor Day Mon–Tues and Fri 9am–6pm; Wed–Thurs 9am–8pm; Sat–Sun and holidays 9am–7pm. Day after Labor Day to June Mon–Fri 9am–5pm; Sat–Sun and holidays 9am–6pm. T: Blue Line to Aquarium.

This entertaining complex is home to more than 7,000 fish and aquatic mammals. At busy times in the summer, it seems to contain at least that many people—in July and August, try to make this your first stop of the day, especially on weekends, and consider investing in a Boston CityPass (see "Let's Make a Deal," above), which allows you to skip the ticket line. Inside, buy an exhibit guide and plan your route as you commune with the penguin colony.

The focal point of the main building is the aptly named **Giant Ocean Tank.** A four-story spiral ramp encircles the cylindrical glass tank, which contains 187,000 gallons of salt water, a replica of a Caribbean coral reef, and a conglomeration of sea creatures who seem to coexist amazingly well. Part of the reason for the peace might be that scuba divers feed the sharks five times a day (for a person's-eye view, check at your video store for the 1998 romantic comedy *Next Stop Wonderland*). Other exhibits show off freshwater specimens, the Aquarium medical center, denizens of the Amazon, and the ecology of Boston Harbor. At the ***Edge of the Sea*** exhibit, you're encouraged to touch the sea stars, sea urchins, and horseshoe crabs in the tide pool. Be sure to leave time for a show at the floating marine mammal pavilion, **Discovery,** where sea lions perform every 90 minutes throughout the day.

The aquarium is growing; the first stage of its expansion is the dramatic West Wing, which echoes the waves on adjacent Boston Harbor. It holds exhibit space, the gift shop, and a cafe with views of the city and the harbor. The complex is scheduled to gain an **IMAX theater** with 3-D capability in 2001; call for admission fees.

The aquarium runs **harbor tours** that teach "Science at Sea" daily in the spring, summer, and fall. Tickets are $9 for adults, $7 for seniors and youths 12 to 18, and $6.50 for children under 12. Discounts are available when you combine a visit to the aquarium with a harbor tour or a whale watch (see "Organized Tours," below).

2 More Museums & Attractions

Boston Public Library. 700 Boylston St., Copley Sq. ☎ **617/536-5400.** www.bpl.org. Free admission. Mon–Thurs 9am–9pm; Fri–Sat 9am–5pm; Sun (Oct–May only) 1–5pm. Closed Sun June–Sept and legal holidays. T: Green Line to Copley.

The central branch of the city's library system is an architectural and intellectual monument. The original 1895 building, a Charles F. McKim National Historic Landmark, is an Italian Renaissance–style masterpiece that fairly drips with art. The lobby doors are the work of Daniel Chester French (who also designed the Abraham Lincoln statue in the memorial in Washington, the *Minute Man* statue in Concord, and the John Harvard statue in Cambridge). The recently restored murals are by John Singer Sargent and Pierre Puvis de Chavannes, among others. Visit the lovely courtyard or peek at it from a window on the stairs. The adjoining addition, of the same height and material (pink granite), was designed by Philip Johnson and opened in 1972. It's a utilitarian building with a dramatic skylit atrium.

Free **Art & Architecture Tours** are conducted year-round Monday at 2:30pm, Tuesday and Thursday at 6pm, Friday and Saturday at 11am, and September through May on Sunday at 2pm. Call ☎ **617/536-5400,** ext. 216, to arrange group tours.

The Institute of Contemporary Art. 955 Boylston St. ☎ **617/266-5152.** www.culturefinder.com. Admission $6 adults, $4 students and seniors, free for children under 12; free to all Thurs 5–9pm. Wed and Sat–Sun noon–5pm; Thurs noon–9pm; Fri noon–7pm. Closed major holidays. T: Green Line B, C, or D to Hynes/ICA.

Eye in the Sky

For a smashing view of the airport, the harbor, and the South Boston waterfront, stroll along the harbor (or Atlantic Avenue) to the Boston Harbor Hotel complex. Above the landmark arch is Foster's Rotunda. Enter through the lobby of 30 Rowes Wharf, immediately turn right, and take the elevator that runs straight to the ninth-floor rotunda. Step out onto the balcony and soak up the scenery. There's no admission charge, but open hours are limited: Monday to Friday 11am to 4pm.

Across from the Hynes Convention Center, the ICA hosts rotating exhibits of 20th-century art, including painting, sculpture, photography, and video and performance art. The institute also offers films, lectures, music, video, poetry, and educational programs for children and adults. "Docent Teens"—participants in the institute's nationally recognized program for urban youth—lead tours on Thursday afternoons, and staff members lead tours on Friday at 12:30pm. The 1886 building, originally a police station, is a showpiece in its own right.

In 2000, the ICA's proposal won a competition to select an arts institution for the South Boston waterfront, near the new federal courthouse on Fan Pier. Check here for details and updates as the project proceeds.

Mapparium. World Headquarters of the First Church of Christ, Scientist, 250 Mass. Ave. (at Huntington Ave.). ☎ **617/450-3793.** www.tfccs.com. Admission free. Mon–Sat 10am–4pm. Mother Church Sun 11:15am–2pm; Mon–Sat 10am–4pm. Closed major holidays. MBTA: Green Line E to Symphony or Orange Line to Mass. Ave.

One of Boston's most unusual attractions is undergoing renovation; it's scheduled to reopen in early 2001. The Mapparium offers a real insider's view of the world . . . from inside. The unique hollow globe 30 feet across is a work of both art and history. The 608 stained-glass panels are connected by a bronze framework and surrounded by electric lights. Because sound bounces off the nonporous surfaces, the acoustics are as unusual as the aesthetics. As you cross the glass bridge just south of the equator, you'll see the political divisions of the world from 1932 to 1935, when the globe was constructed.

Also in the 14-acre Christian Science complex is the Romanesque 1894 Mother Church, notable for its stained-glass windows. The domed Mother Church Extension (1906), is in Renaissance-Byzantine style and has one of the largest pipe organs in the world.

Massachusetts Archives. 220 Morrissey Blvd., Columbia Point. ☎ **617/727-2816.** Free admission. Mon–Fri 9am–5pm; Sat 9am–3pm. Closed legal holidays. T: Red Line to JFK/UMass.

The nearby Kennedy Library explores the history of one of Boston's most famous families; here, you might find your own family's history. The state archives contain passenger lists for ships that arrived in Boston from 1848 to 1891; state census schedules that date to 1790; and documents, maps, and military and court records starting with the Massachusetts Bay Company (1628 to 1629). Knowledgeable staff members are on hand to answer researchers' questions in person, by mail, or by phone.

In the same building, you'll find the **Commonwealth Museum** (☎ 617/727-9150), which has videos, slide shows, and other interactive exhibits on the state's people, places, and politics. Topics covered recently in the regularly changing exhibits include the archaeology of the Big Dig, war photography, and the history of Massachusetts labor unions.

Museum of Transportation. 15 Newton St., Larz Anderson Park, Brookline. ☎ **617/ 522-6547.** www.mot.org. Admission $5 adults; $3 seniors, students with valid ID, and children 6–16. Tues–Sun and Mon holidays 10am–5pm. T: Green Line D to Reservoir, then take bus no. 51 (Forest Hills); museum is 5 blocks from intersection of Newton and Clyde sts. Call for driving directions.

Automobile buffs will delight in this museum, which is based in an 1888 carriage house modeled after a French château. Beginning in 1899, Larz and Isabel Anderson acquired the antique cars that form the core of the collection, now the country's oldest private assemblage of antique autos. The cars boast what was then the latest equipment, from a two-cylinder engine (in a 1901 Winton race car) to a full lavatory (in a 1906 CGV). Autos and memorabilia from the collection and from other sources are on display.

On most Sundays from May through October, car shows take over the lawn, with themes such as Corvettes, Cadillacs, Triumphs, German cars, or Italian imports. Call to find out what's featured during your visit.

3 Historic Houses

The home in Boston imbued with the most history is the ✪ **Paul Revere House,** 19 North Sq. (☎ 617/523-2338; www.paulreverehouse.org). Best known as a stop on the Freedom Trail, it's the oldest home in downtown Boston, dating to about 1680. Many people know no more about Revere than the first few lines of Henry Wadsworth Longfellow's poem "Paul Revere's Ride"—many people don't even know that—but his house brings the legendary revolutionary to life. The tour is self-guided, with staff members on hand to answer questions, and is exceptionally thought-provoking. The format allows you to linger on the artifacts that hold your interest. Revere had eight children (he called them "my lambs") with each of his two wives, and he supported the family with his thriving silversmith's trade. At his home, you'll get a good sense of the risks he took with his role in the events that led to the Revolutionary War.

The house is open daily April 15 through October from 9:30am to 5:15pm, and November through April 14 from 9:30am to 4:15pm. It's closed Mondays from January through March. Admission is $2.50 for adults, $2 for seniors and students, $1 for children 5 to 17. Special programs and events are scheduled to coincide with Patriots Day, Fourth of July, and Christmas; call for details.

The adjacent **Pierce/Hichborn House,** a suitably furnished Georgian structure built around 1711 and occupied by Revere's cousins, is shown by guided tour only. There are usually two tours a day at busy times; call the Paul Revere House for schedules.

On **Beacon Hill,** you'll find houses that are as interesting for their architecture as for their occupants. The south slope, facing Boston Common, has been a fashionable address since the 1620s; excellent tours of two houses (one on the north slope) focus on the late 18th and early 19th centuries. The homes were designed by Charles Bulfinch, the architect of the State House, which sits at the hill's summit.

Bulfinch designed the ✪ **Harrison Gray Otis House,** 141 Cambridge St. (☎ 617/227-3956), in 1796 for an up-and-coming young lawyer who later became mayor of Boston. The restoration was one of the first in the country to use computer analysis of paint, and the result was revolutionary. It revealed that the colors on the walls were drab because the paint was faded, not because they started out dingy. Furnished in the style to which a wealthy family in the young United States would have been accustomed, the restored Federal-style mansion is a colorful, elegant treasure. It is at the foot of Beacon Hill, near the Government Center and Charles/MGH T stops.

> ### ❷ Did You Know?
>
> - Robert Newman, who hung the lanterns in the steeple of the Old North Church to signal to Paul Revere, was a great-grandson of George Burroughs, one of the victims of the Salem witch trials of 1692.
> - The Boston subway system, which opened in 1897, was the first in the Western Hemisphere.
> - The first public school in America, attended by John Hancock and Benjamin Franklin, among others, was on School Street in Boston. Other alumni include Charles Bulfinch, Ralph Waldo Emerson, George Santayana, Arthur Fiedler, and Leonard Bernstein.

Guided tours (the only way to see the house) discuss its architecture and post-Revolutionary social, business, and family life, and touch on the history of the neighborhood. They cost $4 and start on the hour Wednesday through Sunday from 11am to 4pm.

The **Society for the Preservation of New England Antiquities** (SPNEA) makes its headquarters at the Otis House, which is just the tip of the iceberg. SPNEA owns and operates 34 historic properties throughout New England, and the results of its restoration techniques can be seen at museums all over the area. Contact the society, 141 Cambridge St., Boston, MA 02114 (☎ 617/227-3956; www.spnea.org), for brochures, visiting hours, and admission fees.

The **Nichols House Museum,** 55 Mount Vernon St. (☎ 617/227-6993), is an 1804 Beacon Hill home with beautiful antique furnishings collected by several generations of the Nichols family. From May through October, it's open Tuesday through Saturday; November through April, Thursday through Saturday (open days may vary, so call ahead). Tours start at 12:15pm and continue every 30 minutes on the quarter hour through 4:15pm. Admission is $5.

In the Back Bay, the **Gibson House Museum,** 137 Beacon St. (☎ 617/267-6338), is an 1859 brownstone that embodies the word *Victorian.* You'll see dozens of family photos and portraits, petrified-wood hat racks, a sequined pink-velvet pagoda for the cat, a Victrola, and all manner of decorations. The museum is open for tours at 1, 2, and 3pm Wednesday through Sunday from May to October, and weekends only from November to April. It's closed on major holidays. Admission is $5.

At the **John F. Kennedy National Historic Site,** 83 Beals St., Brookline (☎ 617/566-7937; www.nps.gov/jofi), the 35th president's birthplace is restored to its appearance in 1917. It affords a fascinating look at domestic life of the period and the roots of the Kennedy family. A unit of the National Park Service, the house is shown only by guided ranger tour, at 10:45 and 11:45am and 1, 2, 3, and 4pm. Guided tours are $2 for adults and free for children under 17. The house is open from 10am to 4:30pm, Wednesday to Sunday from mid-March to November, Friday to Sunday December to mid-March. T: Green Line C to Coolidge Corner, then walk 4 blocks north on Harvard Street.

4 African-American History

Before you leave home, contact the **Greater Boston Convention & Visitors Bureau,** 2 Copley Place, Suite 105, Boston, MA 02116 (☎ 888/SEE-BOSTON or

617/536-4100; fax 617/424-7664; www.bostonusa.com), and ask for a copy of the 22-page "Boston African American Discovery Guide," which lists many cultural and historical activities and events.

The **Black Heritage Trail** covers sites on Beacon Hill that are part of the history of 19th-century Boston. You can take a free 2-hour guided tour with a ranger from the National Park Service's **Boston African American National Historic Site,** which starts at the Visitor Center, 46 Joy St. (☎ 617/742-5415; www.nps.gov/boaf). Or go on your own, using a brochure that includes a map and descriptions of the buildings. The sites include stations of the Underground Railroad, homes of famous citizens, and the first integrated public school.

One of the most interesting sites on the Black Heritage Trail is the **African Meeting House,** 8 Smith Court. Opened in 1806, it's the oldest standing black church in the United States. William Lloyd Garrison founded the New England Anti-Slavery Society in this building, where Frederick Douglass made some of his great abolitionist speeches. Once known as the "Black Faneuil Hall," it offers an informative audiovisual presentation and schedules lectures, concerts, and church meetings.

The meetinghouse is the chief artifact of the **Museum of Afro-American History,** 46 Joy St. (☎ 617/742-1854; www.afroammuseum.org), which has the most comprehensive information on the history and contributions of blacks in Boston and Massachusetts. It's open 10am to 4pm, daily from Memorial Day to Labor Day, weekdays the rest of the year. The suggested donation is $5 for adults, $3 for seniors, students, and children.

5 Parks & Gardens

Green space is an important part of Boston's appeal, and the public parks are hard to miss. The world-famous **Emerald Necklace,** Frederick Law Olmsted's vision for a loop of green spaces, runs through the city. (See "Organized Tours," below, for information about seeing part or all of the Emerald Necklace with a Boston Park Ranger.)

The best-known park, for good reason, is the spectacular ✪ **Public Garden,** bordered by Arlington, Boylston, Charles, and Beacon streets. Something lovely is in bloom at the country's first botanical garden at least half the year. The spring flowers are particularly impressive, especially if your visit happens to coincide with the first really warm day of the year. It's hard not to enjoy yourself when everyone around you seems ecstatic just to be seeing the sun.

For many people, the official beginning of spring coincides with the return of the **swan boats** (☎ 617/522-1966; www.swanboats.com). The pedal-powered vessels— the attendants pedal, not the passengers—plunge into the lagoon on the Saturday before Patriots Day (the third Monday of April). Although they don't move fast, they'll transport you. They operate daily 10am to 5pm in the summer; daily 10am to 4pm in the spring; weekdays noon to 4pm and weekends 10am to 4pm from Labor Day to mid-September. The cost for the 15-minute ride is $1.75 for adults, $1.50 for seniors, 95¢ for children under 13.

Across Charles Street is **Boston Common,** the country's first public park. The property was purchased in 1634 and officially set aside as public land in 1640, so if it seems a bit run-down (especially compared to the Public Garden), it's no wonder. The Frog Pond, where there really were frogs at one time, makes a pleasant spot to splash around in the summer and skate in the winter. At the Boylston Street side is the **Central Burying Ground,** where you can see the grave of famed portraitist Gilbert Stuart. There's also a bandstand where you might take in a free concert, and many beautiful shade trees.

Focus on Women's History

Public art and politics have come together in recent years to honor women's contributions to local and national society—a late but welcome development in Boston's history. Its most prominent manifestation is in the State House (see chapter 8), where a permanent installation, "Hear Us," is mounted outside Doric Hall. The portrait gallery celebrates the accomplishments of social reformer Dorothea Dix, abolitionist and feminist Lucy Stone, antislavery activist Sarah Parker Remond, union organizer Mary Kenney O'Sullivan, journalist and suffragist Josephine St. Pierre Ruffin, and political activist Florence Hope Luscomb. Remond and Ruffin are the first African Americans commemorated in the State House.

Underground Railroad leader Harriet Tubman is the subject of a new sculpture in the South End, at Columbus Avenue and West Newton Street.

The Boston Women's Heritage Trail is a walking tour with stops at the homes, churches, and social and political institutions where 20 women lived, made great contributions to society, or both. Subjects include Julia Ward Howe, Dorothea Dix, the colonial religious leader Anne Hutchinson, and less famous Bostonians, such as Phillis Wheatley, a slave who became the first African-American published poet, and Lucy Stone. You can buy a guidebook (be sure you get the 1999 edition) at the National Park Service Visitor Center at 15 State St., at local bookstores, and at historic sites, such as the Paul Revere House and the Old South Meeting House. For more detailed information, call ☎ 617/522-2872.

March is Women's History Month; special events include lectures, walking tours, museum events, and workshops. Check with the Greater Boston Convention & Visitors Bureau (☎ 800/SEE-BOSTON; www.bostonusa.com) for details.

The most spectacular garden is the ✪ **Arnold Arboretum,** 125 Arborway, Jamaica Plain (☎ 617/524-1718; www.arboretum.harvard.edu). One of the oldest parks in the United States, founded in 1872, it is open daily from sunrise to sunset. Its 265 acres contain more than 15,000 ornamental trees, shrubs, and vines from all over the world. In the spring, the air fills with the dizzying scent of dogwood, azaleas, rhododendrons, and hundreds of varieties of lilacs, for which the arboretum is especially famous. Lilac Sunday, in May, is the only time picnicking is allowed in the arboretum. This is definitely a place to take a camera.

There is no admission fee for the National Historical Landmark, which Harvard University administers in cooperation with the Boston Department of Parks and Recreation. To get there, take the MBTA Orange Line to the Forest Hills stop and follow the signs to the entrance. The visitor center is open weekdays from 9am to 4pm, weekends from noon to 4pm. Call for information about educational programs.

6 Cambridge

Boston and Cambridge are so closely associated that many people believe they're the same—a notion both cities' residents and politicians would be happy to dispel. Cantabrigians are often considered more liberal and better educated than Bostonians, which is another idea that's sure to get you involved in a heated discussion. Take the Red Line across the river and see for yourself.

Cambridge Attractions

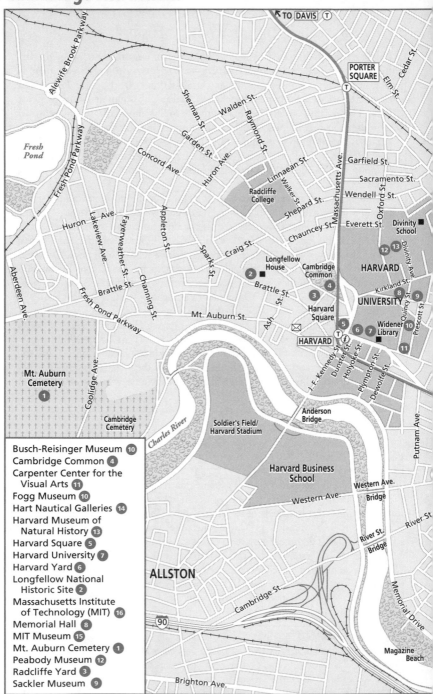

Busch-Reisinger Museum ⑩
Cambridge Common ④
Carpenter Center for the
  Visual Arts ⑪
Fogg Museum ⑩
Hart Nautical Galleries ⑭
Harvard Museum of
  Natural History ⑬
Harvard Square ⑤
Harvard University ⑦
Harvard Yard ⑥
Longfellow National
  Historic Site ②
Massachusetts Institute
  of Technology (MIT) ⑯
Memorial Hall ⑧
MIT Museum ⑮
Mt. Auburn Cemetery ①
Peabody Museum ⑫
Radcliffe Yard ③
Sackler Museum ⑨

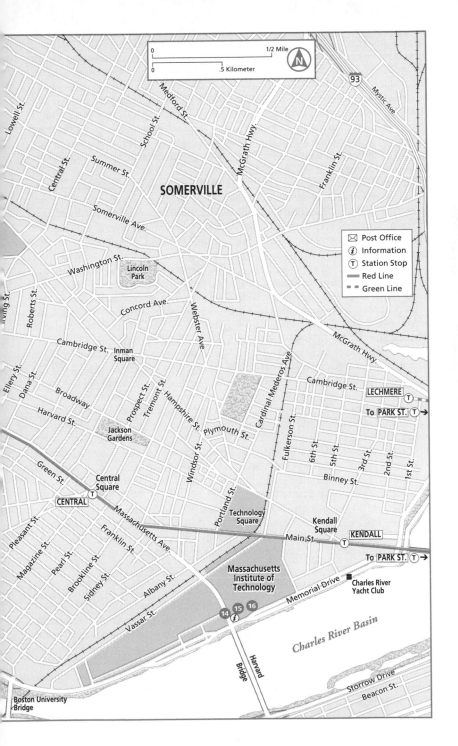

SOMERVILLE

Legend

- ⊠ Post Office
- ⓘ Information
- Ⓣ Station Stop
- — Red Line
- -- Green Line

Lowell St.

Central St.

Summer St.

Medford St.

School St.

McGrath Hwy.

Franklin St.

93

Mystic Ave.

Somerville Ave.

Washington St.

Lincoln Park

Concord Ave.

Webster Ave.

McGrath Hwy.

Irving St.

Roberts St.

Cambridge St.

Inman Square

Cardinal Mederos Ave.

Cambridge St.

LECHMERE Ⓣ

To **PARK ST.** Ⓣ →

Ellery St.

Dana St.

Broadway

Prospect St.

Tremont St.

Hampshire St.

Plymouth St.

Fulkerson St.

6th St.

5th St.

3rd St.

2nd St.

1st St.

Harvard St.

Jackson Gardens

Windsor St.

Binney St.

Green St.

Central Square

CENTRAL Ⓣ

Massachusetts Ave.

Portland St.

Technology Square

Kendall Square

KENDALL Ⓣ

Main St.

Pleasant St.

Magazine St.

Pearl St.

Brookline St.

Franklin St.

Sidney St.

Albany St.

Massachusetts Institute of Technology

Memorial Drive

Charles River Yacht Club

To **PARK ST.** Ⓣ →

14 15 16 ⓘ

Vassar St.

Harvard Bridge

Charles River Basin

Boston University Bridge

Storrow Drive

Beacon St.

1/2 Mile

.5 Kilometer

For a good overview, begin at the main Harvard T entrance. Follow the **walking tour** described in chapter 8, or set out on your own. At the **information booth** (☎ 617/497-1630) in the middle of Harvard Square at the intersection of Mass. Ave., John F. Kennedy Street, and Brattle Street, trained volunteers dispense maps and brochures and answer questions Monday through Saturday from 9am to 5pm and Sunday from 1 to 5pm. From mid-June through Labor Day, there are guided tours that include the entire old Cambridge area. Check at the booth for rates, meeting places, and times, or call ahead. If you prefer to sightsee on your own, you can buy an Old Cambridge or East Cambridge walking guide prepared by the **Cambridge Historical Commission** (☎ 617/349-4683).

Whatever you do, spend some time in **Harvard Square.** It's a hodgepodge of college and high school students, instructors, commuters, street performers, and sightseers. Near the information booth are two well-stocked newsstands, **Nini's Corner** and **Out of Town News** (where you can find out what's happening at home from the extensive collection of newspapers and magazines), and the **Harvard Coop.** There are restaurants and stores along all three streets that spread out from the center of the square and on the streets that intersect them. If you follow **Brattle Street** to the residential area just outside the square, you'll come to a part of town known before and during the American Revolution as **"Tory Row"** because the residents were loyal to King George.

By the time you read this, the ravishing yellow mansion at 105 Brattle St. should have reopened after extensive refurbishment. The house is the ✪ **Longfellow National Historic Site** (☎ 617/876-4491; www.nps.gov/long), where the books and furniture have remained intact since the poet Henry Wadsworth Longfellow died there in 1882. Now a unit of the National Park Service, during the siege of Boston in 1775–76 the house served as the headquarters of Gen. George Washington, with whom Longfellow was fascinated. The poet first lived there as a boarder in 1837. When he and Fanny Appleton married in 1843, her father made it a wedding present. On a tour—the only way to see the house—you'll learn about the history of the building and its famous occupants.

The house is open from mid-March through mid-December. Tours are offered Wednesday through Sunday at 10:45 and 11:45am, and 1, 2, 3, and 4pm from June to October and on weekends from mid-March to May and November to mid-December, and Wednesday through Friday spring and fall at 12:30, 1:30, 2:30, and 3:30pm. Admission is $2 for adults, free for children under 17 and seniors.

Farther west, near where Brattle Street and Mount Auburn Street intersect, is **Mount Auburn Cemetery** (see the box "Celebrity Cemetery"). It's a pleasant but long walk; you might prefer to drive or take the bus. Or you can return to the square and investigate Harvard.

HARVARD UNIVERSITY

The **walking tour** in chapter 8 describes many of the buildings you'll see on the Harvard campus. Free, student-led tours leave from the **Events & Information Center** in Holyoke Center, 1350 Mass. Ave. (☎ 617/495-1573), during the school year twice a day on weekdays and once on Saturday, except during vacations, and during the summer four times a day Monday to Saturday and twice on Sunday. Call for exact times; reservations aren't necessary. The Events & Information Center has maps, illustrated booklets, and self-guided walking-tour directions, as well as a bulletin board where campus activities are publicized. You may want to check out the university Web site (www.harvard.edu) before your trip.

Celebrity Cemetery

Three important colonial burying grounds—Old Granary, King's Chapel, and Copp's Hill—are in Boston on the Freedom Trail (see chapter 8). The most famous cemetery in the area, however, is in Cambridge.

Mount Auburn Cemetery, 580 Mount Auburn St. (☎ **617/547-7105**), the final resting place of many well-known people, is also famous simply for existing. Dedicated in 1831, it was the first of America's rural, or garden, cemeteries. The establishment of burying places removed from city and town centers reflected practical and philosophical concerns. Development was encroaching on urban graveyards, and the ideas associated with the Greek revival (the word *cemetery* derives from the Greek for "sleeping place") and Transcendentalism dictated that communing with nature take precedence over organized religion. Since the day it opened, Mount Auburn has been a popular place to retreat and reflect—in the 19th century, it was often the first place out-of-town visitors asked to go.

A modern visitor will find history and horticulture coexisting with celebrity. The graves of Henry Wadsworth Longfellow, Oliver Wendell Holmes, Julia Ward Howe, and Mary Baker Eddy are here, as are those of Charles Bulfinch, James Russell Lowell, Winslow Homer, Transcendentalist leader Margaret Fuller, and abolitionist Charles Sumner. In season, you'll see gorgeous flowering trees and shrubs (the Massachusetts Horticultural Society had a hand in the design). Stop at the office or front gate to pick up brochures and a map. You can rent a 60-minute audiotape tour ($5; a $12 deposit is required) and listen in your car or on a portable tape player. **The Friends of Mount Auburn Cemetery** (☎ **617/864-9646**) conduct workshops and lectures and coordinate walking tours. Call for topics, schedules, and fees.

The cemetery is open daily from 8am to dusk; there is no admission charge. Animals and recreational activities such as jogging and picnicking are not allowed. MBTA bus routes no. 71 and 73 start at Harvard station and stop near the cemetery gates; they run frequently on weekdays, less often on weekends. By car (5 min.) or on foot (30 min.), take Mount Auburn Street or Brattle Street west from Harvard Square; just after the streets intersect, the gate is on the left.

The best-known part of the university is **Harvard Yard,** actually two large quadrangles. The **John Harvard statue,** a rendering of one of the school's original benefactors, is in the Old Yard, which dates to the college's founding in 1636. Most first-year students live in the dormitories here—even in the school's oldest building, **Massachusetts Hall** (1720). The other side of the Yard (sometimes called Tercentenary Theater because the college's 300th-anniversary celebration was held there) is home to the imposing **Widener Library,** named after a Harvard graduate who perished when the *Titanic* sank.

Also on campus are two engaging museum complexes:

Harvard University Art Museums. 32 Quincy St. and 485 Broadway (at Quincy St.). ☎ **617/495-9400.** www.artmuseums.harvard.edu. Admission to all 3 museums $5 adults, $4 seniors, $3 students, free for children under 18; free to all Wed 10am–5pm, Sat 10am–noon. Mon–Sat 10am–5pm; Sun 1–5pm. Closed major holidays. T: Red Line to Harvard. Cross Harvard Yard diagonally from the middle of the T station and cross Quincy St., or turn your back on the Coop and follow Mass. Ave. to Quincy St., then turn left.

Impressions

*I should sooner live in a society governed by the first 2,000 names in the Boston
telephone directory than in a society governed by the 2,000 faculty members of
Harvard University.*
　　　　　　—Yale alumnus William F. Buckley, Jr., *Rumbles Left and Right,* 1963

The Harvard art museums house a total of about 150,000 works of art in three collections: the Fogg Art Museum, the Busch–Reisinger Museum, and the Arthur M.
Sackler Museum. The exhibit spaces also serve as teaching and research facilities. You
can take a 1-hour guided tour on weekdays September through June, and Wednesdays
only in July and August.

The **Fogg Art Museum** (32 Quincy St., near Broadway) centers on an impressive
16th-century Italian stone courtyard, with two floors of galleries opening off it. You'll
see something different in each of the 19 rooms—17th-century Dutch and Flemish
landscapes, 19th-century British and American paintings and drawings, French paintings and drawings from the 18th century through the Impressionist period, contemporary sculpture, and changing exhibits.

The **Busch–Reisinger Museum** in Werner Otto Hall (enter through the Fogg) is
the only museum in North America devoted to the painting, sculpture, and decorative art of northern and central Europe, specifically Germany. Its encyclopedic collection also includes prints and illustrated books. Particularly notable are the
early-20th-century collections, including works by Klee, Feininger, Kandinsky, and
artists and designers associated with the Bauhaus.

The **Arthur M. Sackler Museum** (485 Broadway, at Quincy St.) houses the university's collections of Asian, ancient, and Islamic art. Included is an assemblage of
Chinese jades and cave reliefs that's considered the best in the world, as well as Korean ceramics, Roman sculpture, Greek vases, and Persian miniature paintings and
calligraphy.

Harvard Museum of Natural History. 26 Oxford St. ☎ **617/495-3045.**
www.hmnh.harvard.edu.

Peabody Museum of Archaeology & Ethnology. 11 Divinity Ave. ☎ **617/496-1027.**
www.peabody.harvard.edu. Admission to both $5 adults, $4 seniors and students, $3 children
3–13, free for children under 3; free to all Sat 9am–noon. Mon–Sat 9am–5pm; Sun 1–5pm.
T: Red Line to Harvard. Cross Harvard Yard, keeping John Harvard statue on right, and turn
right at Science Center. First left is Oxford St.

These fascinating museums house the university's collections of items and artifacts
related to the natural world. The world-famous academic resource offers interdisciplinary programs and exhibitions that tie in elements of all the associated fields. You'll
certainly find something interesting here, be it a dinosaur skeleton, a hunk of mete-
orite, a Native American artifact, or the world-famous Glass Flowers.

The Museum of Natural History comprises three institutions. The best-known is
the **Botanical Museum,** whose most popular display is the **Glass Flowers,** 3,000
models of more than 840 plant species devised between 1887 and 1936 by the German father-and-son team of Leopold and Rudolph Blaschka. You might have heard
about them, and you might be skeptical, but it's true: They look real. Children love
the **Museum of Comparative Zoology,** where the dinosaurs share space with preserved and stuffed insects and animals that range in size from butterflies to giraffes.
The **Mineralogical & Geological Museum** is the most specialized—hold off unless
there's an interesting interdisciplinary display or you're really into rocks.

Young visitors also enjoy the dollhouse-like "Worlds in Miniature" display at the **Peabody Museum of Archaeology & Ethnology,** which represents people from all over the world in scaled-down homes. The museum also boasts the **Hall of the North American Indian,** where 500 artifacts representing 10 cultures are on display. The museum also has a terrific gift shop (☎ **617/495-2248**) packed with reasonably priced folk art and crafts.

MASSACHUSETTS INSTITUTE OF TECHNOLOGY (MIT)

The public is welcome at the Massachusetts Institute of Technology campus, a mile or so from Harvard Square, across the Charles River from Beacon Hill and the Back Bay. Visit the **Information Office,** 77 Mass. Ave. (☎ **617/253-4795**), to take a free guided tour (weekdays, 10am and 2pm), or pick up a copy of the "Walk Around MIT" map and brochure. At the same address, the **Hart Nautical Galleries** (open daily 9am to 5pm) contain ship and engine models that trace the development of marine engineering. The school has an excellent outdoor sculpture collection, which includes works by Picasso and Alexander Calder, and notable modern architecture by Eero Saarinen and I. M. Pei. Even more modern are the holography displays at the **MIT Museum,** 265 Mass. Ave. (☎ **617/253-4444;** http://web.mit.edu/museum), where you'll also find works in more conventional mediums. The museum is open Tuesday through Friday from 10am to 5pm, weekends from noon to 5pm; it's closed on major holidays. Admission is $5 for adults, $3 for students and seniors, $1 for children 5 to 18.

To get to MIT, take the MBTA Red Line to Kendall/MIT. The scenic walk from the Back Bay takes you along Mass. Ave. over the river straight to the campus. By car from Boston, cross the river at the Museum of Science, Cambridge Street, or Mass. Ave. and follow signs to Memorial Drive, where you can usually find parking during the day.

7 Boston Neighborhoods to Explore

This section attempts to answer briefly the second most-asked question visitors have for Boston residents: "Where do people who live here go?" (The most-asked question is "Why aren't there more public bathrooms?" We wish we knew.)

Boston is a city of neighborhoods, some of which you'll learn about in the walking tours described in chapter 8. Here are several other areas that are fun to explore. Bear in mind that many of the buildings you will see are private homes, not tourist attractions. See chapter 6 for dining suggestions and chapter 9 for shopping tips.

BEACON HILL

The original Boston settlers, clustered around what are now the Old State House and the North End, considered Beacon Hill outlandishly distant. Today the distance is a matter of atmosphere; climbing "the Hill" is like traveling back in time. Lace up your walking shoes (the brick sidewalks gnaw at anything fancier, and driving is next to impossible), wander the narrow streets, and admire the brick and brownstone architecture.

Impressions

For we must consider that we shall be as a city upon a hill. The eyes of all people are upon us. . . .

—John Winthrop, "A Model of Christian Charity" (sermon), 1630

Beacon and Park streets is a figurative high point (literally, it's *the* high point): Charles Bulfinch's magnificent **State House.** The 60-foot **monument** at the rear illustrates the hill's original height, before the top was shorn off to use in the landfill projects of the 19th century. **Beacon and Mount Vernon streets** run downhill to commercially dense **Charles Street,** but if ever there was an area where there's no need to head in a straight line, it's this one. Your travels may take you past former homes of Louisa May Alcott (10 Louisburg Sq.), Henry Kissinger (1 Chestnut St.), Julia Ward Howe (13 Chestnut St.), Edwin Booth (29A Chestnut St.), or Robert Frost (88 Mount Vernon St.). One of the oldest black churches in the country, the **African Meeting House,** is at 8 Smith Court.

These days, Alcott probably wouldn't be able to afford even the rent for a home on **Louisburg Square** (say "Lewis-burg"). The lovely private park is surrounded by 22 homes where a struggling writer would more likely be an employee than a resident. The iron-railed square is open only to tenants with keys.

Your wandering will probably lead you down to Charles Street. After you've had your fill of the shops and restaurants, you may want to investigate the architecture of the **"flats,"** between Charles Street and the Charles River. Built on landfill, the buildings are younger than those higher up, but many are just as eye-catching. This is the area where you can look for signs that MTV's **"The Real World"** passed through. You might recognize the converted firehouse where the cast of the 1997 show lived; also a one-time "Spenser: For Hire" set, it's at Mount Vernon and River streets.

T: Red Line to Charles/MGH, Green Line to Park Street, or Blue Line to Bowdoin.

CHINATOWN

This close-knit residential and commercial community is constantly pushing its borders, expanding into the nearly defunct "Combat Zone" (the red-light district) on Washington Street and crossing the Massachusetts Turnpike extension into the South End. It's also including more Vietnamese and Cambodian residents. The Expressway, the downtown shopping district, the Theater District, and the Tufts University medical complex border the heart of Chinatown. You'll know you're there when the phone booths suddenly sprout pagoda tops.

Start your visit at Beach Street and the Surface Artery. There aren't many street signs, but you can't miss the three-story **Chinatown Gateway.** The gate with four marble lions was a bicentennial gift from the government of Taiwan.

Beach Street is the closest thing Chinatown has to a main drag, and the streets that cross it and run parallel are nearly as congested and equally interesting. You'll see fish tanks full of entrees-to-be, produce stands, gift shops, and markets. After wandering around for a while and working up an appetite, stop for **dim sum** (see chapter 6 for pointers). If you have room for dessert, stop at a bakery—perhaps **Hing Shing Pastry,** 67 Beach St. (☎ 617/451-1162), or **Ho Yuen Bakery,** 54 Beach St. (☎ 617/426-8320)—for giant walnut cookies, pastries in the shape of animals, fried sesame balls, and moon cakes. The wares in the gift shops run from classic to cartoonish, and prices tend to be quite reasonable.

During the celebration of **Chinese New Year** (January or February, depending on the moon), masses of people turn out even in the harshest weather to watch the parade. Dragons dance in the streets, and firecrackers punctuate the musical accompaniment. In the summer, you'll see the **August Moon Festival,** a local street fair. Call the **Chinese Merchants Association,** 20 Hudson St. (☎ 617/482-3972), for information on special events. The building's bronze bas-reliefs represent the eight immortals of Taoism, and there are mirrored plaques along Oxford Alley to ward off evil spirits.

Impressions

And this is good old Boston,
The home of the bean and the cod,
Where the Lowells talk to the Cabots,
And the Cabots talk only to God.
  —John Collins Bossidy, toast at the Holy Cross College alumni dinner, 1910

As a family, the Bradlees had been around for close to three hundred years, but well
down the totem pole from the Lowells and the Cabots. Proper enough as proper
Bostonians went, but not that rich, and not that smart.
  —Former *Washington Post* executive editor Ben Bradlee, *A Good Life,* 1995

Before you leave, you may want to stop at a food store for supplies to take home. One of the largest in size and selection, the **88 Supermarket,** 50 Herald St., at Washington Street (☎ **617/423-1688**), is across the Pike extension. It's not just Chinese—every ingredient of every Asian cuisine seems to be on the shelves somewhere, and the fresh produce ranges from lemons to lemongrass. In Chinatown proper, **See Sun Co.,** 25 Harrison Ave. (☎ **617/426-0954**), isn't as large, but the selection and prices are good.

   T: Orange Line to Chinatown, or Green Line to Boylston.

THE SOUTH END

One of the city's most diverse neighborhoods is also one of its largest, but fans of Victorian architecture won't mind the sore feet they have after trekking around the South End.

   The South End was laid out in the mid-19th century, before the Back Bay; while the newer area's grid echoes the boulevards of Paris, the South End tips its hat to London. The main streets are broad, the side streets dotted with pocket parks. The gentrification movement of the 1970s saw many South End brownstones reclaimed from squalor and converted into luxury condominiums, a trend that caught fire in the late '90s. Even on run-down buildings, you'll see wonderful details.

   With Back Bay Station to your left, walk down **Dartmouth Street,** crossing Columbus Avenue. Proceed on Dartmouth and explore some of the streets that extend to the left, including **Chandler, Lawrence, and Appleton streets.** This area is known as **Clarendon Park.** Turn left on any of these streets and walk to **Clarendon Street.** Its intersection with Tremont Street is the part of the South End you're most likely to see if you're not out exploring. This is the area where businesses and restaurants surround the **Boston Center for the Arts** (☎ **617/426-7700** for events; 617/426-0320 for box office). The BCA's **Cyclorama** building (the interior is dome-shaped), at 539 Tremont St., is listed on the National Register of Historic Places. Here you can see a show, have a meal, or continue your expedition. This is not the greatest neighborhood to roam through at night, but in daylight you can feel comfortable taking **Tremont Street** or **Columbus Avenue** (and wandering down the streets that run between them) all the way to Mass. Ave. From there, you can take the no. 1 bus to the Back Bay or into Cambridge, or the Orange Line downtown.

   T: Orange Line to Back Bay, or Green Line to Copley.

JAMAICA PLAIN

You can combine a visit to the Arnold Arboretum (see "Parks & Gardens," above) with a stroll around Jamaica Pond or along Centre Street. Culturally diverse Jamaica Plain abounds with interesting architecture and open space. The pond is especially pleasant in good weather, when people walk, run, skate, fish, picnic, and sunbathe. Many of

Photo Synthesis

Boston is such a shutterbug magnet that residents sometimes offer to snap a picture of a visiting family even before being asked. Arrange Junior and Sissy in the lap of one of the area's numerous portrait sculptures, or take a step back and capture the juxtaposition of a 19th-century steeple silhouetted against a 20th-century office tower.

Say "Cheese": At the bronze **teddy bear** in front of FAO Schwarz, 440 Boylston St. (at Berkeley Street). Arm-in-arm or deep in thought with Mayor **James Michael Curley,** in the park on Union Street across North Street from Faneuil Hall. Pulling the cigar away from Celtics legend **Red Auerbach,** between the South Canopy of Quincy Market and the South Market building, Faneuil Hall Marketplace. Comparing your tiny sneakers to **Larry Bird's** clodhoppers, captured in bronze right next to Red. Falling at the feet of a Colonial hero— pedestals support **Benjamin Franklin** (School Street, in front of Old City Hall), **Paul Revere** (Hanover Street at Clark, across from St. Stephen's Church), and **George Washington** (in the Public Garden at the foot of the Commonwealth Avenue Mall). Perched on Mrs. Mallard (or one of her babies if you fit) of *Make Way for Ducklings* fame, in the Public Garden near the corner of Beacon and Charles streets. Outdistancing the winner (or the runner-up) captured in *The Tortoise and Hare at Copley Square,* in front of Trinity Church. And at a spot so popular that the grass on the area favored by photographers had to be paved over, in front of **John Harvard,** Harvard Yard, Cambridge.

Say "Ooh": Always remember to look up for a quirky perspective. Capture a church against a backdrop of skyscrapers on **Tremont Street** (with the Boston Common Visitor Information Center at your back, turn left toward Park Street Church) or **Boylston Street** (in front of the Four Seasons Hotel, turn left toward the Arlington Street Church; across from Trinity Church, focus on the Hancock Tower). Kill two birds with one stone: Pointing up at the **Paul Revere** statue on Hanover Street, you can lock in the **Old North Church** in the background, or walk around the statue for a new perspective on **St. Stephen's Church.** The **Old North Church** crops up all over the North End and Charlestown, as the **Hancock Tower** does throughout the Back Bay. And if your travels take you to the area around the Charles/MGH T stop, wander out onto the **Longfellow Bridge,** especially at twilight—the views of the river are splendid, and if you hit it just right, the moon appears to shine out of the Hancock Tower.

the 19th-century mansions overlooking the pond date to the days when families fled the oppressive heat downtown and moved to the "country" for the summer.

After you've had your fill of nature (or before you set out), Centre Street makes a good destination for wandering and snacking. Our favorite target, black-and-white cow motif and all, is **JP Licks Homemade Ice Cream,** 674 Centre St. (☎ 617/ 524-6740). You'll find excellent vegetarian and vegetarian-friendly food at the **Centre Street Café,** 669 Centre St. (☎ 617/524-9217), and nouveau Italian at **Bella Luna,** 405 Centre St. (☎ 617/524-6060). Across the street from the T stop is the **Dogwood Café,** 3712 Washington St. (☎ 617/522-7997), a family-friendly bar and restaurant with plenty of beers on tap and tasty pizza.

T: Orange Line to Forest Hills.

8 Especially for Kids

What can the children do in Boston? A better question might be "What *can't* the children do in Boston?" Just about every major destination in the city either is specifically designed to appeal to youngsters or can easily be adapted to do so.

I wouldn't ordinarily make such an insulting suggestion, but experience tells me that some parents need reminding: Please allow your kids some input while you're planning your trip. A great deal of anecdotal evidence tells me that incorporating suggestions (especially from teenagers) cuts down on eye-rolling and sighing. And the college tour, whale watch, or day trip that you wouldn't have considered might turn out to be one of the highlights of your vacation.

The following attractions are covered extensively elsewhere in this chapter; here's the boiled-down version for busy parents.

Destinations with something for every member of the family include **Faneuil Hall Marketplace** (☎ 617/338-2323) and the **Museum of Fine Arts** (☎ 617/267-9300), which offers special weekend and after-school programs.

Hands-on exhibits are a big draw at the **Boston Tea Party Ship & Museum** (☎ 617/338-1773) and the **New England Aquarium** (☎ 617/973-5200). The **Museum of Science** (☎ 617/723-2500) not only is a hands-on paradise, but also is home to the Hayden Planetarium and the Mugar Omni Theater.

You might get your hands on a baseball at a **Red Sox game** (see "Spectator Sports," below) or the **Sports Museum of New England** (☎ 617/624-1234).

The allure of seeing people the size of ants draws young visitors to the **John Hancock Observatory** (☎ 617/572-6429) and the **Prudential Center Skywalk** (☎ 617/859-0648). And they can see actual ants—although they may prefer dinosaurs—at the Museum of Comparative Zoology, part of the **Harvard University Museum of Natural History** (☎ 617/495-3045).

Older children who have studied modern American history will enjoy a visit to the **John F. Kennedy Library and Museum** (☎ 617/929-4523). And kids interested in cars will like the **Museum of Transportation** (☎ 617/522-6547).

Middle-schoolers who enjoyed Esther Forbes's *Johnny Tremain* might get a kick out of the **Paul Revere House** (☎ 617/523-2338). Young visitors who have read Robert McCloskey's children's classic, *Make Way for Ducklings,* will relish a visit to the **Public Garden,** and fans of E. B. White's *The Trumpet of the Swan* certainly will want to ride on the **swan boats** (☎ 617/522-1966; see "Parks & Gardens," above). Considerably less tame and much longer are **whale watches** (see "Organized Tours," below).

More Kid Stuff

For more suggestions, check (or let the kids check) elsewhere in this book. Chapter 10 lists nightlife destinations; before night falls (and sometimes after), the whole family can have a great time at Jillian's Boston (pool and all manner of arcade and virtual-reality games), the House of Blues or the Hard Rock Cafe (food and music), *Shear Madness* (audience-participation theater), and Blue Man Group (performance art).

Turn to chapter 9 for shopping recommendations—the CambridgeSide Galleria mall, Beadworks, Curious George Goes to WordsWorth, Pearl Art & Craft Supplies, and the various college bookstores can be as fun as toy stores.

Finally, check chapter 11 for information about day trips. Particularly fun destinations include Salem (at least according to my 13-year-old cousin Kurt, who now wants to be a witch), Plymouth, and Concord.

The walking-tour company ❂ **Boston By Foot,** 77 N. Washington St. (☎ 617/ 367-2345, or 617/367-3766 for recorded information; www.bostonbyfoot.com), has a special program, "Boston By Little Feet," that's geared to children 6 to 12 years old. The 60-minute walk gives a child's-eye view of the architecture along the Freedom Trail and of Boston's role in the American Revolution. Children must be accompanied by an adult, and a map is provided. Tours run from May through October and meet at the statue of Samuel Adams on the Congress Street side of Faneuil Hall, Saturday at 10am, Sunday at 2pm, and Monday at 10am, rain or shine. The cost is $6 per person.

The **Historic Neighborhoods Foundation** (☎ 617/426-1885) offers a 90-minute "Make Way for Ducklings" tour ($7 adults, $5 children 5 and up, free for children under 5). The tour follows the path of the Mallard family described in Robert McCloskey's famous book and ends at the Public Garden. Every year on Mother's Day, Historic Neighborhoods organizes the Ducklings Day Parade.

❂ **Children's Museum.** 300 Congress St. (Museum Wharf). ☎ **617/426-8855.** www.bostonkids.org. Admission $7 adults, $6 children 2–15 and seniors, $2 children age 1, free for children under 1; Fri 5–9pm $1 for all. June–Aug Mon–Thurs 10am–7pm, Fri 10am–9pm, Sat–Sun 10am–5pm; Sept–May Sat–Thurs 10am–5pm, Fri 10am–9pm. T: Red Line to South Station. Walk north on Atlantic Ave. 1 block (past Federal Reserve Bank), turn right onto Congress St., walk 2 blocks (across bridge). Call for information about discounted parking.

As you approach the Children's Museum, don't be surprised to see adults suddenly being dragged by the hand when their young companions realize how close they are and start running. You know the museum is near when you see the 40-foot-high red-and-white milk bottle out front. It makes both children and adults look small in comparison—which is probably part of the point. No matter how old, everyone behaves like a little kid at this delightful museum.

Children can stick with their parents or wander on their own, learning, doing, and role-playing. The centerpiece of the renovated warehouse building is a new two-story-high maze, the **New Balance Climb,** which incorporates motor skills and problem-solving. Other favorites include **Grandparents' Attic,** a souped-up version of playing in Grandma's closet; **Under the Dock,** an environmental exhibit that teaches about the Boston waterfront and allows youngsters to dress up in a crab suit; hands-on physical experiments (such as creating giant soap bubbles) in **Science Playground;** and **Boats Afloat,** which has an 800-gallon play tank and a replica of the bridge of a working boat. **Supermercado** is a marketplace that immerses children in Hispanic culture, surrounding them with Spanish newspapers, ethnic food products, and salsa music. You can also explore a Japanese house and subway train from Kyoto (Boston's sister city) and learn about young adults in **Teen Tokyo.** Children under 4 and their caregivers have a special room, **Playspace,** that's packed with toys and activities.

Call or surf ahead for information about traveling exhibitions, KidStage participatory plays, and special programs. And be sure to check out the excellent gift shop (as if you have a choice).

Franklin Park Zoo. 1 Franklin Park Rd. ☎ **617/541-LION.** www.zoonewengland.com. Admission $7 adults, $4 children 2–15, free for children under 2. Apr–Sept Mon–Fri 10am–5pm, Sat–Sun and holidays 10am–6pm; Oct–Mar daily 10am–4pm. T: Orange Line to Forest Hills, then bus no. 16 to the main entrance. Call for driving directions.

The Franklin Park Zoo constantly becomes more enjoyable—for animals as well as people. From June to September, you can visit the popular, colorful **Butterfly Landing** enclosure. On the new **Outback Trail,** you can see kangaroos, wallabies, emus, and cockatoos. **Bongo Congo** is home to bongo antelopes, zebras, aoudad sheep, ibex, ostriches, warthogs, and vultures. Other installations house cheetahs, lions, and snow leopards. The **African Tropical Forest** exhibit is a sprawling complex where you'll see more than 50 species of animals. This is the domain of the western lowland gorillas (including a baby born in August 1999), who appear to be roaming free in an approximation of their natural habitat. If you're traveling with animal-mad youngsters, the Children's Zoo is both entertaining and educational.

Be sure to leave plenty of time—at least half a day—for a visit to the zoo. Franklin Park is 40 minutes from downtown by public transportation, and the walk from the main gate and the parking area to the entrance is fairly long, especially for those with little legs.

Blue Hills Trailside Museum. 1904 Canton Ave., Milton. ☎ **617/333-0690.** www. massaudubon.org. Admission $3 adults, $2 seniors, $1.50 children 3–15, free for children under 3 and Mass. Audubon Society members. Tues–Sun and Mon holidays 10am–5pm. By car, take I-93 south to Exit 2B (Rte. 138 north).

This outdoor spot at the foot of Great Blue Hill is especially popular with younger children. It's at the 7,500-acre Blue Hills Reservation, a 20-minute drive south of Boston. There's room to hike, climb hills, and study replicas of the natural habitats found in the area. Visitors can climb the lookout tower, crawl through logs, visit a Native American wigwam, and explore the new pond walk exhibit. Resident native animals include owls, honeybees, deer, otters, foxes, bobcats, snakes, and turtles. Children can feed the ducks and deer.

Weekend activities include story time (11am) and educational programs run by staff naturalists: a live "mystery animal" presentation (1pm) and a monthly theme program (3pm). Special events and family programs change with the seasons. They include maple sugaring in early spring, honey harvest and hawk study in the fall, and owl prowls in January. Call ahead to register.

Puppet Showplace Theatre. 32 Station St., Brookline. ☎ **617/731-6400.** E-mail: ShoPuppets@aol.com. Tickets $6. T: Green Line D to Brookline Village.

The Puppet Showplace stages programs of favorite fables, ethnic legends, and folktales and fairy tales from around the world. Professional puppeteers mount the shows year-round in a lovely theater that seats 120. Historic puppets and puppet posters are on display, puppet-making workshops are offered, and toy puppets are for sale. Call for schedules and reservations.

9 Organized Tours

ORIENTATION TOURS

GUIDED WALKING TOURS   Even if you usually prefer to explore on your own, consider an excellent walking tour with ✪ **Boston By Foot,** 77 N. Washington St. (☎ **617/367-2345,** or 617/367-3766 for recorded information; www.bostonbyfoot. com). From May through October, the nonprofit educational corporation conducts historical and architectural tours that focus on particular neighborhoods or themes. The rigorously trained guides are volunteers who encourage questions. Buy tickets ($8 per person) from the guide; reservations are not required. The 90-minute tours take place rain or shine. *Note:* All excursions from Faneuil Hall start at the statue of Samuel Adams on Congress Street.

The **"Heart of the Freedom Trail"** tour starts at Faneuil Hall Tuesday through Saturday at 10am. Tours of **Beacon Hill** begin at the foot of the State House steps on Beacon Street weekdays at 5:30pm, Saturday at 10am, and Sunday at 2pm. **"Boston Underground"** looks at subterranean technology, including crypts, the subway, and

The Boston History Collaborative

An umbrella organization that promotes historic tourism and development, the nonprofit **Boston History Collaborative** (☎ 617/574-5950) is the force behind several new heritage trails. The Literary Trail (www.Lit-Trail.org) and Boston by Sea: The Maritime Trail (www.bostonbysea.org) are up and running. Tours that focus on immigration (www.BostonFamilyHistory.org), the African-American community, and inventions are in the pipeline.

the depression of the Central Artery. It starts at Faneuil Hall Sunday at 2pm. Other tours and meeting places are **Victorian Back Bay,** on the steps of Trinity Church, 10am Friday and Saturday; the **Waterfront,** at Faneuil Hall, Friday at 5:30pm and Sunday at 10am; and the **North End,** at Faneuil Hall, Saturday at 2pm.

Once a month, a special tour ($9) covers a particular theme or area. Special theme tours—they include "Great Women of Boston," "Literary Landmarks," and a China-town tour—can be scheduled if there are enough requests. Off-season tours for groups only (minimum 10 people; $10 per person) are available.

The **Society for the Preservation of New England Antiquities** (☎ 617/227-3956; www.spnea.org) offers a fascinating tour that describes and illustrates life in the mansions and garrets of Beacon Hill in 1800. "Magnificent and Modest," a 2-hour program, costs $10 and starts at the Harrison Gray Otis House, 141 Cambridge St., at 11am on Saturday and Sunday from May through October. The price includes a tour of the Otis House, and reservations are recommended.

The **Historic Neighborhoods Foundation** (☎ 617/426-1885) offers 90-minute walking tours in several neighborhoods, including Beacon Hill, the North End, Chinatown, the Waterfront, and the Financial District. Schedules change with the season, and reservations are required. The programs highlight points of interest to visitors while covering history, architecture, and topographical development. Tours usually cost about $6 per person; check ahead for schedules and meeting places.

Boston by Sea: The Maritime Trail (☎ 617/574-5950; www.bostonbysea.org) is a walk near the Waterfront with a costumed guide. The 45-minute land-only version is currently free. Plans call for a version with a cruise component; check ahead.

The **Boston Park Rangers** (☎ 617/635-7383; www.ci.boston.ma.us/parks) offer free guided walking tours. The best-known focus is the **Emerald Necklace,** a loop of green spaces designed by pioneering American landscape architect Frederick Law Olmsted. You'll see and hear about the city's major parks and gardens, including Boston Common, the Public Garden, the Commonwealth Avenue Mall, the Muddy River in the Fenway, Olmsted Park, Jamaica Pond, the Arnold Arboretum, and Franklin Park. The full 6-hour walk includes a 1-hour tour of any of the sites. Call for schedules. The **MDC Charles River Rangers** (☎ 617/727-9650, ext. 445) occasionally lead tours that focus on the river and the issues that affect it.

TROLLEY TOURS   The ticket-sellers who clamor for your business wherever tourists gather (notably in front of the Aquarium and on Boston Common) will claim no visit is complete without a day on a trolley. For many people, this is simply not true. A narrated tour on a trolley (actually a bus chassis with a trolley body) can give you an overview before you focus on specific attractions, or you can use the all-day pass to hit as many places as possible in 8 hours or so. Because Boston is so pedestrian friendly, a trolley tour isn't the best choice for the able-bodied and unencumbered making a long visit. In some neighborhoods, notably the North End, the trolleys stop a long way away from the attractions, so don't believe a ticket-seller who tells you otherwise. But if you're unable to walk long distances, or traveling with children, a trolley tour can be worth the money.

The business is extremely busy and competitive, with various firms offering different stops in an effort to distinguish themselves from the rest. All cover the major attractions and offer informative narratives and anecdotes in their 90- to 120-minute tours; most offer free reboarding if you want to visit the attractions.

Each tour is only as good as its guide, and quality varies widely—every few years a TV station or newspaper runs an "exposé" of the wacky information a tour guide is passing off as fact. Have a grain of salt ready.

Trolley tickets cost $18 to $24 for adults, $12 or less for children. Boarding spots are at hotels, historic sites, and tourist information centers. There are busy waiting areas near the New England Aquarium, the Park Street T stop, and the corner of Boylston Street and Charles Street South. Each company paints its cars a different color. Orange-and-green **Old Town Trolleys** (☎ 617/269-7150; www.historictours.com) are the most numerous. Minuteman Tours' **Boston Trolley Tours** (☎ 617/867-5539; www.historictours.com) are blue; **Beantown Trolleys** (☎ 800/343-1328 or 617/236-2148) say "Gray Line" but are red; and **CityView Luxury Trolleys** (☎ 617/363-7899, or 800/525-2489 outside 617) are silver. The **Discover Boston Multilingual Trolley Tours** (☎ 617/742-1440) vehicle is white; it conducts tours in Japanese, Spanish, French, German, and Italian.

"DUCK" TOURS   The most unusual way to see Boston is with ✪ **Boston Duck Tours** (☎ 800/226-7442 or 617/723-DUCK; www.bostonducktours.com). The tours, offered only from April to November, are pricey but great fun. Sightseers board a "duck," a reconditioned Second World War amphibious landing craft, on the Boylston Street side of the Prudential Center. The 80-minute narrated tour begins with a quick but comprehensive jaunt around the city. Then the duck lumbers down a ramp, splashes into the Charles River, and goes for a spin around the basin.

Tickets, available at the Prudential Center, are $21 for adults, $18 for seniors and students, $11 for children 4 to 12, and 25¢ for children under 4. Tours run every 30 minutes from 9am to 1 hour before sunset. Reservations are not accepted (except for groups of 16 or more), and tickets usually sell out, especially on weekends. Try to buy same-day tickets early in the day, or plan ahead and ask about the limited number of tickets available 2 days in advance.

SIGHTSEEING CRUISES

Take to the water for a taste of Boston's rich maritime history or a daylong break from walking and driving. You can cruise around the harbor or go all the way to Provincetown or Gloucester. The season runs from **April through October,** with spring and fall offerings often restricted to weekends. If you're traveling in a large group, call ahead for information about reservations and discounted tickets. If you're prone to seasickness, check the size of the vessel for your tour before buying tickets; larger boats provide more cushioning and comfort than smaller ones.

The largest company is **Boston Harbor Cruises,** 1 Long Wharf (☎ 617/227-4321; www.bostonboats.com). It runs 30-minute lunchtime cruises on weekdays at 12:15pm; tickets are $2. Ninety-minute **historic sightseeing cruises,** which tour the Inner and Outer Harbor, depart daily at 1 and 3pm, at 7pm (the sunset cruise), and at 11am on weekends and holidays. Tickets are $15 for adults, $12 for seniors, $10 for children under 12. The 45-minute *Constitution* cruise takes you around the Inner Harbor and docks at the Charlestown Navy Yard so that you can go ashore and

---

On the Cheap

You don't have to take a tour to take a cruise. The MBTA—as in the subway—runs a ferry that connects Long Wharf, the Charlestown Navy Yard, and Lovejoy Wharf (near North Station). It costs $1 (free if you have a visitor passport) and makes a good final leg of the Freedom Trail.

---

visit "Old Ironsides." Tours leave Long Wharf hourly from 10:30am to 4:30pm, and on the hour from the navy yard from 11am to 5pm. The cruise is $8 for adults, $7 for seniors, and $6 for children. The same company offers service to **Georges Island,** where free water-taxi service to the rest of the Boston Harbor Islands is available (see the box "A Vacation in the Islands").

Massachusetts Bay Lines (☎ 617/542-8000; www.massbaylines.com) offers 55-minute **harbor tours** from Memorial Day through Columbus Day. Cruises leave from Rowes Wharf on the hour from 10am to 6pm; the price is $8 for adults, $5 for children and seniors. The 90-minute sunset cruise departs at 7pm. Tickets are $15 for adults, $10 for children and seniors.

The **Charles Riverboat Company** (☎ 617/621-3001; www.charlesriverboat. com) offers 55-minute narrated cruises around the **lower Charles River basin** and in the opposite direction, through the **Charles River locks to Boston Harbor.** Boats depart from the CambridgeSide Galleria mall; river tours leave on the hour from noon to 5pm, harbor tours once a day, at 10:30am. Tickets for either tour are $8 for adults, $6 for seniors, and $5 for children 2 to 12.

DAY TRIPS   Bay State Cruises (☎ 617/748-1428; www.baystatecruises.baweb. com) operates conventional and high-speed service to Provincetown. Trips leave from Commonwealth Pier at the World Trade Center, 164 Northern Ave. The water shuttle from Long Wharf has been discontinued, but there's ferry service (☎ 617/ 227-4321; www.mbta.com) to Commonwealth Pier from Lovejoy Wharf, behind North Station, and water taxi service (☎ 617/422-0392) from around the harbor. You can also take a regular old land taxi; when you reserve your cruise, ask the clerk the best way to reach the pier from your hotel.

MV *Provincetown II* sails daily from mid-June to Labor Day, and on weekends late May to mid-June and September to Columbus Day. It leaves at 9am for the 3-hour trip to Provincetown, at the tip of Cape Cod. The return trip leaves at 3:30pm, giving you 3¹/₂ hours for shopping and sightseeing in P-town. Same-day round-trip fares are $30 for adults, $23 for senior citizens, and $21 for children 3 to 12. Bringing a bike costs $5 extra each way. High-speed service takes 1 hour and 50 minutes, and operates twice a day from late May to Columbus Day. Trips leave Boston at 8am and 4pm, and Provincetown at 10:30am and 6:30pm. The round-trip fare is $75, plus $5 each way for your bike. Reservations are recommended.

A.C. Cruise Line (☎ 800/422-8419 or 617/261-6633; www.accruiseline.com) offers an excursion to **Gloucester.** The *Virginia C II* leaves Pier 7, 290 Northern Ave., daily from late June through Labor Day at 10am and returns at 5pm. You'll have about 2¹/₂ hours to explore Gloucester. Tickets are $18 for adults, $14 for seniors, $10 for children.

WHALE WATCHING

For whale-watching trips from Cape Ann, see the box "A Whale of an Adventure," in chapter 11.

Trip the Light Fantastic

The oldest lighthouse in North America, Boston Light is the only one in the country that's still staffed (by the Coast Guard). Built on Little Brewster Island in 1716, it fell to the British in 1776 and was rebuilt in 1783. Tours of the 102-foot lighthouse include a round-trip cruise and a chance to climb the spiral stairs to the top (you must be 50 in. tall). The 3-hour excursions leave from the Harbor Islands Discovery Center at Fan Pier on summer Saturdays at 9am and 1pm. Tickets are $25 for adults, $20 for seniors, $15 for children under 12. Reservations (☎ 617/ 223-8666) are recommended.

The **New England Aquarium** (☎ 617/973-5281; see "The Top Attractions," above) runs whale watches daily from May through mid-October and on weekends in April and late October. You'll travel several miles out to sea to Stellwagen Bank, the feeding ground for the whales as they migrate from Newfoundland to Provincetown. Tickets (cash only) are $26 for adults, $21 for senior citizens and college students, $19 for youths 12 to 18, and $16.50 for children 3 to 11. Children must be 3 years old and at least 30 inches tall. Reservations are strongly recommended and can be held with a MasterCard or Visa.

Boston Harbor Whale Watch (☎ 617/345-9866; www.bostonwhale.com) promises more time watching whales than trying to find them. Tours depart from Rowes Wharf beginning in mid-June and operate Friday through Sunday until the end of the month. From July through early September, there's daily service. Departure times are 10am on weekdays, 9am and 2pm on weekends. Expect to spend about 4¹/₂ hours at sea. Tickets are $21 for adults, $18 for seniors and children under 13. Reservations are suggested.

Several other companies offer whale watches: **Boston Harbor Cruises** (☎ 617/ 227-4321; www.bostonboats.com), which has a high-speed catamaran; **A.C. Cruise Line** (☎ 800/422-8419 or 617/261-6633; www.accruiseline.com); and **Massachusetts Bay Lines** (☎ 617/542-8000; www.massbaylines.com).

SPECIALTY TOURS

THE LITERARY TRAIL   A tour of pertinent sites in Boston, Cambridge, and Concord, the Literary Trail (☎ 617/574-5950; www.Lit-Trail.org) was an instant hit in 1999. You can take a narrated trolley tour or visit on your own, using a guide that's available at local bookstores. The 4-hour, 20-mile trolley excursion begins and ends at the Omni Parker House hotel (you can also exit in Harvard Square). It explores locations associated with authors and poets such as Emerson, Thoreau, Longfellow, and Louisa May Alcott, among others. The fare is $35 for adults, $31.50 for students and children under 18; reservations are required.

FOR HORROR-MOVIE FANS   "Ghosts and Gravestones" covers burial grounds and other shiver-inducing areas in a trolley and on foot. Presented by Minuteman Tours (☎ 617/269-3626; www.historictours.com), the 2-hour tour starts at dusk on summer and fall weekends. It costs $28 for adults, $15 for children.

MORE SPECIAL-INTEREST TOURS   Boston's busiest operator of theme tours is **Old Town Trolley** (☎ 617/269-7150; www.historictours.com). Schedules and offerings vary according to the season and level of visitor interest. Prices vary according to what's included but are usually at least $20 for adults, a little less for seniors and children. Call ahead for reservations, meeting places, and details of the tours. At press time, options included **"JFK's Boston"** (with stops at John F. Kennedy's birthplace in Brookline and the presidential library), separate tours for **seafood** lovers and **chocolate** lovers, a tour that stops at several **brew pubs,** and a December **"Holiday Lights"** tour.

10 Outdoor Pursuits

The incredibly helpful site maintained by the ✪ **Metropolitan District Commission** (www.magnet.state.ma.us/mdc) includes descriptions of properties and activities and has a planning area to help you make the most of your time.

BEACHES

The beaches in Boston proper (discussed below) are decent places to catch a cool breeze and splash around, but for real ocean surf, you need to head out of town.

NORTH SHORE BEACHES   North of Boston are sandy beaches that complement the rocky coastline. Two caveats: (1) It's not Florida, so don't expect 70° water (the operative word is *refreshing*), and (2) parking can be scarce, especially on weekends, and pricey—as much as $15 per car. If you can't set out early, wait till mid-afternoon and hope that the people who beat you to the beach in the morning have had enough. During the summer, lifeguards are on duty 9am to 5pm at larger public beaches. Surfing is generally permitted outside of those hours.

Probably the best-known North Shore beach is **Singing Beach** (off Masconomo Street in Manchester-by-the-Sea), named for the sound the sand makes under your feet. The legions of people walking six-tenths of a mile on Beach Street from the downtown commuter rail station attest to both the beach's reputation and the difficulty and expense of parking. Save some cash and bother by taking the MBTA (☎ **617/222-3200;** www.mbta.com) from Boston's North Station.

Nearly as famous and equally popular is **Crane Beach,** off Argilla Road in Ipswich, part of a 1,400-acre barrier beach reservation. Expanses of white sand and fragile dunes lead down to Ipswich Bay, and the surf is calmer than that at less sheltered Singing Beach, but still quite chilly. Also on Ipswich Bay is Gloucester's **Wingaersheek Beach,** on Atlantic Street off Route 133. It has its own exit (no. 13) off Route 128, about 15 minutes away on winding roads with low speed limits. When you finally arrive, you'll find beautiful white sand, a glorious view, and more dunes.

The beach at the **Parker River National Wildlife Refuge** (☎ **508/465-5753**) is *not* open all summer—it closes April 1 for piping plover nesting season. The areas not being used for nesting reopen July 1, and the rest of the beach opens in August when the birds are through with it. The currents are strong and can be dangerous, and there are no lifeguards—you might prefer to stick to surf fishing and exploring the trails that crisscross the gorgeous marshes and dunes and allow you to view the extraordinary variety of birds and wildlife.

Swimming or not, watch out for the **greenhead flies** at North Shore beaches in late July and early August. They don't sting—they actually take little bites of flesh. Plan to bring or buy insect repellent.

Closer to Boston are **Nahant Beach** (follow the signs from the intersection of Route 1A and Route 129, near the Lynn–Swampscott border), which is large and extremely popular, and **Revere Beach.** Revere Beach is better known for its pickup scene than its narrow strip of sand, but the cruising crowds are friendly, and parking on the boulevard is free. The Blue Line of the T has a Revere Beach stop; if you're driving, head north to **Point of Pines,** which has smaller crowds and its own exit off Route 1A.

Meat Me at the Beach

No trip to Revere Beach is complete without a stop at **Kelly's Roast Beef,** 410 Revere Beach Blvd. (☎ **781/284-9129**). Open all year, not just in the summer, Kelly's is a local legend for its onion rings, fried clams, and roast beef sandwiches— and the double burger from the "sandwich welfare" scene in *Good Will Hunting*.

SOUTH SHORE BEACHES   Private beaches dominate the southern suburbs, but there are a couple of pleasant public options. In Hull (take Route 3 or 3A to Route 228), **Nantasket Beach** (☎ **617/925-4905**) is right in town. It's popular with families for its fairly shallow water and the historic wooden carousel in a building across the street from the main parking lot. Nine-mile-long **Duxbury Beach** (take Route 3A to Route 139 north, and go right on Canal Street) makes an enjoyable stop on the way to Plymouth, if that's in your plans. **Plymouth Beach,** off Route 3A south of downtown at Warren Avenue, is smaller, with mild surf.

BOSTON BEACHES   The condition of Boston Harbor has improved considerably since its pollution was an issue in the 1988 presidential campaign. The **Metropolitan District Commission** (☎ **617/727-9547**) is working to restore the run-down beaches. Red flags fly when swimming is not recommended; blue flags mean the water's fine. These are very much neighborhood hangouts. In Dorchester, off Morrissey Boulevard, **Malibu Beach** and **Savin Hill Beach** are within walking distance of the Savin Hill stop on the Red Line. South Boston beaches are off Day Boulevard; you reach them by taking the Red Line to Broadway or Green Line to Copley, then a bus marked "City Point" (routes 9, 10, and 11). Among them are **Castle Island, L Street,** and **Pleasure Bay.**

BIKING

Expert cyclists who feel comfortable with the layout of the city (a tiny group) shouldn't have too much trouble navigating in traffic. Recreational bikers will be much better off sticking to Cambridge, which has bike lanes, or the area's many bike paths. State law requires that children under 12 wear helmets. Bicycles are forbidden on MBTA buses and the Green Line at all times, and during rush hours on the other parts of the system. You must have a $5 permit (☎ **617/222-3302**) to bring your bike on the Blue, Orange, and Red lines and commuter rail during nonrush hours.

On summer Sundays from 11am to 7pm, a flat 1½-mile stretch of **Memorial Drive** in Cambridge from Western Avenue to the Eliot Bridge (Central Square to west Cambridge) is closed to cars. It's also popular with pedestrians and in-line skaters, and can get quite crowded. The **Dr. Paul Dudley White Charles River Bike Path** is a 17.7-mile circuit that begins at Science Park (near the Museum of Science) and loops along both sides of the river to Watertown and back. You can enter and exit at many points along the way. Bikers share the path with joggers and in-line skaters, especially in Boston near the Esplanade and in Cambridge near Harvard Square. The **Metropolitan District Commission,** or MDC (☎ **617/727-9547**), maintains this path. It also maintains the 5-mile **Pierre Lallement Bike Path,** in Southwest Corridor Park, which starts behind Copley Place and runs through the South End and Roxbury along the route of the MBTA Orange Line to Franklin Park. The 10½-mile **Minuteman Bikeway** starts at Alewife station at the end of the Red Line in Cambridge. It runs through Arlington and Lexington to Bedford along an old railroad bed, a wonderful way to head out to the historic sites in Lexington.

Rental shops require you to show a driver's license or passport and leave a deposit using a major credit card. Most charge around $5 an hour, with a minimum of at least 2 hours, or a flat daily rate of about $25. In Boston, try **Earth Bikes 'n' Blades,** 35 Huntington Ave., near Copley Square (☎ **617/267-4733**); **Back Bay Bikes & Boards,** 333 Newbury St., near Mass. Ave. (☎ **617/247-2336**); and **Community Bicycle Supply,** 496 Tremont St., near East Berkeley Street (☎ **617/542-8623**).

For additional information, contact **MassBike** (☎ **617/491-7433;** www.massbike. org), also known as the Bicycle Coalition of Massachusetts.

BOATING

Technically, riding a **swan boat** is boating—it has been a classic Boston experience since 1877. The lagoon at the Public Garden (☎ **617/522-1966;** www.swanboats. com; see "Parks & Gardens," above) turns into a fiberglass swan habitat every spring and summer. Steel-thighed attendants do the pedaling as you go on a 15-minute cruise.

There are also plenty of less tame options (see "Sailing," below). The **Charles River Canoe and Kayak Center** (☎ **617/965-5110;** www.ski-paddle.com) has two locations, on Soldiers Field Road in Allston and at 2401 Commonwealth Ave. in Newton. Both centers rent canoes and kayaks (the Newton location also rents sculls) and offer lessons. From April through October, they open at 10am on weekdays and 9am on weekends and holidays, and close at dusk.

FISHING

For information on locations and regulations, call the Sport Fishing Information Line (☎ **800/ASK-FISH**). Information is also available from the state **Division of Fisheries and Wildlife,** 100 Cambridge St., Room 1902, Boston, MA 02202 (☎ **617/ 727-3151**), and in the fishing columns in the *Globe* and *Herald* on Fridays in the spring, summer, and fall.

Charter fishing in Boston Harbor is a growth industry. The main attraction from May to October is striped bass. Reserve at least a week ahead. **Reel Pursuit Fishing Charters** (☎ **617/731-1172** or 617/922-3474; www.bostonfishing.com) uses a 34-foot boat that holds up to six people. Expect to pay about $350 for a 4-hour charter. For fly-fishing, try **Firefly Outfitters** (☎ **617/423-3474;** www. firefly-outfitters.net). A half-day excursion in an 18-foot boat costs $295 for two people, $345 for three.

GOLF

You won't get far in the suburbs without seeing a golf course, and with the recent explosion in the sport's popularity, you won't be the only one looking. Given a choice, opt for the lower prices and smaller crowds you'll find on weekdays. The **Massachusetts Golf Association,** 175 Highland Ave., Needham, MA 02192 (☎ **781/ 449-3000;** www.mgalinks.org), represents more than 310 golf courses around the state and will send you a list of courses on request.

At **Newton Commonwealth Golf Course,** 212 Kenrick St., Newton (☎ **617/ 630-1971;** www.newtongolf.com/newton), an excellent 18-hole layout designed by Donald Ross, par is 70 and greens fees are $23 on weekdays and $30 on weekends. At the 9-hole, par-35 **Fresh Pond Golf Course,** 691 Huron Ave., Cambridge (☎ **617/ 349-6282;** www.freshpondgolf.com), it's $16, or $23 to go around twice, on weekdays, and $19 and $29 on weekends. Two 18-hole, par-70 courses lie within the city limits: the **William J. Devine Golf Course,** in Franklin Park, Dorchester (☎ **617/ 265-4084;** www.newtongolf.com/franklinpark), where greens fees are $22 on

A Vacation in the Islands

Majestic ocean views, hiking trails, historic sites, rocky beaches, nature walks, campsites, and picnic areas abound in New England. To find them all together, take a 45-minute trip east (yes, east) of Boston. The **Boston Harbor Islands** (☎ 617/223-8666; www.bostonislands.com) were under your nose if you arrived by plane, but until recently their accessibility wasn't widely known. They became a National Recreation Area in 1997, and summer travelers can now take better advantage of their unspoiled beauty and easy access.

There are 30 islands in the Outer Harbor, and at least a half dozen are open for exploring, camping, or swimming. Bring a sweater or jacket. You can investigate on your own or take a ranger-led tour. Plan a day trip or even an overnight stay, but note that fresh water is available only on Georges Island, and management suggests that you bring your own.

Ferries run to the most popular, **Georges Island,** home of Fort Warren (1834), where Confederate prisoners were kept during the Civil War. Tours are offered periodically. The island has a visitor center, refreshment area, fishing pier, picnic area, and wonderful view of Boston's skyline. From there, free water taxis run to **Lovell, Gallops, Peddocks, Bumpkin,** and **Grape islands,** which have picnic areas and campsites. Lovell Island also has the remains of a fort (Fort Standish) and a sandy beach; it's the only harbor island with supervised swimming in the chilly water.

For more information, stop at the **Discovery Center** in the courthouse on Fan Pier, on Northern Avenue across the Fort Point Channel from the Boston Harbor Hotel. You can also consult the staff at the **kiosk on Long Wharf,** the Web site, or the sources below.

Boston Harbor Cruises (☎ 617/227-4321; www.bostonboats.com) serves Georges Island from Long Wharf; the trip takes 45 minutes, and tickets are $8 for adults, $7 for seniors, $6 for children under 12. Cruises depart at 10am, noon, and 2pm on spring and fall weekends, and daily on the hour from 10am to 4pm in the summer. In the off-season, check ahead for a winter wildlife excursion (scheduled occasionally). Water taxis and admission to the islands are free.

Administered as a National Park Partnership, the Boston Harbor Islands National Recreation Area (www.nps.gov/boha) is the focus of a public-private project designed to make the islands more interesting and accessible. For more information, contact the **Friends of the Boston Harbor Islands** (☎ 617/740-4290; www.fbhi.org). The **Metropolitan District Commission** (☎ 617/727-7676; www.magnet.state.ma.us/mdc/harbor.htm) administers Georges, Lovell, and Peddocks islands; the state **Department of Environmental Management** (☎ 617/740-1605) oversees Gallops, Grape, and Bumpkin islands.

---

weekdays and $25 on weekends, and **George Wright Golf Course,** 420 West St., Hyde Park (☎ 617/361-8313), where fees are $24 on weekdays and $27 on weekends.

GYMS

If your hotel doesn't have a health club, the concierge or front desk staff can recommend one nearby and possibly give you a pass good for free or discounted admission. The best combination of facilities and value is at the **Central Branch YMCA,** 316 Huntington Ave., near Symphony Hall (☎ 617/536-7800). A $10 1-day pass includes the use of the pool, gym, weight room, fitness center, and indoor track. Closer to downtown,

Fitcorp (☎ 617/375-5600; www.fitcorp.com) charges $12 for a guest pass that includes well-equipped facilities but not a pool. It has branches at 1 Beacon St. (☎ 617/248-9797), near Government Center; 133 Federal St. (☎ 617/542-1010), in the Financial District; and in the Prudential Center (☎ 617/262-2050).

HIKING

The **Bay Circuit Trail** is a 200-mile corridor of open space that curves around Boston from Newburyport, near the New Hampshire border, to Kingston Bay, a bit north of Plymouth. In early 2000, the last pieces of this giant ribbon of conservation land were just falling into place, but you probably won't be hiking the whole thing (will you?). The trail touches on 50 cities and towns; it comes closest to the areas covered in this book when it cuts through **Concord** along the north shore of Walden Pond (see chapter 11). For information, contact the nonprofit Bay Circuit Alliance, 3 Railroad St., Andover, MA 01810 (☎ 978/470-1982; www.serve.com/baycircuit).

The **Boston Harbor Islands** also offer great hiking; it takes a half-day's hike to circle the largest island, Peddocks. See the box "A Vacation in the Islands," above.

ICE-SKATING & IN-LINE SKATING

The skating rink at the Boston Common **Frog Pond** (☎ 617/635-2197) is a popular cold-weather destination. It's an open surface with an ice-making system and a clubhouse where you can rent skates for $5; admission is $3 for adults, free for children under 14. It gets unbelievably crowded on weekend afternoons, so try to go in the morning or on a weekday.

A favorite spot for in-line skaters is the **Esplanade,** between the Back Bay and the Charles River. It continues onto the bike path that runs to Watertown and back, but after you leave the Esplanade the pavement isn't totally smooth, which can lead to mishaps. Your best bet is to wait for a Sunday in the summer, when **Memorial Drive** in Cambridge is closed to traffic from 11am to 7pm. It's a perfect surface. Unless you're confident of your ability and your knowledge of Boston traffic, staying off the streets is a good idea.

If you didn't bring your skates, you have several options for renting. A former Olympic cyclist and speed skater runs **Eric Flaim's Motion Sports,** 349 Newbury St. (☎ 617/247-3284). Or try **Back Bay Bikes & Boards,** 333 Newbury St. (☎ 617/247-2336); the **Beacon Hill Skate Shop,** 135 Charles St. S. (☎ 617/482-7400); **Earth Bikes 'n' Blades,** 35 Huntington Ave. (☎ 617/267-4733); or **Ski Market,** 860 Commonwealth Ave. (☎ 617/731-6100).

The **InLine Club of Boston's** Web site (www.sk8net.com) offers up-to-date event and safety information and an extremely clever logo.

JOGGING

The 17.7-mile **Dr. Paul Dudley White Charles River Bike Path** is also a popular jogging route. The bridges that connect Boston and Cambridge allow for circuits of various lengths. Don't jog at night, try not to go alone, and always be careful around abutments, where you can't see far ahead. If you're not staying near the river, the concierge or desk staff at your hotel may be able to provide a map with suggested jogging routes.

Other sources of information include the **Metropolitan District Commission** (☎ 617/727-1300) and the **Bill Rodgers Running Center** in Faneuil Hall Marketplace (☎ 617/723-5612). As in any large city, stay out of park areas (including the Esplanade) at night.

SAILING

Sailboats fill the Charles River basin all summer and skim across the Inner Harbor in all but the coldest weather. Your options during a short stay aren't especially cost-effective, but they are fun.

The best deal is with **Community Boating, Inc.,** 21 Embankment Rd., on the Esplanade (☎ 617/523-1038; www.community-boating.org). Visitors pay $50 for 2 days of unlimited use. The oldest public sailing facility in the country offers lessons and boating programs for children and adults from April to November. The **Boston Sailing Center,** 54 Lewis Wharf (☎ 617/227-4198; www.bostonsailingcenter.com), offers lessons for sailors of all ability levels. The center is open all year (even for "frost-bite" racing in the winter). The least expensive 30-day "mini-membership" costs $325. Prices for chartering a boat with a captain start at $100 an hour, with a 2-hour minimum and a six-person maximum.

TENNIS

Public courts maintained by the **Metropolitan District Commission** (☎ 617/727-1300) are available throughout the city at no charge. To find the one nearest you, call the MDC or ask the concierge or desk staff at your hotel. Well-maintained courts near downtown that seldom get busy until after work are at several spots on the **Southwest Corridor Park** in the South End (there's a nice one near West Newton Street) and off Commercial Street near the North Washington Street bridge in the **North End.** The courts on **Boston Common** and in **Charlesbank Park,** overlooking the river next to the bridge to the Museum of Science, are more crowded during the day.

11 Spectator Sports

Boston's well-deserved reputation as a great sports town derives in part from the days when at least one of the city's professional teams was one of the world's best. With the exception of the Patriots, who play in suburban Foxboro, none of them has done much lately. Passions still run deep, though: Insult the local teams and be ready to defend yourself. That enthusiasm applies to some college sports as well, particularly hockey, in which the Division I schools are fierce rivals.

The new (as of 1995) **FleetCenter** and **Boston Garden History Center,** 150 Causeway St. (☎ 617/624-1518; www.fleetcenter.com), are open for tours; call for schedules during your visit. Tickets are $6 for adults, $5 for seniors and students, $4.50 for children under 12.

On the FleetCenter's fifth- and sixth-floor concourses, the **Sports Museum of New England** (☎ 617/624-1234 or 617/787-7678; www.townonline.com/sportsmuseum) highlights local teams and athletes (especially the Celtics and Bruins, who play in the building). Always call ahead; there's no access during events. Hours usually are Tuesday to Saturday 10am to 5pm, Sunday noon to 5pm. Admission is $5 adults, $4 seniors and children 6 to 17, free for children under 6.

BASEBALL

No other experience in sports matches watching the **Boston Red Sox** play at ✪ **Fenway Park,** which they do from early April to early October, and later if they make the playoffs. The quirkiness of the oldest park in the major leagues (1912) and the fact that (at press time) the team last won the World Series in 1918 only add to the mystique. A hand-operated scoreboard is built into the Green Monster, or left-field wall (watch carefully during a pitching change—the left fielder from either team might suddenly disappear into the darkness to cool off), and the wall itself is such a celebrity that it's often

Boston's quirky little Fenway Park . . . has been the scene of so many heartbreaks and dashed hopes that it is to Beantowners what the Bridge of Sighs is to Venetians.
—Charles McGrath, *The New York Times Book Review,* 1999

called simply The Wall. It's 37 feet tall, a mere 298 feet from home plate (don't believe the sign), and irresistibly tempting to batters who ought to know better. On two vertical white lines on the scoreboard you'll see Morse code for the initials of late owners Thomas A. and Jean R. Yawkey.

The crowds can be as interesting as the architecture. Fans wedge themselves into narrow, uncomfortable seats close to the field, bond with total strangers, reminisce, and make bold predictions. The "Friendly Fenway" fan-relations campaign has produced better-mannered employees, a greater variety of concession items (but not lower prices), and expanded family-seating sections, but that's not why you're here. You're in an intensely green place that's older than your grandparents, inhaling a Fenway Frank and wishing for a home run—what could be better?

Practical concerns: Compared with its modern brethren, Fenway is tiny. Tickets go on sale in January, and the earlier you order, the better chance you'll have of landing seats during your visit. Forced to choose between tickets for a low-numbered grandstand section (say, 10 or below) and bleacher seats, go for the bleachers. They can get rowdy during night games, but the view is better from there than from the deep right-field corner. Every ticket is expensive—during the 2000 season, after a third straight price hike, the cheapest seat was $14. Throughout the season, a limited number of standing-room tickets go on sale the day of the game, and presold tickets sometimes are returned. It can't hurt to check, especially if the team isn't playing well. The fans are incredibly loyal, but they're not all obsessed.

The **Fenway Park ticket office** (☎ 617/267-8661 for information, 617/267-1700 for tickets, 617/482-4SOX for touch-tone ticketing; www.redsox.com) is at 4 Yawkey Way, near the corner of Brookline Avenue. Tickets for people with disabilities and in no-alcohol sections are available. Smoking is not allowed in the park. Games usually begin at 6 or 7pm on weeknights and 1pm on weekends. Take the MBTA Green Line B, C, or D to Kenmore, or D to Fenway.

You can also take a **Fenway Park tour** (☎ 617/236-6666), which includes a walk on the warning track. From May to September, tours begin on weekdays only at 10am, 11am, noon, and 1pm, plus 2pm when the team is away. There are no tours on holidays or before day games. Admission is $5 for adults, $4 for seniors, $3 for children under 16.

BASKETBALL

Sixteen National Basketball Association championship banners hang from the ceiling of the FleetCenter, testimony to the glorious history of the **Boston Celtics.** Unfortunately, the most recent is from 1986.

The Celtics play from early October to April or May; when a top contender is visiting, you may have trouble buying tickets. Prices are as low as $10 for some games and top out at $70. For information, call the FleetCenter (☎ 617/624-1000; www.nba.com/celtics); for tickets, contact Ticketmaster (☎ 617/931-2000; www.ticketmaster.com). To reach the FleetCenter, take the MBTA Green or Orange Line or commuter rail to North Station.

Going Out of Business . . . Maybe

Plans are afoot to tear down most of Fenway Park (preserving the legendary Wall) and move the Red Sox into a new facility nearby. The project is only a couple of steps beyond theoretical, but the wheels are in motion. If you want to see it, see it now, while you still can.

The local college teams are competitive but (with the exception of the Harvard women) not world-beaters. The schools and venues: **Boston College,** Conte Forum, Chestnut Hill (☎ **617/552-3000**); **Boston University,** Walter Brown Arena, 285 Babcock St. (☎ **617/353-3838**); **Harvard University,** Lavietes Pavilion, North Harvard Street, Allston (☎ **617/495-2211**); and **Northeastern University,** Matthews Arena, St. Botolph Street (☎ **617/373-4700**).

FOOTBALL

The **New England Patriots** (☎ **800/543-1776;** www.patriots.com) were playing to standing-room-only crowds even before they went to (and lost) the Super Bowl in 1997. The Patriots play from August through December (or January if they make the playoffs) at Foxboro Stadium on Route 1, about a 45-minute drive south of the city. Tickets ($23 to $60) almost always sell out. Plan as far in advance as you can.

Work on a new stadium has begun, so watch out for construction-related traffic. You can drive (leave lots of extra time even if there isn't construction) or catch a bus from the entrance of South Station, the Riverside T station, or Shopper's World in Framingham, west of the city.

Boston College, another tough ticket, is New England's only Division I-A college football team. The Eagles play at Alumni Stadium in Chestnut Hill (☎ **617/ 552-3000**). The area's Division I-AA teams are **Harvard University,** Harvard Stadium, North Harvard Street, Allston (☎ **617/495-2211**), and **Northeastern University,** Parsons Field, Kent Street, Brookline (☎ **617/373-4700**).

GOLF TOURNAMENTS

Two of the three major tours get within about an hour of downtown Boston. The tournaments have changed their schedules several times in recent years; at press time, both are in August, but call ahead for dates and other information. The LPGA Tour visits Pleasant Valley Country Club in Sutton (☎ **508/865-5244;** www.pleasantvalleyycc. com), and the Senior PGA Tour hits Nashawtuc Country Club in Concord (☎ **978/369-3457**). The *Globe* and *Herald* regularly list numerous amateur events for fun and charity.

HOCKEY

The **Boston Bruins** are in roughly the same condition as the Celtics—burdened by history and looking to the future. In 1997, for the first time in 3 decades, the Bruins failed to make the playoffs. Their games are exciting, especially if you happen to be in town at the same time as the arch-rival Montréal Canadians, but incredibly expensive ($43 to $70). Tickets for many games sell out early despite being among the priciest in the league. For information, call the FleetCenter (☎ **617/624-1000;** www. bostonbruins.com); for tickets, contact Ticketmaster (☎ **617/931-2000;** www. ticketmaster.com). To reach the FleetCenter, take the MBTA Green or Orange Line or commuter rail to North Station.

Economical fans who don't have their hearts set on seeing a pro game will be pleasantly surprised by the quality of local **college hockey.** Even for sold-out games, standing-room tickets are usually available the night of the game. Women's games usually don't sell out. The local teams regularly hit the national rankings; they include **Boston College,** Conte Forum, Chestnut Hill (☎ 617/552-3000); **Boston University,** Walter Brown Arena, 285 Babcock St. (☎ 617/353-3838); **Harvard University,** Bright Hockey Center, North Harvard Street, Allston (☎ 617/495-2211); and **Northeastern University,** Matthews Arena, St. Botolph Street (☎ 617/373-4700). These four are the Beanpot schools, whose men's teams play a tradition-steeped tournament on the first two Mondays of February at the FleetCenter.

HORSE RACING

✪ **Suffolk Downs,** 111 Waldemar Ave., East Boston (☎ 617/567-3900; www.suffolkdowns.com), is one of the best-run smaller tracks in the country. It's an excellent family destination (really), sparkling clean, and the home of the Massachusetts Handicap, run in early June. Horse of the Year Cigar won the MassCap in 1995 and 1996, conferring instant cachet on the event and the facility. The season runs from late September to early June, and there are extensive simulcasting options during and after the live racing season. The day's entries appear in the *Globe* and the *Herald.* The track is off Route 1A, about a mile from Logan Airport. The Blue Line of the T has a Suffolk Downs station; wait for the shuttle bus or walk about 10 minutes to the track entrance.

THE MARATHON

Every year on Patriots Day (the third Monday in April), the ✪ **Boston Marathon** rules the roads from suburban Hopkinton to Copley Square in Boston. Cheering fans line the entire route. An especially nice place to watch is tree-shaded Commonwealth Avenue between Kenmore Square and Mass. Ave., but you'll be in a crowd wherever you stand, particularly near the finish line in front of the Boston Public Library. For information about qualifying, contact the **Boston Athletic Association** (☎ 617/236-1652; www.bostonmarathon.org).

ROWING

In late October, the **Head of the Charles Regatta** (☎ 617/864-8415; www.hocr.org) attracts more rowers than any other crew event in the country to Boston and Cambridge. Some 4,000 oarsmen and oarswomen race against the clock for 4 miles from the Charles River basin to the Eliot Bridge in west Cambridge. Tens of thousands of spectators socialize and occasionally watch the action, which runs nonstop on Saturday afternoon and all day Sunday.

Spring crew racing is far more exciting than the "head" format; the course is 1¼ miles, and races last just 5 to 7 minutes. Men's and women's collegiate events take place on Saturday mornings in April and early May in the Charles River basin. You'll have a perfect view of the finish line from Memorial Drive between the MIT boathouse and the Hyatt Regency. To find out who's racing, check the Friday *Globe* sports section.

SOCCER

The **New England Revolution** (☎ 508/543-0350; www.nerevolution.com) of Major League Soccer plays at Foxboro Stadium on Route 1 from April through July. Tickets are available through Ticketmaster (☎ 617/931-2000; www.ticketmaster.com). Unless the team or its opponent is doing incredibly well, buying tickets the day of the match shouldn't be too difficult. Be sure to leave extra time to negotiate the congested roads near the stadium.

Boston Strolls

Walking is the best way to see Boston. The narrow, twisting streets that make driving such a headache are a treat for pedestrians, who are never far from something worth seeing. The central city is compact—walking east to west quickly from one end to the other takes about an hour—and dotted with historically and architecturally interesting buildings and neighborhoods.

In this chapter you'll find three tours of **Boston** and one of **Harvard Square** in Cambridge. Tours 1 and 2 include (with some detours) the ✪ **Freedom Trail,** which links 16 historical sights with a 3-mile red line on the sidewalk first painted in 1958.

Be sure to wear comfortable walking shoes, and if you're not inclined to pay designer prices for designer water, bring your own bottle and fill it with ice at the hotel. By the time it's ready for you, you'll be ready for it.

Walking Tour 1:
Downtown Boston & Beacon Hill

Start: Boston Common (T: Green or Red Line to Park Street).
Finish: Faneuil Hall (Congress and North streets).
Time: At least 2 hours. Allow 3 if the attractions sound especially appealing. If you elect to continue to Museum Wharf, add at least $1^{1}/_{2}$ hours.
Best Times: Early morning to early afternoon.
Worst Times: Mid-afternoon, when closing times and rush hour quickly approach.

Park Street station, at the corner of Park and Tremont streets, sits at the edge of:

1. **Boston Common.** In 1634, when their settlement was just 4 years old, the town fathers paid the Rev. William Blackstone £30 for this property. In 1640 it was set aside as common land. The 45 or so acres of the country's oldest public park have served as a cow pasture, a military camp, and the site of hangings, protest marches, and visits by dignitaries. Today the Common is a bit run-down, especially compared with the adjacent Public Garden, but it buzzes with activity all day. You might see a

Caught in the Web

The nonprofit **Freedom Trail Foundation** (☎ **617/227-8800;** www.thefreedom-trail.org) makes an excellent jumping-off point while you're planning your visit. Call for a guide or, even better, check out the interactive Web site. If you're interested, it's the only way to rub gravestones legally.

demonstration, a musical performance, a picnic lunch, or a game of tag—almost everything but a cow (except during the Boston Dairy Festival in early June). Cows have been banned since 1830, which seems to be one of the few events related to the Common that isn't commemorated with a plaque.

One of the loveliest markers is on this route; head up the hill from the train station inside the fence, not on the sidewalk. At Beacon Street is a memorial designed by **Augustus Saint-Gaudens** to celebrate the deeds (indeed, the very existence) of Col. Robert Gould Shaw and the Union Army's **54th Massachusetts Colored Regiment,** who fought in the Civil War. You might remember the story of this first American army unit made up of free black soldiers from the movie *Glory.*

Across Beacon Street is the:

2. Massachusetts State House (☎ **617/727-3676**). Boston is one of the only American cities where a building whose cornerstone was laid in 1795 (by Governor **Samuel Adams**) would be called the "new" anything. Nevertheless, this is the new State House, as opposed to the Old State House (stop no. 11 on this tour). The great Federal-era architect **Charles Bulfinch** designed the central building of the state capitol, and in 1802 copper sheathing manufactured by **Paul Revere** replaced shingles on the landmark dome. Gold leaf now covers the dome; during the blackouts of the Second World War, it was painted black. The state legislature, formally named the Massachusetts General Court, meets here. The House of Representatives congregates under a wooden fish, the **Sacred Cod.** John Rowe, known as "Merchant" Rowe (Rowes Wharf bears his name), donated the carving in 1784 as a reminder of fishing's importance to the local economy. Free tours (guided and self-guided) leave from the second floor. The newest art installation, **"Hear Us,"** honors women's contributions to the state (see "Focus on Women's History" in chapter 7). Whether or not you decide to go inside, be sure to study some of the many statues outside. Subjects range from **Mary Dyer,** a Quaker hanged on the Common in 1660 for refusing to abandon her religious beliefs, to President **John F. Kennedy.** The 60-foot monument at the rear (off Bowdoin Street) illustrates Beacon Hill's original height, before the top was shorn off to use in 19th-century landfill projects.

Leaving the State House, walk down **Park Street**—laid out by Bulfinch in 1804—and look back at the second-floor balcony, where the governor sometimes steps outside for a breath of air. At the foot of the hill at Tremont Street is:

3. Park Street Church, 1 Park St. (☎ **617/523-3383**). Henry James described the 1809 structure with the 217-foot steeple as "the most interesting mass of bricks and mortar in America." The church has accumulated an impressive number of firsts: The first missionaries to Hawaii left from here in 1819; the prominent abolitionist **William Lloyd Garrison** gave his first antislavery speech here on July 4, 1829; and **"America"** ("My Country 'Tis of Thee") was first sung here on July 4, 1831. You're standing on **"Brimstone Corner,"** named either for the passion of the Congregational ministers who have declaimed from the pulpit or for the fact

1. Boston Common
2. Massachusetts State House
3. Park Street Church
4. Old Granary
   Burying Ground
5. King's Chapel
6. Site of the First Public School
7. Statue of Benjamin Franklin
8. 3 School St.
9. Old South
   Meeting House
10. Benjamin Franklin's
    Birthplace
11. Old State House
12. Boston Massacre Site
13. Faneuil Hall

(T) Free transfer   (i) Information   —— Red Line   —— Blue Line
(T) Station Stop   😊 "Take a Break"   ▪▪▪ Orange Line   ▪ ▪ ▪ Green Line

that during the War of 1812, gunpowder (made from brimstone) was stored in the basement. This was part of the site of a huge granary that became a public building after the Revolutionary War, when it was no longer needed for grain storage. In the 1790s, the sails for USS *Constitution* ("Old Ironsides") were manufactured in that building.

From late June to August, the church is open from 9:30am to 4pm Tuesday through Saturday. Sunday services are at 9 and 10:45am and 5:30pm year-round.

Walk away from the Common on Tremont Street. On your left is the:

4. **Old Granary Burying Ground.** This cemetery, established in 1660, was once part of Boston Common. You'll see the graves of patriots **Samuel Adams, Paul Revere, John Hancock,** and **James Otis;** merchant **Peter Faneuil** (spelled "Funal"); and Benjamin Franklin's parents. Also buried here are the victims of the **Boston Massacre** (see stop no. 12 on this tour) and the wife of Isaac Vergoose, who is believed to be **"Mother Goose"** of nursery rhyme fame. Note that gravestone rubbing, however tempting, is illegal in Boston's historic cemeteries. Open daily from 8am to 5pm (until 3pm in the winter).

Turn left as you leave the cemetery and continue 1¹/₂ blocks on Tremont Street. At the corner of School Street, diagonally across from where you'll wind up, is:

5. **King's Chapel,** 58 Tremont St. (☎ **617/523-1749**). Architect **Peter Harrison** sent the plans for this building from Newport, Rhode Island, in 1749. Rather

than replacing the existing wooden chapel, the granite edifice was constructed around it. Completed in 1754, it was the **first Anglican church in Boston.** George III sent gifts, as did Queen Anne and William and Mary, who presented the communion table and chancel tablets (still in use today) before the church was even built. The Puritan colonists had little use for the royal religion; after the Revolution, this became the **first Unitarian church in America.** Unitarian Universalist services are conducted here, using the Anglican Book of Common Prayer. The chapel is open Tuesday through Saturday from 10am to 2pm; services are Sunday at 11am. The **burying ground,** on Tremont Street, is the oldest in the city; it dates to 1630. Among the scary colonial headstones (winged skulls are a popular decoration) are the graves of **John Winthrop,** the first governor of the Massachusetts Bay Colony; **William Dawes,** who rode with Paul Revere; **Elizabeth Pain,** the model for Hester Prynne in Nathaniel Hawthorne's novel *The Scarlet Letter;* and **Mary Chilton,** the first female colonist to step ashore on Plymouth Rock. The burying ground is open daily 8am to 5:30pm (until 3pm in the winter).

Now follow the trail back along Tremont Street and turn left onto School Street. On the sidewalk a short distance ahead is a colorful folk-art mosaic marking the:

6. Site of the First Public School. **Samuel Adams, Benjamin Franklin, John Hancock,** and **Cotton Mather** were students here. It was founded in 1634, 2 years before Harvard College. The original building (1645) was demolished to make way for the expansion of King's Chapel, and the school was moved across the street. Now called Boston Latin School, the prestigious institution is in the Fenway neighborhood.

The fence to your left encloses a courtyard where you'll see a:

7. Statue of Benjamin Franklin. This was the first portrait statue erected in Boston, in 1856. Franklin was born in Boston in 1706 and apprenticed to his half-brother James, a printer, but they got along so poorly that in 1723 Benjamin ran away to Philadelphia. Plaques on the base describe his numerous accomplishments. The lovely granite building behind the statue is **Old City Hall** (1865), designed in Second Empire style by Arthur Gilman (who laid out the Back Bay) and Gridley J. F. Bryant, and opened in 1865. The administration moved to Government Center in 1969, and the building now houses offices and an excellent French restaurant, **Maison Robert.**

TAKE A BREAK   At the corner of School and Washington streets, stop into the second-floor cafe at **Borders Books & Music,** 24 School St. (☎ 617/ 557-7188), for a snack or light meal and a cup of coffee. Order tea if you're feeling rebellious—at stop no. 9, you'll be reminded that in Boston, drinking tea was once considered unpatriotic. The store and cafe are open Monday through Saturday 7am to 8pm, Sunday 10am to 8pm.

School Street ends at Washington Street. On the left is:

8. 3 School St. This is the former Old Corner Bookstore, which also held the publishing house of Ticknor & Fields. Built in 1712, it's on a plot of land that was once home to the religious reformer **Anne Hutchinson,** who was excommunicated and expelled from Boston in 1638 for heresy. In the middle of the 19th century, the little brick building was the literary center of America. Publisher James Fields, known as "Jamie," counted among his friends Henry Wadsworth

Longfellow, James Russell Lowell, Henry David Thoreau, Ralph Waldo Emerson, Nathaniel Hawthorne, and Harriet Beecher Stowe.

Turn right and walk 1 block. On your left at the corner of Milk Street is the clock tower of the:

 9. **Old South Meeting House,** 310 Washington St. (☎ **617/482-6439**). The Old South, as it's known, was a religious and political gathering place, and it is best known today as the site of one of the events leading to the Revolution. On December 16, 1773, a crowd of several thousand, too big to fit into Faneuil Hall, gathered here for word from the governor about whether the three ships full of tea in the harbor would be sent back to England. They were not, and the tea, priced to undercut the cost of smuggled tea and force the colonists to trade with merchants approved by the Crown, was cast into the harbor by revolutionaries poorly disguised as Mohawks. That uprising, the **Boston Tea Party,** is commemorated here, and you can even see a vial of the tea.

Originally built in 1670 and replaced by the current structure in 1729, the building underwent extensive renovations in the 1990s. In 1872 the devastating fire that destroyed most of downtown stopped at the Old South, a phenomenon considered to be a testament to the building's power. Its storied history is told in an interactive multimedia exhibit, *Voices of Protest.* The building is open daily, April to October from 9am to 5:30pm, November through March weekdays from 10am to 4pm, weekends from 10am to 5pm. Admission is $3 for adults, $2.50 for seniors, $1 for children 6 to 12, free for children under 6.

Around the corner on Milk Street, opposite the exit from the gift shop, is:

10. **Benjamin Franklin's Birthplace.** In a little house at 17 Milk St., Franklin was born in 1706, the 15th child of Josiah Franklin. The house is long gone, but step to the edge of the curb across the street, and look at the second floor of the office building that's in its place. When the building went up after the fire of 1872, the architect guaranteed that the Founding Father wouldn't be forgotten: A bust and the words "Birthplace of Franklin" are worked into the facade.

Backtrack on Washington Street away from the pedestrian mall. On your right just before the first intersection (with Water Street), you'll pass what appears to be an alley but is actually one of the first streets in Boston, **Spring Lane.** For the first 2 centuries of the settlement, it was home to a real spring.

Two long blocks from the Old South Meeting House, you'll come to the:

11. **Old State House,** 206 Washington St. (☎ **617/720-3290;** www.bostonhistory. org). Built in 1713, it served as the seat of colonial government before the Revolution and as the state capitol until 1797. For many years, it was considered a tall building. From its balcony the **Declaration of Independence** was first read to Bostonians on July 18, 1776. In 1789 President **George Washington**

Impressions

I do not speak with any fondness, but the language of coolest history, when I say that Boston commands attention as the town which was appointed in the destiny of nations to lead the civilization of North America.
                    —Ralph Waldo Emerson, *The Natural History of Intellect,* 1893

From John Adams to George Apley, Bostonians are smugly apt to like their own town best.
                    —Esther Forbes, *Paul Revere and the World He Lived In,* 1942

Something Old, Something New

The Freedom Trail isn't just about colonial Boston. If you need proof, stop into the city's new museum of immigration, the **Dreams of Freedom Center,** 1 Milk St., off Washington Street (☎ **617/338-6022;** www.dreamsoffreedom.org). Ben Franklin is the "host" of a multimedia show about the changing face of the city's population; other exhibits include a gallery of bags and suitcases that offers a look at what people brought with them on their long journey to the New World, and the interiors of two important modes of transportation: an early-20th-century ship, and a jet liner. At press time, the center was expected to open in the summer of 2000. It's open daily, with extended hours in the summer; call ahead for exact times. Admission is $7 for adults, $5 for seniors and students, $3 children 6 to 17, and free for children under 6.

---

reviewed a parade from the building. The exterior decorations are particularly interesting—the clock was installed in place of a sundial, and the gilded lion and unicorn are reproductions of the original symbols of British rule that were ripped from the facade and burned the day the Declaration of Independence was read.

Inside, you'll find the **Bostonian Society's** museum of the city's history. The society was founded in 1881 to save this building, which was badly deteriorated and, incredibly, about to be sold and shipped to Chicago. There are an introductory video on the history of the building and regularly changing exhibits that draw on the society's extensive collections of historic artifacts and documents. The Old State House is open daily from 9am to 5pm. Admission is $3 for adults, $2 for seniors and students, $1 for children 6 to 18, free for children under 6.

As you leave the building, turn left and walk half a block. On a traffic island in State Street, across from the T station under the Old State House, a ring of cobblestones marks the:

12. **Boston Massacre Site.** This skirmish on March 5, 1770, helped consolidate the spirit of rebellion in the colonies. Angered at the presence of royal troops in Boston, colonists threw snowballs, garbage, rocks, and other debris at a group of redcoats. The soldiers panicked and fired into the crowd, killing five men. Their graves, including that of Crispus Attucks, the first black man to die in the Revolution, are in the Old Granary Burying Ground.

Continue on the trail by turning left onto Congress Street and walking down the hill. Near the corner of Congress and North streets is:

13. **Faneuil Hall.** Built in 1742 (and enlarged using a Charles Bulfinch design in 1805), it was a gift to the town from prosperous merchant **Peter Faneuil.** The "Cradle of Liberty" rang with speeches by orators such as **Samuel Adams**— whose statue is on the Congress Street side—in the years leading to the Revolution. Abolitionists, temperance advocates, and suffragists used it as a pulpit in the years after. The upstairs is still a public meeting (and sometimes concert) hall, and the downstairs area is a market, all according to Faneuil's will. The grasshopper **weather vane,** the sole remaining detail from the original building, is modeled after the weather vane on London's Royal Exchange.

National Park Service rangers give **free 20-minute talks** every half hour from 9am to 5pm in the second-floor auditorium and operate a visitor center on the first floor. On the top floor is a small museum that houses the weapons collection and historical exhibits of the **Ancient and Honorable Artillery Company** of Massachusetts. Admission is free.

🍵 **WINDING DOWN   Faneuil Hall Marketplace** spreads out before you, and the **Quincy Market Colonnade** overflows with takeout food. Two good places to picnic lie nearby, on the other side of the Big Dig. Cross Atlantic Avenue and head down **Long Wharf,** Boston's principal wharf since 1710 and a busy sightseeing-cruise dock, past the Marriott to the ✪ **brick plaza** at the very end of the wharf. The granite building dates to 1846, and the whole plaza affords a great view of the harbor and the airport. Or stay at **Christopher Columbus Park,** on the other side of the hotel, watch the action at the marina, and play in the playground.

If you prefer a sit-down restaurant, **Durgin-Park** is in the middle of the marketplace, and **Ye Olde Union Oyster House** is a block away.

DETOUR   If you want to continue to the **Waterfront** and **Museum Wharf,** set out from here and be ready to negotiate many construction-clogged areas. See chapter 7 for descriptions of the New England Aquarium, the Children's Museum, and the Boston Tea Party Ship & Museum.

Walking Tour 2: The North End & Charlestown

Start: Faneuil Hall Marketplace (T: Green Line to Government Center, Orange Line to State Street, or Blue Line to Aquarium).
Finish: Bunker Hill Monument, Charlestown.
Time: 2 to 3 hours.
Best Time: Morning and early afternoon. Aim for Friday or Saturday if you want to see Haymarket.
Worst Time: Late afternoon, when you'll be in the midst of rush-hour gridlock.

Facing the statue of **Samuel Adams** on the Congress Street side of Faneuil Hall, turn left and cross North Street. Walk up Union Street past the two statues of **James Michael Curley.** Looming above are the six glass columns that make up:
1. **The New England Holocaust Memorial.** Erected in 1995, the towers spring up in the midst of attractions that celebrate freedom, reminding visitors of the consequences of a world without it. The pattern on the glass, which at first appears merely decorative, is actually six million random numbers, one for each Jew who died during the Holocaust.
    Across the street is:
2. **Ye Olde Union Oyster House,** 41 Union St. (☎ **617/227-2750**). First opened in 1826, the Union Oyster House is the oldest restaurant in Boston that's still in operation. (See chapter 6 for a review.)

Get Lost!: A Pep Talk

There's almost nothing as stereotypical or as distressing as seeing tourists shuffling along in lockstep, looking only at what's described in their travel guides and going only where the Freedom Trail takes them. This is a *guide*book, not the boot-camp curriculum, and getting really lost in downtown Boston is nearly impossible—it's just too small. Wander away from the line, if time allows, and poke around on your own. I promise you won't be sorry.

Continue on Union Street, or explore a bit in the narrow cobbled streets and alleys that branch off it. This area is the "Blackstone Block," and the buildings are among the oldest in the city—you'll get a sense of the scale of 18th- and 19th-century Boston. Make your way to Hanover Street (at the end of Union Street) and turn right. If it's Friday or Saturday, you'll be in the midst of:

3. Haymarket. The open-air market consists of stalls piled high with fruit, vegetables, and seafood, but shoppers aren't allowed to touch anything they haven't bought. It's a great scene and a favorite with photographers. Two blocks up, you can turn right onto Blackstone Street and explore the merchandise further (the market runs to North Street), or cross Blackstone Street and take the **pedestrian passage** beneath the Central Artery (Fitzgerald Expressway). You'll probably walk near, over, or around indications that the Big Dig is in the works; if construction appears to block your way, look for signs pointing to the North End.

You'll emerge at Cross and Salem streets, one of several gateways to:

4. The North End. This is Boston's Little Italy (although it's never called that), home to natives of Italy and their assimilated children, numerous Italian restaurants and private social clubs, and many historic sights. This is one of the oldest neighborhoods in the city. It was home in the 17th century to the **Mather family** of Puritan ministers, who certainly would be shocked to see the merry goings-on at the festivals and street fairs that take over a different section of the North End each weekend in July and August.

The Italians (and their yuppie neighbors who have made inroads since the 1980s) are only the latest immigrant group to dominate the North End. In the mid–19th century, this was an eastern European Jewish enclave, and later an Irish stronghold. In 1894, **Rose Fitzgerald,** mother of President John F. Kennedy, was born on Garden Court Street and baptized at St. Stephen's Church.

Turn right onto Cross Street, following the Freedom Trail (if you can find it amid the construction debris). Walk 1 block to Hanover Street, where you must turn left. At the first traffic light, turn right onto Richmond Street, still following the Freedom Trail. Walk 1 block and turn left onto North Street. Wharves ran up almost this far in colonial days; in the 19th century, this was a notorious red-light district. Half a block up on the left is:

5. The Paul Revere House, 19 North Sq. (☎ **617/523-2338;** www. paulreverehouse.org). One of the most pleasant stops on the Freedom Trail, it presents history on a human scale. Revere was living here when he set out for Lexington on April 18, 1775, a feat immortalized in **Henry Wadsworth Longfellow's poem "Paul Revere's Ride"** ("Listen, my children, and you shall hear, / Of the midnight ride of Paul Revere"). The oldest house in downtown Boston, it was built around 1680, bought by Revere in 1770, and put to a number of uses before being turned into a museum in the early 20th century. The two-and-a-half-story wood structure is filled with neatly arranged and identified 17th- and 18th-century furnishings and artifacts, including the famous Revere silver, considered some of the finest anywhere. The self-guided tour—with staff members around in case you have questions—allows you to linger over the objects that particularly interest you.

The house is open daily from April 15 through October from 9:30am to 5:15pm, and November through April 14 from 9:30am to 4:15pm; it's closed Mondays from January to March, as well as January 1, Thanksgiving Day, and December 25. Admission is $2.50 for adults, $2 for seniors and students, $1 for children 5 to 17.

Get Away For Less.

Avis features GM cars.

With great offers and services from Avis, you'll get more out of your vacation! And now you can **save $20 on a weekly rental**. All the information you need is on the coupon below. Plus most rentals come with free unlimited mileage to save you even more.

As an added touch you can count on our famous "We try harder." service for a fast, hassle-free rental. Because speed and personal service is what everyone at Avis is dedicated to delivering.

For more information and reservations, call your travel agent or Avis toll free at **1-800-831-8000**.

Save $20 On A Weekly Rental

Reserve an Avis Intermediate through Full Size 4-Door car for a minimum of five consecutive days. At time of rental, present this coupon at the Avis counter and you can save $20. **An advance reservation is required.** Subject to complete Terms and Conditions below. Rental must begin by 06/30/01.

For reservations and information, call your travel consultant or Avis toll free at **1-800-831-8000**.

Terms and Conditions: Coupon valid on an Intermediate (Group C) through a Full Size 4-Door (Group E) car. Dollars off applies to the cost of the total rental with a minimum of 5 days. A Saturday night overstay is required. Coupon must be surrendered at time of rental; one per rental. Coupon valid at Avis participating locations in the U.S. An advance reservation is required. Cars subject to availability. Taxes, local government surcharges, vehicle licensing and an airport recruitment fee at some locations, optional items such as LDW, additional driver fee and refueling fee are extra. Renter must meet Avis driver and credit requirements. Minimum age is 25 but may vary by location. Rental must begin by 6/30/01.

Coupon #: **MUNA002**

Rental Sales Agent Instructions
At checkout:
In AWD, enter AWD number.
In CPN, enter **MUNA002**.
Complete this information:
RA # _____
Rental location _____
Attach to COUPON tape.

AVIS

www.avis.com

It's a Whole New World with

Frommer's

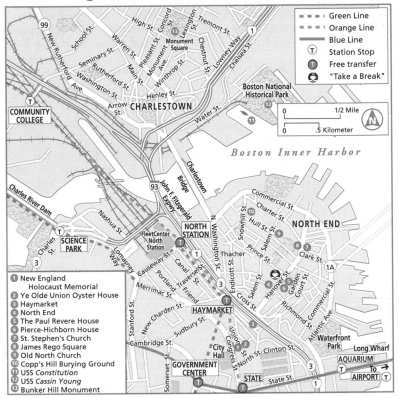

Across the courtyard from Revere's house is the home of his Hichborn cousins, the:

6. **Pierce/Hichborn House.** The 1711 Georgian-style home is a rare example of 18th-century middle-class architecture. It's suitably furnished and is shown only by guided tour (usually twice a day at busy times). Call the Paul Revere House for schedules.

Before you leave North Square, look across the cobblestone plaza at **Sacred Heart Church.** It was established in 1833 as the Seamen's Bethel, a church devoted to the needs of the mariners who frequented the area. Today it's Roman Catholic, and one Mass every Sunday is said in Italian.

Turn left as you exit the Paul Revere House and walk to the corner of Prince Street. Here you can turn left and walk 1 block to Hanover Street, or take a few steps onto Garden Court Street and look for no. 4, on the right. The private residence was the **birthplace of Rose Fitzgerald** (later Kennedy). Pause when you get to the corner of Prince and Hanover streets.

☕ **TAKE A BREAK**   You're in the heart of North End *caffè* country, the perfect place to have a cup of coffee or a soft drink and feast on sweets. Across the street is **Mike's Pastry,** 300 Hanover St. (☎ 617/742-3050), which does a frantic take-out business and also has tables where you can sit down and order one of the confections on display in the cases. Mike's claim to fame is its **cannoli** (tubes of crisp-fried pastry filled with sweetened ricotta cheese); the cookies, cakes, and other pastries are excellent, too. You can also sit and relax at **Caffè dello Sport** and **Caffè Vittoria,** on either side of Mike's, or across the street at **Caffè Graffiti.**

Back at Prince and Hanover streets, with North Square behind you, turn right and walk 2 blocks on Hanover Street to Clark Street. At the corner is:

7. St. Stephen's Church, the only **Charles Bulfinch**–designed church still standing in Boston. The church was Unitarian when it was dedicated in 1804, and the next year the congregation bought a **bell from Paul Revere's foundry** for $800. Architecture buffs will get a kick out of the design, a paragon of Federal-style symmetry. St. Stephen's became Roman Catholic in 1862 and was moved back when Hanover Street was widened in 1870. During refurbishment in 1965, it regained its original appearance, with clear glass windows, red carpets, white walls, and gilded organ pipes. It's one of the plainest Catholic churches you'll ever see.

Cross Hanover Street to reach:

8. James Rego Square (Paul Revere Mall), a pleasant little brick-paved park known as the Prado, with an equestrian statue of **Paul Revere.** Take time to read some of the **tablets** on the left-hand wall that describe famous people and places in the history of the North End.

Walk across the mall, around the fountain, and emerge at the side of the:

9. Old North Church, 193 Salem St. (☎ **617/523-6676;** www.oldnorth.com). Officially known as Christ Church, this is the oldest church building in Boston; it dates to 1723. The building is in the style of Sir Christopher Wren. The original steeple was the one where sexton **Robert Newman** hung two lanterns on the night of April 18, 1775, to indicate to **Paul Revere** that British troops were setting out for Lexington and Concord in boats across the Charles River, not on foot ("One if by land, and two if by sea"). The steeple fell victim to hurricanes in 1804 and 1954; the current version is an exact copy of the original. The 175-foot spire, long a reference point for sailors, appears on navigational charts to this day. Members of the Revere family attended this church (their plaque is on pew 54); famous visitors have included **Presidents James Monroe, Theodore Roosevelt, Franklin D. Roosevelt,** and **Gerald R. Ford,** and **Queen Elizabeth II.** There are markers and plaques throughout; note the bust of George Washington, reputedly the first memorial to the first president. The **gardens** on the north side of the church (dotted with more plaques) are open to the public. On the south side of the church, volunteers are re-creating an 18th-century garden. The church is open daily from 9am to 5pm; Sunday services (Episcopal) are at 9 and 11am and 4pm. The quirky **gift shop** and museum (☎ **617/523-4848**), in a former chapel, are open daily from 9am to 5pm, and all proceeds go to support the church. Donations are appreciated.

As you leave the church, bear left and cross Salem Street onto **Hull Street.** Turn right and walk uphill past no. 44, a private residence that's the narrowest house in Boston (10 ft. wide). Across the street is the entrance to:

10. Copp's Hill Burying Ground, the second-oldest cemetery (1659) in the city. No gravestone rubbing is allowed. This is the burial place of **Cotton Mather** and his family, **Robert Newman,** and **Prince Hall.** Hall, a prominent member of the free black community that occupied the north slope of the hill in colonial times, fought at Bunker Hill and established the first black Masonic lodge. The highest point in the North End, Copp's Hill was the site of a windmill and of the British

batteries that destroyed the village of Charlestown during the Battle of Bunker Hill on June 17, 1775. Charlestown is clearly visible (look for the masts of USS *Constitution*) across the Inner Harbor. The burying ground is open daily from 9am to 5pm (until 3pm in winter).

Many people, especially those traveling with fidgety children, opt to skip the next part of the tour. But if your party's not too close to the breaking point, it's a worthwhile excursion.

From the burying ground, it's about a mile to **Charlestown.** Continue on Hull Street and follow it down the hill to Commercial Street (note that there's no crosswalk on Commercial at the dangerous intersection with Hull). Turn left and walk 2 blocks to North Washington Street. Carefully cross busy Commercial Street. Walk across the bridge, and at the end, turn right and follow the signs and the Freedom Trail to the **Charlestown Navy Yard,** home of:

11. USS *Constitution* (☎ 617/242-5670). Active-duty sailors in 1812 dress uniforms give **free tours** daily from 9:30am to 3:50pm.

"Old Ironsides," one of the U.S. Navy's six original frigates, never lost a battle. The ship was constructed in the North End from 1794 to 1797 at a cost of $302,718, using bolts, spikes, and other fittings from **Paul Revere's foundry.** As the new nation made its naval and military reputation, the *Constitution* played a key role, battling French privateers and Barbary pirates, repelling the British fleet during the War of 1812, participating in 40 engagements, and capturing 20 vessels. The frigate earned its nickname during an engagement on August 19, 1812. Shots from the French warship *Guerriere* bounced off its thick oak hull as if it were iron. Retired from combat in 1815, the *Constitution* was rescued from destruction when Oliver Wendell Holmes's poem "Old Ironsides" launched a preservation movement in 1830.

"Old Ironsides" was completely overhauled in 1995 and 1996 in preparation for its bicentennial. It sailed under its own power in 1997 for the first time since 1881, drawing international attention. Tugs tow the *Constitution* into the harbor every **Fourth of July** and turn it to ensure that the ship weathers evenly.

The **USS *Constitution* Museum** (☎ 617/426-1812; www.ussconstititionmuseum.org), just inland from the vessel, has several participatory exhibits that allow visitors to hoist a flag, fire a cannon, and learn more about the ship. The interactive computer displays and naval artifacts make the museum appealing to visitors of all ages. It's open daily from May through October 9am to 6pm, and November to April 10am to 4pm, and closed January 1, Thanksgiving, and December 25. A program that makes admission free to all has been extended until further notice.

Also at the Navy Yard, **National Park Service** rangers (☎ 617/242-5601) staff an **information booth** and give free 1-hour guided tours of the base.

Turn left as you leave the museum (or right as you leave the ship), and follow the big band music to:

12. USS *Cassin Young* (☎ 617/242-5601), a refurbished World War II destroyer. National Park Service rangers give 45-minute **guided tours,** and unescorted visitors can look around on the deck. Admission is free. Call for tour times.

Leave the Navy Yard through gate 4, cross Chelsea Street, and climb the hill, following the Freedom Trail along Tremont Street. Your guidepost is also your destination, the:

13. Bunker Hill Monument (☎ 617/242-5644), a 221-foot granite obelisk built in honor of the colonists who died in the **Battle of Bunker Hill** on June 17,

1775. The rebels lost the battle, but nearly half the British troops were killed or wounded, a loss that contributed to Britain's decision to abandon Boston 9 months later. The **Marquis de Lafayette,** the celebrated hero of the American and French revolutions, helped lay the monument's cornerstone in 1825. He is buried in Paris under soil taken from the hill. A flight of 295 stairs leads to the top—there's no elevator, but the view (away from I-93, anyway) is quite good.

In the lodge at the base of the monument, there are dioramas and exhibits. It's staffed by National Park Service rangers and is open from 9am to 5pm. The monument is open daily from 9am to 4:30pm. Admission is free.

If you don't feel like retracing your steps, you have two public transportation options. At the foot of the hill on Main Street, take **bus no. 92 or 93** to Haymarket (where the Green and Orange lines stop). Even better, return to the Navy Yard for the **water shuttle** to Long Wharf, which leaves every hour on the quarter hour from 6:45am to 7:45pm on weekdays and from 10:15am to 6:15pm on weekends. The 10-minute trip costs $1, and the pier is an easy walk from "Old Ironsides."

Walking Tour 3: The Back Bay

Start: The Public Garden (T: Green Line to Arlington).
Finish: Copley Square.
Time: 2 hours if you make good time, 3 if you detour to the Fiedler statue and the Esplanade, and longer if you take your time while shopping.
Best Time: Any time before late afternoon.
Worst Time: Late afternoon, when the streets are packed with people and cars. And don't attempt the detour on July 4. This is mostly an outdoor walk, so if the weather is bad you might find yourself in lots of shops. Decide for yourself whether that makes an overcast day a "best" or "worst" time.

The Back Bay is the youngest neighborhood in central Boston, the product of a massive landfill project that took place from 1835 to 1882. It's flat, symmetrical, logically designed—the names of the cross streets go in alphabetical order—and altogether anomalous in Boston's crazy-quilt geography.

Begin your walk in the:

1. **Public Garden,** bounded by Arlington, Beacon, Charles, and Boylston streets. Before the Back Bay was filled in, the **Charles River** flowed right up to Charles Street, which separates the Public Garden from Boston Common. On the night of April 18, 1775, the **British troops** bound for Lexington and Concord boarded boats to Cambridge ("two if by sea") at the foot of the Common and set off across what's now the Public Garden.

   Explore the lagoon, the trees and other flora, and the statuary. Take a ride on the **swan boats,** if you like, and then make your way toward the corner of Charles and Beacon streets. A short distance away, within the confines of the Public Garden (listen for the cries of delighted children), you'll see a 35-foot strip of cobblestones topped with the bronze figures that immortalize Robert McCloskey's book:

2. *Make Way for Ducklings.* Installed in 1987 and wildly popular since the moment they were unveiled, Nancy Schön's renderings of **Mrs. Mallard and her eight babies** are irresistible. Mrs. Mallard is 38 inches tall, making her back a bit

Walking Tour 3—The Back Bay

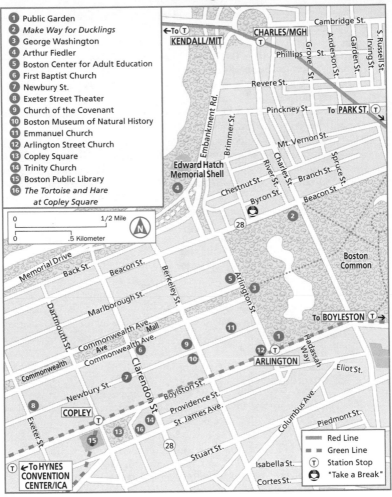

Legend:
1. Public Garden
2. *Make Way for Ducklings*
3. George Washington
4. Arthur Fiedler
5. Boston Center for Adult Education
6. First Baptist Church
7. Newbury St.
8. Exeter Street Theater
9. Church of the Covenant
10. Boston Museum of Natural History
11. Emmanuel Church
12. Arlington Street Church
13. Copley Square
14. Trinity Church
15. Boston Public Library
16. *The Tortoise and Hare at Copley Square*

higher than a tricycle seat, but that doesn't keep people of all ages from climbing on. If you don't know the whole story of the Mallards' perilous trip across town to meet Mr. Mallard at the lagoon, ask one of the parents or children you'll certainly find here.

The city bought the site of the Public Garden from private interests in 1824. Planting began in 1837, but it wasn't until the late 1850s that Arlington Street was built and the land permanently set aside. George F. Meacham executed the design.

Cross the lagoon using the little suspension bridge and look for the statue of:

3. George Washington. Unveiled in 1875, this was Boston's first equestrian statue. It stands 38 feet tall and is considered an excellent likeness of the first president of the United States, an outstanding horseman. The artist, **Thomas Ball,** was a Charlestown native who worked in Italy and numbered among his students noted sculptor and artist Daniel Chester French. Pass through the gate onto

Arlington Street. Before you begin exploring in earnest, this is a good place to detour and:

☕ **TAKE A BREAK**   Turn right and walk up Arlington Street, passing Marlborough Street, to Beacon Street. On your right across the busy intersection is the **Bull & Finch Pub,** 84 Beacon St. (☎ 617/227-9605), also known as the **"Cheers" bar.** The food is quite tasty, but two points must be made: The bar looks nothing like the set of the TV show, and the patrons generally consist of people from everywhere in the universe except Boston.

If you'd rather stay outdoors, turn right on Beacon and walk 1 long block to Charles Street for takeout. **Juice Guys,** 20 Charles St. (☎ 617/367-1166), serves fresh-made smoothies; choose a suggested combination or design your own. You can also pick up something tasty at **Cafe Bella Vita,** 30 Charles St. (☎ 617/720-4505), or **Panificio,** 144 Charles St. (☎ 617/227-4340), or take a shopping break on Charles Street.

When you've found something to eat, backtrack along Beacon Street past Arlington Street to Embankment Road and turn right. Take the **Arthur Fiedler Footbridge** across Storrow Drive to the Esplanade, and unpack your food near the giant head of:

4. **Arthur Fiedler.** Installed in 1985, this sculpture by **Ralph Helmick** consists of sheets of aluminum that eerily capture the countenance of the legendary conductor of the **Boston Pops,** who died in 1979. The amphitheater to the right is the **Hatch Shell,** where the Pops perform free during the week leading up to and including the Fourth of July.

When you're ready, retrace your steps to the corner of Arlington Street and Commonwealth Avenue. This is the:

5. **Boston Center for Adult Education,** 5 Commonwealth Ave. (☎ 617/ 267-4430). Constructed in 1904 as a private residence, the building gained a huge ballroom in 1912. If it's not being used for a class or a function (it's popular for weddings), you're welcome to have a look at the ornate ballroom. The BCAE, established in 1933, is the oldest continuing-education institution in the country.

You're at the foot of the 8-block **Commonwealth Avenue Mall.** This graceful public promenade is the centerpiece of architect **Arthur Gilman's** design of the Back Bay. The mall is 100 feet wide (the entire street is 240) and stretches to Kenmore Square. The elegant Victorian mansions on either side—almost all divided into apartments or in commercial or educational use—are generally considered a great asset, but the attitude toward the apparently random collection of sculpture along the mall is hardly unanimous. Judge for yourself as you inspect the art, starting with **Alexander Hamilton** across Arlington Street from **George Washington.** The most moving sculpture is at Dartmouth Street. The **Vendome Memorial** honors the memory of the nine firefighters who lost their lives in a blaze at the Hotel Vendome in 1972.

Two blocks from the Public Garden at the corner of Clarendon Street is the:

6. **First Baptist Church,** 110 Commonwealth Ave. Built from 1870 to 1872 of Roxbury puddingstone, it originally housed the congregation of the Brattle Street Church (Unitarian), which had been downtown, near Faneuil Hall. The design is notable mainly because its creators went on to much more famous projects. The architect, **H. H. Richardson,** is best known for nearby Trinity Church (stop no. 14 on this tour). The artist who created the frieze, which represents the sacraments, was **Frédéric Auguste Bartholdi,** who designed the Statue of Liberty.

At Clarendon Street or Dartmouth Street, turn left and walk 1 block to:

7. **Newbury Street.** Commonwealth Avenue is the architectural heart of the Back Bay, and Newbury Street is the commercial center. Take some time to roam around here (see chapter 9 for pointers), browsing in the galleries, window-shopping at the expensive clothing stores, and watching the chic shoppers, artists, and students. On Exeter Street you'll see the building that was once the:

8. **Exeter Street Theater,** 26 Exeter St. Designed in 1884 as the First Spiritualist Temple, it was a movie house from 1914 to 1984. Once known for the crowds flocking to the *Rocky Horror Picture Show*, it's now the home of a TGI Friday's restaurant.

   When you're ready to continue your stroll (or when your credit cards cry for mercy), head back toward the Public Garden and seek out three of Newbury Street's oldest buildings, starting with the:

9. **Church of the Covenant,** 67 Newbury St., a Gothic revival edifice built from 1866 to 1867 and designed by **Richard Upjohn.** The stained-glass windows are the work of **Louis Comfort Tiffany.**

   Across the street, set back from the sidewalk at 234 Berkeley St., is an opulent store in an equally opulent setting. The luxury clothing emporium Louis, Boston occupies the original home of the:

10. **Boston Museum of Natural History,** a forerunner of the Museum of Science. Built from 1861 to 1864 using **William Preston's** French Academic design, it was originally two stories. It still has the original roof, preserved when the third floor was added.

    Cross Newbury Street again and continue walking back toward the Public Garden. On your left is:

11. **Emmanuel Church,** 15 Newbury St. (☎ **617/536-3355**), the first building completed on Newbury Street. The Episcopal church ministers through the arts, so there might be a concert (classical to jazz, solo to orchestral) going on during your visit.

    Now you're almost back at the Public Garden. On your left is the original **Ritz-Carlton** (1927), the pride and joy of the chain. Turn right onto Arlington Street and walk 1 block to Boylston Street. On your right is the:

12. **Arlington Street Church,** 351 Boylston St. It's the oldest church in the Back Bay, completed in 1861. An interesting blend of Georgian and Italianate details, it's the work of architect **Arthur Gilman,** who laid out the neighborhood. Here you'll see more Tiffany stained glass. Step inside to see the pulpit that was in use in 1788 (when the congregation worshipped downtown on Federal Street).

    Follow Boylston Street away from the Public Garden. You'll pass the famous **FAO Schwarz** toy store, with the huge **bronze bear** out front at the corner of Berkeley Street. At the end of the block is:

13. **Copley Square.** Enjoy the fountain, visit the farmers' market (Tuesday and Friday afternoons from July through November), but whatever you do, don't miss:

14. **Trinity Church** (to your left), **H. H. Richardson's** Romanesque masterpiece, completed in 1877. It's built on 4,502 pilings driven into the mud that was once the Back Bay. If you happen to visit on a Friday, organ recitals begin at 12:15pm. Otherwise, brochures and guides are available to help you find your way around a building considered one of the finest examples of church architecture in the country. It's open daily from 8am to 6pm.

    Across Dartmouth Street is the:

15. **Boston Public Library.** The work of architect **Charles Follen McKim** and many others, the Renaissance revival building was completed in 1895 after

10 years of construction. Its design reflects the significant influence of the Bibliothèque Nationale in Paris. Wander up the steps to check out the building's impressive interior (see chapter 7 for more details).

Leave through the doors facing Dartmouth Street, which were designed by **Daniel Chester French,** and head across the street to Copley Square. In a sense, you've come full circle; as at the Public Garden, you'll see a playful and compelling sculpture:

16. *The Tortoise and Hare at Copley Square,* also by **Nancy Schön.** Designed to signify the end of the **Boston Marathon** (the finish line is on Boylston Street between Exeter and Dartmouth streets), it was unveiled for the 100th anniversary of the event in 1996 and immediately became another shutterbug magnet.

From here you're in a good position to set out for any other part of town, or just walk a little way in any direction and continue exploring. **Copley Place** and the **Shops at Prudential Center** are nearby, **Newbury Street** is 1 block over, and there's a Green Line T station at Boylston and Dartmouth streets.

Walking Tour 4: Harvard Square

Start: Harvard Square (T: Red Line to Harvard).
Finish: John F. Kennedy Park.
Time: 2 to 4 hours, depending on how much time you spend in shops and museums.
Best Time: Almost any time during the day (see below); the Harvard museums are free on Saturday mornings, and the art museums are also free all day Wednesday.
Worst Time: The first full week of June. You may have trouble gaining admission to Harvard Yard during commencement festivities. The ceremony is Thursday morning, and without a ticket, you won't be allowed in.

Popular impressions to the contrary, Cambridge is not exclusively Harvard. Harvard Square isn't even exclusively Harvard. During a walk around the area, you'll see historic buildings and sights, interesting museums, and notable architecture on and off the university's main campus.

Ride the Red Line to Harvard Square. Leave the station by the **main entrance** (take the ramp to the turnstiles and the escalators to the outside) and emerge in the heart of:

1. **Harvard Square.** Town and gown meet at this lively intersection, where you'll get a taste of the improbable mix of people drawn to the crossroads of Cambridge. To your right is the landmark **Out of Town News** kiosk. It stocks newspapers and magazines from all over the world and tons of souvenirs (beefed up when the rise of the Internet cut into the demand for non-virtual journalism). At the booth in front of you, you can request information about the area. Step close to it so that you're out of the flow of pedestrian traffic, and look around.

The store across Mass. Ave. is the **Harvard Coop.** The name rhymes with *hoop*—say "*co*-op" and risk being taken for a Yale student. On the far side of the intersection at the corner of John F. Kennedy Street and Brattle Street, look up at the third floor of the brick building, and find the sign for **"Dewey Cheetham & Howe"** (say it out loud). National Public Radio's hilarious show **"Car Talk"** originates here.

Turn around so that the Coop is at your back, and walk half a block, crossing Dunster Street. Across Mass. Ave. you'll see the:

Walking Tour 4—Harvard Square

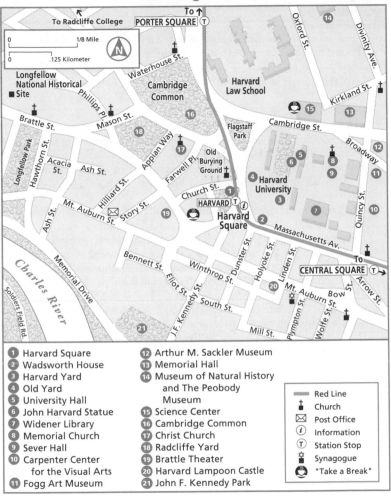

1. Harvard Square
2. Wadsworth House
3. Harvard Yard
4. Old Yard
5. University Hall
6. John Harvard Statue
7. Widener Library
8. Memorial Church
9. Sever Hall
10. Carpenter Center for the Visual Arts
11. Fogg Art Museum
12. Arthur M. Sackler Museum
13. Memorial Hall
14. Museum of Natural History and The Peabody Museum
15. Science Center
16. Cambridge Common
17. Christ Church
18. Radcliffe Yard
19. Brattle Theater
20. Harvard Lampoon Castle
21. John F. Kennedy Park

— Red Line
✝ Church
✉ Post Office
ⓘ Information
Ⓣ Station Stop
⚲ Synagogue
☕ "Take a Break"

2. Wadsworth House, 1341 Mass. Ave. Most of the people waiting for the bus in front of this yellow wood building probably don't know it was built in 1726 as a residence for Harvard's fourth president—but then, neither do most Harvard students. Now the headquarters of the alumni association, its biggest claim to fame is a classic: **George Washington** slept here.

Cross the street and go left. Follow the outside of the brick wall past one gate until you see another T exit. Turn right and use Johnston Gate to enter:

3. Harvard Yard. This is the oldest part of **"the Yard."** It was just a patch of grass with animals grazing on it when Harvard College was established in 1636 to train young men for the ministry. It wasn't much more when the **Continental Army** spent the winter of 1775–76 here. Harvard is the oldest college in the United States, with the most competitive admissions process, and if you suggest aloud that it's not the best, you might run up against the attitude that inspired the saying, "You can always tell a Harvard man, but you can't tell him much."

One emerged, as one still does, from the subway exit in the Square and faced an old red-brick wall behind which stretched, to my fond eye, what remains still the most beautiful campus in America, the Harvard Yard. If there is any one place in all America that mirrors better all American history, I do not know of it.
—Theodore H. White, *In Search of History,* 1978

Harvard, a private institution since 1865, includes the college and 10 graduate and professional schools located in more than 400 buildings scattered around Boston and Cambridge. Some of the most interesting are around the perimeter of this quadrangle, the classroom and administration buildings and dormitories that make up the:

4. Old Yard. To your right is **Massachusetts Hall.** Built in 1720, this National Historic Landmark is the university's oldest surviving building. First-year students share the building with the first-floor office of the university president (or perhaps it's the other way around), who is traditionally invited upstairs for tea once a year. To your left, across from Massachusetts Hall, is **Harvard Hall,** a classroom building constructed in 1765. Turn left and walk down the side of Harvard Hall. The matching side-by-side buildings here are **Hollis and Stoughton halls.** Hollis dates to 1763 (Stoughton "only" to 1805), and has been home to many students who went on to great fame, among them **Ralph Waldo Emerson, Henry David Thoreau,** and **Charles Bulfinch.** Almost hidden across the tiny lawn between these two buildings is **Holden Chapel,** a Georgian-style gem built in 1745. It has been an anatomy lab, a classroom building, and, of course, a chapel, and it is now home to the Harvard Glee Club.

Cross the Yard to the building opposite the gate where you entered. This is:

5. University Hall. Designed by **Charles Bulfinch** and constructed in 1812 and 1813 of granite quarried in nearby Chelmsford, it's the college's main administration building. In 1969 it was occupied by students protesting the Vietnam War, but it's best known as the backdrop of the:

6. John Harvard Statue, one of the most photographed objects in the Boston area. Designed by **Daniel Chester French** in 1884, it's known as the "Statue of Three Lies" because the inscription reads "John Harvard—Founder—1638." In fact, the college was founded in 1636; Harvard (one of many involved in its formation) didn't really establish the university, but donated money and his library; and this isn't John Harvard, anyway. No portraits of him survive, so the model for this benevolent-looking bronze gentleman was, according to various accounts, either his nephew or a student.

Walk around University Hall into the adjoining quadrangle. This is still the Yard, but it's the **"New Yard,"** sometimes called **Tercentenary Theater** because the college's 300th-anniversary celebration was held here. This is where commencement and other university-wide ceremonies take place. On your right is:

7. Widener Library. The centerpiece of the world's largest university library system was built in 1913 as a memorial to **Harry Elkins Widener,** a 1907 Harvard graduate. Legend has it that he died when the *Titanic* sank in 1912 because he was unable to swim 50 yards to a lifeboat, and his mother donated $2 million for the library on the condition that every undergraduate prove his ability to swim 50 yards.

Today the library holds more than 3 million volumes, including 3,500 rare volumes collected by Harry Elkins Widener, on 50 miles of shelves. Don't even think about trying to swipe Harry's **Gutenberg Bible.** The last person to try, in 1969, gained access from above but couldn't climb back out. With the 70-pound Bible in his knapsack, he fell six stories to the courtyard below. The library was designed by **Horace Trumbauer** of Philadelphia, whose primary design assistant was **Julian Francis Abele,** a student of architecture at the University of Pennsylvania and the first black graduate of L'Ecole des Beaux Arts in Paris. At press time, the library was in the midst of a massive renovation, and access to the lobby (which sits within view of the locked **memorial room** that holds Widener's collection) was restricted. Check to see if you're allowed to take a peek, or just stop at the top of the outside staircase and enjoy the view. Facing the library is:

8. **Memorial Church,** built in 1931 and topped with a tower and weather vane 197 feet tall. You're welcome to look around this Georgian Revival–style edifice unless services are going on, or to attend them if they are. Morning prayers are said daily from 8:45 to 9am, and the Sunday service is at 11am. The building is also used for private weddings and funerals. The entrance is on the left. On the **south wall,** toward the Yard, the names of the Harvard graduates who died in the world wars, Korea, and Vietnam are listed. One is Joseph P. Kennedy, Jr., the president's brother, class of 1938.

With Memorial Church behind you, turn left toward:

9. **Sever Hall,** a classroom building designed by **H. H. Richardson** (the architect of Boston's Trinity Church) and built from 1878 to 1880. Notice the gorgeous brickwork that includes roll moldings around the doors, the fluted brick chimneys, and the arrangement of the windows. The front door is set back in the **"whispering gallery."** Stand on one side of the entrance arch, station a friend or willing passerby on the opposite side, and speak softly into the facade. Someone standing next to you can't hear what you say, but the person at the other side of the arch can.

Facing Sever Hall, turn right and go around to the back. The building to the right is Emerson Hall, which appeared in the movie *Love Story* as Barrett Hall, named after the family of Ryan O'Neal's character. Cross this quadrangle, go through the gate, and step onto **Quincy Street.** On your right on the other side of the street is the:

10. **Carpenter Center for the Visual Arts,** a concrete-and-glass structure at 24 Quincy St. There are art exhibitions in the lobby, movies from the extensive Harvard Film Archive are shown in the basement (you can pick up a schedule on the main floor), and the building itself is a work of art. It was constructed from 1961 to 1963 and designed by the Swiss-French architect **Le Corbusier,** along with the team of **Sert, Jackson, and Gourley.** It's the only building in North America designed by Le Corbusier. Just up Quincy Street is the:

11. **Fogg Art Museum,** founded in 1895 and located at 32 Quincy St. since the building was completed in 1927. The Fogg's excellent collection of painting, sculpture, and decorative art runs from the Middle Ages to the present. See chapter 7 for a complete description of the Fogg, the adjacent Busch-Reisinger Museum, and the next stop on our walk, the:

12. **Arthur M. Sackler Museum,** 485 Broadway, to the left as you face the Fogg. The university's spectacular collection of Asian art is housed here.

Continue on Quincy Street with the Fogg behind you and cross Broadway, then cross Cambridge Street, watching out for the confused drivers emerging from the underpass to your left. Covering the block between Cambridge Street and Kirkland Street is:

13. **Memorial Hall,** a Victorian structure built from 1870 to 1874. The entrance on Cambridge Street puts you in the actual hall of memorials, a transept where you can read the names of the Harvard men who died fighting for the Union during the Civil War—but not of their Confederate counterparts. To the right is **Sanders Theatre,** prized as a performance space and lecture hall for its excellent acoustics and clear views. To the left is **Annenberg Hall,** originally Alumni Hall. It's a dining hall that's technically closed to visitors, but you might be able to look in at the gorgeous stained-glass windows. Harvard graduates **William Ware** and **Henry Van Brunt** won a design competition for Memorial Hall, which was constructed for a total cost of $390,000 (most of it donated by alumni). The colorful tower is a replica of the original, which was destroyed by fire in 1956 and not rebuilt until 1999.

Facing in the same direction you were when you entered, walk through the transept and exit onto Kirkland Street. Turn left and take the first right, onto Oxford Street. One block up on the right you'll see an entrance to the:

14. **Harvard Museum of Natural History,** 26 Oxford St. (☎ **617/495-3045**), which adjoins the **Peabody Museum of Archaeology & Ethnology,** 11 Divinity Ave. (☎ **617/496-1027**). The Museum of Natural History consists of the **Botanical Museum,** the **Museum of Comparative Zoology,** and the **Mineralogical & Geological Museum.** See chapter 7 for a full description.

Leave through the back door at 11 Divinity Ave. and look around. Across the street at 6 Divinity Ave. is the **Semitic Museum** (☎ **617/495-4631**), where the second- and third-floor galleries hold displays of archaeological artifacts and photographs from the Near and Middle East. You might want to detour here. The building next door, **2 Divinity Ave.,** was designed by **Horace Trumbauer,** the architect of Widener Library. It's home to the Harvard-Yenching Institute, which promotes East Asian studies and facilitates scholar exchange programs. For every person who can tell you that, there are several thousand who know this building only for the pair of **Chinese stone lions** flanking the front door.

Turn right and return to Kirkland Street, then go right again. At the intersection of Kirkland and Oxford streets is the university's:

15. **Science Center,** Zero Oxford St. The 10-story monolith is said to resemble a Polaroid camera (Edwin H. Land, founder of Cambridge-based Polaroid Corporation, was one of its main benefactors). The Science Center was designed by the Spanish architect **Josep Luis Sert** and built from 1970 to 1972. Sert, the dean of the university's Graduate School of Design from 1953 to 1969, was a disciple of Le Corbusier, whose Carpenter Center for the Visual Arts you've already seen. On the plaza between the Science Center and the Yard is the **Tanner Rock Fountain,** a group of 159 New England field boulders artfully arranged around a small fountain. Since 1985 this has been a favorite spot for students to relax and watch unsuspecting passersby get wet; the fountain sprays a fine mist, which begins slowly and gradually intensifies.

☕ **TAKE A BREAK**   The main level of the Science Center is open to the public and has several options if you want a soft drink, gourmet coffee, or chicken sandwich. Go easy on the sweets, though, in anticipation of the next break.

Leave the Science Center near the fountain and turn right. Keeping the underpass on your left, follow the walkway for the equivalent of 1¹/₂ blocks as it curves around to the right. The **Harvard Law School** campus is on your right. You're back at Mass. Ave., which, when you saw it last, took a right at the Coop and turned north. Cross carefully to:

16. **Cambridge Common.** Memorials and plaques dot this well-used plot of greenery and bare earth. Follow the sidewalk along Mass. Ave. to the left, and after a block or so you'll walk near or over horseshoes embedded in the concrete. This is the path **William Dawes,** Paul Revere's fellow alarm-sounder, took from Boston to Lexington on April 18, 1775. Turn right onto Garden Street and continue following the Common for 1 block. On your right you'll see a monument marking the place where Gen. **George Washington** took control of the Continental Army on July 3, 1775. The elm under which he assumed command is no longer standing.

Cross Garden Street and backtrack to:

17. **Christ Church,** Zero Garden St., the oldest church in Cambridge. **Peter Harrison** of Newport, Rhode Island (also the architect of King's Chapel in Boston), designed the church, which opened in 1761. Note the square wooden tower. Inside the vestibule you can still see bullet holes made by British muskets. At one time the church was used as the barracks for troops from Connecticut, who melted down the organ pipes to make ammunition.

Facing the church, turn right and proceed on Garden Street to the first intersection. This is Appian Way. Turn left and take the first right into:

18. **Radcliffe Yard.** Radcliffe College was founded in 1879 as the "Harvard Annex" and named for **Ann Radcliffe, Lady Mowlson,** Harvard's first female benefactor. Undergraduate classes merged with Harvard's in 1943, Radcliffe graduates first received Harvard degrees in 1963, and in 1977 Harvard officially assumed responsibility for educating undergraduate women. Radcliffe remained an independent corporation until 1999; it's now the university's Radcliffe Institute for Advanced Study. After you've strolled around, return to Appian Way and turn right. You'll emerge on Brattle Street.

You might want to call ahead to see if the **Longfellow National Historic Site,** 105 Brattle St. (☎ 617/876-4491; see chapter 7), has reopened after renovations. It makes for an interesting and scenic detour, and adds about an hour to your walk. If you can't or don't want to detour, turn left and continue walking along Brattle Street. There are excellent shops on both sides of the street.

☕ TAKE A BREAK   Yes, **Billings & Stover Apothecaries,** 41A Brattle St. (☎ 617/547-0502), on your left, is a drugstore. Look harder—the front of the store is an old-fashioned soda fountain.

Across the street is the:

19. **Brattle Theater,** 40 Brattle St. Opened in 1890 as Brattle Hall, it was founded by the Cambridge Social Union and used as a venue for cultural entertainment. In 1953, it was converted to a movie hall and quickly became known as Cambridge's center for art films. The Brattle Theater, one of the oldest independent movie houses in the country, started the *Casablanca* revival craze, which explains the name of the restaurant in the basement.

You're now in the **Brattle Square** part of Harvard Square. You might see street musicians or performers, a protest, a speech, or just more stores to explore. Cross Brattle Street at **WordsWorth Books,** bear right, and follow the curve of the building all the way around the corner to Mount Auburn Street. Stay on the left-hand side of the street as you cross John F. Kennedy Street, Dunster Street, Holyoke Street, and Linden Street. On your left between Dunster and Holyoke streets is **Holyoke Center,** an administration building designed by **Josep Luis**

Sert that has commercial space on the ground floor. The corner of Mount Auburn and Linden streets is a good vantage point for viewing the:

20. Harvard Lampoon Castle, constructed in 1909 and designed by **Wheelwright & Haven,** architects of Boston's Horticultural Hall. Listed on the National Register of Historic Places, this is the home of Harvard's undergraduate humor magazine, the *Lampoon.* The main tower looks like a face, with windows as the eyes, nose, and mouth, topped by what looks like a miner's hat. The *Lampoon* and the daily student newspaper, the *Crimson,* share a long history of reciprocal pranks and harmless vandalism. Elaborate security measures notwithstanding, *Crimson* editors occasionally make off with the bird that might be atop the castle (it looks like a crane but is actually an ibis), and *Lampoon* staffers have absconded with the huge wood president's chair from the *Crimson.*

You'll pass the *Crimson* building on your right if you decide to detour for a visit to the **Harvard Book Store** (turn left onto Plympton Street and follow it to the corner of Mass. Ave.). Otherwise, follow Mount Auburn Street back to John F. Kennedy Street. Alternatively, cross Mount Auburn Street and walk away from Holyoke Center on Holyoke Street or Dunster Street to get a sense of some of the rest of the campus. Turn right on Winthrop Street or South Street, and proceed to Kennedy Street.

Turn left onto Kennedy Street, cross it at some point, and follow it toward the Charles River, almost to Memorial Drive. On your right is:

John F. Kennedy Park. This lovely parcel of land was an empty plot near the MBTA train yard in the 1970s (at that time the Red Line ended at Harvard), when the search was on for a site for the Kennedy Library. Traffic concerns led to the library's being built in Dorchester, but the **Graduate School of Government** and this adjacent park bear the president's name. Walk away from the street to enjoy the **fountain,** which is engraved with excerpts from the president's speeches. This is an excellent place to take a break and plan the rest of your day.

Shopping 9

Boston's shopping scene is a harmonious blend of classic and contemporary. You'll find intimate boutiques and sprawling malls, esoteric bookshops and national chain stores, classy galleries and snazzy secondhand-clothing outlets. In this chapter I'll point you to areas that are great for shop-hopping, and specific destinations that are great for specific items.

1 The Shopping Scene

One of the best features of shopping in Massachusetts is that there's no sales tax on clothing priced below $175, or on food. Just about every store will ship your purchases home for a fee, but if it's part of a chain that operates in your home state, you'll probably be subject to that sales tax. Be sure to ask first. All other items are taxed at 5% (as are restaurant meals and takeout food).

In the major shopping areas, stores usually open at 10am on weekdays and Saturday. Malls keep their own hours (noted below); smaller shops stay open weeknights and Saturday until 6 or 7pm, and Sunday until 5 or 6pm. Winter open days and Sunday open hours may vary. The state no longer prohibits stores from opening before 12 on Sunday, but many still wait till noon or don't open at all. If a business sounds too good to pass up, call to make sure it's open before venturing out.

GREAT SHOPPING AREAS

The area's premier shopping area is Boston's **Back Bay.** Dozens of classy galleries, shops, and boutiques make **Newbury Street** a world-famous destination. Nearby, the **Shops at Prudential Center** and **Copley Place** (linked by a weatherproof walkway across Huntington Avenue), **Neiman Marcus, Lord & Taylor,** and **Saks Fifth Avenue** form the backbone of a giant retail complex.

Another popular destination is **Faneuil Hall Marketplace.** The shops, boutiques, and pushcarts at Boston's busiest attraction sell everything from cosmetics to costume jewelry, sweaters to souvenirs.

If the prospect of the hubbub at Faneuil Hall is too much for you, stroll over to **Charles Street,** at the foot of Beacon Hill. It's a short but commercially dense (and picturesque) street noted for its gift shops and antiques dealers.

One of Boston's oldest shopping areas is **Downtown Crossing.** The traffic-free pedestrian mall along Washington, Winter, and Summer streets near Boston Common is home to two major department stores (**Filene's** and **Macy's**), tons of smaller clothing and shoe stores, food and merchandise pushcarts, outlets of two major bookstore chains (**Barnes & Noble** and **Borders**), and the original **Filene's Basement** (see below).

Harvard Square in Cambridge, with its bookstores, boutiques, and T-shirt shops, is about 15 minutes from downtown Boston by subway. Over the neighborhood association's objections, chain stores have swept into "the Square," driving up rents and driving out many of the businesses that contributed to its legendary bohemian atmosphere. Today you'll find a mix of national and regional outlets, and more than a few persistent independent retailers.

For a less generic experience, stroll along shop-lined **Massachusetts Avenue** in either direction to the next T stop (**Porter Square** to the north, **Central Square** to the southeast). The walk takes an hour or so—time well spent for dedicated consumers.

2 Shopping A to Z

Here we've singled out establishments we especially like and neighborhoods that suit shoppers interested in particular types of merchandise. Unless otherwise indicated, addresses are in Boston.

ANTIQUES & COLLECTIBLES

No antiques hound worthy of the name will leave Boston without an expedition along both sides of **Charles Street** from Cambridge Street to Beacon Street.

✪ **Boston Antique Cooperative I & II.** 119 Charles St. ☎ **617/227-9810.** T: Red Line to Charles/MGH.

Merchandise from Europe, Asia, and the United States fills these shops. They specialize in furniture, vintage clothing and photographs, jewelry, and porcelain, but you might come across just about anything. The traffic is heavy and the turnover rapid, so if you see something you like, buy it immediately or risk losing out.

Bromfield Pen Shop. 5 Bromfield St. ☎ **617/482-9053.** T: Red or Orange Line to Downtown Crossing.

This shop's selection of antique pens will thrill any collector. It also sells new pens, including Mont Blanc, Pelikan, Waterman, and Omas.

Danish Country Antique Furniture. 138 Charles St. ☎ **617/227-1804.** T: Red Line to Charles/MGH.

Owner James Kilroy specializes in Scandinavian antique furnishings dating from the 1700s onward. You'll also see folk art, crafts, Royal Copenhagen porcelain, and 19th-century Chinese furniture and home accessories.

Shreve, Crump & Low. 330 Boylston St. ☎ **800/324-0222** or 617/267-9100. T: Green Line to Arlington.

This Boston institution, founded in 1796, is best known for new jewelry, china, silver, crystal, and watches. The antiques department specializes in 18th- and 19th-century American and English furnishings, British and American silver, and Chinese porcelain.

ART

Everyone has to start somewhere, and the artists whose work you'll find in the big museums years from now might be showing at galleries in Boston today. You'll find the greatest concentration of galleries along ✪ **Newbury Street** (remember to look up

Back Bay & Beacon Hill Shopping

Alpha Gallery ㉟
Anne Fontaine ㊺
Artful Hand Gallery ⑥
Avenue Victor Hugo
  Bookshop ⑮
Barbara Krakow
  Gallery ㊷
Beadworks ⑱
Boston Antique
  Cooperative I & II ㊽
Brooks Brothers ㊱
Chanel ㊺
Copley Place ⑦
CP Shades ㉘
Crate & Barrel ④
Danish Country
  Antique Furniture ㊿
E6 Apothecary ㉗
Emporio Armani ⑫
Ermenegildo Zegna ㊲
FAO Schwarz ㉟
Farmer's Market ⑨
The Flat of the Hill ㊼
Gallery NAGA ㉜
Gargoyles, Grotesques
  & Chimeras ⑰
Gianni Versace ㊶
Giorgio Armani ㊳
Globe Corner
  Bookstore ㉞
Haley & Steele ㉛

Helen's Leather Shop ㊾
International Poster Gallery ⑭
Jasmine/Sola ⑲
John Lewis, Inc. ㉚
Koo De Kir ㊻
La Ruche ⑬
Lord & Taylor ⑪
Louis, Boston ㉝
Museum of Fine Arts
  Gift Shop ⑤
Neiman Marcus ⑧
Newbury Comics ⑳
Nielsen Gallery ㉔
Oilily ㊵
Pucker Gallery ㉖
Restoration Hardware ⑩
Robert Klein Gallery ㊳
Saks Fifth Avenue ③
Savenor's Supermarket ㉛
Shops at
  Prudential Center ①
Shop at the Union ㊸
Shreve, Crump & Low ㊹
Society of Arts & Crafts ㉕
Swatch Kiosk ②
Sweet Peas Home ㉙
Tower Records ㉑
Vose Galleries of Boston ㉒
Waterstone's Booksellers ㉓

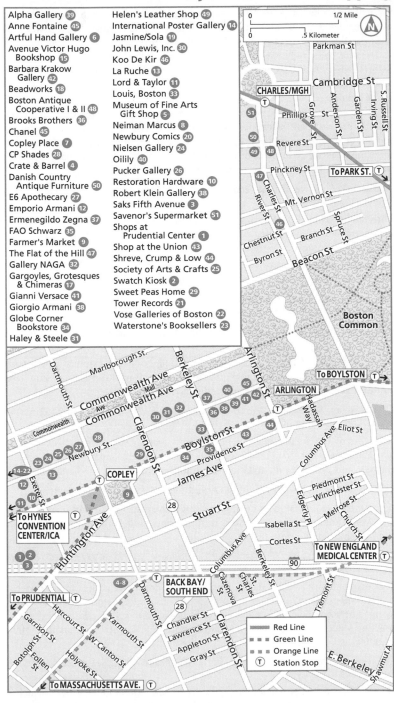

for galleries on higher floors). Browsers and questions are welcome. Most galleries are open Tuesday through Sunday from 10 or 11am to 5:30 or 6pm. For specifics, check with the **Newbury Street League** (☎ 617/267-7961; www.newbury-st.com).

Tremont Street and Harrison Avenue in the South End is a budding gallery area, as is the Leather District around South Street (between South Station and Chinatown), which is muddling through the Big Dig. You'll find galleries, but you're equally likely to see bulldozers.

One excellent way to see artists at work is to check listings in the *Globe* and *Herald* for information about neighborhood **open studio** days. The artists' communities in the South End, the Fort Point Channel area, Somerville, and even tony Brookline stage the weekend events once or twice a year. You may be asked to make a contribution to charity in exchange for a map of the studios.

Alpha Gallery. 14 Newbury St., 2nd floor. ☎ **617/536-4465.** E-mail: alphagall@aol.com. T: Green Line to Arlington.

Directed by Joanna E. Fink, daughter of founder Alan Fink, Alpha Gallery specializes in contemporary American paintings, sculpture, and works on paper, as well as modern master paintings and prints.

Barbara Krakow Gallery. 10 Newbury St., 5th floor. ☎ **617/262-4490.** www. barbarakrakowgallery.com. T: Green Line to Arlington.

This prestigious gallery, established more than 30 years ago, specializes in paintings, sculpture, drawings, and prints created after 1945.

Gallery NAGA. 67 Newbury St. ☎ **617/267-9060.** www.gallerynaga.com. T: Green Line to Arlington.

In the neo-Gothic Church of the Covenant, Gallery NAGA exhibits contemporary painting, prints, sculpture, photography, furniture, and works in glass. A stop here is a must if you want to see holography (trust me, you do).

✪ **Gargoyles, Grotesques & Chimeras.** 262 Newbury St. ☎ **617/536-2362.** T: Green Line B, C, or D to Hynes/ICA.

Gargoyles of all sizes decorate this intentionally gloomy space. You'll also see plaster reproductions of details on the facades of famous cathedrals and other buildings, non-gargoyle home decorations, and haunting photographs that set the Gothic mood.

Haley & Steele. 91 Newbury St. ☎ **617/536-6339.** T: Green Line to Arlington.

If you prefer traditional to contemporary, this is the place. You'll find maritime, military, botanical, ornithological, and historical prints, and 19th-century oil paintings and British sporting prints.

✪ **International Poster Gallery.** 205 Newbury St. ☎ **617/375-0076.** www. internationalposter.com. T: Green Line to Copley.

This extraordinary gallery's Italian vintage poster collection is the largest anywhere, and the thousands of other pieces include posters and ephemera from around the world. The accommodating staff will comb its databases (cyber and cerebral) to help you find the exact image you want. Prices start at $50, with most in the $500 to $2,000 range.

✪ **Nielsen Gallery.** 179 Newbury St. ☎ **617/266-4835.** www.nielsengallery.com. T: Green Line to Copley.

Owner Nina Nielsen personally selects the artists who exhibit in her gallery (which has been here for more than 35 years), and she has great taste. You might come across the work of a young, newly discovered talent or that of a more established artist.

✪ **Pucker Gallery.** 171 Newbury St. ☎ **617/267-9473.** E-mail: puckergall@aol.com. T: Green Line to Copley.

Pucker Gallery's eclectic offerings include Inuit, African, and Israeli art; contemporary paintings, prints, drawings, and ceramics by regional and international artists; and excellent photographs. The staff is eager to show off and discuss the art, which spreads over four floors.

Robert Klein Gallery. 38 Newbury St., 4th floor. ☎ **617/267-7997.** T: Green Line to Arlington.

For 19th- and 20th-century photography, head to Robert Klein Gallery. Among the artists represented are Diane Arbus, Robert Mapplethorpe, Man Ray, and Ansel Adams.

Vose Galleries of Boston. 238 Newbury St. ☎ **617/536-6176.** T: Green Line B, C, or D to Hynes/ICA.

One of the specialties here is Hudson River School paintings—fitting, because the business and the mid-19th-century movement are about the same age. The oldest continuously operating gallery in the United States opened in 1841 and is still run by the Vose family (now in its fifth generation). You'll see works of the Boston School and American Impressionists among the 18th-, 19th-, and early-20th-century American paintings.

BOOKS

The Boston area is a book lover's paradise. **Harvard Square** is to books as Newbury Street is to art, but bibliophiles will unearth treasures on both sides of the Charles River.

Avenue Victor Hugo Bookshop. 339 Newbury St. ☎ **617/266-7746.** www. avenuevictorhugobooks.com. T: Green Line B, C, or D to Hynes/ICA.

This two-story shop buys, sells, and trades new and used books and estate libraries. The stock of 150,000 books is comprehensive; the primary specialty is science fiction. You'll also find periodicals, with back issues of magazines that date to 1850, and a selection of general fiction titles that's billed as the largest north of New York City.

Barnes & Noble. 395 Washington St. ☎ **617/426-5184.** www.barnesandnoble.com. T: Red or Orange Line to Downtown Crossing.

The downtown branch of the national chain carries a large selection of local-interest titles and has a huge periodicals section. Barnes & Noble runs the bookstore operations at Boston University and Harvard (see "College Paraphernalia," below). There's also a branch at 325 Harvard St., Coolidge Corner, Brookline (☎ **617/232-0594**).

Borders Books & Music. 24 School St. ☎ **617/557-7188.** www.borders.com. T: Orange or Blue Line to State.

Two levels of books and one of music, plus an in-house cafe and occasional author appearances, make this sprawling store near Downtown Crossing a popular destination.

✪ **Brattle Book Shop.** 9 West St. ☎ **800/447-9595** or 617/542-0210. E-mail: brattle@tiac.net. T: Red or Orange Line to Downtown Crossing or Green Line to Boylston.

This marvelous store near Macy's buys and sells used, rare, and out-of-print titles, and owner Kenneth Gloss does free appraisals. Be sure to check the carts out front (in all but the nastiest weather) for good deals on books of all ages. *Warning:* Book lovers and collectors who make this their first stop may not get any other shopping done.

Going, Going . . . : A Famous Auction House

Antiques Roadshow fans, this one's for you. The rotating cast of appraisers on PBS's smash hit includes staff members from New England's best-known auction house, **Skinner,** Heritage on the Garden, 63 Park Plaza (☎ **617/350-5400;** www.skinnerinc.com). Skinner mounts about 60 auctions a year in Boston—usually on weekends—and suburban Bolton, and visitors can bid or just observe. You might see fine art, antiques, collectibles, jewelry, furniture, textiles, rugs, or even musical instruments. Call or check the Web site for information about buying a catalog, or just show up. Heritage on the Garden is at the corner of Boylston and Arlington streets (T: Green Line to Arlington).

✪ **Brookline Booksmith.** 279 Harvard St., Brookline. ☎ **617/566-6660.** www. brooklinebooksmith.com. T: Green Line C to Coolidge Corner.

The huge, varied selection makes this award-winning store a polymath's dream. *Publishers Weekly* named it the best bookstore in the country in 1998. It boasts a great gift and card section, and stages tons of events.

Globe Corner Bookstore. 500 Boylston St. ☎ **617/859-80008.** www.globecorner. com. T: Green Line to Copley. 28 Church St., Cambridge. ☎ **617/497-6277.** T: Red Line to Harvard.

These overstuffed stores (offspring of the dear departed original on the Freedom Trail) carry huge selections of travel guides and essays, maps, atlases, globes, and nautical charts.

✪ **Harvard Book Store.** 1256 Mass. Ave., Cambridge. ☎ **800/542-READ** outside 617, or 617/661-1515. www.harvard.com. E-mail: hbs-info@harvard.com. T: Red Line to Harvard.

The excellent scholarly selection and discounted best-sellers attract shoppers to the main level of this independent bookstore, and the basement is the draw for those in the know. Prices on remainders are good, and used paperbacks (many bought for classes and hardly opened) are 50% off their original price.

Rand McNally Map & Travel Store. 84 State St. ☎ **617/720-1125.** www. randmcnallystore.com. T: Orange or Blue Line to State.

Armchair travelers who get as far as Faneuil Hall Marketplace can go one more block for guides, maps, games, software, travel accessories, and a great variety of globes.

Schoenhof's Foreign Books. 76A Mt. Auburn St., Cambridge. ☎ **617/547-8855.** www.schoenhofs.com. E-mail: info@schoenhofs.com. T: Red Line to Harvard.

Schoenhof's stocks books for both children and adults in more than two dozen languages, as well as dictionaries and language-learning materials for more than 300 languages and dialects. After a recent expansion, it also carries gifts, greeting cards, calendars, and the like. The multilingual staff arranges special orders at no extra charge.

✪ **WordsWorth Books.** 30 Brattle St., Cambridge. ☎ **800/899-2202** or 617/354-5201. www.wordsworth.com. E-mail: info@wordsworth.com. T: Red Line to Harvard.

This sprawling store stocks more than 100,000 volumes, all (except textbooks) discounted at least 10%. It's a great place for browsing; if you prefer, the information desk staff will brainstorm with you until the database generates the title you want. The excellent selection of children's books and gifts is up the street at ✪ **Curious George Goes to WordsWorth,** 1 John F. Kennedy St. (☎ **617/498-0062;** www.curiousg.com).

COLLEGE PARAPHERNALIA

The centrally located big names are BU and Harvard (you'll see Boston College merchandise downtown, too), but why stop there? Look like a real insider with a T-shirt from the **Emerson College Book Store,** 80 Boylston St. (☎ 617/728-7700; T: Green Line to Boylston); the **MIT Coop,** 3 Cambridge Center (☎ 617/499-3200; T: Red Line to Kendall/MIT); the **Northeastern University Bookstore,** 360 Huntington Ave. (☎ 617/373-2286; T: Green Line E to Northeastern); or the **Suffolk University Bookstore,** 148 Cambridge St., Beacon Hill (☎ 617/227-4085; T: Blue Line to Bowdoin).

Barnes & Noble at Boston University. 660 Beacon St. ☎ **617/267-8484.** www.bkstore.com/bu. T: Green Line B, C, or D to Kenmore.

The BU crest, mascot (a terrier), or name appears somewhere on at least a floor's worth of clothing and just about any other item with room for a logo. The author series (☎ 617/236-7421) brings writers to campus year-round.

The Harvard Coop. 1400 Mass. Ave., Cambridge. ☎ **617/499-2000.** www.thecoop.com. T: Red Line to Harvard.

The Coop (rhymes with *hoop*), or Harvard Cooperative Society, is student-oriented but not a run-of-the-mill college bookstore. You'll find Harvard insignia merchandise, stationery, prints and posters, and music. As at BU, Barnes & Noble runs the book operation.

✪ **The Harvard Shop.** 52 John F. Kennedy St., Cambridge. ☎ **617/864-3000.** T: Red Line to Harvard.

Kids in shopping malls from Jacksonville to Juneau wear Harvard shirts in every color and outlandish pattern under the sun. Visit this shop for authentic gear in the shadow of the school.

CRAFTS

✪ **The Artful Hand Gallery.** Copley Place. ☎ **617/262-9601.** T: Orange Line to Back Bay or Green Line to Copley.

The Artful Hand specializes, as you might guess, in handcrafted items. It shows and sells work by an excellent roster of artists. You'll see wonderful jewelry, ceramics, blown glass, wood pieces (including boxes), and sculpture, plus furniture, folk art, and books.

Pearl Art & Craft Supplies. 579 Mass. Ave., Cambridge. ☎ **617/547-6600.** E-mail: cambridge@pearlart.com. T: Red Line to Central.

The Central Square branch of this national discount chain stocks everything you need to do it yourself, from pens and pencils to stamps and stencils to beads and fittings.

✪ **Society of Arts and Crafts.** 175 Newbury St. ☎ **617/266-1810.** www. societyofcrafts.org. T: Green Line to Copley.

Contemporary American work, much created by New Englanders, is the focus at the oldest nonprofit craft organization in the country. The jewelry, furniture, home accessories, glass, and ceramics range from practical to purely decorative. The **Downtown Crossing** branch, open on weekdays only, is on the second floor of 101 Arch St. (☎ 617/345-0033), off Summer Street.

DEPARTMENT STORES

There's so much else going on in the Back Bay that you might forget it's home to branches of three elegant chains. We particularly like **Lord & Taylor,** 760 Boylston

St. (☎ 617/262-6000), for its great sales and costume jewelry. The high-end **Saks Fifth Avenue,** Prudential Plaza (☎ 617/262-8500), would be the classiest department store in town if not for **Neiman Marcus,** 5 Copley Place (☎ 617/536-3660), which charges Texas-size prices for the trappings of true luxury.

Filene's. 426 Washington St. ☎ **617/357-2100.** T: Red or Orange Line to Downtown Crossing.

Filene's (say "Fie-*leen's*") is a full-service department store with all the usual trappings, plus an exceptional cosmetics department.

Macy's. 450 Washington St. ☎ **617/357-3000.** T: Red or Orange Line to Downtown Crossing.

Across Summer Street from Filene's stands New England's largest store. It bears the hallmarks of the New York–based chain, including excellent selections of housewares, china, and silver.

DISCOUNT SHOPPING

✪ **Filene's Basement.** 426 Washington St. ☎ **617/542-2011.** T: Red or Orange Line to Downtown Crossing.

Dedicated discount shoppers had no trouble picking the biggest story of 1999—not the rise of e-tailing, but that Filene's Basement declared Chapter 11 bankruptcy. The overextended chain was retrenching at press time, closing many branches and publicly vowing to keep this location, the original, as its flagship. Deals worth bragging about are harder to track down, but still possible. I happen to love that sort of thing, but if you don't, you may find that battling the no-holds-barred crowds isn't worth the payoff—the selling floors are still pretty wild at busy times.

New England's most famous discount retailer opened in 1908. Its automatic-markdown policy (25% off after 2 weeks on the selling floor, up to 75% after 7 weeks) applies to everything from lingerie to overcoats. The most ego-boosting quarries are designer and other top-quality clothes at a fraction of their original prices. Try to beat the lunchtime crowds, and check the papers for early opening times during special sales (notably the $249 wedding-dress blowout at least twice a year).

Syms. 55 Summer St. ☎ **617/556-0820.** www.syms.com. T: Red or Orange Line to Downtown Crossing.

Discounted designer duds for men and women are Syms' calling card. As at Filene's Basement, prices drop automatically, but Syms uses longer intervals. The merchandise here is of more consistent quality—fewer disasters, but fewer great finds.

FASHION
Also see "Shoes" and "Vintage & Secondhand Clothing," below.

ADULTS
Newbury Street is ground zero for if-you-have-to-ask-you-can't-afford-it designer shopping. Bring your platinum card to **Chanel,** 15 Arlington St., in the Ritz-Carlton, Boston (☎ 617/859-0055); **Ermenegildo Zegna,** 39 Newbury St. (☎ 617/424-6657); and **Gianni Versace,** 12 Newbury St. (☎ 617/536-8300).

Anne Fontaine. Heritage on the Garden, 318 Boylston St. ☎ **617/423-0366.** T: Green Line to Arlington.

This is the first U.S. outlet for the designer's "perfect white blouse collection from Paris." We wanted to laugh, but then we saw for ourselves—almost every item *is* a perfect (for one reason or another) white blouse. A few darker tops have sneaked in, too. Prices start at $80.

Brooks Brothers. 46 Newbury St. ☎ **617/267-2600**. T: Green Line to Arlington. 75 State St. ☎ **617/261-9990**. T: Orange or Blue Line to State.

Blue blazers, gray flannels, and seersucker suits are widely available, but only at Brooks Brothers will you find the business and casual styles that mark you as a "proper Bostonian." The stores carry women's clothes and sportswear, too. Brooks is also the only place for exactly the right preppy shade of pink button-down oxford shirts—something I've never seen at the outlet stores.

CP Shades. 139B Newbury St. ☎ **617/421-0846**. T: Green Line to Copley.

No, not sunglasses—comfortable knits and natural fabrics that women can wear for everything from board meetings to baby-sitting.

Dakini. 1704 Mass. Ave., Cambridge. ☎ **617/864-7661**. www.dakini.com. T: Red Line to Porter.

Come here for fleece in every imaginable incarnation, from shearling-like jackets to velvety gloves, high-fashion women's separates to kids' pullovers. It's not cheap, but it's top quality, and the regular sales can make you feel both toasty and thrifty.

Giorgio Armani. 22 Newbury St. ☎ **617/267-3200**. T: Green Line to Arlington.

Here you'll find Armani's sleek, sophisticated men's and women's clothing—in addition to ski, golf, and bridal collections—at true Armani prices. If your taste (and budget) is less grand, head down the street to **Emporio Armani,** 210–214 Newbury St. (☎ **617/262-7300**). It carries sportswear, jeans, eveningwear, and home accessories.

Louis, Boston. 234 Berkeley St. ☎ **800/225-5135** or 617/262-6100. T: Green Line to Arlington.

This ultraprestigious store (with prices to match) sells designer men's suits that can be coordinated with handmade shirts, silk ties, and Italian shoes. Louis, Woman, at the same address, caters to an equally elegant female clientele. Also on the premises are a full-service hair salon and Café Louis, which serves lunch and dinner.

CHILDREN

Calliope. 33 Brattle St., Cambridge. ☎ **617/876-4149**. T: Red Line to Harvard.

The must-see window displays at this Harvard Square shop use stuffed animals, clothes, and toys to illustrate sayings and proverbs, often twisted into hilarious puns. The merchandise inside—clothing, shoes, and a huge selection of plush animals—is equally delightful.

Oilily. 31 Newbury St. ☎ **800/964-5459** or 617/247-9299. www.oilily.nl. T: Green Line to Arlington.

At this end of Newbury Street, even kids must be *au courant.* Lend a hand with a visit to the Boston branch of the chichi international chain, which specializes in brightly colored fashions and accessories for ages newborn to 14 years. There's also a women's store at 32 Newbury St. (☎ **617/247-2386**).

Saturday's Child. 1762 Mass. Ave., Cambridge. ☎ **617/661-6402**. T: Red Line to Porter.

Never mind the nursery rhyme—"Saturday's child works hard for a living," my foot. You won't want your little angel lifting a finger in these precious (in both senses of the word) outfits. You'll also find top-quality shoes, accessories, and toys.

Varese Shoes. 285 Hanover St. ☎ **617/523-6530.** T: Green or Orange Line to Haymarket.

One window holds men's shoes, but that's not why you hear oohing and aahing all the way from the Freedom Trail (10 steps away). The other window is full of the most adorable Italian leather children's shoes. So they're not necessarily practical—are all of *your* shoes practical?

FOOD

Cardullo's Gourmet Shoppe. 6 Brattle St., Cambridge. ☎ **617/491-8888.** T: Red Line to Harvard.

A veritable United Nations of fancy food, Cardullo's carries specialties (including a huge variety of candy) from just about everywhere. If you can't afford the big-ticket items, order a tasty sandwich to go.

✪ **Dairy Fresh Candies.** 57 Salem St. ☎ **800/336-5536** or 617/742-2639. www.dairyfreshcandies.com. T: Green or Orange Line to Haymarket.

This North End hole-in-the-wall is crammed with decadent sweets and other delectables, from bagged nuts and dried fruit to imported Italian specialties. Before sweet-tooth-oriented holidays (especially Easter), it's irresistible. The store is too small for turning the children loose, but they'll be happy they waited outside when you return with confections to fortify them along the Freedom Trail.

J. Pace & Son. 42 Cross St. ☎ 617/227-9673. T: Green or Orange Line to Haymarket.

Imported Italian food items, from fine meats and cheeses to pasta and cookies, overflow the shelves and cases at this bustling market on the threshold of the North End. Prices are good, especially for olive oil, and there's never a dull moment at the front counter. Order a sandwich if you don't feel like hauling groceries around—you can eat outside with the Big Dig workers.

Le Saucier. Quincy Market, North Canopy. ☎ 617/227-9649. www.lesaucierinc.com. T: Green or Blue Line to Government Center.

The sauces collected in this little space might bring tears to your eyes. The variety verges on infinite, and the hot sauces (check the front counter for free samples) are concocted from positively diabolical ingredients. The shop also carries regional and international specialty foods.

Savenor's Supermarket. 160 Charles St. ☎ 617/723-6328. T: Red Line to Charles/MGH.

Long a Cambridge institution (and a Julia Child favorite), Savenor's moved to Beacon Hill after a fire in 1993. It's the perfect place to load up on provisions before a concert or movie on the nearby Esplanade. And it's *the* local purveyor of exotic meats—if you crave buffalo or rattlesnake meat, this is the place.

✪ **Trader Joe's.** 727 Memorial Dr., Cambridge. ☎ **617/491-8582.** 1317 Beacon St., Brookline. ☎ **617/278-9997.** www.traderjoes.com. T: Green Line C to Coolidge Corner.

This celebrated California-based retailer stocks a great selection of natural and organic products, wine, cheese, nuts, baked goods, and other edibles, at excellent prices. The Cambridge location is a good place to stop for picnic provisions if you're driving. Get a preview from the Web site or just ask devotees—they can't shut up about it.

GIFTS & SOUVENIRS

Boston has dozens of shops and pushcarts that sell T-shirts, hats, and other souvenirs. At the stores listed here, you'll find gifts that say Boston without actually *saying* "Boston" all over them. Remember to check out museum shops for unique items, including crafts and games. Particularly good retail outlets include those at the **Museum of Fine Arts,** the **Museum of Science,** Harvard's **Peabody Museum,** the **Isabella Stewart Gardner Museum,** the **Concord Museum,** and the **Peabody Essex Museum** in Salem.

The Flat of the Hill. 60 Charles St. ☎ **617/619-9977.** E-mail: theflatofthehill@juno.com. T: Red Line to Charles/MGH.

A folk-art wooden dog stands watch at the door of this jam-packed shop, which overflows with fun tchotchkes—home accessories, picture frames, stuffed animals, toys, and all manner of candles.

✪ **Joie de Vivre.** 1792 Mass. Ave., Cambridge. ☎ **617/864-8188.** T: Red Line to Porter.

Joie de Vivre's selection of gifts and toys for adults and sophisticated children is beyond compare. The kaleidoscope collection alone is worth the trip to this shop outside Porter Square; you'll also find salt and pepper shakers, jewelry, note cards, and puzzles.

Koo De Kir. 34 Charles St. ☎ **617/723-8111.** www.koodekir.com. T: Red Line to Charles/MGH.

In the heart of 19th-century Beacon Hill, Koo De Kir is a splash of the 21st century. Its selection of contemporary home accessories, furniture, lighting, and sculpture ranges from classics-to-be to downright whimsical.

Museum of Fine Arts Gift Shop. Copley Place. ☎ **617/536-8818.** T: Orange Line to Back Bay or Green Line to Copley. South Market Building, Faneuil Hall Marketplace. ☎ **617/720-1266.** T: Green or Blue Line to Government Center.

For those without the time or inclination to visit the museum, the satellite shops carry posters, prints, cards and stationery, books, educational toys, scarves, mugs, T-shirts, and reproductions of jewelry in the museum's collections. You might even be inspired to pay a call on the real thing.

Only the Best. 75 Commercial St. ☎ **888/296-3330** or 617/367-7411. www.bostongiftbaskets.com. T: Blue Line to Aquarium.

Half a block from Quincy Market, this North End shop is easy to miss, yet worth a detour. Owner Nancy George specializes in creating gift baskets (and more exciting containers). The individual components—cards, gifts, home accessories, jewelry, toiletries, pet-related items, and more—are available un-basketed, too.

The Shop at the Union. 356 Boylston St. ☎ **617/536-5651.** T: Green Line to Arlington.

This large, crowded store has a wide selection of high-quality home, garden, and personal accessories. You'll see jewelry, greeting cards, antiques, needlework, handmade children's clothes, toys, and confections. Most of the merchandise is manufactured by women or by woman-owned firms. Proceeds benefit the human services programs of the Women's Educational and Industrial Union, a nonprofit educational and social-service organization founded in 1877.

HOME & GARDEN

Crate & Barrel. www.crateandbarrel.com. South Market Building, Faneuil Hall Marketplace. ☎ **617/742-6025.** T: Green or Blue Line to Government Center. Copley Place. ☎ **617/536-9400.** T: Orange Line to Back Bay or Green Line to Copley. 777 Boylston St.. ☎ **617/262-8700.** T: Green Line to Copley. 48 Brattle St., Cambridge. ☎ **617/876-6300.** T: Red Line to Harvard.

This is wedding-present heaven, packed with contemporary and classic housewares. The sleek merchandise, from juice glasses and linen napkins to top-of-the-line knives and roasting pans, suits every budget. The Boylston Street location, which also carries furniture, is the newest in the immediate Boston area (there are five others in the suburbs and 50 or so nationwide). A branch that stocks only furniture and home accessories is at 1045 Mass. Ave., Cambridge (☎ 617/547-3994).

La Ruche. 168 Newbury St. ☎ **617/536-6366.** T: Green Line to Copley.

If you've never dreamed of living in a birdhouse, that might be because you've never been to this boutique. It stocks European and American glassware and pottery (including the complete line of Mackenzie–Childs majolica ware), unusual home and garden accessories, hand-painted furnishings, and dazzling architectural birdhouses.

Restoration Hardware. 711 Boylston St. ☎ **617/578-0088.** www.restorationhardware. com. T: Green Line to Copley.

This national chain specializes in old-fashioned style at new-fashioned prices. The merchandise runs more to home accessories than to hardware (although there's plenty of that, too) and makes for great browsing.

Stoddard's. 50 Temple Place. ☎ **617/426-4187.** T: Red or Orange Line to Downtown Crossing.

The oldest cutlery shop in the country (since 1800), Stoddard's is full of items you don't know you need until you see them. You'll find sewing scissors, nail scissors, scissors for any other use you can think of, knives of all descriptions—including a spectacular selection of Swiss army knives—shaving brushes, binoculars, fishing tackle, and fly rods. There's also a branch at Copley Place (☎ **617/536-8688**).

Sweet Peas Home. 216 Clarendon St. ☎ **617/247-2828.** www.sweetpeashome.com. T: Green Line to Copley.

Just off Newbury Street, this little shop carries engagingly funky home and bath accessories, picture frames, lamps, candles, and furniture. You'll see a lot of faux rustic items, many made or painted by hand.

JEWELRY & WATCHES

Beadworks. 349 Newbury St. ☎ **617/247-7227.** T: Green Line B, C, or D to Hynes/ICA. 23Church St., Cambridge. ☎ **617/868-9777.** T: Red Line to Harvard.

The jewelry at these shops will suit you exactly—you make it yourself. Prices for the dazzling variety of raw materials start at 5¢ a bead, fittings (hardware) are available, and you can assemble your finery at the in-store worktable.

High Gear Jewelry. 139 Richmond St. ☎ **617/523-5804.** T: Green or Orange Line to Haymarket.

Don't be put off by the sign that says this little shop around the corner from the Paul Revere House (and right on the Freedom Trail) is a wholesale outlet. Retail shoppers are welcome to peruse the impressive selection of reasonably priced costume jewelry and watches.

✪ **John Lewis, Inc.** 97 Newbury St. ☎ **617/266-6665.** T: Green Line to Arlington.

John Lewis's imaginative women's and men's jewelry—crafted on the premises—suits both traditional and trendy tastes, and the staff is cordial and helpful. The pieces that mark you as a savvy Bostonian are earrings, necklaces, and bracelets made of hammered silver or gold circles.

Swatch Store. 57 John F. Kennedy St., in the Galleria Mall, Cambridge. ☎ **617/864-1227.** T: Red Line to Harvard.

Swatchdogs will revel in the largest Swatch store in the world, also the home of the Swatch Museum (a collection of every design since 1983). There are also Swatch kiosks at the Shops at Prudential Center and Faneuil Hall Marketplace.

MALLS & SHOPPING CENTERS

CambridgeSide Galleria. 100 CambridgeSide Place, Cambridge. ☎ **617/621-8666.** T: Green Line to Lechmere, or Red Line to Kendall/MIT and free shuttle bus (every 10 to 20 min.).

This three-level mall has two large department stores—**Filene's** (☎ **617/621-3800**) and **Sears** (☎ **617/252-3500**)—and more than 100 specialty stores. Pleasant but quite generic, it might be just the bargaining chip you need to lure your teenager to the nearby Museum of Science.

There's trendy sportswear at **Abercrombie & Fitch** (☎ 617/494-1338), outdoors gear at **Eastern Mountain Sports** (☎ 617/374-4787), audio and video equipment at **Cambridge SoundWorks** (☎ 617/225-3900), casual clothing at **J. Crew** (☎ 617/225-2739), and music and appliances at **Best Buy** (☎ 617/225-2004). There are three restaurants, a food court that opens onto an outdoor plaza, and seating along a pleasant canal. Strollers and complimentary wheelchairs are available.

Open Monday through Saturday 10am to 9:30pm, Sunday 11am to 7pm. Garage parking rates start at $1 for an hour.

☺ Copley Place. 100 Huntington Ave. ☎ **617/369-5000.** T: Orange Line to Back Bay or Green Line to Copley.

Copley Place has set the standard for upscale shopping in Boston since 1985. Connected to the Westin and Marriott hotels and the Prudential Center, it's a crossroads for office workers, moviegoers, out-of-towners, and enthusiastic consumers. You can while away a couple of hours or a whole day shopping and dining here and at the adjacent Shops at Prudential Center (see below) without ever going outdoors.

Some of Copley Place's 100-plus shops will be familiar from the mall at home, but this is emphatically not a suburban shopping complex that happens to be in the city. You'll see famous stores that don't have another branch in Boston: **Caswell-Massey** (☎ 617/437-9292), **Gucci** (☎ 617/247-3000), **Joan & David** (☎ 617/536-0600), **Liz Claiborne** (☎ 617/859-3787), **Louis Vuitton** (☎ 617/437-6519), **Polo Ralph Lauren** (☎ 617/266-4121), **Tiffany & Co.** (☎ 617/353-0222), and a suitably classy "anchor" department store, **Neiman Marcus** (☎ 617/536-3660). There's also an 11-screen movie theater, but beware: Some of the screens are almost comically tiny.

Open Monday through Saturday 10am to 8pm, Sunday noon to 6pm. Some stores have extended hours, and the theaters and some restaurants are open through late evening.

By car, the Massachusetts Turnpike eastbound has a Copley exit. Park in the **Copley Place Garage** (☎ 617/375-4488), off Huntington Avenue at Exeter Street. To

Flying Lobsters

If you relished the fresh seafood in Boston and want to share some with a friend, you can send a top-quality live lobster and make someone at home very happy. **James Hook & Co.,** 15 Northern Ave. at Atlantic Avenue (☎ **617/423-5500;** T: Blue Line to Aquarium or Red Line to South Station), and **Legal Seafoods Fresh by Mail,** Logan Airport Terminal C (☎ **800/477-5342** or 617/569-4622; T: Blue Line to Airport) will handle the overnight shipping.

pay a reduced rate, have your ticket validated when you make a purchase. Time limits may apply during the day.

Faneuil Hall Marketplace. Between North, Congress, and State sts. and I-93. ☎ **617/ 338-2323.** T: Green or Blue Line to Government Center or Orange Line to Haymarket.

The original festival market is both wildly popular and widely imitated, and Faneuil Hall Marketplace changes constantly to appeal to visitors as well as natives wary of its touristy reputation. The original part of **Faneuil Hall** itself dates to 1742, and the lower floors take it back to its retail roots. The **Quincy Market Colonnade,** in the central building, houses a gargantuan selection of food and confections. The bars and restaurants always seem to be crowded, and the shopping is terrific, if a tad generic. Many long-term leases expired in 1999 and 2000, so turnover has been high recently—look for grand-opening and going-out-of-business sales.

In and around the five buildings surrounded by brick-and-stone plazas, the shops combine "only in Boston" with "only at every mall in the country." **Marketplace Center** and the ground floors of the **North Market and South Market buildings** have lots of chain outlets—a magnet for many, a distraction to some. Most of the unique offerings are under **Quincy Market's canopies** on the pushcarts piled high with crafts and gifts, and upstairs or downstairs in the market buildings. The only way to find what suits you is to explore.

Shop hours are Monday through Saturday from 10am to 9pm and Sunday from noon to 6pm. The Colonnade opens earlier, and most bars and restaurants close later. If you must drive, there's parking in the Government Center garage off Congress Street and the marketplace's own crowded garage off Atlantic Avenue.

The Garage. 36 John F. Kennedy St., Cambridge. No phone. T: Red Line to Harvard.

Wander up the corkscrew ramp to the boutiques and shops (a record store, a clothing store, a jewelry store, and two stores carrying sci-fi paraphernalia) on the upper levels of this little mall. On the main floor, you can have a light or filling meal at **Formaggio's** (☎ 617/547-4795) or **Bruegger's Bagel Bakery** (☎ 617/661-4664).

The Shops at Prudential Center. 800 Boylston St. ☎ **800/SHOP-PRU** or 617/267-1002. T: Green Line to Copley, E to Prudential, or B, C, or D to Hynes/ICA.

The main level of the city's second-tallest tower holds this sprawling complex. In addition to **Lord & Taylor** (☎ 617/262-6000) and **Saks Fifth Avenue** (☎ 617/ 262-8500), there are more than 40 shops and boutiques, a food court, a "fashion court," a post office, and five restaurants, including Legal Sea Foods and California Pizza Kitchen. Vendors sell gifts, souvenirs, and novelty items off pushcarts in the arcades, and there's outdoor space in front if you need some fresh air. If you're planning a picnic, at ground level on Boylston Street is a **Star Market** supermarket (☎ 617/267-9721). **Restaurant Marché Mövenpick** (☎ 617/578-9700; www.marcheusa.com), near the Huntington Avenue and Belvidere Street entrances, is an enormous, frantic "food theater." It serves everything from salad and sushi to grilled meats and fresh baked goods at islands and stations where your meal or snack is cooked to order while you wait.

Hours are Monday through Saturday 10am to 8pm, Sunday 11am to 6pm. The restaurants and food court stay open later.

MARKETS

Farmers' Markets. City Hall Plaza, Mon and Wed. T: Green or Blue Line to Government Center. Copley Sq., Tues and Fri. T: Green Line to Copley or Orange Line to Back Bay.

Massachusetts farmers and growers under the auspices of the state **Department of Food and Agriculture** (☎ 617/227-3018) dispatch trucks filled with whatever's in season to the heart of the city from July through November. Depending on the time of year, you'll have your pick of berries, herbs, tomatoes, squash, pumpkins, apples, corn, and more, all fresh and reasonably priced.

MEMORABILIA

✪ **Boston City Store.** Faneuil Hall, lower level. ☎ **617/635-2911.** T: Green or Blue Line to Government Center.

A great, wacky idea, the Boston City Store sells the equivalent of the contents of the municipal attic and basement, from old street signs (look for your name) to used office equipment and furniture. The selection changes regularly according to what has out-lived its usefulness or been declared surplus, but you'll always find lucky horseshoes from the mounted police for $5 apiece. Closed Sunday.

✪ **Nostalgia Factory.** 51 N. Margin St. ☎ **800/479-8754** or 617/720-2211. www. nostalgia.com. T: Green or Orange Line to Haymarket.

The Nostalgia Factory has gained national attention for its million-piece collection of posters and advertising pieces. Long a Newbury Street fixture, the store moved to the North End in 1997 and gained more room for its enormous collections. They include original movie posters of all ages and in many languages, vintage war and travel posters, and political memorabilia.

MUSIC

Looney Tunes Records & Tapes. 1106 Boylston St. ☎ **617/247-2238.** T: Green Line B, C, or D to Hynes/ICA. 1001 Mass. Ave., Cambridge. ☎ **617/786-5624.** T: Red Line to Harvard.

Where there are college students, there are pizza places, copy shops, and used-record (and CD) stores. These two specialize in jazz and classical, and they have tons of other tunes at excellent prices.

Newbury Comics. 332 Newbury St. ☎ **617/236-4930.** www.newbury.com. T: Green Line B, C, or D to Hynes/ICA.

You'll find a wide selection of CDs, tapes, posters, and T-shirts—and, of course, comics—at the branches of this funky chain. The music is particularly cutting-edge, with lots of independent labels and imports. There are also stores at 1 Washington Mall, near City Hall (☎ 617/248-9992), and in Harvard Square at 36 John F. Kennedy St., in the Garage mall (☎ 617/491-0337).

Tower Records. 360 Newbury St. (at Mass. Ave.). ☎ **617/247-5900.** www. towerrecords.com. T: Green Line B, C, or D to Hynes/ICA.

One of the largest record stores in the country, Tower boasts three floors of records, tapes, CDs, videos, periodicals, and books. It's open until midnight every night. The Harvard Square branch, 95 Mount Auburn St. (☎ 617/876-3377), is smaller but still quite impressive.

PERFUME & COSMETICS

✪ **Colonial Drug.** 49 Brattle St., Cambridge. ☎ **617/864-2222.** T: Red Line to Harvard.

The perfume counter at this family business puts the "special" in "specialize." You can choose from more than 1,000 fragrances—plus cosmetics, soap, and countless other body-care products—with the help of the gracious staff members. They remain unflap-pable even during Harvard Square's equivalent of rush hour, Saturday afternoon.

E6 Apothecary. 167 Newbury St. ☎ **800/664-6635** or 617/236-8138. www. e6apothecary.com. T: Green Line to Copley.

This place is the exact opposite of scary department store cosmetic counters. The friendly staffers can guide you toward the right formula for your face, and they're equally helpful if you're spending 5 bucks or 500. E6 is the exclusive Boston supplier of Shu Uemura and Lorac products, and it carries many other brands that are hard (or impossible) to find north of New York.

SHOES

Berk's. 50 John F. Kennedy St. ☎ **617/492-9511.** T: Red Line to Harvard.

"Trendy" only scratches the surface in describing the wares at this Harvard Square institution. Come here for Doc Martens (the largest selection in New England), outrageous platforms, and whatever else is fashionable right this red-hot minute.

Helen's Leather Shop. 110 Charles St. ☎ **617/742-2077.** T: Red Line to Charles/MGH.

Homesick Texans visit Helen's just to gaze upon the boots. Many are handmade from exotic leathers, including ostrich, buffalo, and many varieties of snakeskin. Name brands such as Tony Lama and Dan Post are also available, along with a large selection of other leather goods.

Jasmine/Sola. 329 Newbury St. ☎ **617/437-8465.** T: Green Line B, C, or D to Hynes/ICA. 37A and 35 Brattle St., Cambridge. ☎ **617/354-6043.** T: Red Line to Harvard.

These boutiques sell men's and women's fashions that are as chic as the spectacular shoe collections.

TOYS & GAMES

FAO Schwarz. 440 Boylston St. (at Berkeley St.). ☎ **617/262-5900.** T: Green Line to Copley.

The giant teddy bear out front is the first indication that you're in for a rollicking good time, and a teddy bear wouldn't steer you wrong. A branch of the famed New York emporium, FAO Schwarz stocks top-quality toys, dolls, stuffed animals, games, books, and vehicles (motorized and not).

The Games People Play. 1100 Mass. Ave., Cambridge. ☎ **800/696-0711** or 617/492-0711. T: Red Line to Harvard.

Just outside Harvard Square, this 25-year-old business carries enough board games to outfit every country, summer, and beach house in New England. There are puzzles, playing cards, and backgammon sets, too.

The Magic Hat. Marketplace Center, Faneuil Hall Marketplace. ☎ **617/439-8840.** T: Green or Blue Line to Government Center or Orange Line to Haymarket.

Bring your Houdini fantasies to this small shop with a big "wow" factor. At least one staff member practices sleight-of-hand at the counter, and the stock of props, tricks, gifts, and other fun merchandise is (literally) incredible.

VINTAGE & SECONDHAND CLOTHING

✪ **Boomerangs.** 60 Canal St. ☎ **617/723-2666.** T: Green or Orange Line to North Station.

It's not all used, and it's not all clothing—you'll also find gifts, home furnishings, books, CDs, and other bargains. The designer duds and other merchandise are so classy, you'll forget you're in a warehouse building near North Station. Proceeds benefit the AIDS Action Committee.

The Garment District. 200 Broadway, Cambridge. ☎ **617/876-5230.** T: Red Line to Kendall/MIT.

You're hitting the clubs and you want to look cool, but you have almost no money. You'll be right at home among the shoppers here, paying great prices for a huge selection of contemporary and vintage clothing. Merchandise on the first floor is sold (no kidding) by the pound.

Keezer's. 140 River St., Cambridge. ☎ **617/547-2455.** T: Red Line to Central.

Generations of local college students have bought their first (and often only) tuxedo at this institution just south of Central Square. The terrific prices also extend to excellent nonformal designer menswear and a decent women's section.

✪ **Oona's.** 1210 Mass. Ave., Cambridge. ☎ **617/491-2654.** T: Red Line to Harvard.

From funky accessories and costume jewelry to vintage dresses nice enough to get married in, Oona's, just outside Harvard Square, has an extensive selection of "experienced clothing" at good prices.

10 Boston After Dark

Countless musicians, actors, and comedians went to college or otherwise got their start in the Boston area, and it's still a good place to check out rising stars and promising unknowns. You might get an early look at the next Rosie O'Donnell, Jack Lemmon, Paula Cole, or Jay Mohr. And you'll certainly be able to enjoy the work of many established artists.

The nightlife scene is, to put it mildly, not exactly world-class—you can be back from a night of club-hopping when your friends in New York are still drying their hair. Closing time for clubs is 2am, which means packing a lot into 4 hours or so.

For up-to-date entertainment listings, consult the "Calendar" section of the Thursday *Boston Globe*, the "Scene" section of the Friday *Boston Herald*, and the Sunday arts sections of both papers. The weekly *Boston Phoenix* (published on Thursday) has especially good club listings, and the free biweekly *Improper Bostonian* offers extensive live music listings. Before your visit, you can check with Boston's tourism offices (see "Visitor Information" in chapter 2), to see if big events are scheduled during your visit.

GETTING TICKETS   Some companies or venues sell tickets over the phone or the Internet; many will refer you to a ticket agency.

The major agencies that serve Boston, **Ticketmaster** (☎ 617/931-2000; www.ticketmaster.com), **Next Ticketing** (☎ 617/423-NEXT; www.nextticketing.com), and **Tele-charge** (☎ 800/447-7400), calculate service charges per ticket, not per order. To avoid the charge, visit the box office in person. If you wait until the day before or the day of a performance, you'll sometimes have access to tickets that were held back for one reason or another and have just gone on sale.

1 The Performing Arts

Year-round, you can find a performance that fits your taste and budget, be it a touring theater company or a children's chorus.

CONCERT HALLS & AUDITORIUMS

The ✪ **Hatch Shell** on the Esplanade (☎ 617/727-9547, ext. 450) is an amphitheater best known as the home of the Boston Pops' Fourth of July concerts. Almost every night in the summer, free music

Let's Make a Deal

Yankee thrift gains artistic expression at the ✪ **BosTix** booths at Faneuil Hall Marketplace (on the south side of Faneuil Hall) and in Copley Square (at the corner of Boylston and Dartmouth streets). Same-day tickets to musical and theatrical performances are half price, subject to availability. A **coupon book** with discounted and two-for-one admission to many area museums is available, too. Credit cards are not accepted, and there are no refunds or exchanges. Check the board for the day's offerings.

BosTix (☎ **617/423-4454;** www.boston.com/artsboston) also offers full-price advance tickets; discounts on more than 100 theater, music, and dance events; and tickets to museums, historic sites, and attractions in and around town. The booths are Ticketmaster outlets, too. They're open Tuesday through Saturday from 10am to 6pm (half-price tickets go on sale at 11am), and Sunday from 11am to 4pm. The Copley Square location is also open Monday from 10am to 6pm.

---

and dance performances and films take over the stage to the delight of crowds on the lawn.

The **Emerson Majestic Theatre,** 219 Tremont St. (☎ **617/824-8000;** www. emerson.edu/majestic), may be under renovation as you read this. The popular dance and music performance space also handles Emerson College student productions.

Berklee Performance Center. 136 Mass. Ave. ☎ **617/266-1400**, ext. 8820. www.berklee.edu/calen/database.html. T: Green Line B, C, or D to Hynes/ICA.

The Berklee College of Music's theater features the work of faculty members, students, and professional recording artists (many of them former Berklee students). Offerings are heavy on jazz and folk, with plenty of other options.

Boston Center for the Arts. 539 Tremont St. ☎ **617/426-7700** (events line) or 617/426-2787 (box office). www.bcaonline.org. T: Orange Line to Back Bay.

Five performance spaces and an anything-goes booking policy make the BCA a leading venue for contemporary theater, music and dance performances, visual arts exhibitions, and poetry and prose readings.

Jordan Hall. 30 Gainsborough St. ☎ **617/536-2412,** or 617/262-1120, ext. 700 (concert line). www.newenglandconservatory.edu/jordanhall. T: Green Line E to Symphony.

The New England Conservatory of Music's auditorium features both students and professionals; it presents classical instrumental and vocal soloists, chamber music, and occasionally, contemporary artists.

Sanders Theatre. 45 Quincy St. (corner of Cambridge St.), Cambridge. ☎ **617/496-2222.** www.fas.harvard.edu/~memhall. T: Red Line to Harvard.

In Memorial Hall on the Harvard campus, Sanders Theatre was a multipurpose facility before there was such a thing. It's a lecture hall and a performance space that features big names in classical, folk, and world music, as well as student performances.

Symphony Hall. 301 Mass. Ave. (at Huntington Ave.). ☎ **617/266-1492** or 617/ CONCERT (program information). SymphonyCharge ☎ 888/266-1200 (from outside the 617 area code) or 617/266-1200. www.bso.org. T: Green Line E to Symphony, or Orange Line to Mass. Ave.

Acoustically perfect Symphony Hall is home to the Boston Symphony Orchestra. When the orchestra is away, top-notch classical and chamber music artists from elsewhere take over.

Boston After Dark

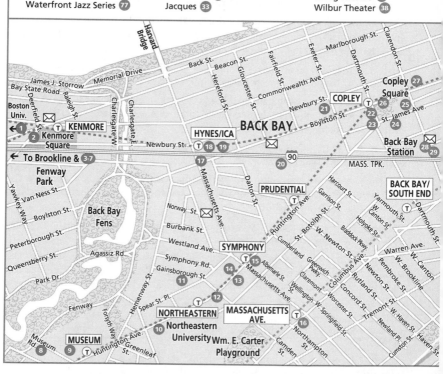

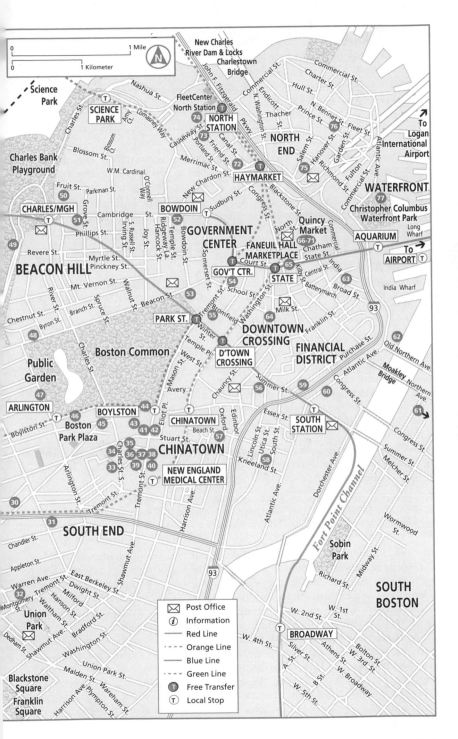

Wang Theatre. 270 Tremont St. ☎ **617/482-9393** or 800/447-7400 (Tele-charge). www.boston.com/wangcenter. T: Green Line to Boylston or Orange Line to New England Medical Center.

Also known as the Wang Center, this art deco palace is home to Boston Ballet, and books numerous and varied national companies. On some Monday evenings in the winter, it reverts to its roots as a movie theater and shows classic films on its enormous screen.

CLASSICAL MUSIC

✪ **Boston Pops.** Performing at Symphony Hall, 301 Massachusetts Ave. (at Huntington Ave.). ☎ **617/266-1492** or 617/CONCERT (program information). SymphonyCharge ☎ 888/266-1200 (outside 617) or 617/266-1200. www.bso.org. Tickets $33–$45 for tables; $12.50–$28 for balcony seats. T: Green Line E to Symphony.

From early May to early July, members of the Boston Symphony Orchestra lighten up. Tables and chairs replace the floor seats at Symphony Hall, and drinks and light refreshments are served. The Pops play a range of music from light classical to show tunes to popular music (hence the name), sometimes with celebrity guest stars. Conductor Keith Lockhart is so popular that he could almost give the orchestra its name all by himself. Performances are Tuesday through Sunday evenings. Special holiday performances in late December ($18 to $65) usually sell out well in advance, but it can't hurt to check.

The regular season ends with a week of free outdoor concerts at the Hatch Shell on the Charles River Esplanade, including the traditional Fourth of July concert, which features fireworks.

✪ **Boston Symphony Orchestra.** Symphony Hall, 301 Mass. Ave. (at Huntington Ave.). ☎ **617/266-1492** or 617/CONCERT (program information). SymphonyCharge ☎ 888/266-1200 (outside 617) or 617/266-1200. www.bso.org. Tickets $24–$79. Rush tickets $8 (on sale 9am Fri; 5pm Tues, Thurs). Rehearsal tickets $14.50. T: Green Line E to Symphony.

The Boston Symphony Orchestra, one of the world's greatest, was founded in 1881. The repertoire includes contemporary music, but classical is the BSO's calling card— you may even want to schedule your trip to coincide with a particular performance, or with a visit by a celebrated guest artist or conductor. Seiji Ozawa, the latest in a line of distinguished conductors, has announced that he'll end his tenure as music director in 2003—so you may unwittingly be watching an audition.

The season runs from October through April, with performances most Tuesday, Thursday, and Saturday evenings; Friday afternoons; and some Friday evenings. Half-hour talks (included in the ticket price) precede some performances; check ahead to see if yours is one. If you couldn't get tickets in advance, check at the box office 2 hours before show time, when returns from subscribers go on sale. A limited number of rush tickets (one per person) are available on the day of the performance for Tuesday and Thursday evening and Friday afternoon programs. Wednesday evening and Thursday morning rehearsals are sometimes open to the public.

The World on a String

From November 2000 to February 2001, keep an eye out for special concerts that coincide with the Museum of Fine Arts exhibition "Dangerous Curves: The Art of the Guitar." Styles from classical to jazz to flamenco will be in the spotlight at venues all over town.

○ **Handel & Haydn Society.** 300 Mass. Ave. ☎ **617/266-3605.** www.handeland-haydn.org. Tickets $25–$65. T: Green Line E to Symphony.

The Handel & Haydn Society uses period instruments and techniques in its orchestral and choral performances, yet is as cutting-edge as any other ensemble in town. Established in 1815, it's the oldest continuously performing arts organization in the country. Under the direction of Christopher Hogwood, the society prides itself on its creative programming of "historically informed" concerts. The season runs year-round, with most performances at Symphony Hall and Jordan Hall.

The society was the first American group to perform Handel's *Messiah,* in 1818, and made it an annual holiday tradition in 1854. If you'll be in town in December, check for ticket availability as soon as you start planning your trip.

ADDITIONAL OFFERINGS

The repertoire of the **Boston Lyric Opera** (☎ 617/542-6772 or 617/542-4912; www.blo.org) includes classical and contemporary works. The season runs from October through March. Performances are at the Shubert Theatre, 265 Tremont St., and tickets cost $26 to $108.

Students and faculty members at two prestigious institutions perform frequently during the academic year; admission is usually free. For information, contact the **New England Conservatory of Music,** 290 Huntington Ave. (☎ 617/585-1100), and Cambridge's **Longy School of Music,** 1 Follen St. (☎ 617/876-0956, ext. 500; www.longy.edu). Also check listings when you arrive in town for the particulars of other student performances at area colleges; most are free or cheap, and the quality is often surprisingly high.

CONCERT SERIES

The biggest names in classical music, dance, theater, jazz, and world music appear as part of the **FleetBoston Celebrity Series,** 20 Park Plaza, Boston, MA 02116 (☎ 617/482-2595, or 617/482-6661 for Celebrity Charge; www.celebrityseries.org). It's a subscription series that also offers tickets to individual events, which take place at Symphony Hall, Jordan Hall, the Wang Theatre, and other venues.

FREE (OR ALMOST FREE) CONCERTS

Radio station–sponsored outdoor music is a summer staple. Specifics change from year to year, but you can count on hearing jazz, classical, oldies, and sometimes pop at various convenient venues, including City Hall Plaza, Copley Square, and the Hatch Shell, at lunch, after work, and in the evening. Check the papers when you arrive, or just follow the crowds and the music.

Federal Reserve Bank of Boston. 600 Atlantic Ave. ☎ **617/973-3453.** www.bos.frb.org. T: Red Line to South Station.

Local groups and artists perform jazz, classical, and contemporary music in the bank's ground-floor auditorium on Thursdays and some Fridays at 12:30pm.

A Major Music Festival in the Bucolic Berkshires

When the Boston Symphony Orchestra goes on summer vacation, it goes to J Tanglewood (☎ **413/637-5165,** or 617/266-1492 out of season; www.bso.org) in Lenox, Mass., a 3-hour drive from Boston. Popular weekend concerts sell out far in advance, but tickets for weeknight shows are usually available at the box office. If you can't get a seat inside the shed, bring a blanket and picnic on the lawn (consult *Frommer's New England* for in-depth coverage of western Massachusetts).

Fridays at Trinity. Trinity Church, Copley Sq. ☎ **617/536-0944.** Donations accepted. T: Green Line to Copley or Orange Line to Back Bay.

This landmark church features organ recitals by local and visiting artists on Fridays at 12:15pm. Take advantage of the chance to look around this architectural showpiece.

King's Chapel Noon Hour Recitals. 58 Tremont St. ☎ **617/227-2155.** $2 donation requested. T: Red or Green Line to Park St.

Organ, instrumental, and vocal solos fill this historic building with music and make for a pleasant break along the Freedom Trail. Concerts are at 12:15pm on Tuesdays.

MUSIC IN THE MUSEUMS

A treat for the eyes and the ears, live music could be the offering that helps you schedule your visit to a museum.

✪ **Isabella Stewart Gardner Museum.** 280 The Fenway. ☎ **617/734-1359.** www.boston.com/gardner. Tickets (including museum admission) $16 adults, $11 seniors, $9 students with ID, $7 youths 12–17, $5 children 5–11. T: Green Line E to Museum.

This gorgeous museum, originally a home modeled after a 15th-century Venetian palace, features soloists, local students, chamber music, and sometimes jazz in the Tapestry Room. Performances are Saturday and Sunday at 1:30pm, from late September to early May.

Museum of Fine Arts. 465 Huntington Ave. ☎ **617/267-9300** or 617/369-3300. Tickets $14, $12 seniors and students, $5 children under 12. T: Green Line E to Museum.

The "Concerts in the Courtyard" series brings folk and jazz artists to the MFA on Wednesday evenings from June through September at 7:30pm. The courtyard opens to picnickers at 6pm; bring dinner, or buy it there. Chair seating is limited, and you're encouraged to bring a blanket or lawn chair.

ROCK & POP CONCERTS

✪ **FleetBoston Pavilion.** 290 Northern Ave., Wharf 8, South Boston. ☎ **617/374-9000,** or 617/931-2000 (Ticketmaster). www.bankbostonpavilion.com.

One of the most congenial venues in the area is this giant white tent. The 5,000-seat pavilion, formerly Harborlights, moved here in 1999. It schedules pop, rock, country, rap, folk, and jazz performers on evenings from May through September. Call ahead for information about water transportation and shuttle buses from South Station.

FleetCenter. 1 FleetCenter (Causeway St.). ☎ **617/624-1000** (events line), or 617/931-2000 (Ticketmaster). www.fleetcenter.com. T: Orange or Green Line to North Station.

The state-of-the-art FleetCenter opened in 1995, replacing legendary Boston Garden. It's the home of the Bruins (hockey), the Celtics (basketball), the circus (in October), ice shows (at least once a year), and touring rock and pop artists of all stripes. Concerts are in the round or in the arena stage format.

Orpheum Theater. 1 Hamilton Place. ☎ **617/679-0810,** or 617/423-NEXT for tickets. www.dlclive.com/orpheum.html. T: Red or Green Line to Park St.

Although it's old (the building went up in 1852) and cramped, the Orpheum offers an intimate setting for big-name performers. Most of the time, it books top local acts and national artists such as Sheryl Crow, Elvis Costello, Sting, and Smashmouth. Each fall, the "Comics Come Home" charity event attracts top talent (the live show is taped for Comedy Central). Hamilton Place is off Tremont Street, across from the Park Street Church.

Tweeter Center for the Performing Arts. Rte. 140, Mansfield. ☎ **508/339-2333** or 617/931-2000 (Ticketmaster). www.tweetercenter.com.

For major mainstream and alternative-rock acts on summer tours—with a smattering of folk, pop, country, reggae, and light classical—head about an hour south of Boston. The Tweeter Center, formerly Great Woods, is a sheltered (it has a roof but no sides) auditorium surrounded by a lawn. Shows are held rain or shine.

DANCE

✪ **Boston Ballet.** 19 Clarendon St. ☎ **617/695-6955** or 800/447-7400 (Tele-charge). www.bostonballet.org. Performing at the Wang Theatre, 270 Tremont St., and Shubert Theatre, 265 Tremont St. (both box offices, Mon–Sat 10am–6pm). Tickets $23–$73. Student rush tickets (1 hr. before curtain) $12.50, except for *The Nutcracker.* T: Green Line to Boylston.

Boston Ballet's reputation seems to jump a notch every time someone says, "So it's not just *The Nutcracker.*" The country's fourth-largest dance company is a holiday staple, and during the rest of the season (October through May), it presents an eclectic mix of classic story ballets and contemporary works. Because the Wang was built as a movie theater, the pitch of the seats makes the top two balconies less-than-ideal locations—paying more for a better seat is a good investment.

Dance Umbrella. 515 Washington St., 5th floor. ☎ **617/482-7570** or 617/824-8000 (MajesTix). www.danceumbrella.org. Tickets $17–$50; students and children $15.

Contemporary dance aficionados will want to check out the latest offerings sponsored by Dance Umbrella. It commissions and presents international, culturally diverse works—a broad definition that covers everything from acrobats and jazz tap dancers to well-known groups such as the Mark Morris and Bill T. Jones/Arnie Zane companies. Performances take place at venues in Boston, most often at the **Emerson Majestic Theatre,** 219 Tremont St.

ADDITIONAL OFFERINGS

The best-known offering by **Ballet Theatre of Boston** (☎ 617/262-0961) is *The Nutcracker,* performed throughout December at the Emerson Majestic Theatre,

Planning Pointer

Some hotel packages—the best-known are *Nutcracker* weekends—include tickets to a cultural event. Find a deal that offers what you want to see, and you won't have to worry about getting tickets.

219 Tremont St. Although Boston Ballet's production has more impressive sets, BTB's has a reputation as a good "starter" ballet. Tickets run $9 to $29.

THEATER

Local and national companies, professional and amateur actors, classic and experimental drama combine to make the theater scene in Boston and Cambridge a lively one, and in the past few years it has positively exploded. Call ahead or check the papers or BosTix (see "Let's Make a Deal," above) after you arrive—you're sure to find something of interest.

Boston is one of the last cities for pre-Broadway tryouts, allowing an early look at a classic (or classic flop) in the making. It's also a popular destination for touring companies of established Broadway hits. You'll find most of the shows headed to or coming from Broadway in the Theater District, at the **Colonial Theatre,** 106 Boylston St. (☎ 617/426-9366); the **Shubert Theatre,** 265 Tremont St. (☎ 617/482-9393); the **Wang Theatre,** 270 Tremont St. (☎ 617/482-9393); and the **Wilbur Theater,** 246 Tremont St. (☎ 617/423-4008).

The excellent local theater scene boasts the **Huntington Theatre Company,** which performs at the Boston University Theatre, 264 Huntington Ave. (☎ 617/266-0800; www.bu.edu/huntington), and the **American Repertory Theatre (ART),** which makes its home at Harvard University's Loeb Drama Center, 64 Brattle St., Cambridge (☎ 617/547-8300; www.amrep.org). Both stage classic and contemporary productions; the ART is more likely to put on the work of a living playwright.

The **Lyric Stage,** 140 Clarendon St. (☎ 617/437-7172), mounts contemporary and modern works in an intimate second-floor setting. The **Copley Theatre,** 225 Clarendon St. (☎ 617/266-7262), stages revues, concerts, and one-person shows. The **57 Theatre,** 200 Stuart St., in the Radisson Hotel Boston (☎ 800/233-3123), often books one-person shows. Some ART projects and independent productions are at the **Hasty Pudding Theatre,** 12 Holyoke St., Cambridge (☎ 617/496-8400).

The Loeb and the Hasty Pudding also feature student productions. Other college venues include Suffolk University's **C. Walsh Theatre,** 55 Temple St., Beacon Hill (☎ 617/573-8680); various performance spaces at **MIT** (☎ 617/253-4720, Theater Arts Hotline; web.mit.edu/arts); and Northeastern's **Blackman Theater,** 360 Huntington Ave. (☎ 617/373-2247).

FAMILY THEATER/AUDIENCE PARTICIPATION

Two other local institutions offer entertaining, long-running productions that appeal to adults and children. Kids love them, and they make a good introduction to live theater.

Charles Playhouse. 74 Warrenton St. ☎ 617/426-5225. www.blueman.com and www.shearmadness.com. Blue Man Group $49 and $39; *Shear Madness* $34. T: Green Line to Boylston.

The off-Broadway sensation **Blue Man Group** began selling out as soon as it arrived on the Charles Playhouse's Stage I in 1995. Famous for reducing even the most eloquent theatergoer to one-syllable sputtering, the troupe of three cobalt-colored entertainers backed by a rock band uses music, percussion, food, and audience members in its overwhelming performance art. Shows are at 8pm Wednesday and Thursday, 7 and 10pm Friday and Saturday, and 3 and 6pm Sunday. Tickets are available at the box office and through Ticketmaster.

Shear Madness, on Stage II (downstairs), is the longest-running nonmusical play in theater history. The zany "comic murder mystery" has turned the stage into a unisex

Dessert Alert

I don't want to boss you around; I'm here to suggest. So I *suggest* that after the theater, you run right over to **Finale Desserterie,** 1 Columbus Ave. (☎ **617/ 423-3184**), in the pointy end of the Park Plaza Building. It serves fruit desserts, dessert wines, pastry desserts, flavored coffees, and, best of all, chocolate desserts. (Oh, and some real food selections for spoilsports.) And it's open all day, not just after the theater. Yes, it's expensive. No, this is not a balanced meal. The name doesn't come from unapologetic (and pronunciation-challenged) chocoholics chorusing, "Finally, a restaurant that serves the thing I really want" . . . but it could.

hairdressing salon for over 20 years (it opened in January 1980), and the show's never the same twice. One of the original audience-participation productions, the play changes at each performance as spectator-investigators question suspects, reconstruct events, and then name the murderer. Performances are Tuesday through Friday at 8pm, Saturday at 6:30 and 9:30pm, and Sunday at 3 and 7:30pm.

Le Grand David and His Own Spectacular Magic Company. Cabot Street Cinema Theater, 286 Cabot St., Beverly; and Larcom Theatre, 13 Wallis St., Beverly. ☎ **978/927-3677.** E-mail: lgdmagico@aol.com. Tickets $10–$20.

Three generations of magicians make up this company, a nationally acclaimed troupe of illusionists who have staged more than 2,000 performances since 1977. The 2-hour shows take place at two theaters in Beverly, about 40 minutes from Boston by car. Le Grand David has received national attention for his sleight-of-hand and has performed at Easter parties at the White House.

2 The Club & Music Scene

The Boston-area club scene is multifaceted and constantly changing, and somewhere out there is a good time for everyone, regardless of age, musical taste, or budget. Check the "Calendar" section of the Thursday *Globe,* the "Scene" section of the Friday *Herald,* the *Phoenix,* or the *Improper Bostonian* while you're making plans.

A night on the town in Boston is relatively brief: Most bars close by 1am, clubs close at 2am, and the T shuts down around 12:30am. The drinking age is 21; a valid driver's license or passport is required as proof of age, and the law is strictly enforced, especially near college campuses.

COMEDY CLUBS

The days when every motel and truck stop had a "laff lounge" are, mercifully, behind us. Boston was one of the first cities with a hopping comedy-club scene, and as the fad fades, the quality clubs are hanging in there and skimming off the cream. The goal is to emulate Jay Leno, Steven Wright, Paula Poundstone, Rosie O'Donnell, Denis Leary, Jimmy Tingle, and others who parlayed success in Boston into careers in film and TV (or at least TV commercials).

✪ **Comedy Connection at Faneuil Hall.** Quincy Market, Upper Rotunda. ☎ **617/ 248-9700.** http://go.boston.com/comedyconnection. Cover $8–$30. T: Green or Blue Line to Government Center or Orange Line to Haymarket.

A large room with a clear view from every seat, the oldest original comedy club in town (established in 1978) draws top-notch talent from near and far. Big-name national acts lure enthusiastic crowds, and the openers are often just as funny but not as famous—yet. Shows are nightly at 8pm, plus Friday and Saturday at 10:15pm. The cover charge seldom tops $12 during the week but jumps for a big name appearing on a weekend. The Backstage restaurant-club next door, under the same ownership, offers dinner-show packages that include preferred seating.

Comedy Studio. At the Hong Kong restaurant, 1236 Mass. Ave., Cambridge. ☎ **617/661-6507.** Cover $5–$7. T: Red Line to Harvard.

Nobody here is a sitcom star—yet. With a growing reputation for ferreting out undiscovered talent, the no-frills Comedy Studio draws connoisseurs, college students, and network scouts. It's not just setup-punchline-laugh, either; sketches and improv spice up the standup.

Improv Asylum. 216 Hanover St. ☎ **617/263-6887.** Tickets $10–$15. T: Green or Orange Line to Haymarket.

The posters that catch your eye on the Freedom Trail may draw you back to the North End later for raucous improv and sketch comedy in a subterranean setting. Performances are Thursday through Saturday evenings, and reservations are recommended.

DANCE CLUBS

Many clubs are in the areas surrounding Boston's **Kenmore Square** (especially along Lansdowne Street) and Cambridge's **Central Square.** That makes club-hopping easy, but it also means students overrun the neighborhoods on Friday and Saturday. If you don't feel like dealing with huge crowds of loud teenagers and recent college grads, stick to slightly more upscale and isolated nightspots. If you do like loud teenagers, seek out a place where admission is 18- or 19-plus (policies change regularly, sometimes from night to night, so call ahead).

✪ **Avalon.** 15 Lansdowne St. ☎ **617/262-2424.** Cover $5–$15. T: Green Line B, C, or D to Kenmore.

A cavernous space divided into several levels, with a full concert stage, private booths and lounges, large dance floors, and a spectacular light show, Avalon is either great fun or sensory overload. It recently expanded, allowing more concert bookings (the Chemical Brothers, Semisonic, and Fiona Apple have played recently); when the stage is not in use, DJs take over.

Friday is **"Avaland,"** with national names in the booth and costumed house dancers on the floor. On Saturday (suburbanites' night out), expect more mainstream dance hits. The dress code calls for jackets, shirts with collars, and no jeans or athletic wear. The crowd is slightly older than at Axis. Open Thursday (international night) to Sunday (gay night) 10pm to 2am.

Axis. 13 Lansdowne St. ☎ **617/262-2437.** Cover $7–$10. T: Green Line B, C, or D to Kenmore.

Progressive rock at bone-rattling volume and "creative dress"—break out the leather—attract a young crowd. There are special nights for alternative rock, house, techno, soul, and funk music, and for international DJs. Open Tuesday through Sunday (gay night with adjoining Avalon) 10pm to 2am.

The Big Easy Bar. 1 Boylston Place. ☎ **617/351-7000.** Cover $7–$10. T: Green Line to Boylston.

Buttoned-up Boston meets let-it-all-hang-out New Orleans—it could get ugly. Not here, however, in a large, inviting space with a balcony (great for people watching), a billiard room, a dance floor, and music by top local DJs that runs from soul to alternative rock. Tuesday is international night. The lower level is the **Sugar Shack;** at both, the crowd tends to be on the young (collegiate and post-) side. No ripped jeans or athletic shoes.

Cosmopolitan. 54 Canal St. ☎ **617/720-2889.** Cover $10. T: Green or Orange Line to North Station.

A classy, cavernous space near the FleetCenter, the Cosmopolitan—a restaurant and an after-work and postgame hangout—books DJs and live music on weekends. Friday is the extremely popular urban-soul night, which attracts the largest African-American crowd in town.

Karma/Mambo Lounge. 5 Lansdowne St. ☎ **617/421-9595.** Cover $5–$15. T: Green Line B, C, or D to Kenmore.

Dancing machines, this one's for you. Pack something eye-catching, but not too fancy, and your dancing shoes. Thursday is Top 40 hip-hop night; big-name DJs take over on Friday (American) and Saturday (international) night.

☀ **The Roxy.** In the Tremont Boston hotel, 279 Tremont St. ☎ **617/338-7699.** www.gbcx.com/roxy. Cover $10–$15. T: Green Line to Boylston.

This former hotel ballroom boasts excellent DJs and live music, a huge dance floor, a concert stage, and a balcony (perfect for checking out the action below). Occasional concerts take good advantage of the acoustics and sight lines. Call for the latest schedule—swing recently yielded to disco on Fridays, and specific offerings change regularly. Open 8pm (entertainment starts at 10) to 2am Thursday to Saturday, and some Wednesdays and Sundays for special events. No jeans or athletic shoes.

ECLECTIC

☀ **Johnny D's Uptown Restaurant & Music Club.** 17 Holland St., Davis Sq., Somerville. ☎ **617/776-2004** or 617/776-9667 (concert line). www.johnnyds.com. Cover $2–$16, usually $5–$10. T: Red Line to Davis.

This family-owned and -operated establishment is one of the best in the area. Live-music aficionados, you'll kick yourself if you don't at least check out who's performing while you're in town. Johnny D's draws a congenial crowd for acts on international tours and acts that haven't been out of eastern Massachusetts. The music ranges from zydeco to rock, rockabilly to jazz, blues to ska. The food's even good (try the weekend brunch). This place is worth a long trip, but it's only two stops past Harvard Square on the Red Line, about a 15-minute ride at night. Open daily from 11:30am to 1am. Brunch starts at 9am on weekends; dinner runs from 4:30 to 9:30pm Tuesday through Saturday, with lighter fare until 11pm.

Kendall Café. 233 Cardinal Medeiros Way, Cambridge. ☎ **617/661-0993.** Cover $5–$10. T: Red Line to Kendall/MIT.

This friendly neighborhood bar near the 1 Kendall Square office-retail complex showcases three up-and-coming artists each night. Folk predominates, and you might also hear rock, country, or blues in the tiny back room. Or just stay at the bar—you won't be able to see, but it's such a small place that you'll have no trouble hearing. Shows are Monday through Saturday at 8pm, Sunday at 4pm.

The Western Front. 343 Western Ave., Cambridge. ☎ **617/492-7772.** Cover $5–$10. T: Red Line to Central.

A 30-ish friend swears by this legendary reggae club for one reason: "You're never the oldest one there." A casual spot on a nondescript street south of Central Square, it attracts an integrated crowd for world-beat music, blues, and especially reggae. Sunday is dance-hall reggae night, and the infectious music makes every night dancing night. Open Tuesday through Sunday from 5pm to 2am; live entertainment begins at 9pm.

FOLK

Boston is one of the only cities where folk musicians consistently sell out larger venues that usually book rock and pop performers. If an artist you want to see is out touring, check ahead for Boston-area dates. The music listings in the "Calendar" section of the Thursday *Globe* include information about **coffeehouses,** which are the main area outlets for folk. Curiously, the streets around Harvard Square are another promising venue—Tracy Chapman is just one famous "graduate" of the scene. Also check the papers to see whether the **Nameless Coffee House** is open during your visit. A local legend for 30 years, the Nameless pops up periodically from September to June at the First Parish in Cambridge, 3 Church St. (☎ 617/864-1630).

✪ **Club Passim.** 47 Palmer St., Cambridge. ☎ **617/492-7679.** Cover $5–$22; most shows $12 or less. T: Red Line to Harvard.

Passim has launched more careers than the mass production of acoustic guitars—Joan Baez, Suzanne Vega, and Tom Rush started out here. In a basement on the street between buildings of the Harvard Coop, this coffeehouse (which doesn't serve alcohol) enjoys an international reputation built on more than 30 years of nurturing new talent and showcasing established musicians. Patrons who have been regulars since day one mix with college students. There's live music 4 to 6 nights a week and Sunday afternoons, and coffee and light meals are available all the time. Tuesday is open-mike poetry night. Open Sunday through Thursday from 11am to 11pm, Friday and Saturday from 11am to 4am.

JAZZ & BLUES

If you're partial to these genres, consider timing your visit to coincide with the **Boston Globe Jazz & Blues Festival** (☎ 617/267-4301; www.boston.com/jazzfest), usually scheduled for the third week of June. Constellations of jazz and blues stars (large and small) appear at events, some of them free, many of them outdoors. The festival wraps up with a free Sunday-afternoon program at the Hatch Shell.

On summer Fridays at 6:30pm, the ✪ **Waterfront Jazz Series** (☎ 617/635-3911) brings amateurs and professionals to Christopher Columbus Park on the waterfront for a refreshing interlude of music and cool breezes.

Cantab Lounge. 738 Mass. Ave., Cambridge. ☎ **617/354-2685.** Cover $3–$6. T: Red Line to Central.

Follow your ears to this friendly neighborhood bar, which attracts a three-generation crowd. When the door swings open at night, deafening music (usually R&B or rock, sometimes jazz) spills out. The source on weekends often is Little Joe Cook and the Thrillers, headliners since the early '80s whose catchy tunes you'll dance to all night and hum all the next day—because your ears will still be ringing. Downstairs is the Third Rail, where you can hear blues and, on Wednesday, poetry.

✪ **House of Blues.** 96 Winthrop St., Cambridge. ☎ **617/491-2583,** or 617/497-2229 for tickets. Dining reservations (☎ 617/491-2100) accepted only for parties of 25 or more. www.hob.com. Cover $7–$30; Sat matinee $5. T: Red Line to Harvard.

The original House of Blues, a blue clapboard house near Harvard Square, packs 'em in every evening and on weekend afternoons. It attracts tourists, music buffs, and big names—Mighty Sam McClain, Junior Brown, NRBQ, and the Fabulous Thunderbirds have played recently. And there's no telling when an audience member will turn out to be someone famous who winds up onstage jamming. The restaurant is open 11:30am to 11pm Monday to Saturday, 4:30 to 11pm on Sunday; the music hall until 1am Sunday to Wednesday, 2am Thursday to Saturday. ✪ **Sunday gospel buffet brunch** seatings are at 10am, noon, and 2pm; advance tickets ($26 adults, $13 children) are highly recommended.

✪ **Regattabar.** In the Charles Hotel, 1 Bennett St., Cambridge. ☎ **617/661-5000** or 617/876-7777 (Concertix). Tickets $6–$25. T: Red Line to Harvard.

The Regattabar's selection of local and international artists is considered the best in the area—a title that Scullers (see below) is happy to dispute. Tito Puente, the Count Basie Orchestra, McCoy Tyner, Rebecca Parris, and Karen Akers have appeared recently. The large third-floor room holds about 200 and, unfortunately, sometimes gets a little noisy. Buy tickets in advance from Concertix (there's a $2 per ticket service charge), or try your luck at the door an hour before performance time. Open Tuesday through Saturday and some Sundays, with one or two performances per night.

Ryles Jazz Club. 212 Hampshire St., Inman Sq., Cambridge. ☎ **617/876-9330.** www.rylesjazz.com. Cover $5 weeknights; $7–$15 weekends.

This popular spot books local, regional, and national acts—Maynard Ferguson played recently. Hard-core music buffs of every stripe turn out for a wide variety of first-rate jazz, R&B, world beat, and Latin in two rooms. Both levels offer top-notch music and a friendly atmosphere. The Sunday jazz brunch runs from 10am to 3pm. Open Tuesday through Sunday; shows start at 9pm.

✪ **Scullers Jazz Club.** In the Doubletree Guest Suites hotel, 400 Soldiers Field Rd. ☎ **617/562-4111** or 617/931-2000 (Ticketmaster). www.scullersjazz.com. Tickets $10–$35.

Overlooking the Charles River, Scullers is a lovely, comfortable room that books top singers and instrumentalists—recent notables include Branford Marsalis, Abbey Lincoln, Livingston Taylor, and (quite a coup) Bobby Short. Patrons tend to be more hard-core and quieter than the crowds at the Regattabar, but it really depends on who's performing. There are usually two shows a night from Tuesday through Saturday; the box office is open those days from 11am to 6:30pm. Ask about dinner packages, which include preferred seating.

Wally's. 427 Mass. Ave. ☎ **617/424-1408.** No cover. T: Orange Line to Mass. Ave.

Wally's is scheduled to expand, which should only increase the fame of this Boston institution, near a busy corner in the South End. It draws a notably diverse crowd—

Rock of Ages

Bring an ID, bring an ID, bring an ID—you must be 21 to drink alcohol, and the law is strictly enforced. Even if you look older, bouncers won't risk a fine or license suspension, especially at 18-plus shows.

gay, straight, black, white, affluent, indigent—for performances by students and instructors from the Berklee College of Music, local ensembles, and, infrequently, internationally renowned musicians. Although there is no cover, patrons are expected to buy at least one drink (alcoholic or non).

ROCK

Bill's Bar. 5^1/$_2$ Lansdowne St. ☎ **617/421-9678.** Cover $5–$10. T: Green Line B, C, or D to Kenmore.

Long known as the only real hangout on Lansdowne Street, Bill's has transformed itself into a live-music destination and kept its friendly atmosphere and great beer menu. It books locals and touring up-and-comers or DJs most nights at 9:30 or 10pm. Monday is hard-rock night; Tuesday is hip-hop, funk, and soul. Open nightly 8pm to 2am.

Lizard Lounge. 1667 Mass. Ave., Cambridge. ☎ **617/547-0759.** Cover $2–$7. T: Red Line to Harvard.

In the basement of the Cambridge Common restaurant, the Lizard Lounge features well-known local rock and folk musicians who draw a postcollegiate-and-up crowd (Harvard Law School is next door). Shows Wednesday through Saturday at 10pm; Sunday is open-mike poetry jam night.

✪ **The Middle East.** 472–480 Mass. Ave., Central Sq., Cambridge. ☎ **617/864-EAST** or 617/931-2000 (Ticketmaster). www.mideastclub.com. Cover $7–$15. T: Red Line to Central.

The Middle East books an impressive variety of progressive and alternative rock in two rooms (upstairs and downstairs) every night. Showcasing top local talent as well as bands with international reputations—keep an eye out for the Mighty Mighty Bosstones, who usually pass through in December—it's a popular hangout that gets crowded, hot, and *loud*. There's also Middle Eastern food and gallery space with rotating art exhibits. The bakery next door, under the same management, features acoustic artists most of the time and belly dancers on Wednesdays. Some music shows are all ages (most are 18-plus); the age of the crowd varies with the performer.

T.T. the Bear's Place. 10 Brookline St., Cambridge. ☎ **617/492-0082** or 617/492-BEAR (concert line). www.mindspring.com/~ttthebears. Cover $3–$15, usually less than $10. T: Red Line to Central.

This no-frills spot generally attracts a young crowd, but 30-somethings will feel comfortable, too. Bookings range from cutting-edge alternative rock and roots music to ska and funk shows to up-and-coming pop acts. New bands predominate early in the week, with more established artists on weekends. Open Monday 7pm to midnight, Tuesday through Sunday 6pm to 1am.

3 The Bar Scene

Bostonians had some quibbles with the TV show "Cheers," but no one ever complained that the concept of a neighborhood bar where the regulars practically lived was implausible. From the Littlest Bar (a closet-size downtown watering hole) to the Bull & Finch (on which "Cheers" is based), the neighborhood bar occupies a vital niche. It tends to be a fairly insular scene—as a stranger, don't expect to be welcomed with open arms. This is one area where you can and probably should judge a book by its cover. If you poke your head in the door and see people who look like you and your friends, give it a whirl.

Theme a Little Theme

The **Hard Rock Cafe,** 131 Clarendon St. (☎ 617/424-ROCK; www.hardrock. com), is a fun link in the fun chain—just ask the other tourists in line with you. The two-level space boasts a guitar-shaped bar and stained-glass windows that glorify rock stars. You'll see memorabilia of Jimi Hendrix, Elvis Presley, Madonna, local heroes Aerosmith and the Cars, and others. The kid-friendly restaurant menu favors salads, burgers, and sandwiches (including the legendary "pig sandwich"). There's live acoustic music downstairs on weekends, and T-shirts and other goods for sale.

BARS & LOUNGES

The Bay Tower. 60 State St. ☎ **617/723-1666.** www.baytower.com. No cover. T: Green or Orange Line to State or Blue Line to Aquarium.

The view from the 33rd floor of any building is bound to be amazing; sitting atop 60 State St., you'll be mesmerized by the harbor, the airport, and Faneuil Hall Marketplace directly below. There's dancing to live music Monday through Saturday (piano on weeknights, jazz quartet Friday and Saturday). No denim or athletic shoes.

Bull & Finch Pub. 84 Beacon St. ☎ **617/227-9605.** www.cheersboston.com. T: Green Line to Arlington.

If you're out to impersonate a native, try not to be shocked when you walk into "the 'Cheers' bar" and realize that inside it looks nothing like the bar on the TV show. (The outside does, though—bring a camera.) The Bull & Finch really is a neighborhood bar, but today it's far better known for attracting legions of out-of-towners, who find good pub grub, drinks, and plenty of souvenirs. Food is served from 11am to 1:15am, and there's a kids' menu ($3.50 to $4.50).

Casablanca. 40 Brattle St., Cambridge. ☎ **617/876-0999.** T: Red Line to Harvard.

Students and professors jam this legendary Harvard Square watering hole, especially on weekends. You'll find excellent food (see chapter 6), an excellent jukebox, and excellent eavesdropping.

Cornwalls. 510 Commonwealth Ave. ☎ **617/262-3749.** T: Green Line B, C, or D to Kenmore.

This subterranean spot is an entertaining dash of England in a city noted for its Irish bars. It's known for expertly dispensed brews, authentic pub fare, and its habit of requesting ID from everyone under, oh, 50 or so (Boston University is a stone's throw away).

The Good Life. 28 Kingston St. ☎ **617/451-2622.** www.the-goodlife-us.com. T: Red or Orange Line to Downtown Crossing.

The city's premier retro hot spot, the Good Life is a 1950s-style lounge and restaurant, where the roar of the crowd often drowns out the Sinatra music playing in the background. Two blocks from Downtown Crossing, it's also popular with office workers who flock here for the burgers. There's live jazz Sunday to Wednesday. The **Good Life Uptown,** 99 St. Botolph St. (☎ **617/266-3030**), near the Prudential Center, is larger and somewhat calmer.

Green Street Grill/Charlie's Tap. 280 Green St., Cambridge. ☎ **617/876-1655.** No cover for music. T: Red Line to Central.

This atmospheric Central Square hangout draws a congenial crowd for live blues, rock, and jazz on weekends and, on Tuesdays (we kid you not), magicians. Blues and jazz aficionados will find perhaps the best jukebox on the planet, and there's also excellent food (see chapter 6). Open nightly until 1am.

Harvard Gardens. 320 Cambridge St. ☎ **617/523-2727.** T: Red Line to Charles/MGH.

A new incarnation of a run-down Beacon Hill standby, Harvard Gardens remains a neighborhood favorite. In this neighborhood, that means students, yuppies, and medical professionals of every stripe (Mass. General Hospital is across the street). It's more lounge than tavern, with plenty of beers on tap, great margaritas, and food until 11pm (midnight on weekends).

O'Leary's. 1010 Beacon St., Brookline. ☎ **617/734-0049.** T: Green Line C to St. Mary's.

This congenial bar attracts folk-music fans, law students from BU and Northeastern, local professionals, and plenty of people who hate smelling like an ashtray the morning after a night out. Good news: Brookline forbids smoking at restaurants *and bars*.

Purple Shamrock. 1 Union St. ☎ **617/227-2060.** Cover $3–$6 Thurs–Sat. T: Green or Blue Line to Government Center, or Orange Line to Haymarket.

Across the street from Faneuil Hall Marketplace, the Purple Shamrock packs in wall-to-wall 20-somethings. This is a rowdy, fun place that schedules DJs, cover bands, and, I'm obliged to report, karaoke (on Tuesday).

Radius. 8 High St. ☎ **617/426-1234.** No cover. T: Red Line to South Station.

The high-tech bar at this hot, *haute* restaurant offers almost everything the dining room does—the chic crowd, the noise, the perfect martinis—without the sky-high food bill.

Top of the Hub. Prudential Center. ☎ **617/536-1775.** No cover. T: Green Line E to Prudential.

Boasting a panoramic view of greater Boston, Top of the Hub is 52 stories above the city; the view is especially beautiful at sunset. There is music and dancing nightly. Dress is casual but neat. Open until 1am Sunday through Wednesday, 2am Thursday to Saturday. (See chapter 6 for restaurant listing.)

BREW PUBS

One of the first cities to develop microbrewery overload was Boston, where hanging copper tubing on a brick wall and proclaiming yourself a master brewer is practically an industry. If you're harboring aspirations, check out these places first. Most don't charge a cover, but beer will set you back at least $3 a mug, more if something fancy is involved. These are also popular dining destinations—they serve full meals, some as good as the brews, and all a step up from burgers and nachos.

Boston Beer Works. 61 Brookline Ave. ☎ **617/536-2337.** T: Green Line B, C, or D to Kenmore.

Across the street from Fenway Park, this cavernous, cacophonous space is even more frantic before and after Red Sox games. Don't plan to be able to hear anything your friends are saying. It has a full food menu and 14 brews on tap, including excellent bitters and ales, and seasonal concoctions such as Red Oktoberfest: lager with blueberries floating in it (not as dreadful as it sounds). Especially good are the cask-conditioned offerings, seasoned in wood till they're as smooth as fine wine. Sweet-potato fries make a terrific snack. Open daily from 11:30am to 1am.

✪ **Brew Moon Restaurant & Microbrewery.** 115 Stuart St. ☎ **617/742-BREW.** T: Green Line to Boylston.

Handcrafted beer meets tasty edibles at this popular Theater District spot, where bar food, sandwiches, and salads accompany freshly made brews. The Munich Gold won a gold medal at the 1996 Great American Beer Festival; if you're looking for something lighter, try the Grasshopper IPA or the out-of-this-world house-brewed root beer. Open daily from 11:30am to 2am. The equally busy Harvard Square branch, at 50 Church St. (☎ 617/499-BREW), stays open till 1am (midnight on Sunday). Both have live music at the ✪ **Sunday jazz brunch,** 11am to 3pm.

John Harvard's Brew House. 33 Dunster St., Cambridge. ☎ **617/868-3585.** www. johnharvards.com. No cover. T: Red Line to Harvard.

This subterranean Harvard Square hangout pumps out terrific English-style brews in a clublike setting (try to find the sports figures in the stained-glass windows) and prides itself on its food. The beer selection changes regularly; it includes at least one selection from each "family" (ambers, porters, seasonals, and more), all brewed on the premises. Order a sampler if you can't decide. Open daily from 11:30am to 1:30am; food is served until 11:30pm.

Samuel Adams Brew House. In the Lenox Hotel, 710 Boylston St. ☎ **617/536-2739.** T: Green Line to Copley.

This dark, sometimes noisy spot boasts excellent pretzels, friendly service, and the signature local brew, guaranteed to be served fresh. Choose from the dozen beers on tap or order a sampler of four. Open daily from 11:30am to 1:30am.

HOTEL BARS

Many popular nightspots are associated with hotels and restaurants (see chapters 5 and 6); the following are particularly agreeable, albeit pricey, places to while away an hour or three.

The Atrium. Bostonian Hotel, at Faneuil Hall Marketplace, 40 North St. ☎ **617/523-3600.** T: Green or Blue Line to Government Center or Orange Line to State.

The floor-to-ceiling windows of this ground-floor room across the street from Faneuil Hall Marketplace allow for great people watching. There is champagne by the glass, live piano music on weeknights, and cushy furnishings that encourage lingering. This is one of the only places in Boston that allows cigar-smoking, so it can be smoky. Open daily until midnight.

The Bar at the Ritz. 15 Arlington St. (in the Ritz-Carlton, Boston). ☎ **617/536-5700.** T: Green Line to Arlington.

The Bar at the Ritz is an elegant room with walnut paneling, a fireplace, live piano music, and a magnificent view of the Public Garden. The spectacular setting and service make it an excellent place for a celebration. Open Monday through Saturday 11:30am to 1am, Sunday noon to midnight. No sneakers or athletic wear.

Bar 10. In the Westin Copley Place Boston, 10 Huntington Ave. ☎ **617/424-7446.** T: Green Line to Copley or Orange Line to Back Bay.

Cushy seating, sleek decor, huge windows, and French doors that open off the lobby lend an air of being away from it all yet in the middle of everything. The bistro menu is Mediterranean, the atmosphere smoker-friendly. Open daily until midnight.

Boston Harbor Hotel. 70 Rowes Wharf (entrance on Atlantic Ave.). ☎ **617/439-7000.** T: Blue Line to Aquarium, or Red Line to South Station.

You have two appealing options on the ground floor: **Intrigue,** which looks like a comfortable living room and boasts a harbor view, and the **Rowes Wharf Bar,** with a serious businesslike atmosphere and serious martinis.

❂ **Bristol Lounge.** 200 Boylston St. (in the Four Seasons Hotel). ☎ **617/351-2053.** T: Green Line to Arlington.

This is a perfect choice after the theater, after work, or after anything else. An elegant room with soft lounge chairs, a fireplace, and fresh flowers, it features a fabulous Viennese Dessert Buffet on weekend nights. There's live jazz every evening. An eclectic menu is available until 11:30pm (12:30am on Friday and Saturday).

Oak Bar. In the Fairmont Copley Plaza Hotel, Copley Sq. ☎ **617/267-5300.** T: Green Line to Copley or Orange Line to Back Bay.

This paneled, high-ceilinged room is a haven for cigar smokers. The lighting is muted, the leather seating soft and welcoming, the oyster bar picture-perfect. There's live entertainment nightly. Proper dress is required. Open Sunday through Thursday 4:30pm to 12:30am, Friday and Saturday until 1am.

IRISH BARS

The Black Rose. 160 State St. ☎ **617/742-2286.** www.irishconnection.com. Cover $3–$5. T: Orange or Blue Line to State.

Purists might sneer at the Black Rose's touristy location, but performers don't. Sing along with the authentic entertainment—you might be able to make out the tune on a fiddle over the din—at this jam-packed pub and restaurant at the edge of Faneuil Hall Marketplace.

The Burren. 247 Elm St., Somerville. ☎ **617/776-6896.** Cover (back room only) $5–$10. T: Red Line to Davis.

If you saw the 1998 movie *Next Stop Wonderland,* you'll recognize the Burren as the place where Hope Davis met her loser blind dates under the scrutiny of the bartender (Jimmy Tingle of *60 Minutes II*) . There's traditional Irish music in the front room, and acoustic rock in the large back room.

Mr. Dooley's Boston Tavern. 77 Broad St. ☎ **617/338-5656.** Cover $3 Fri–Sat. T: Blue Line to Aquarium.

Sometimes an expertly poured Guinness is all you need. If one of the nicest bartenders in the city pours it, so much the better. This Financial District spot also offers a wide selection of imported beers on tap, live music, and a menu of "pub favourites."

GAY & LESBIAN CLUBS & BARS

In addition to the clubs listed below, there's a weekly gay night at some mainstream clubs. On Sunday, **Avalon** and **Axis** play host to the largest gathering of gay men in town. On Thursday and Sunday nights, women congregate and play pool upstairs at the **Hideaway Pub,** 20 Concord Lane, off Fresh Pond Parkway, Cambridge (☎ 617/ 661-8828). For up-to-date listings, check *Bay Windows* and the monthly *Phoenix* supplement "One in 10."

Club Café. 209 Columbus Ave. ☎ **617/536-0966.** T: Green Line to Arlington or Orange Line to Back Bay.

This trendy South End spot draws a chic crowd of men and women for conversation (the noise level is reasonable), dining, live music in the front room, and video entertainment in the back room. Open daily from 2pm to 1am; lunch is served weekdays from 11:30am to 2:30pm, and dinner from 5:30 to 10pm Sunday through Wednesday, and until 11pm Thursday through Saturday. Sunday brunch starts at 11:30am.

Fritz. In the Chandler Inn Hotel, 26 Chandler St. ☎ **617/482-4428.** T: Orange Line to Back Bay.

This popular South End hangout is a neighborhood favorite. The friendly crowd bonds over sports—there's even a satellite dish.

Jacques. 79 Broadway, Bay Village. ☎ **617/426-8902.** T: Green Line to Arlington.

The only drag venue in town, Jacques draws a friendly crowd of gay and straight patrons who mix with the "girls" and sometimes engage in a shocking activity—that's right, disco dancing. The eclectic entertainment includes live bands, performance artists, and, of course, drag shows. Open daily from noon to midnight.

Man-Ray. 21 Brookline St., Cambridge. ☎ **617/864-0400.** Cover $3–$10. T: Red Line to Central.

The area's best goth scene is at Man-Ray, which has regular fetish nights and an appropriately gloomy atmosphere. Thursday is "Campus" night, when the crowd is 21-plus and mostly men. Open Wednesday until 1am, Thursday through Saturday until 2am.

Paradise. 180 Mass. Ave., Cambridge. ☎ **617/494-0700.** No cover. T: Red Line to Central, 10-min. walk.

Not to be confused with the Boston rock club (well, you can, but it won't be quite the same experience), the Paradise attracts an all-ages male crowd. It's also a good place to see strippers. Thursday is college night. Open daily 5pm to 1am.

4 More Entertainment

COFFEEHOUSES

As in most other American cities, you can't get far in Boston or Cambridge without seeing a **Starbucks.** We'll submit to the passive-aggressive counter routine if it ends in a frozen drink, but even then, we're happier at **Dunkin' Donuts.** For coffee, tea, and hanging out, there are plenty of less generic options. Many are in the North End (see chapter 6), and other favorites are listed here. At all of them, hours are long, and loitering is encouraged—these are good places to bring your journal.

1369 Coffee House. 757 Mass. Ave., Central Sq., Cambridge. ☎ **617/576-4600.** T: Red Line to Central.

A long, narrow room that often attracts an (ahem) eccentric clientele, the 1369 offers excellent baked goods, a Crayola-like range of coffee flavors, and great people watching. The original location is at 1369 Cambridge St., Inman Square (☎ **617/ 576-1369**), hence the name.

Algiers Coffeehouse. 40 Brattle St. ☎ **617/492-1557.** T: Red Line to Harvard.

Middle Eastern food and music, plain and flavored coffees, and the legendary atmosphere make this a classic Harvard Square hangout. Your "quick" snack or drink (try the mint coffee) might turn into a longer stay, as the sociologist in you studies the resident and would-be intellectuals. This a good spot to eavesdrop while you sample terrific soups, sandwiches, homemade sausages, falafel, and hummus.

BeanTowne Coffee House. 1 Kendall Sq., Cambridge. ☎ **617/621-7900.** T: Red Line to Kendall.

A splash of the bohemian in a buttoned-up office-retail complex, this is a good stop before or after a film at the Kendall Square Cinema. There's only one problem—it's too popular. If a table empties, make your move fast.

Curious Liquids Café. 22-B Beacon St. ☎ **617/720-2836.** www.liquids.com. T: Red or Green Line to Park St.

Beacon Hill's newest hangout offers a view of the Common and the State House from the handful of tables upstairs, and plenty of comfortable seating in the basement. Government workers and Suffolk University students come for the huge selection of beverages, many of which are indeed curious, plus sandwiches and baked goods.

☉ **Someday Café.** 51 Davis Sq., Somerville. ☎ **617/623-3323.** T: Red Line to Davis.

If "Friends" featured real people of all ages, they might hang out here, up the street from the Somerville Theater. The coffee and tea selections are impressive, and there's great lemonade in summer, cider in winter, and brownies all the time.

Trident Booksellers & Café 338 Newbury St. ☎ **617/267-8688.** T: Green Line B, C, or D to Hynes/ICA.

This Back Bay institution has a view of the funkier end of Newbury Street, a browsing-friendly book selection, and a soothing, New Age-y atmosphere. Open until midnight daily.

POOL PLUS

Plenty of bars have pool tables, but at Boston's relatively upscale pool palaces, drinking is what you do while you're playing pool, not the other way around.

Boston Billiard Club. 126 Brookline Ave. ☎ **617/536-POOL.** Weekend evenings $11 an hour for 2 players, $2 an hour for each additional person. Daytime and weeknight discounts. T: Green Line B, C, or D to Kenmore.

Decorated with hunting prints, brass wall sconces, and a mahogany bar, this club has 42 tables with full liquor service. If you don't want to wait for a table, ask about taking a back room (they can't be reserved) for $16 an hour. Open Monday through Saturday 11am to 2am, Sunday noon to 2am.

Flat Top Johnny's. 1 Kendall Sq., Cambridge. ☎ **617/494-9565.** Weekend evenings $10 an hour for 1 or 2 players, $12 for 3 or more. Daytime and weeknight discounts. T: Red Line to Kendall.

A spacious but loud room with a bar and 12 red-topped tables, Flat Top Johnny's has a neighborhood feel despite being in a rather sterile office-retail complex. Open weekdays from 3pm to 1am, weekends at noon.

The Rack. 24 Clinton St. (at North St.). ☎ **617/725-1051.** www.therackboston.com. $6 an hour before 4:30pm, $12 an hour after 4:30pm. T: Green Line to Government Center, Blue Line to Aquarium or Orange Line to Haymarket.

Across the street from Faneuil Hall Marketplace and the Regal Bostonian Hotel, the Rack is an enormous space. It courts the after-work crowd with 22 tournament-size tables, two bars, and a lounge. You can order food from 11am to 1am and maybe do a little star-gazing—pro athletes turn up here periodically. In good weather, the action spills onto the patio out front.

A Multimedia Experience

The owners of ✪ **Jillian's Boston,** 145 Ipswich St. (☎ **617/437-0300;** www. jilliansboston.com), revived an interest in pool in Boston and continue expanding their horizons as entertainment technology becomes more sophisticated. The 70,000-square-foot complex, which anchors the Lansdowne Street strip, contains a 52-table pool parlor, a virtual-reality movie "ride," slot machines (for fun, not profit), and an interactive aviation game. The 250-game video midway includes classic arcade games. There are dartboards, a table tennis area, a dance club, five full bars, and a restaurant. If you can't scare up some fun here, check your pulse.

Jillian's is open Monday through Saturday 11am to 2am, Sunday noon to 2am. Children under 18 accompanied by an adult are admitted before 7pm. Pool costs $12 an hour for 1 or 2 people, $14 for 3 or more. Valet parking is available Wednesday to Sunday after 6pm except during Red Sox games. T: Green Line B, C, or D to Kenmore.

FILMS

✪ **Free Friday Flicks at the Hatch Shell** (☎ **617/727-9547,** ext. 450) are family films shown on a large screen in the amphitheater on the Esplanade. On the lawn in front of the Hatch Shell, hundreds of people picnic while the sky grows dark, then watch a classic crowd pleaser (*The Wizard of Oz* and *Raiders of the Lost Ark* are favorites). Bring sweaters in case the breeze off the river grows chilly.

The **Screen on the Green** film festival (☎ **877/262-5866;** www. screenonthegreen.com) brings classic movies to Boston Common, at Beacon and Charles streets, on early-summer Tuesdays at dusk.

True revival houses—they feature lectures and live performances in addition to foreign and classic films—are the **Brattle Theater,** 40 Brattle St., Cambridge (☎ **617/876-6837;** www.beaconcinema.com/brattle), and the **Coolidge Corner Theater,** 290 Harvard St., Brookline (☎ **617/734-2500;** www.coolidge.org/Coolidge). Classic and foreign films are the tip of the iceberg at the quirky **Harvard Film Archive,** 24 Quincy St., Cambridge (☎ **617/495-4700**), which also shows student films.

For first-run independent and foreign films, head to the ✪ **Kendall Square Cinema,** 1 Kendall Sq., Cambridge (☎ **617/494-9800**). The best movie theater in the immediate Boston area, it offers five excellent screening rooms and discounted parking in the adjoining garage.

LECTURES & READINGS

The Thursday *Globe* "Calendar" section is the best place to check for listings of lectures, readings, and talks on a wide variety of subjects, often at local colleges and libraries. Many are free or charge a small fee. Most of the bookstores listed in chapter 9 sponsor author readings; check their Web sites or in-store displays, or call ahead.

5 Late-Night Bites

There aren't a lot of ways to slice it: Boston's late-night scene needs to climb a couple of notches to reach pathetic, and Cambridge's wee-hour diversions are even skimpier. The only plus is that just about every cab driver out cruising knows how to reach the places that are still open.

If you're starving after the clubs close, you might be glad to know that the fry cooks work 24/7 at **Buzzy's Fabulous Roast Beef,** 327 Cambridge St. (☎ **617/242-7722**). The cheese steak is famous (and actually pretty fabulous), but not as famous as the onion rings. Don't infer anything from the number of medical professionals—it's only because Mass. General Hospital is nearby. The Buzzy's at 647 Mass. Ave., in **Central Square,** Cambridge (☎ **617/864-2333**), is open until midnight Wednesday and Thursday, 2am Friday and Saturday.

Near the Theater District and Chinatown, the 24-hour **Blue Diner,** 150 Kneeland St. (☎ **617/338-4639**), is the only place in town where you might have to wait for a table at 3am. A number of **Chinatown** restaurants don't close until 3 or 4am. The hottest scene at the moment is at **Ginza Japanese Restaurant,** 14 Hudson St. (☎ **617/338-2261**). In the North End, **Caffe Pompeii,** 280 Hanover St. (☎ **617/ 523-9438**), draws European club-hoppers and neighborhood shift workers until 4am. And if you have a car, make like a college student and road-trip to the **International House of Pancakes** at 1850 Soldiers Field Rd. in Brighton (☎ **617/787-0533**). It's open 24 hours.

Side Trips from Boston

11

Sights and attractions of great beauty and historical significance surround Boston. The destinations in this chapter—**Lexington** and **Concord,** the **North Shore** and **Cape Ann,** and **Plymouth**—make fascinating, manageable day trips and offer enough diversions to fill several days.

1 Lexington & Concord

The shooting stage of the Revolutionary War began here, and parts of the towns still look much as they did in April 1775, when the fight for independence began. Start your visit in **Lexington,** where colonists and British troops first clashed. On the border with **Concord,** spend some time at **Minute Man National Historical Park,** investigating the battle that raged there more than 200 years ago. Decide for yourself where the "shot heard 'round the world" rang out—bearing in mind that Ralph Waldo Emerson, who wrote those words, lived in Concord. Emerson's house and Louisa May Alcott's family home (also in Concord) are just two of the fascinating destinations in this area.

Some attractions are closed from November through March or mid-April, opening after **Patriots Day,** which is celebrated on the third Monday in April. Information about both towns is available from the **Greater Merrimack Valley Convention & Visitors Bureau,** 9 Central St., Suite 201, Lowell, MA 01582 (☎ **800/443-3332** or 978/459-6150; www.lowell.org).

LEXINGTON
6 miles NW of Cambridge, 9 miles NW of Boston

Lexington, a country village turned Boston suburb, takes great pride in its history. The **Battle Green,** next to a bustling business district, is an open common where you can see the famous Minuteman Statue and several other memorials.

British troops marched from Boston to Lexington late on April 18, 1775 (no need to memorize the date; you'll hear it everywhere), preceded by patriots Paul Revere and William Dawes, who sounded the warning. Members of the local militia, called "Minutemen" for their ability to assemble quickly, were waiting at the **Buckman Tavern.** John Hancock and Samuel Adams, leaders of the revolutionary movement, were sleeping (or trying to) at the nearby **Hancock–Clarke House.** The warning came around midnight, followed about 5 hours later by some 700 British troops, headed to Concord to destroy the rebels' military supplies. Ordered to disperse, the patriots—fewer than 100, and some accounts say 77—stood their ground. Nobody knows who started the shooting, but when it was over, 8 militia members were dead, including a drummer boy, and 10 were wounded.

ESSENTIALS

GETTING THERE   Route 2A approximates Paul Revere's path, but if you attempt to follow it during rush hour, you'll wish you had a horse of your own. Instead, take Route 2 from Cambridge through Belmont and follow signs for Route 4/225 into the center of Lexington. (To reach Route 2 from downtown Boston, take Storrow or Memorial Drive.) Or take Route 128 (I-95) to Exit 31 and follow signs. Mass. Ave. (the same street you might have seen in Boston and Cambridge) runs through Lexington.

The **MBTA** (☎ 617/222-3200; www.mbta.com) runs bus routes nos. 62 (Bedford) and 76 (Hanscom) to Lexington from Alewife station, the last stop on the Red Line. The one-way fare is 60¢, and the trip takes about 25 minutes. Buses leave every hour during the day and every half hour during rush periods, Monday through Saturday. They pass the Munroe Tavern and the Museum of Our National Heritage, if you prefer not to walk from the center of town. There is no service on Sundays, and no public transportation between Lexington and Concord.

VISITOR INFORMATION   The **area code** is 781. The **Chamber of Commerce Visitor Center,** 1875 Mass. Ave., Lexington, MA 02473 (☎ 978/862-1450), distributes sketch maps and information. The community Web site (www. lexingtonweb.com) has an area with visitor information.

Before you set out, you might want to read **"Paul Revere's Ride,"** Henry Wadsworth Longfellow's classic but historically questionable poem that dramatically chronicles the events of April 18 and 19, 1775.

SEEING THE SIGHTS

Minute Man National Historical Park is in Lexington, Concord, and Lincoln (see also "Concord," below).

Start your visit to Lexington at the **Visitor Center,** on the Battle Green. It's open daily from 9am to 5pm (9:30am to 3:30pm October through June). A diorama and accompanying narrative illustrate the Battle of Lexington. The **Minuteman Statue** on the Green is of Capt. John Parker, who commanded the militia. When the British confronted his troops, Parker called: "Stand your ground. Don't fire unless fired upon, but if they mean to have a war, let it begin here!"

Three important destinations in Lexington were among the country's first "historic houses" when restoration of them began in the 1920s.

The ✪ **Buckman Tavern,** 1 Bedford St. (☎ 781/862-5598), built around 1710, is the only building still on the Green that was there on April 19, 1775. The interior has been restored to approximate its appearance that day. The Minutemen gathered here to await word of British troop movements, and brought their wounded here after the conflict. The tour, by costumed guides, is educational and entertaining. If time is short and you have to pick just one house to visit, this is the one.

Within easy walking distance, the **Hancock–Clarke House,** 36 Hancock St. (☎ 781/861-0928), is where Samuel Adams and John Hancock were staying when Paul Revere arrived. They fled to nearby Woburn. The 1698 house, furnished in colonial style, contains the Historical Society's museum of the Revolution.

The British took over the **Munroe Tavern,** 1332 Mass. Ave. (about 1 mile from the Green), to use as their headquarters and, after the battle, as their field hospital. The

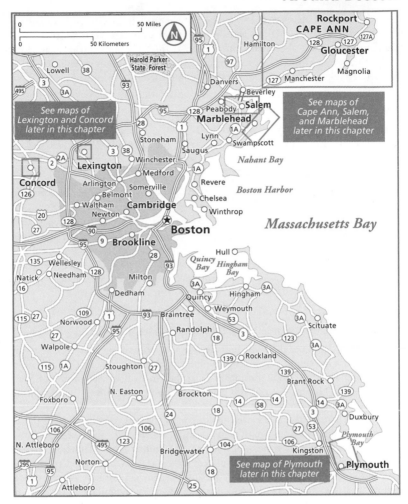

building (1690) is packed with fascinating artifacts and furniture carefully preserved by the Munroe family, including the table and chair President George Washington used when he dined here in 1789. The gardens in the rear are beautifully planted and maintained.

All three houses are open for guided tours Monday through Saturday from 10am to 5pm and Sunday from 1 to 5pm, April through October. Admission for adults is $4 per house, $10 for all three; for children 6 to 16, $2 per house, $4 for all three. The last tour starts at 4:30pm; tours take 30 to 45 minutes. Call for information about group tours, which are offered by appointment. The Munroe Tavern houses the **Lexington Historical Society** (☎ **781/862-1703;** www.lexingtonhistory.org), which operates all three.

The fascinating exhibits at the **Museum of Our National Heritage,** 33 Marrett Rd., Route 2A, at Mass. Ave. (☎ **781/861-6559** or 781/861-9638; www.mnh.org), explore history through popular culture. The installations in the six exhibition spaces change regularly; you can start with another dose of the Revolution, the permanent exhibit *Lexington Alarm'd*. Other topics have ranged from George Washington to Frank Lloyd Wright, American circus posters to Navajo rugs. Lectures, concerts, and family programs are also offered. Admission is free. The museum is open Monday through Saturday from 10am to 5pm and Sunday from noon to 5pm; closed January 1, Thanksgiving, and December 25. The museum is sponsored by the Scottish Rite of Freemasonry.

WHERE TO DINE

Bertucci's, 1777 Mass. Ave. (☎ 781/860-9000), is a branch of the family-friendly pizzeria chain. **Aesop's Bagels,** 1666 Mass. Ave. (☎ 781/674-2990), is a good place to pick up a light meal.

Lemon Grass. 1710 Mass. Ave. ☎ 781/862-3530. Main courses $5.50–$8.25 at lunch; $7.25–$15.50 at dinner. AE, DISC, MC, V. Mon–Fri 11:30am–3pm; Mon–Thurs 5–9:30pm; Fri–Sat 5–10pm; Sun 4–9pm. THAI.

A welcome break: The only revolution going on here is in Americans' culinary habits. The space is a former coffee shop disguised with bamboo decorations and the aroma of Asian spices. You might start with *satay* (skewers of meat served with a delectable peanut sauce) or chicken coconut soup, with a kick of pepper and plenty of poultry. Entrees include a tasty rendition of traditional pad Thai and excellent curry dishes. The accommodating staff will adjust the heat and spice to suit your taste.

CONCORD

18 miles NW of Boston, 15 miles NW of Cambridge, 6 miles W of Lexington

Concord (say "conquered") revels in its legacy as a center of groundbreaking thought and its role in the country's political and intellectual history. The first official battle of the Revolutionary War took place in 1775 at the North Bridge (now part of Minute Man National Historical Park); 100 years later, Concord became an important literary and intellectual center.

After just a little time in this lovely town, you might find yourself adopting the local attitudes toward two of its most famous residents: **Ralph Waldo Emerson,** who comes across as a well-respected uncle figure, and **Henry David Thoreau,** everyone's favorite eccentric cousin. The contemplative writers wandered the countryside nearby and did much of their writing and reflecting in Concord, forming the nucleus of a group of important writers who settled in the town. By the middle of the 19th century, Concord was the center of the Transcendentalist movement; sightseers can visit the former **homes of Emerson, Thoreau, Nathaniel Hawthorne, and Louisa May Alcott.** Lovers of literature can also visit **Sleepy Hollow Cemetery,** the final resting place of all these authors. Consider starting your visit at the **Concord Museum,** which offers an excellent overview.

ESSENTIALS

GETTING THERE   From Lexington, take Route 2A west from Mass. Ave. (Rte. 4/225) at the Museum of Our National Heritage; follow the BATTLE ROAD signs. From Boston and Cambridge, take Route 2 into Lincoln and stay in the right lane. Where the main road makes a sharp left, go straight onto Cambridge Turnpike, and follow signs to HISTORIC CONCORD.

The **MBTA commuter rail** (☎ 617/222-3200; www.mbta.com) takes about 45 minutes from North Station in Boston, with a stop at Porter Square in Cambridge. The round-trip fare is $6.50. There is no bus service from Boston to Concord, and no public transportation between Lexington and Concord. The station is about three-quarters of a mile over flat terrain from the town center.

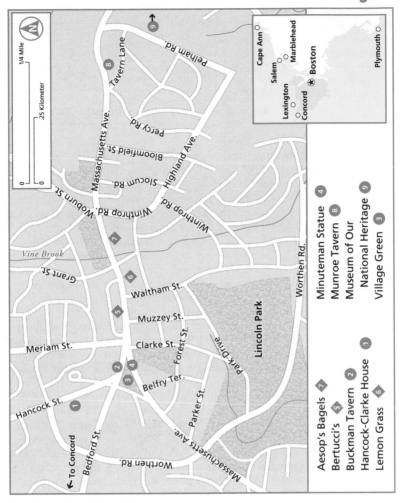

Minuteman Statue 4
Munroe Tavern 8
Museum of Our National Heritage 9
Village Green 3

Aesop's Bagels 7
Bertucci's 5
Buckman Tavern 2
Hancock-Clarke House 1
Lemon Grass 6

VISITOR INFORMATION The **area code** is 978. The **Chamber of Commerce,** 2 Lexington Rd., Concord, MA 01742 (☎ **978/369-3120;** www.ultranet.com/ ~conchamb), maintains an information booth on Heywood Street, 1 block southeast of Monument Square. It's open weekends in April and daily May through October, 9:30am to 4:30pm. One-hour tours are available starting in May on Saturday, Sunday, and Monday holidays, or on weekdays by appointment. Group tours are available by appointment. The community (www.concordma.com) and town (www.concordnet. org) Web sites include visitor information.

EXPLORING THE AREA

Minute Man National Historical Park

This 900-acre park preserves the scene of the first Revolutionary War battle at Concord on (all together now) April 19, 1775. After the skirmish at Lexington, the British moved on to Concord in search of stockpiled arms, which militia members had already moved. Warned of the troops' advance, the colonists were preparing to confront them. The Minutemen crossed the North Bridge, evading the "regulars" who were standing guard, and waited for reinforcements on a nearby hilltop. In Concord, the British searched homes and burned any guns they found. The Minutemen saw the smoke and, mistakenly thinking the troops were torching the town, attacked the soldiers standing guard at the bridge. The gunfire that ensued is remembered as "the shot heard 'round the world," the opening salvo of the Revolution.

The park is open daily, year-round. To reach the **North Bridge,** follow Monument Street out of Concord Center until you see the parking lot on the right. Park and walk a short distance to the bridge (a reproduction), stopping along the unpaved path to read the narratives and hear the audio presentations. On one side of the bridge is a plaque commemorating the British soldiers who died in the Revolutionary War; on the other is Daniel Chester French's **Minute Man statue**.

You can also start your visit at the **North Bridge Visitor Center,** 174 Liberty St., off Monument Street (☎ **978/369-6993;** www.nps.gov/mima), which overlooks the Concord River and the bridge from a hilltop. A diorama and video program illustrate the battle, and exhibits include uniforms, weapons, and tools of colonial and British soldiers. Park rangers are on duty if you have questions. Outside, picnicking is allowed, and the scenery is lovely, especially in the fall. The center is open daily from 9am to 5:30pm (until 4pm in winter), and closed January 1 and December 25.

At the Lexington end of the park, the **Minute Man Visitor Center,** off Route 2A, one-half mile west of I-95 Exit 33B (☎ **781/862-7753;** www.nps.gov/mima), is open daily from 9am to 5pm (until 4pm in winter), and closed January 1 and December 25. The park includes the first 4 miles of the Battle Road, the route the defeated British troops took as they left Concord. At the visitor center, you'll see informational displays, a new multimedia program about the Revolution, and a new 40-foot mural illustrating the battle. On summer weekends, rangers lead tours of the park—call ahead for times. The new **Battle Road Trail,** a 5$^1/_2$-mile interpretive path, carries pedestrian, wheelchair, and bicycle traffic. Exhibit panels and granite markers bear information about the military, social, and natural history of the area and point the way along the trail.

Walden Pond State Reservation. 915 Walden St. (Rte. 126). ☎ **978/369-3254.** www.state.ma.us/dem/parks/wldn.htm. From Concord Center, take Walden St. (Rte. 126) south, cross Rte. 2, and follow signs to the parking lot.

A pile of stones marks the site of the cabin where Henry David Thoreau lived from 1845 to 1847. Today the picturesque park is an extremely popular destination for walking (a path circles the pond), swimming, and fishing. Call for the schedule of ranger-led interpretive programs. No dogs or bikes are allowed. From Memorial Day through Labor Day, a daily parking fee is charged and the lot still fills early every day—call before setting out.

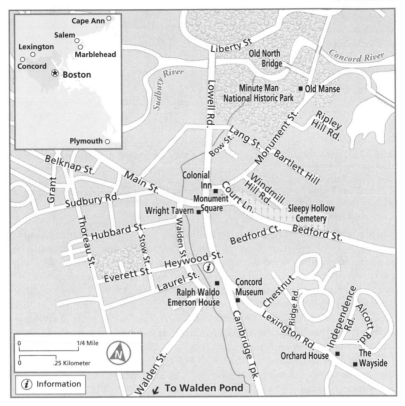

Museums & Literary Sites

⭘ **Concord Museum.** Lexington Rd. and Cambridge Tpk.. ☎ **978/369-9763.** www.
concordmuseum.org. Admission $7 adults, $6 seniors and students, $3 children under 16,
$16 families. Apr–Dec Mon–Sat 9am–5pm, Sun noon–5pm; Jan–Mar Mon–Sat 11am–4pm,
Sun 1–4pm. Parking allowed on road. Follow Lexington Rd. out of Concord Center and bear
right at museum onto Cambridge Tpk.; entrance is on left.

Just when you're (understandably) suspecting that everything interesting in this area
started on April 18, 1775, and ended the next day, this superb museum sets you
straight. A visit makes a great way to start your visit to the town.

The History Galleries explore the question "Why Concord?" Artifacts, murals,
films, maps, documents, and other presentations illustrate the town's changing roles.
It has been a Native American settlement, Revolutionary War battleground, 19th-
century intellectual center, and focal point of the 20th-century historic preservation
movement. Items on display include archaeological artifacts, silver from colonial
churches, a fascinating collection of embroidery samplers, and rooms furnished with
period furniture and textiles. Explanatory text places the exhibits in context. One of
the lanterns that signaled Paul Revere from the steeple of the Old North Church is on
display. You'll also see the contents of Ralph Waldo Emerson's study, arranged the way
it was at his death in 1882, and a large collection of Henry David Thoreau's belong-
ings. There are changing exhibits in the New Wing throughout the year, special events
such as "tea and tour" (call for reservations), and an outstanding gift shop.

By the rude bridge that arched the flood,
Their flag to April's breeze unfurled,
Here once the embattled farmers stood,
And fired the shot heard round the world.

—Ralph Waldo Emerson, *Concord Hymn*, 1836

DeCordova Museum and Sculpture Park. 51 Sandy Pond Rd., Lincoln. ☎ **781/259-8355.** www.decordova.org. Museum $6 adults; $4 seniors, students, and children 6–12; free for children under 6. Tues–Sun and Mon holidays 11am–5pm. Sculpture park admission free. Daily 8am–10pm. Closed Jan 1, July 4, Thanksgiving, Dec 25. From Rte. 2 east, take Rte. 126 to Baker Bridge Rd. (1st left after Walden Pond). When it ends, go right onto Sandy Pond Rd.; museum is on left. From Rte. 2 west, take I-95 to Exit 28B, follow Trapelo Rd. 2¹/₂ miles to Sandy Pond Rd., then follow signs.

Indoors and out, the DeCordova shows the work of American contemporary and modern artists, with an emphasis on living New England residents. The main building, on a leafy hilltop, overlooks a pond and the area's only outdoor public sculpture park. Recent renovations added several galleries, room for interactive exhibits, a video space, a roof garden, and a sculpture terrace that displays the work of one sculptor per year. Picnicking is allowed in the sculpture park; bring lunch, or buy it at the cafe (open 11am to 4pm, Wednesday through Sunday). Free guided tours of the main galleries start at 1pm Wednesday and 2pm Sunday, year-round; sculpture park tours run from May to October on Saturday and Sunday at 1pm.

The **Store @ DeCordova** (☎ 617/259-8692) carries an excellent selection of gifts, toys, prints, jewelry, clothing, and other work by local artists, including instructors at the Museum School.

The Old Manse. 269 Monument St. (at North Bridge). ☎ **978/369-3909.** www.thetrustees.org. Guided tour $6 adults, $5 seniors, $4 children 6–12. Mid-Apr to Oct Mon–Sat 10am–5pm; Sun and holidays noon–5pm. Closed Nov to mid-Apr. From Concord Center, follow Monument St. to North Bridge parking lot (on right); Old Manse is on left.

The Rev. William Emerson built the Old Manse in 1770 and watched the Battle of Concord from his yard. He died during the Revolutionary War, and for almost 170 years the house was home to his widow, her second husband, their descendants, and two famous friends. Nathaniel Hawthorne and his bride, Sophia Peabody, moved in after their marriage in 1842 and stayed for 3 years. As a wedding present, Henry David Thoreau sowed the vegetable garden for them; in 1997 cultivation resumed after a 49-year break. This is also where William's grandson Ralph Waldo Emerson wrote the essay "Nature." Today you'll see mementos and memorabilia of the Emerson and Ripley families and of the Hawthornes, who scratched notes on two windows with Sophia's diamond ring.

◐ Orchard House. 399 Lexington Rd. ☎ **978/369-4118.** www.louisamayalcott.org. Guided tours $6 adults, $5 seniors and students, $4 children 6–17, $16 families (up to 2 adults and 4 children). Apr–Oct Mon–Sat 10am–4:30pm, Sun 1–4:30pm; Nov–Mar Mon–Fri 11am–3pm, Sat 10am–4:30pm, Sun 1–4:30pm. Closed Jan 1–15, Easter, Thanksgiving, Dec 25. Follow Lexington Rd. out of Concord Center and bear left at Concord Museum; house is on the left. Overflow parking lot is across the street.

With the release of the 1994 movie *Little Women* (which was filmed elsewhere), Louisa May Alcott's best-known and most popular work moved from the world of preadolescent girls into the mainstream. The 1868 book was written and set at Orchard

House, although most of the events took place about 10 to 20 years earlier—Louisa was in her mid-30s when *Little Women* appeared. Seeing the Alcotts' home brings the author and her family to life for legions of female visitors and their pleasantly surprised male companions. Fans won't want to miss the excellent tour, copiously illustrated with heirlooms. (Serious buffs can call ahead for information on holiday programs and many other special events, some of which require reservations.)

Louisa's father, Amos Bronson Alcott, was a writer, educator, philosopher, and leader of the Transcendentalist movement. He created Orchard House by joining and restoring two homes already on the 12 acres of land he bought in 1857. The family lived here from 1858 to 1877, socializing in the same circles as Emerson, Thoreau, and Hawthorne. Bronson Alcott's passion for educational reform eventually led to his being named superintendent of schools, and he ran the Concord School of Philosophy in Orchard House's backyard.

Other family members served as the models for the characters in *Little Women*. Anna ("Meg"), the eldest, was an amateur actress, and May ("Amy") a talented artist. Elizabeth ("Beth"), a gifted musician, died before the family moved to this house. Their mother, the social activist Abigail May Alcott, frequently assumed the role of family breadwinner—Bronson, as Louisa wrote in her journal, had "no gift for money making."

Ralph Waldo Emerson House. 28 Cambridge Tpk.. ☎ **978/369-2236.** Guided tours $5 adults, $3 seniors and children 7–17. Call to arrange group tours (10 people or more). Mid-April to Oct Thurs–Sat 10am–4:30pm; Sun 2–4:30pm. Closed Nov to mid-Apr. Follow Cambridge Tpk. out of Concord Center; just before Concord Museum, house is on right.

Emerson, the philosopher, essayist, and poet, lived here from 1835 until his death, in 1882. He had just married his second wife, Lydia Jackson, whom he called "Lydian"; she called him "Mr. Emerson," as the staff still does. The tour gives a good look at his personal side and at the fashionably ornate interior decoration of the time. You'll see original furnishings and some of Emerson's personal effects. (The contents of his study at the time of his death are in the Concord Museum.)

Sleepy Hollow Cemetery. Entrance on Rte. 62 W. ☎ **978/318-3233.** Daily 7am–dusk. Call ahead for wheelchair access.

Follow the signs for AUTHOR'S RIDGE and climb the hill to the graves of some of the town's literary lights, including the Alcotts, Emerson, Hawthorne, and Thoreau. The graves of military veterans often bear small American flags or other memorial symbols; of this group, only Louisa May Alcott (a Union Army nurse during the Civil War) qualifies. Emerson's grave, fittingly, bears no religious symbols, just an uncarved quartz boulder. Thoreau's grave is nearby; at his funeral in 1862, his old friend Emerson concluded his eulogy with these words: ". . . wherever there is knowledge, wherever there is virtue, wherever there is beauty, he will find a home."

The Wayside. 455 Lexington Rd. ☎ **978/369-6975.** www.nps.gov/mima/wayside. Guided tours $4 adults, free for children under 17. May–Oct Thurs–Tues 10am–4:30pm. Closed Nov–Apr. Follow Lexington Rd. out of Concord Center past Concord Museum and Orchard House; the Wayside is on the left.

The Wayside was Nathaniel Hawthorne's home from 1852 until his death, in 1864. The Alcotts also lived here (the girls called it "the yellow house"), as did Harriett Lothrop, who wrote the *Five Little Peppers* books under the pen name Margaret Sidney and owned most of the current furnishings. The fascinating ranger tour (the house is part of Minute Man National Historical Park) illuminates the occupants' lives and the house's crazy-quilt architecture. The exhibit in the barn consists of audio presentations and figures of Louisa May and Bronson Alcott, Hawthorne, and Sidney.

WHERE TO STAY & DINE

Colonial Inn. 48 Monument Sq., Concord, MA 01742. ☎ **800/370-9200** or 978/369-9200. Fax 978/369-2170. www.concordscolonialinn.com. 45 units (some with shower only). A/C TV TEL. Apr–Oct $185–$195 main inn; $149–$189 Prescott wing; $295–$350 cottage. Nov–Mar $155 main inn; $135 Prescott wing; $250 cottage. AE, CB, DC, DISC, MC, V.

The main building of the Colonial Inn has overlooked Monument Square since 1716. Additions since it became a hotel in 1889 have left the inn large enough to offer modern conveniences and small enough to feel friendly. The 12 original guest rooms—one of which supposedly is haunted—are in great demand, so reserve early if you want to stay in the main inn. Rooms in the three-story Prescott wing are a bit larger and have country-style decor. The public areas, including a sitting room and front porch, are decorated in colonial style. Dry-cleaning and laundry service are available, as are conference rooms.

The inn has two **lounges** that serve drinks and bar food, and a lovely **restaurant** (☎ **978/369-2373**) that offers salads, sandwiches, and pasta at lunch, and traditional American fare at dinner. Afternoon tea is served Wednesday through Sunday; reservations are required.

✪ **Guida's Coast Cuisine.** 84 Thoreau St. (Rte. 126), at Concord Depot. ☎ **978/371-1333.** www.guidas.bizonthe.net. Reservations recommended. Main courses $7–$14 at lunch; $16–$26 at dinner. AE, DISC, MC, V. Wed–Sat 11:30am–2:30pm; Sun–Thurs 5:30–9:30pm; Fri–Sat 5:30–10pm. PORTUGUESE/SEAFOOD.

Concord isn't on a coast, but don't let that keep you away from this excellent restaurant. Guida Ponte, a native of the Azores and a veteran of Legal Sea Foods, oversees a kitchen that works wonders with all manner of fish and shellfish. Clam chowder, creamy and tasting of the sea, is world-class—maybe even better than Legal's, and that's exalted company. A huge portion of mussels swims in flavorful broth meant to be sopped up with fluffy (another neat trick) gnocchi. Home-style Portuguese fish cakes, served with greens, potatoes, and roasted vegetables, are less sophisticated, but equally delectable. Desserts—especially flourless chocolate cake—are superb. This isn't an eat-and-run place, partly because service can be slow, but the food is worth lingering over. Be sure to call before dropping in at lunch—the schedule keeps changing.

Nashoba Brook Bakery & Café. 152 Commonwealth Ave., West Concord. ☎ **978/318-1999.** Sandwiches $5–$6; salads by the pound. Mon–Sat 8am–8pm. From Concord Center, follow Main St. (Rte. 62) west, across Rte. 2; bear right at traffic light in front of train station and go 3 blocks. AMERICAN.

The enticing variety of fresh bread, baked goods, soups, salads, and sandwiches makes this airy cafe a popular destination throughout the day. It offers a good break from the sightseeing circuit. The industrial-looking building off West Concord's main street backs up to little Nashoba Brook, which is visible through the glass back wall. Order and pick up at the counter, then grab a seat along the window or near the children's play area. Or order takeout—this is great picnic food—or a fresh loaf of crusty bread.

2 The North Shore & Cape Ann

The areas north of Boston abound with historic sights and gorgeous ocean vistas. Cape Ann is a rocky peninsula so enchantingly beautiful that when you hear the slogan "Massachusetts's *other* Cape," you might forget what the first one was. Cape Ann and Cape Cod do share some attributes—scenery, shopping, seafood, and traffic. The

North of Boston: Road Tips

The drive from Boston to Cape Ann on I-93 and Route 128 takes about an hour. A more leisurely excursion on Routes 1A, 129, 114, and 127 allows you to explore Marblehead and Salem on your way to Gloucester and Rockport. You can also follow Route 1 to I-95 and 128, but during rush hour the traffic is unbearable. Public transportation in this area is good, but it doesn't go everywhere, and in many towns the train station is some distance from the attractions.

Try to visit on a spring, summer, or fall weekday; many areas are ghost towns from November through March, and traffic is brutal on warm weekends. To go straight to Gloucester and Rockport—or to start there and work your way back—take I-93 north; where it turns into I-95 (signs point to New Hampshire and Maine), stay left and take Route 128 to the end. The last exit, no. 9, puts you in East Gloucester. To take Route 1A, check a map or ask at the front desk of your hotel for directions to the Callahan Tunnel, which is at the heart of the Big Dig. If you miss the tunnel and wind up on I-93, follow signs to Route 1 and pick up Route 1A in Revere.

---

smaller cape's proximity to Boston and manageable scale make it a wonderful day trip as well as a good choice for a longer stay.

The **North of Boston Convention & Visitors Bureau,** 17 Peabody Sq., Peabody, MA 01960 (☎ **800/742-5306** or 978/977-7760; www.northofboston.org), publishes a visitor guide. The **Cape Ann Chamber of Commerce** information center (see "Gloucester," below) can be helpful, too.

MARBLEHEAD

15 miles NE of Boston

Like an attractive person with a great personality, Marblehead has it all. Scenery, history, architecture, and shopping combine to make it one of the area's most popular day trips, for residents and visitors alike. It's even polite—many speed-limit signs say PLEASE. Marblehead is also a good place to spend a night or more.

One of the most picturesque neighborhoods in New England is "Old Town," where the narrow, twisting streets lead down to the magnificent harbor that helps make this the self-proclaimed "Yachting Capital of America." As you walk around Old Town, you'll see plaques on the houses bearing the date of construction, as well as the names of the builder and original occupant—a history lesson without studying. Many of the houses have stood since before the Revolutionary War, when Marblehead was a center of merchant shipping. Two historic homes are open for tours (see below).

ESSENTIALS

GETTING THERE   By car, take Route 1A north through Revere and Lynn; bear right at the signs for Nahant and Swampscott. Take Lynn Shore Drive through Swampscott to Route 129, and follow it into town. Or take I-93 or Route 1 to Route 128, then Route 114 through Salem into Marblehead.

MBTA (☎ **617/222-3200;** www.mbta.com) bus route no. 441/442 runs from Haymarket (Orange or Green Line) to downtown Marblehead. During rush periods on weekdays, the no. 448/449 connects Marblehead to Downtown Crossing. The trip takes about an hour, and the one-way fare is $2.25.

VISITOR INFORMATION   The **area code** is 781. The **Marblehead Chamber of Commerce,** 62 Pleasant St., P.O. Box 76, Marblehead, MA 01945 (☎ 781/631-2868; www.marbleheadchamber.org), is open weekdays from 9am to 5pm. The **information booth** (☎ 781/639-8469) on Pleasant Street near Spring Street is open daily May to October, 10am to 6pm. The chamber publishes a visitor's guide and map that includes a calendar of events; ask for a business directory if you want a description of a walking tour. Marblehead has a community Web site (www.marblehead.com).

SPECIAL EVENTS   There is sailboat racing in the outer harbor all summer, and **Race Week** in mid- to late July attracts enthusiasts from all over the country. The **Christmas Walk,** on the first weekend in December, incorporates music, arts and crafts, shopping, and Santa Claus, who arrives by lobster boat.

EXPLORING THE TOWN

Marblehead is a wonderful place for aimless wandering; to add some structure, consult the Chamber of Commerce's business directory. Whatever else you do, be sure to spend some time in **Crocker Park,** on the harbor off Front Street. Especially in the warmer months, when boats jam the water nearly as far as the eye can see, the view is breathtaking. There are benches and a swing, and picnicking is allowed. You might not want to leave, but snap out of it—the view from **Fort Sewall,** at the other end of Front Street, is equally mesmerizing.

Just inland, the **Lafayette House** is at the corner of Hooper and Union streets. The missing corner of the private home was chopped off to make room for the passage of the Marquis de Lafayette's carriage when he visited the town in 1824. In Market Square on Washington Street, near the corner of State Street, is the **Old Town House,** in use for meetings and gatherings since 1727.

Marblehead is a legendary (or notorious, if you're on a budget) **shopping** destination. All along Washington and Front streets, and scattered on Atlantic Avenue, shops and boutiques will beckon your name.

Abbot Hall. Washington Sq. ☎ 781/631-0528. Free admission. Year-round Mon–Tues, Thurs 8am–5pm, Wed 7:30am–7:30pm, Fri 8am–1pm; May–Oct Fri 8am–5pm, Sat 9am–6pm, Sun 11am–6pm. From the historic district, follow Washington St. up the hill.

The town offices and Historical Commission share Abbot Hall with Archibald M. Willard's famous painting *The Spirit of '76,* on display in the Selectmen's Meeting Room. The thrill of recognizing the ubiquitous drummer, drummer boy, and fife player is the main reason to stop here. The deed that records the sale of the land by the Native Americans to the Europeans in 1684 is also on view. Cases in the halls contain objects and artifacts from the Historical Society's collections. The building's clock tower is visible from all over Old Town.

✪ **Jeremiah Lee Mansion.** 161 Washington St. ☎ 781/631-1768. Guided tours $5 adults, $4.50 students, free for children under 11. Mid-May to Oct Mon–Sat 10am–4pm; Sun 1–4pm. Closed Nov to mid-May. Follow Washington St. until it curves right and heads uphill toward Abbot Hall; house is on right.

The prospect of seeing original hand-painted wallpaper in an 18th-century home is reason enough to visit this house, built in 1768 for a wealthy merchant and considered an outstanding example of pre-Revolutionary Georgian architecture. Original rococo carving and other details complement historically accurate room arrangements, and ongoing restoration and interpretation by the Marblehead Historical Society place the 18th- and 19th-century furnishings and artifacts in context. The friendly guides welcome questions and are well versed in the history of the home. The lawn and gardens are open to the public.

Marblehead

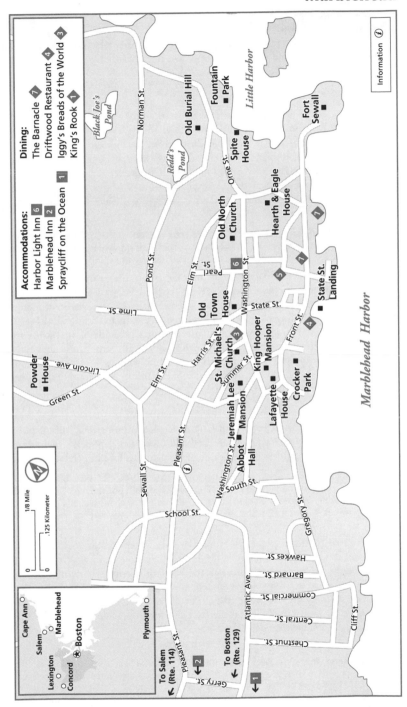

Accommodations:
Harbor Light Inn **6**
Marblehead Inn **2**
Spraycliff on the Ocean **1**

Dining:
The Barnacle **7**
Driftwood Restaurant **4**
Iggy's Breads of the World **3**
King's Rook **1**

Information ⓘ

1/8 Mile
.125 Kilometer

Cape Ann
Salem
Marblehead
Lexington
Concord ✴ Boston
Plymouth

To Salem
(Rte. 114) **2**
To Boston
(Rte. 129) **1**

Norman St.
Black Joe's Pond
Redd's Pond
Old Burial Hill
Fountain Park
Little Harbor
Spite House
Fort Sewall
Orne St.
Old North Church
Hearth & Eagle House
Pond St.
Elm St.
Pearl St. **6**
Washington St.
Lime St.
Old Town House
State St. **5**
State St. Landing **1**
Harris St.
St. Michael's Church **3**
Summer St.
King Hooper Mansion
Front St.
Powder House
Lincoln Ave.
Green St.
Elm St.
Jeremiah Lee Mansion
Lafayette House
Crocker Park
Washington St.
Abbot Hall
Marblehead Harbor
Sewall St.
Pleasant St.
South St.
Gregory St.
School St.
Hawkes St.
Barnard St.
Atlantic Ave.
Commercial St.
Central St.
Chestnut St.
Cliff St.
Pleasant St.
Gerry St.

Architectural Details

On the hill between the Jeremiah Lee Mansion and Abbot Hall, notice the private homes at 185, 181, and 175 Washington St. They are other good examples of the architecture of the pre-Revolutionary period.

The Historical Society's headquarters, across the street at 170 Washington St., house the **J.O.J. Frost Folk Art Gallery** and a changing exhibition gallery. Frost, a noted primitivist painter, was a Marblehead native. The building is open 10am to 4pm, weekdays year-round and Saturday mid-May through December, plus Sunday 1 to 4pm from June to August. Admission is free. The society occasionally offers candlelight tours of the house and sponsors walking tours of Marblehead on Thursdays in July, Sundays in August, and Saturdays in September. Call ahead to see if your schedules match.

King Hooper Mansion. 8 Hooper St. ☎ **781/631-2608.** Donation requested for tour. Mon–Sat 10am–4pm; Sun 1–5pm. Call ahead; no tours during private parties. Where Washington St. curves at the foot of hill near Lee Mansion, look for the colorful sign.

Shipping tycoon Robert Hooper got his nickname because he treated his sailors so well, but it's easy to think he was called "King" because he lived like royalty. Around the corner from the home of Jeremiah Lee (whose sister was the second of Hooper's four wives), the 1728 King Hooper Mansion gained a Georgian addition in 1745. The period furnishings, although not original, give a sense of the life of an 18th-century merchant prince, from the wine cellar to the third-floor ballroom. The building houses the headquarters of the Marblehead Arts Association, which stages monthly exhibits and runs a gift shop that sells members' work. The mansion has a lovely garden; enter through the gate at the right of the house.

WHERE TO STAY

This is B&B heaven; the Chamber of Commerce accommodations listings include many of the town's innumerable inns and bed-and-breakfasts. Check the Web site, call or write for a visitor's guide, or consult one of the agencies listed in chapter 5.

Harbor Light Inn. 58 Washington St., Marblehead, MA 01945. ☎ **781/631-2186.** Fax 781/631-2216. www.harborlightinn.com. 21 units (some with shower only). A/C TV TEL. $105–$175 double; $160–$275 suite. Rates include continental breakfast. Corporate rate available midweek. Minimum 2 nights weekends, 3 nights holiday weekends. AE, MC, V. Free parking.

A stone's throw from the Old Town House, two Federal-era mansions make up this gracious inn. From the wood floors to the 1729 beams (in a third-floor room) to the heated outdoor pool, it's both historical and relaxing. Rooms are comfortably furnished in period style, with some antiques; most have canopy or four-poster beds. Eleven have working fireplaces, and five of those have double Jacuzzis. VCRs and free video rentals are available. Rooms at the back overlook the lawn, sundeck, and pool (open seasonally). There are gorgeous harbor views from some rooms and from the rooftop observation deck, which is open to all guests. There is also a conference room.

✪ **Marblehead Inn.** 264 Pleasant St. (Rte. 114), Marblehead, MA 01945. ☎ **800/ 399-5843** or 781/639-9999. Fax 781/639-9996. www.marbleheadinn.com. 10 units. A/C TV TEL. $139–$199 double. Extra person $25. Rates include continental breakfast. Winter discounts and long-term rates available. 2-night minimum stay busy weekends, 3-night minimum holiday weekends. AE, MC, V. Free parking.

This three-story Victorian mansion just outside the historic district underwent extensive restoration and reopened in 1998 as an all-suite inn. Each attractively decorated unit has a living room, bedroom, workstation, and self-catering kitchenette (the inn supplies breakfast provisions). This is a good choice for families traveling with children or businesspeople making an extended stay. Most suites have Jacuzzis, and some have working fireplaces and small patios. The 1872 building has been an inn since 1923, and once played host to Amelia Earhart.

Spray Cliff on the Ocean. 25 Spray Ave., Marblehead, MA 01945. ☎ **800/626-1530** or 781/631-6789. Fax 781/639-4563. www.spraycliff.com. 7 units (some with shower only). May–Oct $180–$225 double. Extra person $25. Rates include continental breakfast, evening refreshments, and use of bicycles. Off-season discounts available. Minimum 2 nights weekends, 3 nights busy holiday weekends. AE, MC, V. Free parking. Take Atlantic Ave. (Rte. 129) to traffic light at Clifton Ave. and turn east (right driving north, left driving south); parking area is at end of street. No children accepted.

Spray Cliff, a three-story Victorian Tudor built in 1910 on a cliff overlooking the ocean, is 5 minutes from town and a world away. Five of the large, sunny rooms face the water, three have fireplaces, and all are luxuriously decorated in contemporary style with bright accents. Roger and Sally Plauché have run their romantic inn on a quiet residential street 1 minute from the beach since 1994.

WHERE TO DINE

At a number of places in Old Town, you can stock up for a picnic along the water. The best is ✪ **Iggy's Bread of the World,** 5 Pleasant St. (☎ 781/639-4717), which serves fabulous gourmet baked goods and coffee. The store at 78 Front St., near State Street, was between tenants at press time but usually houses an ice-cream shop. Both places have small seating areas—but really, go outside.

The Barnacle. 141 Front St. ☎ 781/631-4236. Reservations not accepted. Main courses $4–$14 at lunch; $12–$17 at dinner. No credit cards. Daily 11:30am–4pm; Sun–Thurs 5–9pm; Fri–Sat 5–10pm. Closed Tues in winter. SEAFOOD.

This unassuming spot doesn't look like much from the street, but at the end of the gangplanklike entrance is a front-row seat for the action on the water. Even if you don't land a seat on the deck or along the counter facing the windows, you'll still have a shorebird's-eye view of the mouth of the harbor and the ocean from the crowded dining room. The food is tasty and plentiful. It's not innovative, but it is fresh—the restaurant's lobster boat delivers daily. The chowder and fried seafood, especially clams, are terrific. This is an ideal place to quaff a beer and watch the boats sail by.

Driftwood Restaurant. 63 Front St. ☎ 781/631-1145. Main courses $2–$10; breakfast items less than $6. No credit cards. Summer daily 6:30am–5pm; winter daily 6:30am–2pm. DINER/SEAFOOD.

At the foot of State Street next to Clark Landing (the town pier) is an honest-to-goodness local hangout. Join the crowd at a table or the counter for generous portions of breakfast (served all day) or lunch. Try pancakes or hash, chowder or a seafood "roll" (a hot dog bun filled with, say, fried clams or lobster salad). The house specialty, served on weekends and holidays, is fried dough, which is exactly as delicious and indigestible as it sounds.

King's Rook. 12 State St. ☎ 781/631-9838. Reservations not accepted. Main courses $5–$9. MC, V. Mon–Fri noon–2:30pm; Tues–Fri 5:30–11:30pm; Sat–Sun noon–11:30pm. Closed Mon in winter. CAFE/WINE BAR.

This cozy spot serves coffees, teas, hot chocolates, soft drinks, and more than 20 wines by the glass, and the food has a sophisticated flair. The intimate side-street atmosphere and racks of newspapers and magazines make this a great place to linger over a pesto pizza, great spinach soup, a salad, or a sinfully rich dessert—and, of course, a beverage.

SALEM

17 miles NE of Boston, 4 miles NW of Marblehead

Settled in 1626 (4 years before Boston) and later known around the world as a center of merchant shipping, Salem is internationally famous today for a 7-month episode in 1692. The witchcraft trial hysteria led to 20 deaths, 3 centuries of notoriety, countless lessons on the evils of prejudice, and innumerable bad puns ("Stop by for a spell" is a favorite slogan).

Unable to live down the association, Salem has embraced it. The high-school sports teams are the Witches, and the logo of the *Salem Evening News* is a silhouette of a sorceress. Today you'll see plenty of witch-associated attractions, plus nearly as many reminders of Salem's seagoing history. The newest is the replica of the 1797 merchant vessel *Friendship* anchored near the Salem Maritime National Historic Site.

ESSENTIALS

GETTING THERE   By car from Marblehead, follow Route 114 west. From Boston, take Route 1A north to Salem, being careful in Lynn, where the road turns left and immediately right. You can also take I-93 or Route 1 to Route 128, then Route 114 into downtown Salem. There's a reasonably priced municipal garage across the street from the Visitor Center.

From Boston, the **MBTA** (☎ 617/222-3200; www.mbta.com) operates commuter trains from North Station and bus route no. 450 from Haymarket (Orange or Green Line). The train takes 30 to 35 minutes; the round-trip fare is $5. The station is about 5 blocks from the downtown area. The one-way fare for the 35- to 55-minute bus trip is $2.25.

Ferries (☎ 617/227-4321; www.bostonharborcruises.com) run from Long Wharf in Boston to the Blaney Street Ferry Terminal, off Derby Street, from June through October. Call ahead, because details of this fairly new service are still in flux. The 75-minute trip costs about $10 for adults, less for seniors and children under 12.

VISITOR INFORMATION   The **area code** is 978. A good place to start is the **National Park Service Visitor Center,** 2 New Liberty St. (☎ 978/740-1650; www.nps.gov/sama), open daily 9am to 5pm. Exhibits highlight early settlement, maritime history, and the leather and textiles industries. The center distributes brochures and pamphlets, including one that describes a **walking tour** of the historic district, and has an auditorium where a free film on Essex County provides a good overview.

Destination Salem (the city's Office of Tourism & Cultural Affairs), 10 Liberty St., Salem, MA 01970 (☎ 877/SALEM-MA or 978/ 744-3663; www.salem.org), collaborates with the Chamber of Commerce to publish a free visitor guide that includes a good map. The **Salem Chamber of Commerce,** 32 Derby Sq., Salem, MA 01970 (☎ 978/744-0004; www.salem-chamber.org), maintains a large rack of brochures and pamphlets at its office on the first floor of Old Town Hall. It's open weekdays 9am to 5pm. Salem has an excellent community Web site (www.salemweb.com).

GETTING AROUND   **Downtown** Salem is spread out but flat. In the immediate downtown area, **walking** is the way to go, but you might not want to hoof it to all the sights, especially if it's hot. At the Essex Street side of the Visitor Center, you can board the **Salem Trolley** (☎ 978/744-5469) for a 1-hour narrated tour. It operates daily 10am to 5pm, April through October, weekends March and November. Tickets ($8

Salem

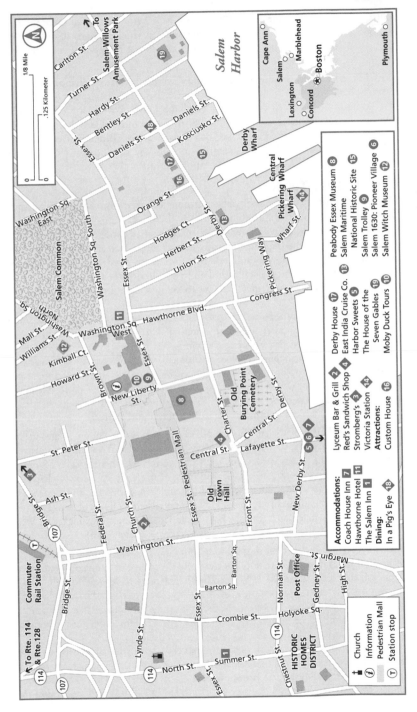

Accommodations:
Coach House Inn **7**
Hawthorne Hotel **11**
The Salem Inn **1**

Dining:
In a Pig's Eye **18**

Lyceum Bar & Grill **2**
Red's Sandwich Shop **4**
Stromberg's **3**
Victoria Station **14**

Attractions:
Custom House **16**

Derby House **17**
East India Cruise Co. **5**
Harbor Sweets **5**
The House of the
  Seven Gables **10**
Moby Duck Tours **10**

Peabody Essex Museum **8**
Salem Maritime
  National Historic Site **15**
Salem Trolley **9**
Salem 1630: Pioneer Village **6**
Salem Witch Museum **12**

Church
Information
Pedestrian Mall
Station stop

255

adults, $7 seniors, $4 children 5 to 12, $20 family of 2 adults and 2 or more children) are good all day, and you can reboard as many times as you like at any of the 15 stops. It's a good deal if you're spending the day and don't want to keep moving the car or carrying leg-weary children.

SPECIAL EVENTS **Haunted Happenings** (www.salemhauntedhappenings.com), the city's Halloween celebration, lasts 2 full weeks. Parades, parties, and tours lead up to a ceremony on the big day. During **Heritage Days,** a weeklong event in mid-August, the city celebrates its multicultural history with musical and theatrical performances, a parade, and fireworks. The 2-day **Winter Island Blues Festival** (☎ 781/639-4040; www.winterislandblues.com) is in mid-July outdoors at Winter Island Park. It books big names and up-and-coming performers.

EXPLORING THE TOWN

The historic district extends well inland from the waterfront. Many 18th-century houses, some with original furnishings, still stand. Ship captains lived near the water at the east end of downtown, in relatively small houses crowded close together. The captains' employers, the shipping company owners, built their homes away from the water (and the accompanying aromas). Many of them lived on **Chestnut Street,** which is a registered National Historic Landmark. Residents along the grand thoroughfare must, by legal agreement, adhere to colonial style in their decorating and furnishings.

Pickering Wharf, at the corner of Derby and Congress streets, is a cluster of shops, boutiques, restaurants, and condos near a marina. The waterfront setting makes it a good place for strolling, snacking, and shopping.

By car or trolley, the **Salem Willows** amusements are 5 minutes away; many signs point the way. The strip of rides and snack bars has a honky-tonk air, and the waterfront park is a good place to bring a picnic and wander along the shore. There's no admission fee; meter parking is available. To enjoy the great view without the arcades and rides, have lunch one peninsula over at **Winter Island Park.**

NARRATED TOURS Salem Trolley offers the best value, but it's land-locked. **Moby Duck Tours** (☎ 978/741-4386; www.mobyduck.com) use amphibious vehicles that cruise the streets of the city, then plunge into the harbor. The 55-minute excursions leave from New Liberty Street in front of the Visitor Center. Tickets (cash only) are $14 for adults, $12 for seniors, $8 for children under 12. Tours operate on weekends in May, daily from Memorial Day to Halloween. You can also take a harbor cruise or go on a whale watch with the **East India Cruise Company,** Pickering Wharf (☎ 800/745-9594 or 978/741-0434; www.salemwhalewatch.com).

SHOPPING Upmarket gift shops throughout New England sell the chocolate confections of ✪ **Harbor Sweets,** and you can go to the source at Palmer Cove, 85 Leavitt St., off Lafayette Street (☎ 978/745-7648). The retail store overlooks the floor of the factory—if you want to see the machinery in action, call ahead to see whether it's running. The sinfully good sweets are pricey, but candy bars and small assortments are available. The shop is open weekdays from 8:30am to 4:30pm and Saturday from 9am to 3pm, with extended hours around candy-centric holidays.

If you can't get witchcraft off your mind, several shops specialize in the necessary accessories. Do bear in mind that Salem is home to many practicing witches who take their beliefs very seriously. The **Broom Closet,** 3–5 Central St. (☎ 978/741-3669), and **Crow Haven Corner,** 125 Essex St. (☎ 978/745-8763), sell everything from crystals to clothing, and cast a modern-day light on age-old customs.

The House of the Seven Gables. 54 Turner St. ☎ **978/744-0991.** www.7gables.org.
Guided tours $8 adults, $5 children 6–17, free for children under 6. Tour and Salem 1630
admission $13 adults, $9 children 6–17. May–Nov daily 10am–5pm; Dec–Apr Mon–Sat
10am–5pm, Sun noon–5pm. Closed Jan 1, Thanksgiving, Dec 25. From downtown, follow
Derby St. east 3 blocks past Derby Wharf.

Nathaniel Hawthorne's cousin lived here, and stories and legends of the house and its
inhabitants inspired his 1851 book of the same name. If you haven't read the eerie
novel, don't let that keep you away—begin your visit with the audiovisual program,
which tells the story. The house, built by Capt. John Turner in 1668, holds six rooms
of period furniture, including pieces referred to in the book, and a narrow, twisting
secret staircase. Tours include a visit to Hawthorne's birthplace (built before 1750 and
moved to the grounds) and describe what life was like for the houses' 18th-century
inhabitants. The costumed guides can get a little silly as they mug for young visitors,
but they're well versed in the history of the buildings and artifacts, and eager to answer
questions. Also on the grounds, overlooking Salem Harbor, are period gardens, the
Retire Beckett House (1655), the **Hooper–Hathaway House** (1682), and a **counting house** (1830).

☉ Peabody Essex Museum. East India Sq. ☎ **800/745-4054** or 978/745-9500.
www.pem.org. Admission (good on 2 consecutive days) $8.50 adults, $7.50 seniors and students with ID, $5 children 6–16, $20 family (2 adults, 1 or more children). Mon–Fri
10am–5pm; Sat–Sun 9am–6pm. Closed Jan 1, Thanksgiving, Dec 25. Take Hawthorne Blvd.
to Essex St., following signs for Visitor Center. Enter on Essex St. or New Liberty St.

The Peabody Essex Museum celebrated its bicentennial in 1999, 7 years after the
merger of the Peabody Museum and the Essex Institute. A massive 2-year expansion
project is scheduled to begin in the fall of 2000; parts of the museum may be closed
during your visit.

The current exhibit, **Odyssey** (up through October 2001), consists of art and artifacts
from throughout the museum's fascinating collections, which illustrate Salem's international adventures and domestic development. In 1799 the East India Marine Society
founded the Peabody Museum, now the nation's oldest in continuous operation. The sea
captains and merchants provided for a "museum in which to house the natural and arti-
ficial curiosities" brought back from their travels. The collections of the Essex Institute
(1821), the county historical society, encompass American art, crafts, furniture, and
architecture (including nine historic houses), as well as dolls, toys, and games.

It all adds up to the impression that you're in Salem's attic, but instead of opening
dusty trunks and musty closets, you find the treasures arranged in well-planned displays that help you understand the significance of each artifact. In the collections—
and perhaps on display when you visit—are objects related to the history of the port
of Salem, the whaling trade, the witchcraft trials, East Asian art, and the practical arts
and crafts of East Asian, Pacific Island, and Native American peoples. Portraits of area
residents include Charles Osgood's omnipresent rendering of Nathaniel Hawthorne.

Sign up for a fascinating tour of one or more houses—the **Gardner–Pingree House**
(1804), a magnificent Federal mansion where a notorious murder was committed in
1830, has been gorgeously restored. You can also take a gallery tour or select from
about a dozen pamphlets for self-guided tours on various topics. The museum has an
excellent gift shop and a cafe that serves lunch daily.

Salem Maritime National Historic Site. 174 Derby St. ☎ **978/740-1660.**
www.nps.gov/sama. Free admission. Guided tours $3 adults, $2 seniors and children 6–16.
Daily 9am–5pm. Closed Jan 1, Thanksgiving, Dec 25. Take Derby St. east; just past Pickering
Wharf, Derby Wharf is on the right.

With the decline of the shipping trade in the early 19th century, Salem's wharves fell into disrepair, a state the National Park Service began to remedy in 1938 when it took over a small piece of the waterfront. **Derby Wharf** is now a finger of parkland extending into the harbor, part of the 9 acres dotted with explanatory markers that make up the historic site.

An exciting addition is a full-size replica of a 1797 East Indiaman merchant vessel, the *Friendship,* a three-masted 171-footer. The hull was laid in Albany, New York, and towed to Salem, where construction was completed in 1999 and 2000. The tall ship is a faithful replica with some concessions to the modern era, such as diesel engines and accessibility for people with disabilities. Fees for visitors were not set at press time, but a tour of the ship likely will be included in the guided ranger tour.

On adjacent **Central Wharf** is a warehouse (ca. 1800) that houses the orientation center. Ranger-led tours, which vary seasonally, expand on Salem's maritime history. Yours might include the **Derby House** (1762), a wedding gift to shipping magnate Elias Hasket Derby from his father, and the **Custom House** (1819). Legend (myth, really) has it that this is where Nathaniel Hawthorne was working when he found an embroidered scarlet *A.* If you prefer to explore on your own, you can see the free film at the orientation center and wander around **Derby Wharf,** the **West India Goods Store,** the **Bonded Warehouse,** the **Scale House,** and **Central Wharf.**

Salem 1630: Pioneer Village. Forest River Park, off West Ave. ☎ **978/744-0991.** www.7gables.org. Admission $7 adults, $5 children 6–17. Admission and House of the Seven Gables tour $13 adults, $9 children 6–17. Late Apr to late Nov Mon–Sat 10am–5pm; Sun noon–5pm. Closed late Nov to late Apr. Take Lafayette St. (Rtes. 114 and 1A) south from downtown to West Ave., turn left and follow signs.

A re-creation of life in Salem just 4 years after European settlement, this Puritan village is staffed by costumed interpreters who lead tours, demonstrate crafts, and tend farm animals. They escort visitors around the various dwellings—wear sneakers, because the village isn't paved—and explain their activities. As with any undertaking of this nature, it takes a while to get used to the atmosphere, but once you do, it's great fun.

Brush with fame: When the 1996 film version of Arthur Miller's play about the witchcraft trials, *The Crucible,* was completed, the village inherited a large collection of authentic and reproduction props that have been put into use.

✪ **Salem Witch Museum.** 19^1/$_2$ Washington Sq. ☎ **978/744-1692.** www. salemwitchmuseum.com. Admission $6 adults, $5.50 seniors, $3.75 children 6–14. July–Aug daily 10am–7pm; Sept–June daily 10am–5pm. Closed Jan 1, Thanksgiving, Dec 25. Follow Hawthorne Blvd. to the northwest corner of Salem Common.

This is one of the most memorable attractions in eastern Massachusetts—it's both interesting and scary. The main draw of the museum (a former church) is a three-dimensional audiovisual presentation with life-size figures. The show takes place in a huge room lined with displays that are lighted in sequence. The 30-minute narration dramatically but accurately tells the story of the witchcraft trials and the accompanying hysteria. The narration is available translated into French, German, Italian, Japanese, and Spanish. There's also a new exhibit that traces the history of witches, witchcraft, and witch hunts.

A Face in the Crowd

On the traffic island across from the entrance to the Witch Museum is a statue that's easily mistaken for a witch. It's really Roger Conant, who founded Salem in 1626.

WHERE TO STAY

The busiest and most expensive time of year is Halloween week; reserve well in advance, even when the holiday falls in the middle of the week (as it does in 2001).

Coach House Inn. 284 Lafayette St. (Rtes. 1A and 114), Salem, MA 01970. ☎ **800/688-8689** or 978/744-4092. Fax 978/745-8031. www.salemweb.com/biz/coachhouse. 11 units, 9 with bathroom (1 with shower only). A/C TV. $75–$95 double with shared bathroom, $95–$135 double with private bathroom; $150–$185 suite. Extra person $20. Rates include continental breakfast. Minimum 2 or 3 nights weekends and holidays. AE, DISC, MC, V. Free parking.

Built in 1879 for a ship's captain, this inn is 2 blocks from the harbor. It's a good choice if you don't mind the 20-minute walk or 5-minute drive from downtown Salem. The pleasant, high-ceilinged rooms in the three-story mansion were redecorated in 1998. They have coffeemakers and elegant furnishings, and most have (nonworking) fireplaces. Breakfast arrives at your door in a basket.

Hawthorne Hotel. 18 Washington Sq. (at Salem Common), Salem, MA 01970. ☎ **800/729-7829** or 978/744-4080. Fax 978/745-9842. www.hawthornehotel.com. 83 units (some with shower only). A/C TV TEL. $99–$182 double; $150–$275 suite. Extra person $12. Children under 16 free in parents' room. Off-season discounts available. Senior discount and weekend and other packages available. Minimum 2 nights holiday weekends. AE, CB, DC, DISC, MC, V. Parking $5. Small pets accepted; $15 charge.

This historic hotel, built in 1925, is both convenient and comfortable. The six-story building is centrally located and well maintained—the lobby was remodeled in 1995, the guest rooms renovated from 1997 to 1999. Rooms are attractively furnished and adequate in size; some overlook Salem Common. Ask to be as high up as possible, because the neighborhood is busy. Guests have the use of an exercise room. There are two restaurants on the ground floor, room service until 10pm, conference rooms, and dry-cleaning and laundry service.

Salem Inn. 7 Summer St. (Rte. 114), Salem, MA 01970. ☎ **800/446-2995** or 978/741-0680. Fax 978/744-8924. www.SalemInnMA.com. 39 units (some with shower only). A/C TV TEL. Nov–Sept $119–$229 double; Oct $160–$290 double. Rates include continental breakfast. Minimum 2 nights during special events and holidays. AE, DC, DISC, JCB, MC, V. Free parking. Pets accepted with prior arrangement.

The Salem Inn occupies the comfortable niche between too-big hotel and too-small B&B. The hubbub of downtown falls away as you enter the inn, which consists of three properties. The 1834 West House and the 1854 Curwen House, former homes of ship captains, are listed on the National Register of Historic Places. The 1874 Peabody House is a recently restored mansion divided into luxury and family suites. The large, tastefully decorated guest rooms all have hair dryers and coffeemakers, and some have fireplaces, canopy beds, and whirlpool baths. Suites have kitchenettes. A peaceful rose garden and brick patio are at the rear of the main building, which also holds a meeting space. The lower-level restaurant, Cuvée, serves dinner Tuesday through Sunday from 6 to 10:30pm.

WHERE TO DINE

Pickering Wharf has a food court as well as a link in the **Victoria Station** chain (☎ 978/744-7644), where the deck has a great view of the marina. **In a Pig's Eye,** 148 Derby St. (☎ 978/741-4436; www.inapigseye.com), is a neighborhood tavern on the way to the House of the Seven Gables that serves excellent Mexican food and bar fare.

○ **Lyceum Bar & Grill.** 43 Church St. (at Washington St.). ☎ **978/745-7665.** www.lyceumsalem.com. Reservations recommended. Main courses $6–$10 at lunch;

$16–$22 at dinner. AE, DISC, MC, V. Mon–Fri 11:30am–3pm; Sun brunch 11am–3pm; daily 5:30–10pm. CONTEMPORARY AMERICAN.

Alexander Graham Bell made the first long-distance telephone call from this building, and you might want to place one of your own to tell the folks at home what a good meal you're having. The elegance of the high-ceilinged front rooms and glass-walled back rooms matches the quality of the food, which attracts local businesspeople and out-of-towners alike. Grilling is a favorite cooking technique—be sure to try the marinated, grilled portabello mushrooms, available as an appetizer. They're also scattered throughout the menu—for example, in delectable pasta with chicken, red peppers, and Swiss chard in wine sauce, or with beef tenderloin, red pepper sauce, and garlic mashed potatoes. Spicy vegetable lasagna is also tasty. Try to save room for one of the traditional yet sophisticated desserts—the brownie sundae is out of this world.

Stromberg's. 2 Bridge St. (Rte. 1A). ☎ **978/744-1863.** Reservations recommended at dinner. Main courses $6–$10 at lunch, $11–$17 at dinner; children's menu $5. AE, DISC, MC, V. Sun, Tues–Thurs 11am–9pm; Fri–Sat 11am–10pm. SEAFOOD.

For generous portions of well-prepared seafood and a view of the water, seek out this popular spot at the foot of the bridge to Beverly. You won't care that Beverly Harbor isn't the most exciting spot, especially if it's summer and you're on the deck enjoying the live entertainment (weekends only). The fish and clam chowders are excellent; daily specials are numerous; and there are more chicken, beef, and pasta options than you might expect. Crustacean lovers in the mood to splurge will fall for the world-class lobster roll.

A DETOUR TO ESSEX

If you approach or leave Cape Ann on Route 128, turn away from Gloucester on Route 133 and head west to **Essex.** It's a beautiful little town known for Essex clams, salt marshes, a long tradition of shipbuilding, an incredible number of antiques shops, and one celebrated restaurant.

Legend has it that ✪ **Woodman's of Essex,** Main Street (☎ **800/649-1773** or 978/768-6451; www.woodmans.com), was the birthplace of the fried clam in 1916. Today the thriving family business is a great spot to join legions of locals and visitors from around the world for lobster "in the rough," steamers, corn on the cob, onion rings, and (you guessed it) superb fried clams. Expect the line to be long, even in the winter, but it moves quickly and offers a good view of the regimented commotion in the food preparation area. Eat in a booth, upstairs on the deck, or out back at a picnic table. Credit cards aren't accepted, but there's an ATM on the premises. You'll want to be well fed before you set off to explore the numerous antiques shops along Main Street.

A DETOUR TO A CASTLE

South of downtown Gloucester on Route 127, you'll see signs for Magnolia and the **Hammond Castle Museum,** 80 Hesperus Ave. (☎ **978/283-2080,** or 978/283-7673 for recorded information; www1.shore.net/~hammond). Eccentric inventor John Hays Hammond, Jr., designed the medieval castle, which was constructed of Rockport granite and cost more than $6 million when it was built from 1926 to 1929. Guided tours aren't offered, so you're on your own with a pamphlet to direct you—not the most fulfilling way to explore such a peculiar place. Still, if you fancy the medieval era, you'll definitely enjoy this. It has 85-foot towers, battlements, stained-glass windows, a great hall 60 feet high, and an enclosed "outdoor" pool and courtyard lined with foliage, trees, and medieval artifacts (including the whole wooden

A Whale of an Adventure

The depletion of New England's fishing grounds has led to the rise of another important seagoing industry: whale watching. The waters off the coast of Massachusetts are prime whale-watching territory, and Gloucester is a center of cruises. Stellwagen Bank, which runs from Gloucester to Provincetown about 27 miles east of Boston, is a rich feeding ground for the magnificent mammals. Species spotted in the area are mainly humpback, finback, and minke whales, who dine on sand eels and other fish that gather along the ridge. Naturalists are on board the cruises to point out the various creatures. The whales often perform for their audience by jumping out of the water, and dolphins occasionally join the show. This is not the most time- or cost-effective activity, especially if children are along, but the payoff is (literally and figuratively) huge.

Dress warmly—it's much cooler at sea than in town—and take sunglasses, sunscreen, a hat, rubber-soled shoes, and a camera with plenty of film. If you're prone to motion sickness, take appropriate precautions (ginger, crystallized or in ginger ale, can help alleviate nausea), because you'll be on the open sea for 4 to 6 hours.

Check the local marinas for sailing times, prices ($24 to $26 for adults, less for seniors and children), and reservations, which are always a good idea. This is an extremely competitive business—most companies guarantee sightings, offer a morning and an afternoon cruise as well as deep-sea fishing excursions, honor other firms' coupons, and offer AARP and AAA discounts. In downtown Gloucester, you'll find **Cape Ann Whale Watch** (☎ **800/877-5110** or 978/283-5110; www.caww.com), **Capt. Bill's Whale Watch** (☎ **800/33-WHALE** or 978/283-6995; www.cape-ann.com/captbill.html), and **Seven Seas Whale Watch** (☎ **800/238-1776** or 978/283-1776; www.7seas-whalewatch.com). At the Cape Ann Marina, off Route 133, is **Yankee Whale Watch** (☎ **800/WHALING** or 508/283-0313; www.yankee-fleet.com/whale.htm).

front of a butcher shop). Many 12th-, 13th-, and 14th-century furnishings, tapestries, paintings, and architectural fragments fill the rooms, and the organ (with more than 8,200 pipes) is used for monthly concerts. Admission to the museum is $6 for adults, $5 for seniors and students, $4 for children 4 to 12, free for children under 4. It's open daily Memorial Day through Labor Day from 10am to 5pm, Labor Day through October Thursday through Sunday from 10am to 4pm, and November through May weekends only from 10am to 4pm.

GLOUCESTER

33 miles NE of Boston, 16 miles NE of Salem

The ocean has been Gloucester's lifeblood since long before the first European settlement in 1623. The French explorer Samuel de Champlain called the harbor "Le Beauport" when he came across it in 1604, some 600 years after the Vikings. Its configuration and proximity to good fishing gave it the reputation it enjoys to this day.

On Stacy Boulevard west of downtown Gloucester (which rhymes with "*roster*") is a reminder of the sea's danger. Leonard Craske's bronze statue of the **Gloucester Fisherman,** known as "The Man at the Wheel," bears the inscription "They That Go Down to the Sea in Ships 1623–1923." More than 10,000 fishermen lost their lives

---

Hollywood Minute: The Perfect Storm

The movie version of Sebastian Junger's best-selling book, *The Perfect Storm,* is scheduled to be in theaters by the time you read this. The thrilling but tragic nonfiction account describes (on paper and film) the travails of the Gloucester fishing fleet during the no-name hurricane of 1991. George Clooney, Mark Wahlberg, and their fellow cast members filmed many scenes in Gloucester. A moving re-creation of the memorial service for the crew of the *Andrea Gail* was attended by many of the same people who were at the real-life observance.

Just about any local resident can tell you more and point you toward the **Crow's Nest,** 334 Main St. (☎ **978/281-2965**). If you've read the book, you'll recognize the neighborhood tavern immediately. It's a no-frills place with a horseshoe-shaped bar and a crowd of regulars who seem amused that their favorite hangout is a tourist attraction. The Crow's Nest plays a major role in Junger's story, but its ceilings aren't high enough for it to be a movie set—so the crew built an exact replica nearby.

---

during the city's first 300 years. A statue honoring the women and children who waited for them is in the works.

ESSENTIALS

GETTING THERE   From Salem, follow Route 1A across the bridge to Beverly, pick up Route 127, and take it through Manchester (near, not on, the water) to Gloucester. From Boston, the quickest path is I-93 or Route 1 to Route 128, which runs directly to Gloucester. Route 128 runs mostly inland; if you'd like a little more scenery along the way, take the Manchester exit from Route 128 and continue the rest of the way to Gloucester on Route 127.

The MBTA **commuter rail** (☎ 617/222-3200; www.mbta.com) runs from Boston's North Station. The trip takes about an hour; the round-trip fare is $7.50. The station is across town from downtown, so allow time for getting to the waterfront area. The **Cape Ann Transportation Authority,** or CATA (☎ 978/283-7916), runs buses from town to town on Cape Ann and operates special routes during the summer.

VISITOR INFORMATION   The **area code** is 978. The **Gloucester Tourism Commission,** 22 Poplar St., Gloucester, MA 01930 (☎ **800/649-6839** or 978/281-8865; www1.shore.net/~nya/gloucester.html), operates an excellent Visitors Welcoming Center at Stage Fort Park, off Route 127 near the intersection with Route 133. It's open during the summer daily from 9am to 5pm. The information center run by the **Cape Ann Chamber of Commerce,** 33 Commercial St., Gloucester, MA 01930 (☎ **800/321-0133** or 978/283-1601; www.cape-ann.com/cacc), is open year-round (summer, weekdays 8am to 6pm, Saturday 10am to 6pm, Sunday 10am to 4pm; winter, weekdays 8am to 5pm) and has a helpful staff. Call or write for the chamber's four-color map and brochure.

SPECIAL EVENTS   Gloucester holds summer festivals and street fairs at the drop of a hat. They honor everything from clams to schooners—check while you're planning to see what's up while you're in town. The best-known event is **St. Peter's Fiesta,** a colorful 4-day event at the end of June. The Italian-American fishing colony's festival has more in common with a carnival midway than a religious observation, but

Cape Ann

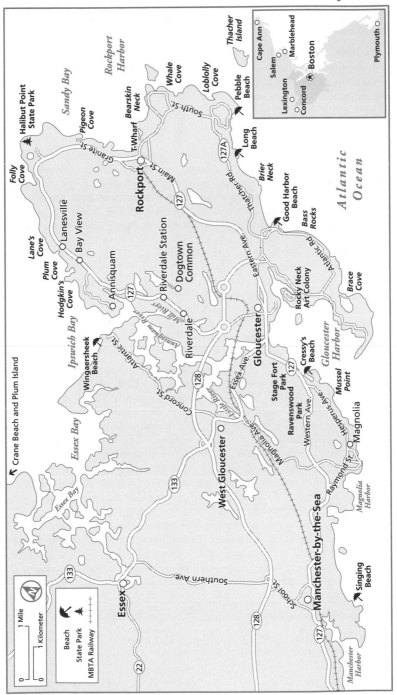

Thacher Island

Cape Ann
Marblehead
Salem
Lexington Boston
Concord
Plymouth

Rockport Harbor

Sandy Bay

Whale Cove
Loblolly Cove
Pebble Beach

Halibut Point State Park
Pigeon Cove

T-Wharf
Bearskin Neck
South St.

Folly Cove

Long Beach
127A

Lanesville
Bay View

Rockport
Main St.
Granite St.
127

Thacher Rd.

Brier Neck
Good Harbor Beach
Bass Rocks

Atlantic Ocean

Lane's Cove
Plum Cove
Hodgkin's Cove

Annisquam

Riverdale Station
Dogtown Common
127

Rocky Neck Art Colony

Brace Cove

Ipswich Bay

Wingaersheek Beach
Atlantic St.
Annisquam River
Mill River

Riverdale

Gloucester
Eastern Ave.

Cressy's Beach
Mussel Point
Gloucester Harbor

Crane Beach and Plum Island

Essex Bay

Concord St.

128

Essex Ave.
Little River

Stage Fort Park
127
Ravenswood Park
Western Ave.
Hesperus Ave.

Magnolia
Magnolia Harbor

Essex Bay

West Gloucester
Magnolia Ave.

133

Raymond St.

Southern Ave.

Manchester-by-the-Sea
Singing Beach

School St.
128
127
Manchester Harbor

133

Essex
22

0 1 Mile
0 1 Kilometer

Beach
State Park
MBTA Railway

263

it's great fun. There are parades, games, music, food, sporting events, and, on Sunday, the blessing of the fleet.

EXPLORING THE TOWN

Business isn't nearly what it once was, but fishing is still Gloucester's leading industry (as your nose will tell you). Tourism is a very close second, and the city is an exceptionally welcoming destination—residents seem genuinely happy to see out-of-towners and to offer directions and insider info. The **"Gloucester Maritime Trail"** brochure, available at visitor information centers, describes four excellent self-guided tours.

To reach East Gloucester, follow signs as you leave downtown, or go directly from Route 128, Exit 9. On East Main Street, you'll see signs for the world-famous **Rocky Neck Art Colony,** the oldest continuously operating art colony in the country. Park in the lot on the tiny causeway and head west along Rocky Neck Avenue, which abounds with studios, galleries, restaurants, and people. The draw is the presence of working artists, not just shops that happen to sell art. Most galleries are open daily in the summer, 10am to 10pm.

The prestigious **North Shore Arts Association,** 197 E. Main St. (☎ 978/283-1857; www.cape-ann.com/nsaa), was founded in 1922 to showcase local artists' work. The exhibits are worth a visit before or after your excursion across the causeway. The building is open late May through October, Monday through Saturday from 10am to 5pm, Sunday from 1 to 5pm. Admission is free.

Stage Fort Park, off Route 127 near the intersection with Route 133, offers an excellent view of the harbor. It's a good spot for a picnic, swimming, or just playing on the cannons in the Revolutionary War fort.

NARRATED CRUISES   The schooner *Thomas E. Lannon* (☎ 978/281-6634; www.schooner.org) is a gorgeous reproduction of a Gloucester fishing vessel. The 65-foot tall ship sails from Seven Seas Wharf, downtown; 2-hour excursions ($25 adults, $22 seniors, $17 children under 17) leave about four times a day from May to October. Reservations are recommended. The company also offers music and dining cruises and "storytelling sails."

Moby Duck Tours (☎ 978/281-3825; www.mobyduck.com) are 55-minute sightseeing expeditions that travel on land before plunging into the water. The amphibious vehicles leave from **Harbor Loop** downtown, where tickets (cash only; $14 adults, $12 seniors, $8 children under 12) are available. They operate weekends from Memorial Day through June, daily from July through Labor Day.

Also at Harbor Loop, you can tour the two-masted schooner *Adventure* (☎ 978/281-8079; www.cape-ann.com/adventure.html), a 121-foot fishing vessel built in Essex in 1926 and currently undergoing extensive restoration. The "living museum," a National Historic Landmark, is open to visitors from Memorial Day to Labor Day, Thursday through Sunday from 10am to 4pm. The suggested donation is $5 adults, $4 children.

✪ **Beauport (Sleeper–McCann House).** 75 Eastern Point Blvd. ☎ **978/283-0800.** www.spnea.org. Guided tour $6 adults, $5.50 seniors, $3 students and children 6–12. Tours on the hour May 15–Sept 15 Mon–Fri 10am–4pm; Sept 16–Oct 15 daily 10am–4pm. Closed Oct 16 to May 14, summer weekends. Take E. Main St. south to Eastern Point Blvd. (a private road), continue ¹/₂ mile to house, park on left.

The Society for the Preservation of New England Antiquities, which operates Beauport, describes it as a "fantasy house," and that's putting it mildly. Interior designer Henry Davis Sleeper used his summer home as a retreat and a repository for his vast collections of American and European decorative arts and antiques. From 1907 to 1934, he decorated the 40 rooms, 26 of which are open to the public, to illustrate literary and historical themes. The entertaining tour concentrates more on the house and rooms in general than on the countless objects on display. You'll see architectural details rescued from other buildings, magnificent arrangements of colored glassware, an early American kitchen, the "Red Indian Room" (with a majestic view of the harbor), and "Strawberry Hill," the master bedroom. Call ahead to see whether there's a special event (such as afternoon tea, a specialty tour, or an evening concert) while you're in town. Note that the house is closed on summer weekends.

Cape Ann Historical Museum. 27 Pleasant St. ☎ **978/283-0455.** Admission $4 adults, $3.50 seniors, $2.50 students, free for children under 6. Mar–Jan Tues–Sat 10am–5pm. Closed Feb. Follow Main St. west through downtown and turn right onto Pleasant St.; the museum is 1 block up on right. Metered parking on street or in lot across street.

This meticulously curated museum makes an excellent introduction to Cape Ann's history and artists. It devotes an entire gallery to the extraordinary work of ☺ **Fitz Hugh Lane,** the Luminist painter whose light-flooded canvases show off the best of his native Gloucester. The nation's single largest collection of his paintings and drawings is here. Other galleries featuring works on paper by 20th-century artists such as Maurice Prendergast and Milton Avery, work by other contemporary artists, and granite-quarrying tools and equipment. On display in the **maritime and fisheries galleries** are entire vessels (including one about the size of a station wagon that actually crossed the Atlantic), exhibits on the fishing industry, ship models, and historic photographs and models of the Gloucester waterfront. The **Capt. Elias Davis House** (1804), decorated and furnished in Federal style with furniture, silver, and porcelains, is part of the museum.

WHERE TO STAY

Atlantis Oceanfront Motor Inn. 125 Atlantic Rd., Gloucester, MA 01930. ☎ **978/283-0014.** Fax 978/281-8994. www.cape-ann.com/atlantis.html. 40 units. TV TEL. Late June–Labor Day $120–$140 double; spring and fall $80–$115 double. Extra person $8. Minimum 2 nights spring and fall weekends, 3 nights holiday and summer weekends. AE, MC, V. Closed Nov to mid-Apr. Follow Rte. 128 to the end (Exit 9, East Gloucester), turn left onto Bass Ave. (Rte. 127A), and follow it ¹/₂ mile. Turn right and follow Atlantic Rd.

This motor inn sits across the street from the water, affording stunning views from every window. That would almost be enough to recommend it, but it also has a heated outdoor pool and a friendly staff. The good-sized guest rooms are decorated in comfortable, contemporary style. Every room has a terrace or balcony and a small table and chairs. The coffee shop on the premises serves breakfast until 11am.

Best Western Bass Rocks Ocean Inn. 107 Atlantic Rd., Gloucester, MA 01930. ☎ **800/528-1234** or 978/283-7600. Fax 978/281-6489. www.bestwestern.com. 48 units. A/C TV TEL. Late Apr–late May $130–$145 double; Memorial Day–late June and early Sept–Oct $140–$170 double; late June–Labor Day $145–$190 double. Extra person $8. Children under 12 free in parents' room. Rollaway $12. Rates include continental breakfast. Minimum 3 nights summer weekends, some spring and fall weekends. AE, CB, DC, DISC, MC, V. Closed Nov to late Apr. Follow Rte. 128 to the end (Exit 9, East Gloucester), turn left onto Bass Ave. (Rte. 127A), and follow it ¹/₂ mile. Turn right and follow Atlantic Rd.

A family operation since 1946, the Bass Rocks Ocean Inn offers modern accommodations in a traditional setting. The spacious guest rooms overlook the ocean from a sprawling, comfortable two-story motel across the road from the rocky shore. A Colonial Revival mansion built in 1899 and known as the "wedding-cake house" holds the office and public areas. The rooftop sundeck, balconies, and heated outdoor pool offer excellent views of the surf. Each guest room has a refrigerator, a balcony or patio, and a king bed or two double beds. In the afternoon, coffee, tea, lemonade, and chocolate-chip cookies are offered. Bicycles, a billiard room, and the library are at the disposal of the guests.

WHERE TO DINE

See "A Detour to Essex," above, for information about the celebrated **Woodman's of Essex,** which is about 20 minutes from downtown Gloucester.

Boulevard Oceanview Restaurant. 25 Western Ave. (Stacy Blvd.). ☎ **978/281-2949.** Reservations recommended at dinner in summer. Sandwiches $3–$7; main courses $6.50–$15; lobster priced daily. DISC, MC, V. Summer daily 11am–10pm; winter daily 11am–9:30pm. PORTUGUESE/SEAFOOD.

This is a friendly, unassuming neighborhood place in a high-tourist-traffic location. Across the street from the waterfront promenade just outside downtown, it's a diner-like spot with water views from the front windows and the small deck. It serves ultra-fresh seafood (crane your neck and you can almost see the processing plants) and lunch-counter sandwiches. Try "Seafood Portuguese style"—shrimp *a la plancha* (in irresistible lemon-butter sauce) and *sao* style (in garlic and wine sauce), and several unusual casseroles. The hostess and I were chatting about where to send visitors to eat in Gloucester when a waitress chimed in: "Send 'em here, dear," she said. "It's the best food they'll ever eat." Even if that's not strictly true, it's good to know an employee thinks so.

The Gull Restaurant. 75 Essex Ave. (Rte. 133), at Cape Ann Marina. ☎ **978/281-6060.** Reservations recommended for parties of 8 or more. Main courses $5–$13 at lunch, $8–$22 at dinner; breakfast $3.45–$7.95. DISC, MC, V. Daily late Apr–Oct 6am–9pm. Closed Nov–late Apr. Take Rte. 133 west from intersection with Rte. 127, or take Rte. 133 east from Rte. 128. SEAFOOD/AMERICAN.

Floor-to-ceiling windows show off the Annisquam River from almost every seat at the Gull. The big, friendly restaurant is known for prime rib as well as seafood. It draws locals, visitors, boaters, and families for large portions at reasonable prices. The seafood chowder is famous (with good reason), appetizers tend toward bar food, and fish is available in just about any variety and style. Ask about daily specials, which run from simple lobster (market price) to sophisticated fish and meat dishes. At lunch, there's an extensive sandwich menu.

ROCKPORT

40 miles NE of Boston, 7 miles N of Gloucester

This lovely little town at the tip of Cape Ann was settled in 1690. Over the years it has been an active fishing port, a center of granite excavation and cutting, and a thriving summer community whose specialty seems to be selling fudge and refrigerator magnets to out-of-towners.

There's more to Rockport than just gift shops. It's popular with photographers, sculptors, jewelry designers, and painters—Winslow Homer is only one of the famous artists who have captured the local color. For every year-round resident who seems genuinely startled when legions of people with cameras around their necks descend on Rockport each June, there are dozens who are proud to show off their town.

ESSENTIALS

GETTING THERE   Rockport is north of Gloucester along Route 127 or 127A. At the end of Route 128, turn left at the signs for Rockport to take 127, which is shorter but more commercial. To take 127A, which runs along the east coast of Cape Ann, continue on Route 128 until you see the sign for East Gloucester and turn left.

The MBTA **commuter rail** (☎ 617/222-3200; www.mbta.com) runs from Boston's North Station. The trip takes 60 to 70 minutes, and the round-trip fare is $8. The station is about 6 blocks from the downtown waterfront. The **Cape Ann Transportation Authority,** or CATA (☎ 978/283-7916), runs buses from town to town on Cape Ann.

VISITOR INFORMATION   The **area code** is 978. The **Rockport Chamber of Commerce and Board of Trade,** 3 Main St. (☎ 978/546-6575; www.rockportusa. com), is open daily in summer 9am to 5pm, and winter weekdays 10am to 4pm. The chamber also operates an information booth on Upper Main Street (Route 127) that's open from mid-May to mid-October. It's about a mile from the town line and a mile from downtown—look for the WELCOME TO ROCKPORT sign. At either location, ask for the pamphlet "Rockport: A Walking Guide," which has a good map and descriptions of three short walking tours. Out of season, Rockport closes up almost as tight as an Essex clam; from January through mid-April, it's pretty but somewhat desolate.

In the summer, if you can schedule only one weekday trip, make it this one. For traffic and congestion, downtown Boston has nothing on Rockport on a Saturday afternoon. If you can't park downtown, there's a parking lot on Upper Main Street (Route 127) on weekends. Parking from 11am to 6pm costs $6 to $7, and a free shuttle takes you downtown and back. The Cape Ann Transportation Authority (see above) also runs within the town.

SPECIAL EVENTS   The **Rockport Chamber Music Festival** (☎ 978/546-7391) takes place over several weeks in June and early July at the Rockport Arts Association, 12 Main St. In addition to performances and family concerts, events include lectures and discussions. The annual **Christmas pageant,** on Main Street in early December, is a crowded, kid-friendly event with carol singing and live animals.

EXPLORING THE TOWN

The most famous example of what to see in Rockport has something of an "Emperor's New Clothes" aura—it's a wooden fish warehouse on the town wharf, or T-Wharf, in the harbor. The barn-red shack known as **Motif No. 1** is the most frequently painted and photographed object in a town filled with lovely buildings and surrounded by rocky coastline. The color certainly catches the eye in the neutrals of the surrounding seascape, but you might find yourself wondering what the big deal is. Originally constructed in 1884 and destroyed during the blizzard of 1978, Motif No. 1 was rebuilt using donations from the local community and tourists. It stands on the same pier, duplicated in every detail, and reinforced to withstand storms.

Nearby is a phenomenon whose popularity is easier to explain. **Bearskin Neck,** named after an unfortunate ursine visitor who drowned and washed ashore in 1800, has perhaps the highest concentration of gift shops anywhere. It's a narrow peninsula with one main street (South Road) and several alleys lined—crammed, really—with galleries, snack bars, antiques shops, and ancient houses. Dozens of little shops stock clothes, gifts, toys, souvenirs, inexpensive novelties, and expensive handmade crafts and paintings.

More than two dozen art galleries display the works of local and nationally known artists. The **Rockport Art Association,** 12 Main St. (☎ 978/546-6604), sponsors major exhibitions and special shows throughout the year. It's open daily year-round.

To get a sense of the power of the sea in this part of the world, take Route 127 north of town to the very tip of Cape Ann. ✪ **Halibut Point State Park** (☎ 978/ 546-2997; www.state.ma.us/dem/parks/halb.htm) has a staffed visitor center, walking trails, tidal pools, and water-filled quarries. Swimming, however, is absolutely forbidden. You can climb around on giant boulders on the rocky beach, or climb to the top of the Second World War observation tower. Guided tours ($2.50 per person) run on Saturday mornings in the summer, and this is a great place just to wander around and admire the scenery. On a clear day, you can see Maine.

If the mansions of Gloucester are too plush for you, or if you want some recycling tips, visit the **Paper House,** 52 Pigeon Hill St., Pigeon Cove (☎ **978/546-2629**). It was built in 1922 entirely out of 100,000 newspapers—walls, furniture, even a piano. Every item is made from papers of a different period. It's open daily May through October from 10am to 5pm. Admission is $1.50 for adults, $1 for children. Follow Route 127 north out of downtown about three-quarters of a mile until you see signs at Curtis Street pointing to the left.

Don't fight the inexplicable craving for fudge that overwhelms otherwise mild-mannered travelers when they get their first whiff of salt water. Give in to temptation, then watch taffy being made at **Tuck's Candy Factory,** 7 Dock Sq. (☎ **800/569-2767** or 978/546-6352), a local landmark since the 1920s.

WHERE TO STAY

When Rockport is busy, it's very busy, and when it's not, it's practically empty. Make summer reservations well in advance, or cross your fingers and call the Chamber of Commerce to ask about cancellations.

If you're not driving, most innkeepers will arrange for guests to be picked up at the train station; be sure to ask about this service when you reserve.

Captain's Bounty Motor Inn. 1 Beach St., Rockport, MA 01966. ☎ **978/546-9557.** www.cape-ann.com/capt-bounty. 24 units. TV TEL. May to mid-June $78 double, $82 efficiency, $88 efficiency suite; mid-June to early Sept $105 double, $120 efficiency, $130 efficiency suite; early Sept–Oct $85 double, $90 efficiency, $95 efficiency suite. Extra person $10; $5 for each child over 5. All rates based on double occupancy. Minimum 2 nights weekends, 3 nights holiday weekends. DISC, MC, V. Closed Nov–Apr.

This modern, well-maintained motor inn is on the water. In fact, it's almost *in* the water, and nearly as close to the center of town as to the harbor. Each rather plain room in the three-story building overlooks the water and has its own balcony and sliding glass door. Ocean breezes provide natural air-conditioning. Although it's hardly plush, and the pricing structure is a bit peculiar (note the charge for children), you can't beat the location. Rooms are spacious and soundproofed, and kitchenette units are available.

Inn on Cove Hill. 37 Mt. Pleasant St., Rockport, MA 01966. ☎ **888/546-2701** or 978/ 546-2701. www.cape-ann.com/covehill. 11 units, 9 with bathroom (4 with shower only, 1 with tub only). A/C TV. $68–$130 double with private bathroom, $50 double with shared bathroom. Extra person $25. Rates include continental breakfast. Minimum 3 nights July–Oct weekends, 2 nights June weekends. MC, V. Closed mid-Oct to mid-Apr. Children not accepted.

This three-story inn was built in 1791 using the proceeds of pirates' gold found nearby. It's an attractive Federal-style home just 2 blocks from the head of the town wharf. Although it's close to downtown, the inn is set back from the road and has a delightful hideaway feel. Innkeepers Marjorie and John Pratt have decorated the guest rooms in period style, with at least one antique piece in each. Most rooms have colonial furnishings and handmade quilts, and some have canopy beds. In warm weather, breakfast (with home-baked breads and muffins) is served on china at the garden tables; in inclement weather, breakfast in bed is served on individual trays.

Peg Leg Inn. 2 King St., Rockport, MA 01966. ☎ **800/346-2352** or 978/546-2352. www.cape-ann.com/pegleg. 33 units (some with shower only). TV. Mid-June to Labor Day, holiday and fall weekends $90–$150 double; $160 2-bedroom unit. Extra person $10. Rates include continental breakfast. Off-season discounts available. Minimum 2 nights summer weekends, 3 nights holiday weekends. AE, MC, V. Closed Nov–Mar.

The Peg Leg Inn consists of five early American houses with front porches, attractive living rooms, and well-kept flower-bordered lawns that run down to the ocean's edge. It's not luxurious, but it is convenient and comfortable. Rooms are good-sized and neatly furnished in colonial style, and some have excellent ocean views. Breakfast is served in the main building's dining room. Guests may use the sandy beach across the road.

Yankee Clipper Inn. 96 Granite St. (Rte. 127), P.O. Box 2399, Rockport, MA 01966. ☎ **800/545-3699** or 978/546-3407. Fax 978/546-9730. www.yankeeclipperinn.com. 29 units (some with shower only). A/C TV TEL. Memorial Day to mid-Oct $109–$299 double; weekends spring and fall $131–$169 double; weeknights spring and fall $104–$130 double. Extra person $26. Rates include full breakfast in summer, continental breakfast spring and fall. Minimum 2 nights weekends. AE, DISC, MC, V. Closed mid-Dec to mid-Mar.

Just north of town, the most luxurious destination in Rockport sits on extensive lawns overlooking the sea. The three-story main inn—with its Georgian architecture, outdoor heated saltwater pool (open seasonally), and rooms with private balconies—is the most beautiful of the four buildings. All rooms contain hair dryers and are attractively furnished, with plenty of ruffles and florals. Most are large, and many have views of the water; the least expensive offer neither, but you might not mind feeling like a poor relation at a place this nice. There's a concierge, and room service is available at breakfast and dinner in the summer. Many common rooms, notably the **Veranda** restaurant, face the water. Reservations (☎ **978/546-7795**) are required of guests as well as the public.

WHERE TO DINE

Rockport is a "dry" community—no alcoholic beverages can be sold or served—but you can bring your own bottle, sometimes subject to a corking fee.

On Bearskin Neck, the **Portside Chowder House** (☎ **978/546-7045**) serves Southern barbecue—no, seriously, it serves delicious fresh chowder by the cup, pint, and quart. There's also a small dining room with partial water views.

Brackett's Oceanview Restaurant. 29 Main St. ☎ **978/546-2797**. www.bracketts.com. Reservations recommended at dinner. Main courses $6–$15. AE, DC, DISC, MC, V. Mid-Apr to Memorial Day, Thurs–Sun 11:30am–8pm; Memorial Day–Oct, Sun–Fri 11:30am–8pm, Sat 11:30am–9pm. Closed Nov to mid-Apr. SEAFOOD/AMERICAN.

The dining room at Brackett's has a gorgeous view of the water you glimpsed between buildings as you walked along Main Street. The nautical decor suits the seafood-intensive menu, which offers enough variety to make this a good choice for families—burgers are always available. The service is friendly and the fresh seafood quite good, if not particularly exciting. Try the moist, plump codfish cakes if you're looking for a traditional New England dish, or something with Cajun spices for a little variety. The most exciting offerings are on the extensive dessert menu, where anything homemade is a great choice.

✪ **The Greenery.** 15 Dock Sq. ☎ **978/546-9593**. Reservations recommended at dinner. Main courses $6.25–$12 at lunch, $9.25–$22 at dinner; breakfast items $1.25–$7. AE, CB, DC, DISC, MC, V. Apr–Dec daily 7am–11pm. Closed Jan–Mar. SEAFOOD/AMERICAN.

This is the best restaurant in Rockport, a place that could (but doesn't) get away with serving so-so food because of its great location at the head of Bearskin Neck. The cafe at the front gives no hint that the dining rooms boast great views of the harbor. The terrific food ranges from crab salad quiche at lunch to lobster at dinner to steamers and fresh-caught fish anytime, and the salad bar is available on its own or with many entrees. All baking is done in-house, which explains the lines at the front counter for muffins and pastries. When the restaurant is busy, the cheerful service sometimes drags. This is a good place to launch a picnic lunch on the beach, and an equally good spot for lingering over coffee and a delectable dessert and watching the action around the harbor.

My Place By-the-Sea. 68 South Rd., Bearskin Neck. ☎ **978/546-9667.** Reservations recommended at dinner; accepted same day after noon. Main courses $7–$13 at lunch; $15–$22 at dinner. AE, CB, DC, DISC, JCB, MC, V. Apr–Nov daily 11:30am–9:30pm. Closed Dec–Mar. SEAFOOD.

The lure of My Place By-the-Sea is its location at the very end of Bearskin Neck, where you'll find Rockport's only outdoor oceanfront deck. There are excellent views of Sandy Bay from the two decks and shaded patio. The menu is reliable, with many options dictated by the daily catch. The baked fish and seafood pasta entrees are good choices, and you can also have chicken or beef.

Peg Leg. 18 Beach St. ☎ **978/546-3038.** Reservations recommended. Main courses $7–$19; children's menu $7. AE, CB, DC, MC, V. Late Apr–late Oct Mon–Sat 5:30–9pm; Sun noon–8:30pm. Closed Nov to late Apr. AMERICAN/SEAFOOD.

This pleasant restaurant serves tasty, uncomplicated food in a gardenlike setting, with plants and flowers all around. The romantic greenhouse is behind the cozy main restaurant. Entrees include the house special chicken pie, seafood "pies" (casseroles), fresh fish, steaks, and lobster. All baking is done on the premises, and bread baskets always include sweet rolls.

3 Plymouth

40 miles SE of Boston

Everyone educated in the United States knows at least a little about Plymouth—about how the Pilgrims, fleeing religious persecution, left Europe on the *Mayflower* and landed at Plymouth Rock in December 1620. Many also know that the Pilgrims endured disease and privation, and that just 51 people from the original group of 102 celebrated the first Thanksgiving in 1621 with Squanto, a Pawtuxet Indian associated with the Wampanoags, and his cohorts.

What you won't know until you visit is how small everything was. The *Mayflower* (a replica) seems perilously tiny, and when you contemplate how dangerous life was at the time, it's hard not to marvel at the settlers' accomplishments.

Capt. John Smith sailed along the coast of what he named "New England" in 1614, calling the mainland opposite Cape Cod "Plymouth." The *Mayflower* passengers had secured the title for a tract of land near the mouth of the Hudson River in "Northern Virginia" from the London Virginia Company. In exchange for their passage to the New World, they promised to work the land for the company for 7 years.

On November 11, 1620, rough weather and high seas forced them to make for Cape Cod Bay and anchor there, at Provincetown. On December 16, Provincetown having proven an unsatisfactory location, the weary travelers landed at Plymouth. The captain then announced that they had found a safe harbor, and he refused to continue to their

Plymouth

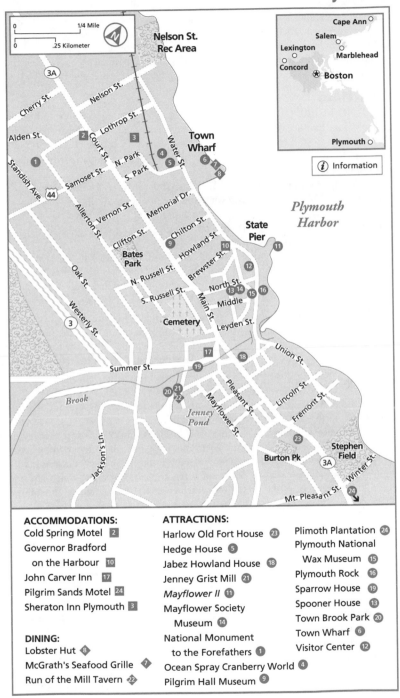

ACCOMMODATIONS:
Cold Spring Motel **2**
Governor Bradford
  on the Harbour **10**
John Carver Inn **17**
Pilgrim Sands Motel **24**
Sheraton Inn Plymouth **3**

DINING:
Lobster Hut **8**
McGrath's Seafood Grille **7**
Run of the Mill Tavern **22**

ATTRACTIONS:
Harlow Old Fort House **23**
Hedge House **5**
Jabez Howland House **18**
Jenney Grist Mill **21**
Mayflower II **11**
Mayflower Society
  Museum **14**
National Monument
  to the Forefathers **1**
Ocean Spray Cranberry World **4**
Pilgrim Hall Museum **9**

Plimoth Plantation **24**
Plymouth National
  Wax Museum **15**
Plymouth Rock **16**
Sparrow House **19**
Spooner House **13**
Town Brook Park **20**
Town Wharf **6**
Visitor Center **12**

original destination. They had no option but to settle in New England. With no one to command them, their contract with the London Virginia Company became void, and they were left on their own to begin life in a new world.

Today, Plymouth is a manageable day-trip destination, particularly enjoyable if you're traveling with children. It also makes a good stop between Boston and Cape Cod.

ESSENTIALS

GETTING THERE By car, follow the Southeast Expressway (I-93) from Boston to Route 3. Take Exit 6A, then Route 44 east, and follow signs to the historic attractions. The trip from Boston takes 45 to 55 minutes if it's not rush hour. Take Exit 5 to the **Regional Information Complex** for maps, brochures, and information. To go directly to **Plimoth Plantation,** take Exit 4.

The MBTA **commuter rail** (☎ 617/222-3200; www.mbta.com) serves Cordage Park, on Route 3A north of downtown, from South Station during the day on weekdays and all day on weekends. (At peak commuting times, service is to nearby Kingston.) The round-trip fare is $8. The 1-hour trip is especially pleasant when the fall foliage and cranberry bogs are at their colorful peak.

Plymouth & Brockton **buses** (☎ 617/773-9401 or 508/746-0378; www.p-b. com) leave from South Station and Park Square, near the Theater District. The fare is $8 one-way, $14 round-trip. You can also make connections at Logan Airport, where buses take on passengers at all terminals ($13 one-way, $23 round-trip).

VISITOR INFORMATION The **area code** is 508. If you haven't visited the Regional Information Complex, you'll want to stop in and at least pick up a map at the **Visitor Center** (☎ 508/747-7525), open seasonally at 130 Water St., across from the town pier. To plan ahead, contact **Destination Plymouth** (also known as Plymouth Visitor Information), P.O. Box ROCK, Plymouth, MA 02361 (☎ **800/ USA-1620** or 508/747-7525; www.visit-plymouth.com).

GETTING AROUND The downtown attractions are accessible on foot. A shallow hill leads from the center of town to the waterfront.

Plymouth Rock Trolley, 22 Main St. (☎ **508/747-3419**), offers a narrated tour and unlimited reboarding daily from Memorial Day through October and weekends through Thanksgiving. It serves downtown and Plimoth Plantation. Tickets are $7 for adults, $3 for children 3 to 12. Trolley markers indicate the stops, which are served every 20 minutes (except the plantation, which is served once an hour in the summer).

SEEING THE SIGHTS

The logical place to begin (good luck talking children out of it) is where the Pilgrims first set foot—at ✪ **Plymouth Rock.** The rock, accepted as the landing place of the *Mayflower* passengers, was originally 15 feet long and 3 feet wide. It was moved on the eve of the Revolution and several times thereafter before assuming its present permanent position at tide level, where winter storms still break over it as they did in Pilgrim days. The Colonial Dames of America commissioned the portico around the rock, designed by McKim, Mead & White and erected in 1920. The rock itself isn't much to look at, but the accompanying descriptions are interesting, and the sense of history is curiously impressive.

To get away from the bustle of the waterfront, make your way to **Town Brook Park,** at Jenney Pond, across Summer Street from the John Carver Inn. Near the tree-bordered pond is the **Jenney Grist Mill,** 6 Spring Lane (☎ **508/747-3715;** admission $2.50 adults, $2 children 5 to 12). It's a working museum where you can see a reconstructed water-powered mill that operates in the summer, daily from 10am to

5pm. The specialty shops in the complex, including the excellent ice-cream shop, are open year-round, daily from 10am to 6pm. Ducks and geese live in the pond, and there's room to run around.

GUIDED TOURS   To put yourself in the Pilgrims' footsteps, take a **Colonial Lantern Tour** offered by New World Tours, 35 North St. (☎ **800/698-5636** or 508/747-4161; www.lanterntours.com). Participants carry pierced-tin lanterns on a 90-minute walking tour of the original settlement under the direction of a knowledgeable guide. It might seem a bit hokey at first, but it's fascinating. Tours run nightly from April through Thanksgiving. The standard history tour leaves the New World office at 7:30pm; the "Ghostly Haunts & Legends" tour leaves from the lobby of the John Carver Inn, 25 Summer St., at 9pm. Tickets are $9 for adults, $7 for children; reservations are recommended.

Narrated **cruises** run from April or May through November. **Splashdown Amphibious Tours** (☎ **508/747-7658**; www.ducktoursplymouth.com) take you around town on land and water. The 1-hour excursions leave from two stops on Water Street—Harbor Place, near the Governor Bradford motor inn, and Village Landing, near the Sheraton—and wind up in the harbor. They cost $15 for adults, $9 for children under 12, $3 for children under 3. **Capt. John Boats,** Town Wharf (☎ **508/ 746-2643**; www.captjohn.com), offers several tours. The most eye-catching option is the *Pilgrim Belle* paddlewheeler. Its 75-minute narrated tours of the harbor ($9 adults, $7 seniors, $6 children) leave from State Pier; dining and entertainment cruises are also available.

Mayflower II. State Pier. ☎ **508/746-1622.** www.plimoth.org. Admission $6.50 adults, $4 children 6–12. *Mayflower II* and Plimoth Plantation admission $19 adults, $17 seniors, $11 children 6–12. Both free for children under 6. Apr–Nov daily 9am–5pm.

Berthed a few steps from Plymouth Rock, *Mayflower II* is a full-scale reproduction of the type of ship that brought the Pilgrims from England to America in 1620. Even at full scale, the 106 ½-foot vessel, constructed in England from 1955 to 1957, seems remarkably small. Although little technical information about the original *Mayflower* survives, William A. Baker, designer of *Mayflower II,* incorporated the few references in Governor Bradford's account of the voyage with other research to re-create the ship as authentically as possible.

Costumed guides provide first-person interpretive narratives about the vessel and voyage. Displays describe and illustrate the voyage and the Pilgrims' experience, including 17th-century navigation techniques, and the history of the *Mayflower II.* The vessel underwent extensive reconstruction and renovation from 1997 to 1999. Plimoth Plantation (see below), which is 3 miles south of the ship, owns and maintains the vessel. Alongside it are museum shops that replicate early Pilgrim dwellings.

Pilgrim Hall Museum. 75 Court St. ☎ **508/746-1620.** www.pilgrimhall.org. Admission $5 adults, $4.50 seniors and AAA members, $3 children 5–17. Feb–Dec daily 9:30am–4:30pm. Closed Dec 25. From Plymouth Rock, walk north on Water St. and up the hill on Chilton St.

This is a great place to get a sense of the day-to-day lives of Plymouth's first European residents. Many original possessions of the early Pilgrims and their descendants are on display, including an uncomfortable chair that belonged to William Brewster (you'll feel just how uncomfortable if you sit in the adjacent replica), one of Myles Standish's swords, and Governor Bradford's Bible. Regularly changing exhibits explore aspects of the settlers' lives, such as home construction or the history of prominent families. Among the permanent exhibits is the skeleton of the *Sparrow-Hawk,* a ship wrecked on Cape Cod in 1626 that lay buried in the sand until 1863. It's even smaller than the *Mayflower II*. Built in 1824, the Pilgrim Hall Museum is the oldest public museum in the United States.

Plimoth Plantation. Rte. 3. ☎ **508/746-1622.** www.plimoth.org. Admission $16 adults, $9 children 6–12. Plimoth Plantation and *Mayflower II* admission $19 adults, $17 seniors, $11 children 6–12. Both free for children under 6. Apr–Nov daily 9am–5pm. From Rte. 3, take Exit 4, Plimoth Plantation Hwy.

Allow at least half a day to explore this re-creation of the 1627 Pilgrim village, which children and adults find equally interesting. You enter by the hilltop fort that protects the villagers and walk down the hill to the farm area, visiting homes and gardens constructed with careful attention to historic detail. Once you get over the feeling that the whole operation is a bit strange (we heard someone mention Pompeii), it's great fun to talk to the "Pilgrims." They're actors who, in speech, dress, and manner, assume the personalities of members of the original community. You can watch them framing a house, splitting wood, shearing sheep, preserving foodstuffs, or cooking a pot of fish stew over an open hearth, all as it was done in the 1600s. They use only the tools and cookware available then. Sometimes you can join the activities—perhaps planting, harvesting, witnessing a trial, or visiting a wedding party. Wear comfortable shoes, because you'll be walking a lot, and the plantation isn't paved.

The community is as accurate as research can make it. Accounts of the original Pilgrim colony were combined with archaeological research, old records, and the history written by the Pilgrims' leader, William Bradford (who often used the spelling "Plimoth" for the settlement). There are daily militia drills with matchlock muskets that are fired to demonstrate the community's defense system. In fact, little defense was needed, because the Native Americans were friendly. Local tribes included the Wampanoags, who are represented near the village at **Hobbamock's Homesite** (included in plantation admission). Members of the museum staff show off native foodstuffs, agricultural practices, and crafts.

At the main entrance, you'll find two modern buildings with an interesting orientation show, exhibits, a gift shop, a bookstore, and a cafeteria. A new **lunch** program offers seasonal menus of 17th-century-style food. Buy tickets ($14.95 adults, $9.95 children under 12) when you arrive. There's also a picnic area. Check in advance for schedules of special events, lectures, and workshops.

✪ **Plymouth National Wax Museum.** 16 Carver St. ☎ **508/746-6468.** Admission $6 adults, $5.50 seniors, $2.75 children 5–12, free for children under 5 accompanied by parents. Daily Mar–May and Nov 9am–5pm; June and Sept–Oct 9am–7pm; July–Aug 9am–9pm. Closed Dec–Feb. From Plymouth Rock, turn around and walk up the hill or the steps.

Adults who visited this museum as children can still tell you all about the Pilgrims. The galleries hold more than 180 life-size figures arranged in scenes. Dramatic soundtracks tell the story of the move to Holland to escape persecution in England, the harrowing trip across the ocean, the first Thanksgiving, and even the tale of Myles Standish, Priscilla Mullins, and John Alden. This museum is a must if children are in your party, and adults will enjoy it, too. On the hill outside is a monument at the gravesite of the Pilgrims who died during the settlement's first winter.

Ocean Spray Cranberry World. 158 Water St. ☎ **508/747-2350.** Free admission. May–Nov daily 9:30am–5pm. Guided tours available; call for reservations. From Plymouth Rock, walk north along the waterfront.

Cranberries aren't just for Thanksgiving dinner, as this interesting center will remind you. Displays include outdoor demonstration bogs, antique harvesting tools, a scale model of a cranberry farm, and interactive exhibits. There are daily cooking demonstrations and free cranberry refreshments. September and October are harvest time.

THE HISTORIC HOUSES

Plymouth's historic homes show how styles of architecture and furnishings have changed since the 1600s. Costumed guides explain the homemaking and crafts of earlier generations. Most of the houses are open Memorial Day weekend through Columbus Day, during Thanksgiving celebrations, and around Christmas; call for schedules.

If you're sightseeing with children, pretend the next sentence is written in capital letters: Unless all of you have a high tolerance for house tours, pick just one or two. Each tour has something to recommend it; the Sparrow and Howland houses are most interesting for those curious about the original settlers.

Six homes are open to visitors: the 1640 **Sparrow House,** 42 Summer St. (☎ **508/ 747-1240;** admission $1); the 1666 **Jabez Howland House,** 33 Sandwich St. (☎ **508/746-9590;** $3 adults, 75¢ children 6 to 12); the 1677 **Harlow Old Fort House,** 119 Sandwich St. (☎ **508/746-0012;** $3 adults, 75¢ children 6 to 12); the 1749 **Spooner House,** 27 North St. (☎ **508/746-0012;** $3 adults, 75¢ children 6 to 12); the 1754 **Mayflower Society Museum,** 4 Winslow St. (☎ **508/746-2590;** $2.50 adults, 75¢ children 6 to 12); and the 1809 **Hedge House,** 126 Water St. (☎ **508/746-0012;** $3 adults, 75¢ children 6 to 12).

WHERE TO STAY

On busy summer weekends, it's not unusual for every room in town to be taken. Make reservations well in advance.

✪ **Cold Spring Motel.** 188 Court St. (Rte. 3A), Plymouth, MA 02360. ☎ **800/678-8667** or 508/746-2222. Fax 508/746-2744. www.coldspringmotel.com. 31 units (some with shower only), 2 two-bedroom cottages. A/C TV TEL. $69–$109 double; $99–$139 suite; $89–$119 cottage. Extra person $10. Off-season discounts available. Mid-May to Oct rates include continental breakfast. AE, DISC, MC, V. Closed Dec–Mar.

Convenient to downtown and the historic sights, this pleasant, fastidiously maintained motel and the adjacent cottages surround a nicely landscaped lawn. Rooms contain hair dryers and coffeemakers, and are big enough for a family to spread out. The location, a bit removed from the water, makes the Cold Spring a great deal. The two-story building is 2 blocks inland, set back from the street in a quiet part of town.

Governor Bradford on the Harbour. 98 Water St., Plymouth, MA 02360. ☎ **800/ 332-1620** or 508/746-6200. Fax 508/747-3032. www.governorbradford.com. 94 units (some with shower only). A/C TV TEL. $89–$139 double. Extra person $10. Children under 16 free in parents' room. Off-season and AAA discounts available. AE, DC, DISC, MC, V.

This well-maintained three-story motor inn is across the street from the waterfront and only a block from Plymouth Rock, the *Mayflower II,* and the center of town. Each attractively decorated room has two double beds, modern furnishings, a refrigerator, and a coffeemaker. More expensive units are higher up and have clearer water views. There are a small heated outdoor pool and coin laundry facilities.

John Carver Inn. 25 Summer St., Plymouth, MA 02360. ☎ **800/274-1620** or 508/746-7100. Fax 508/746-8299. www.johncarverinn.com. 85 units. A/C TV TEL. Mid-Apr to mid-June and mid-Oct to Nov $99–$139 double, $189–$209 suite; mid-June to mid-Oct $119–$159 double, $209–$239 suite; Dec to mid-Apr $89–$119 double, $169–$189 suite. Extra person $10. Rollaway $10. Cribs free. Children under 19 free in parents' room. Packages and senior and AAA discounts available. AE, CB, DC, DISC, MC, V.

A three-story colonial-style building with a landmark portico, this hotel offers comfortable, modern accommodations and plenty of amenities, including room service and meeting facilities. The good-sized guest rooms are regularly renovated and decorated in colonial style. A recent overhaul added six fireplace suites and a fitness center. There's a large outdoor pool and a new indoor "theme pool," with a water slide and Pilgrim ship model. The inn is within walking distance of the main attractions, and the staff is friendly and helpful. Dry-cleaning and laundry service is available. A **Hearth 'n' Kettle** restaurant is on the premises.

Pilgrim Sands Motel. 150 Warren Ave. (Rte. 3A), Plymouth, MA 02360. ☎ **800/ 729-SANDS** or 508/747-0900. Fax 508/746-8066. www.pilgrimsands.com. 64 units. A/C TV TEL. Summer $105–$140 double, spring and early fall $90–$118 double, Apr and late fall $70–$92 double, Dec–Mar $60–$82 double; $100–$200 suite all year. Extra person $6–$8. Minimum 2 nights holiday weekends. Rates may be higher on holiday weekends. AE, CB, DC, DISC, MC, V.

This attractive motel is on a private beach 3 miles south of town, within walking distance of Plimoth Plantation. If you want to avoid the bustle of downtown and still be near the water, it's an excellent choice. The good-sized, modern units have individual climate control and tasteful furnishings; three are accessible for travelers with disabilities. If you can swing it, book a beachfront room—the view is worth the money. In the summer, guests have access to the sundeck, whirlpool spa, and outdoor and indoor swimming pools. Most rooms have two double or queen beds, and many have refrigerators. They're divided into smoking and nonsmoking wings. There's a coffee shop on the premises.

Sheraton Inn Plymouth. 180 Water St., Plymouth, MA 02360. ☎ **800/325-3535** or 508/747-4900. Fax 508/746-2609. www.sheratonplymouth.com. 175 units. A/C TV TEL. Apr–Oct $115–$225 double; Nov–Mar $100–$175 double. Extra person $15. Children under 18 free in parents' room. AE, CB, DC, DISC, JCB, MC, V.

If you need the amenities of a chain and want to be near the historic sights, this is your only choice—and happily, it's a good one. The four-story hotel sits on a hill across the street from the waterfront. Rooms are tastefully furnished in contemporary style and have climate control and in-room movies. Some rooms have small balconies that overlook the indoor swimming pool and whirlpool. The hotel has an exercise room, a business center and conference rooms, room service until 11pm, weekday newspaper delivery, dry-cleaning and laundry service, a restaurant, and a pub. Rooms for travelers with disabilities are available.

WHERE TO DINE

Lobster Hut. Town Wharf. ☎ **508/746-2270.** Reservations not accepted. Luncheon specials $5–$8; main courses $6–$14; sandwiches $3–$7; lobster priced daily. MC, V. Summer daily 11am–9pm; winter daily 11am–7pm. Closed Jan. SEAFOOD.

The Lobster Hut is a self-service restaurant with a great view. Order and pick up at the counter, then take your food to an indoor table or out onto the large deck that overlooks the bay. To start, try clam chowder or lobster bisque. The seafood "rolls" (hot dog buns with your choice of filling) are excellent. The long list of fried seafood includes clams, scallops, shrimp, and haddock. There are also boiled and steamed items, burgers, chicken tenders—and lobster. Beer and wine are served, but only with meals.

McGrath's Seafood Grille. Town Wharf. ☎ **508/746-9751.** Reservations recommended at dinner. Main courses $10–$15. AE, DC, DISC, MC, V. Daily 11:30am–9:30pm. Closed Mon in winter. SEAFOOD.

McGrath's is a big, busy place, popular with families, local businesspeople, and tour groups. Besides fish and seafood dinners, the extensive menu features poultry (including turkey, of course), prime rib, and sandwiches. Ask for a table overlooking the water, because the room facing inland is on the gloomy side, and be sure you're in good company because service can be slow.

Run of the Mill Tavern. Jenney Grist Mill Village, off Summer St. ☎ **508/830-1262.** Reservations not accepted. Main courses $6–$12; children's menu $3–$3.50. AE, MC, V. Sun–Thurs 11:30am–10pm; Fri–Sat 11:30am–11pm. Bar closes at 1am. AMERICAN.

This friendly restaurant sits 3 blocks inland, across from Town Brook Park. You won't mind not having a water view—the food is not only tasty but also reasonably priced, and the wood-paneled tavern is a comfortable destination. The unconventional clam chowder, made with red potatoes, is fantastic. Other appetizers include nachos, potato skins, buffalo wings, and mushrooms. Entrees are well-prepared versions of familiar meat, chicken, and fish dishes, plus sandwiches, burgers, and fresh seafood specials (fried, broiled, or baked).

Appendix:
Boston in Depth

Boston embodies contrasts and contradictions—it's blue blood and blue collar, Yankee and Irish, home to Brahmin bankers and budget-conscious graduate students. It's a proud seaport whose harbor is being reclaimed from crippling pollution. It's home to the country's first public school and to an educational system perpetually on the verge of crisis. It's a one-time hotbed of abolitionism with an intractable reputation for racism. It's a magnet for college students from all over the world and others engaged in intellectual pursuits, yet the traditional, parochial obsessions are "sports, politics, and revenge."

Boston is a living landmark that bears many marks of its colonial heritage, but where it's theoretically possible (this is an observation, not a suggestion) to spend days without going near anything built before 1960, or even going outdoors. How did it get this way?

1 Boston Today

The turn of the century found Boston where it had been at the turn of the other 3 centuries of its existence: in the middle of a transformation. As the 1700s dawned, the town was growing into one of the colonies' most important commercial centers; 100 years later, flush with post-Revolutionary prosperity, it was on its way to becoming a city. The end of the 19th century saw the rise of the "Athens of America" and the rich cultural tradition that endures today in the Museum of Fine Arts, the Boston Symphony Orchestra, and the Boston Public Library, among other institutions.

Today you'll find a city of 574,300 at the heart of the Greater Boston area, which encompasses 83 cities and towns and some 4 million people. The hospitals and medical centers are among the best in the world, and the ongoing health-care revolution is a hot topic. The banking and financial services, computer technology, and insurance industries are thriving. That drives down the unemployment rate, and perhaps not so coincidentally, the crime rate is historically low, too.

WELCOME HOME   As they have for more than a century, immigrants flock to the Boston area, where the Irish, eastern European Jews, Italians, Portuguese, African Americans, Hispanics, West Indians, and, most recently, Asians have made their homes and made their mark.

One pastime that traditionally united many of them was rooting for the city's professional sports teams—an easy task when success seemed to come easily, but less of a common denominator now. Mentioning the Red Sox remains the best opener if you want to strike up a conversation. Although Boston is still a sports town, the glory days of Boston Garden are but a rumor to many current fans. That's good news for visitors, who might find that Celtics or Bruins tickets are no longer so hard to come by.

CONSTRUCTION AHEAD The most prominent feature of downtown Boston, today and for the immediate future, is not an architectural masterpiece or a natural wonder but an enormous construction site. The Central Artery (I-93) is being "depressed"—as are many of the people who travel into and through the city every day—in a massive project whose price recently passed $11 billion. The Big Dig is so big that it even has its own Web site (www.bigdig.com). The ultimate goals are to hide the interstate underground, turn the land it currently occupies into green space and smaller surface roads, and link the Massachusetts Turnpike (I-90) directly to Logan Airport through the Ted Williams Tunnel. (The tunnel is finished; the link is not.) The target completion date is 2004, and although the site is currently a giant eyesore, other parts of the city are pretty enough to help make up for it.

When the project is finished, Boston will, in a sense, have come full circle. The worst of the traffic will be hidden away, the pedestrians who originally owned the city will once again have easy access to the harbor, and the center of commerce will open onto the waterfront as it did 3 centuries ago.

2 History 101

Permanently settled in 1630 by representatives of the Massachusetts Bay Company, Boston was named for the hometown of some of the Puritans who left England to seek religious freedom in the New World. They met with little of the usual strife with the natives, members of the small, Algonquian-speaking Massachuset tribe that roamed the area. They may have used the peninsula they called "Shawmut" (possibly derived from "Mushau-womuk," or "unclaimed land") as a burial place. They grew corn on some harbor islands, but they made their permanent homes farther inland.

In 1632 the little peninsula became the capital of the Massachusetts Bay Colony, and over the next decade the population increased rapidly during the great Puritan migration. Thanks to its excellent location on the deep, sheltered harbor, Boston quickly became a center of shipbuilding, fishing, and trading.

The only thing more important than commerce was religion, and the Puritans exerted such a strong influence that their legacy survives to this day. A concrete reminder is Harvard College's original (1636) mission: preparing young men to be ministers. In 1659 the town fathers officially banned Christmas (the town children apparently had second thoughts—records show

Dateline

- **1614** Capt. John Smith maps the New England coast, names the Charles River after King Charles I of England, and calls the area "a paradise."
- **1621** A party of 11 led by Myles Standish explores Boston Harbor, visits with the Massachuset Indians, and returns to Plymouth.
- **ca. 1624** William Blackstone settles on the Shawmut peninsula (on Beacon Hill) with 200 books and a Brahma bull.
- **1630** John Winthrop leads settlers to present-day Charlestown. Seeking better water, they push on to Shawmut, which they call Trimountain. On September 7, they name it Boston in honor of the English hometown of many Puritans. On October 19, 108 voters attend the first town meeting.

continues

- **1632** Boston becomes the capital of Massachusetts.
- **1635** Boston Latin School, America's first public school, opens.
- **1636** Harvard College founded.
- **1638** America's first printing press established in Cambridge.
- **1639** The country's first post office established in the home of Richard Fairbank.
- **1660** Unrepentant Quaker Mary Dyer hanged on the Common.
- **1704** America's first regularly published newspaper, the *Boston News Letter,* is founded.
- **1721** First smallpox inoculations administered, over the violent objections of the populace.
- **1764** "Taxation without representation" is denounced in reaction to the Sugar Act.
- **1770** On March 5, five colonists are killed outside what is now the Old State House, an incident soon known as the Boston Massacre.
- **1773** On December 16, during the Boston Tea Party, colonists dump 342 chests of tea into the harbor from three British ships.
- **1774** The "Intolerable Acts," which include the closure of the port of Boston and the quartering of British troops in colonists' homes, go into effect.
- **1775** On April 18, Paul Revere and William Dawes spread the word that the British are marching toward Lexington and Concord. The next day, "the shot heard round the world" is fired. On June 17, the British win the Battle of Bunker Hill but suffer heavy casualties.
- **1776** On March 17, royal troops evacuate by ship. On

continues

that the holiday was back in favor within 25 years). Another early example of puritanical stuffiness was recorded in 1673. One Captain Kemble was sentenced to confinement in the stocks for 2 hours because he kissed his wife on their front steps—on a Sunday. He had been away on a voyage for 3 years.

THE ROAD TO REVOLUTION In 1684 the Crown revoked the colony's charter, and the inhabitants came under tighter British control. Laws increasing taxes and restricting trading activities gradually led to trouble. The situation came to a head after the French and Indian War (known in Europe as the Seven Years' War) ended in 1763.

Having helped fight for the British, the notoriously independent-minded colonists were outraged when the Crown expected them to help pay off the war debt. The Sugar Act of 1764 imposed tariffs on sugar, wine, and coffee, mostly affecting those engaged in trade; the 1765 Stamp Act taxed everything printed, from legal documents to playing cards, affecting virtually everyone. Boycotts, demonstrations, and riots ensued. The repeal of the Stamp Act in 1766 was too little, too late—the revolutionary slogan "No taxation without representation" had already taken hold.

The Townshend Acts of 1767 imposed taxes on paper, glass, and tea, sparking more unrest. The following year, British troops occupied Boston. Perhaps inevitably, tension led to violence. In the Boston Massacre of 1770, five colonists were killed in a scuffle with the redcoats. The first to die was a former slave named Crispus Attucks; another was 17-year-old Samuel Maverick. The site, represented by a circle of cobblestones, sits on what is now State Street, and the colonists' graves are nearby.

TEA & NO SYMPATHY Parliament repealed the Townshend Acts but kept the tea tax, and in 1773 granted the nearly bankrupt East India Company a monopoly on the tea trade with the colonies. The idea was to undercut the price of smuggled tea, but the colonists weren't swayed. In December, three British ships sat at anchor in Boston Harbor, waiting for their cargo of tea to be unloaded. Before that could happen, the rabble-rousing Sons of Liberty, some poorly disguised as Indians, boarded the ships and dumped 342 chests of tea into the harbor. (Today, from a replica berthed not far away, you can toss in your own tea.) The

Boston Tea Party became a rallying point for both sides.

The British responded by closing the port until the tea was paid for and forcing Bostonians to house the soldiers who began to flood the community. They soon numbered 4,000 in a town of 16,000. Mutual distrust ran high—Paul Revere wrote of helping form "a committee for the purpose of watching the movements of the British troops." When the royal commander in Boston, General Gage, learned that the patriots were accumulating arms and ammunition, he dispatched men to destroy the stockpiles.

A NEW WORLD ORDER   Troops marched from Boston toward Lexington and Concord late on April 18, 1775. William Dawes and Revere, who alerted the colonists to the British advance on their famous "midnight ride," sounded the warning to the local militia companies, the Minutemen, who mobilized for the impending confrontation. The next day, some 700 British soldiers under Major John Pitcairn emerged victorious from a skirmish in Lexington, then were routed at Concord and forced to retreat to Charlestown.

It took the redcoats almost an entire day to make the trip (along the route now marked "Battle Road"), which you can do in a car in about half an hour. Thanks in no small part to Henry Wadsworth Longfellow's 1863 poem "Paul Revere's Ride" ("Listen my children and you shall hear / Of the midnight ride of Paul Revere"), Lexington and Concord are closely associated with the beginning of the Revolution. In the early stages, military activity left its mark all over eastern Massachusetts, particularly in Cambridge. Royalist sympathizers, or Tories, were concentrated so heavily along one stretch of Brattle Street that it was called "Tory Row." When the tide began to turn, George Washington made his headquarters on the same street (in a house later occupied by Longfellow that's now a National Park Service site). On nearby Cambridge Common is the spot where Washington took command of the Continental Army on July 3, 1775.

The British won the Battle of Bunker Hill (actually fought on Breed's Hill) in Charlestown on June 17, 1775, but at the cost of half their forces. They abandoned Boston the following March 17. On July 4, 1776, the Continental Congress adopted the Declaration of Independence. Although many Bostonians

July 18, the Declaration of Independence is read from the balcony of the Old State House.
- **1790s** The China trade helps bring great prosperity to Boston.
- **1825** The first city census lists 58,277 people.
- **1831** William Lloyd Garrison publishes the first issue of the *Liberator,* a newspaper dedicated to emancipation.
- **1839** Boston University founded.
- **1846** The first operation under general anesthesia (the removal of a jaw tumor) is performed at Massachusetts General Hospital.
- **1861** Massachusetts Institute of Technology founded.
- **1863** Boston College founded. The 54th Massachusetts Colored Regiment of the Union Army suffers heavy casualties in an unsuccessful attempt to capture Fort Wagner in the harbor of Charleston, S.C.
- **1870** Museum of Fine Arts founded.
- **1872** The Great Fire burns 65 acres and 800 buildings and kills 33 people.
- **1876** Boston University professor Alexander Graham Bell invents the telephone.
- **1878** Girls Latin School opens.
- **1881** Boston Symphony Orchestra founded.
- **1895** Boston Public Library opens on Copley Square.
- **1897** The first Boston Marathon is run. The first subway in America opens—a 1.7-mile stretch beneath Boylston Street.
- **1910** John F. "Honey Fitz" Fitzgerald elected mayor.
- **1913** James Michael Curley elected mayor for the first time.
- **1918** The Red Sox celebrate their World Series victory; a championship drought (of

continues

83 years, and counting) begins.

- **1919** A storage tank at the corner of Foster and Commercial streets ruptures. Two million gallons of raw molasses spill into the streets of the North End, killing 21 people and injuring 150.
- **1930s** The Great Depression devastates what remains of New England's industrial base.
- **1938** Guest conductor Nadia Boulanger becomes the first woman to lead the Boston Symphony Orchestra.
- **1940s** World War II and the accompanying industrial frenzy restore some vitality to the economy, particularly the shipyards.
- **1942** A fire at the Cocoanut Grove nightclub kills 491 people.
- **1946** John F. Kennedy is elected to Congress from Boston's 1st Congressional District.
- **1954** The first successful human-to-human organ transplant (of a kidney) is performed at Peter Bent Brigham Hospital.
- **1957** The Boston Celtics win the first of their 16 NBA championships.
- **1958** The Freedom Trail is mapped out and painted.
- **1959** Construction of the Prudential Center begins— and with it, the transformation of the skyline.
- **1962** Scollay Square is razed to make room for Government Center. Doctors at Massachusetts General Hospital carry out the first successful reattachment of a human limb, a 12-year-old boy's right arm.
- **1966** Massachusetts Attorney General Edward Brooke, a Republican, becomes the

continues

fought in the 6-year war that followed, no more battles were fought in Boston.

COMMERCE & CULTURE   After the war, Boston again became a center of business. Fishing, whaling, and trade with the Far East dominated the economy. Exotic spices and fruits, textiles, and porcelain were familiar luxuries in Boston and nearby Salem. The influential merchant families became known as "Boston Brahmins." They spearheaded the cultural renaissance that continued long after the effects of the War of 1812 ravaged international shipping, and banking and manufacturing rose in importance. Boston took a backseat to New York and Philadelphia in size and influence, but the "Athens of America" became known for fine art and architecture, including the luxurious homes on Beacon Hill, and a flourishing intellectual community.

In 1822, Boston became a city. From 1824 to 1826, Mayor Josiah Quincy oversaw the landfill project that moved the waterfront away from Faneuil Hall. The market building constructed at that time was named in his honor. The undertaking was one of many, all over the city, in which hills were lopped off and deposited in the water, transforming the coastline and skyline. For example, the filling of the Mill Pond, now the area around North Station, began in 1807 and in 25 years consumed the summits of Copp's and Beacon hills.

In the 19th century the city tripled in area, creating badly needed space. The largest project, started in 1835 and completed in 1882, was the filling of the Back Bay, the body of mud flats and marshes that gave its name to the present-day neighborhood. Beginning in 1857, much of the fill came by railroad from Needham.

By the mid-1800s, Ralph Waldo Emerson, Oliver Wendell Holmes, Henry Wadsworth Longfellow, Nathaniel Hawthorne, Bronson and Louisa May Alcott, John Greenleaf Whittier, Walt Whitman, Henry David Thoreau, and even Charles Dickens (briefly) and Mark Twain (more briefly) had appeared on the local literary scene. William Lloyd Garrison published the weekly *Liberator* newspaper, a powerful voice in the antislavery and social reform movements. Boston became an important stop on the Underground Railroad, the secret network developed by the abolitionists to smuggle runaway slaves into Canada.

LOCAL GLORY During the Civil War (1861–65), abolitionist sentiment was the order of the day—to such a degree that the rolls listing the names of the war dead in Harvard's Memorial Hall include only members of the Union Army. Massachusetts' contributions to the war effort included enormous quantities of firearms, shoes, blankets, tents, and men.

The famed black abolitionist Frederick Douglass, a former member of the Massachusetts Anti-Slavery Society, helped recruit the 54th and 55th Massachusetts Colored Regiments. The movie *Glory* tells the story of the 54th, the first army unit made up of free black soldiers, and its white commander, Colonel Robert Gould Shaw. The regiment's memorial, a gorgeous bas-relief by Augustus Saint-Gaudens, stands on Boston Common opposite the State House.

A CAPITAL CITY The railroad boom of the 1820s and 1830s and the flood of immigration that began soon after had made New England an industrial center, and Boston, then as now, was its unofficial capital. Thousands of immigrants from Ireland settled in the city, the first ethnic group to do so in great numbers since the French Huguenots in the early 18th century. Signs reading NO IRISH NEED APPLY became scarce as the new arrivals gained political power, and the first Irish mayor was elected in 1885.

By this time the class split in society was a chasm, with the influx of immigrants who swelled the ranks of the local working class adding to the social tension. The Irish led the way and were followed by eastern European Jewish, Italian, and Portuguese immigrants, who had their own neighborhoods, churches, schools, newspapers, and livelihoods that intersected only occasionally with "proper" society.

Even as the upper crust was sowing seeds that would wind up enriching everyone—the Boston Symphony, the Boston Public Library, and the Museum of Fine Arts were established in the second half of the 19th century—it was engaging in prudish behavior that gained Boston a reputation for making snobbery an art form. In 1878 the censorious Watch and Ward Society was founded (as the New England Society for the Suppression of Vice), and the phrase "banned in Boston" soon made its way into the American vocabulary. In 1889 the private St. Botolph Club removed John Singer Sargent's portrait of Isabella Stewart Gardner from public view (it's now at the museum that bears her name) because her dress was too tight.

first black elected to the U.S. Senate in the 20th century.

- **1969** Students protesting the Vietnam War occupy University Hall at Harvard.

- **1974** In September (20 years after the U.S. Supreme Court made school segregation illegal), school busing begins citywide, sparking unrest in Roxbury and Charlestown.

- **1976** The restored Faneuil Hall Marketplace opens.

- **1988** The Central Artery/Third Harbor Tunnel Project is approved.

- **1993** Thomas Menino is elected mayor, becoming the first Italian-American to hold the office.

- **1995** The New England Holocaust Memorial is dedicated. The FleetCenter opens, replacing Boston Garden as the home of the Celtics (basketball) and Bruins (hockey). The first complete piece of the "Big Dig," the Ted Williams Tunnel, opens.

- **1997** Menino runs unopposed, becoming the first mayor in the city's recorded history to do so.

- **1990s** The murder rate plummets, the economy booms, and Boston again becomes a "hot" city.

- **1999** Busing quietly ends, not with a riot but with a court order. The baseball All-Star Game and golf's Ryder Cup focus the attention of the sports world on the Boston area.

- **2000** The Tall Ships return to Boston Harbor and attract millions of spectators.

The Boston Brahmins could keep their new neighbors out of many areas of their lives, but not politics. The forebears of the Kennedy clan had appeared on the scene—John F. "Honey Fitz" Fitzgerald, Rose Kennedy's father, was elected mayor in 1910—and the city was changing.

Although the Second World War bolstered Boston's Depression-ravaged industrial economy, the war's end touched off an economic transformation. Shipping declined, along with New England's textile, shoe, and glass industries, at the same time that students on the G.I. Bill poured into area colleges and universities. The rise of high technology led to new construction, changing the look of the city yet again. The 1960s saw the beginning of a building boom that continues to this day (after a lull during the recession of the late 1980s).

LOSING COMMON GROUND   The mid-1970s brought the Boston busing crisis, sparked by a court-ordered school desegregation plan enacted in 1974 that touched off riots, violence, and a white boycott. Because of "white flight," Boston is now what urban planners call a "doughnut city." It has a relatively large black population (25% of Boston residents are black, compared with 11% of the U.S. population) surrounded by many lily-white suburbs. The city has battled its reputation for racism with varying degrees of success. One of the most integrated neighborhoods, Jamaica Plain, is linked to one of the least integrated, Charlestown—but only by the Orange Line of the subway. The school system has yet to fully recover from the traumatic experience of busing, but every year it sends thousands of students on to the institutions of higher learning that continue to be Boston's greatest claim to fame.

To get a sense of what Boston is (and is not) like today, hit the streets. The puritanical Bostonian is virtually extinct, but you can still uncover traces of the groups, institutions, and events that have shaped history to make Boston the complex city you see before you.

3 Boston Cuisine: A Gift from the Sea (& Land)

SEAFOOD   **Scrod** or **schrod** is a generic term for fresh white-fleshed fish, usually served in fillets. However it's spelled, scrod is served fried (often in fish-and-chips), broiled, poached, and baked. If you see **wolffish** or **cod cheeks** on a menu, jump at the chance to eat fish as tender and sweet as a scallop. Local shellfish includes lobster, clams, scallops, mussels, shrimp, and oysters.

Fish appears in chowder too, but more often you'll see **clam chowder,** a staple at restaurants in every price range. New England clam chowder consists of chopped hard-shell clams, potatoes, cream, salt pork (usually), onions (usually), celery (sometimes), and milk (sometimes)—but never, ever tomatoes. Tomatoes go in Manhattan clam chowder, a New York favorite that's almost impossible to find in restaurants north of Connecticut.

If you want clams but not soup, at many places you can order **steamers** (soft-shell clams cooked in the shell) as an appetizer or main dish. More common on the appetizer menu are hard-shell clams—**littlenecks** (small) or **cherrystones** (medium-size)—served raw, like oysters. At a "raw bar," you can order clams and oysters singly or by the dozen or half dozen. They're opened (a fascinating procedure you may be allowed to watch) and served on a bed of ice with a wedge of lemon, cocktail sauce, and sometimes a dish of horseradish. Technically, all hard-shell clams are quahogs (say "*co*-hogs"), but that term is usually reserved for large specimens. They're often served stuffed—the flesh is chopped, seasoned, mixed with bread crumbs, and cooked in the shells.

New England **fried clams** are particularly good. Fresh, not frozen, they come whole (with the plump belly) or in "strips" (without), lightly battered and served with French fries and coleslaw. You'll probably also see the **roll,** a hot dog bun filled with seafood. A roll is perfect if you're a light eater or on a budget.

Mmm, **lobster.** Lobster was once so abundant off the Massachusetts coast that the resident Indians showed the Pilgrims how to use the ugly crustaceans as fertilizer. Today, it's expensive, so many Bostonians wait for a special occasion to have it. Order lobster boiled or steamed and you'll get a plastic bib, a nutcracker (for the claws and tail), a pick (for the legs), drawn butter (for dipping), and a bowl (for the carcass). If you want someone else to do the dirty work, lobster is also available stuffed, broiled, baked, in a "pie" (usually a casserole), in a cream sauce, over pasta, in salad, and in bisque.

BAKED BEANS & SWEETS   Traditional **Boston baked beans,** which date from the days when cooking on the Sabbath was forbidden, are prepared by soaking dried pea beans or navy beans in water overnight and then boiling them briefly. The cooked beans then go into a crock with dry mustard, brown sugar or molasses, some cooking water or beer, and sometimes onions, ketchup, or vinegar. The mixture is topped with strips of salt pork and cooked for about 8 hours. Made correctly, the dish that earned Boston the nickname "Beantown" is wonderful. In the sort of restaurant that serves real baked beans, you'll probably also see cornbread and **brown bread**—more of a steamed pudding, of whole wheat and rye flour, cornmeal, molasses, buttermilk, and, usually, raisins.

Molasses fiends (this isn't for amateurs) will want to try **Indian pudding,** a heavy dish that's basically very sweet cornmeal mush topped with whipped cream or ice cream.

Be aware that a milk shake in Boston (and other parts of New England) is exactly that: milk, shaken, with some flavored syrup. The concoction the rest of the world considers a milk shake is a **frappe** (say "frap") to Bostonians.

Finally, **Boston cream pie** is actually golden layer cake sandwiched around custard and topped with chocolate glaze—no cream, no pie.

4 Recommended Books, Films & TV

BOOKS   A list of authors with ties to Boston could fill a book of its own and still only scratch the surface. To get in the mood for Boston before visiting, let the impulse that inspired you to make the trip guide you around the library or bookstore. Here are a few suggestions.

For children, *Make Way for Ducklings,* by Robert McCloskey, is a classic that tells the story of Mrs. Mallard and her babies on the loose in the Back Bay. In honor of the book, bronze statues of the family are in the Public Garden. Slightly older kids might know the Public Garden as the setting of part of *The Trumpet of the Swan,* by E. B. White. An excellent historical title is *Johnny Tremain,* by Esther Forbes, a fictional boy's-eye-view account of the Revolutionary War era.

For adults, two splendid Pulitzer Prize winners chronicle the city's history. *Paul Revere and the World He Lived In* is Forbes's look at Boston before, during, and after the Revolution. J. Anthony Lukas's *Common Ground: A Turbulent Decade in the Lives of Three American Families* is the definitive account of the busing crisis of the 1970s.

Architecture buffs will enjoy *Cityscapes of Boston,* by Robert Campbell and Peter Vanderwarker; *Lost Boston,* by Jane Holtz Kay; and Susan and

Michael Southworth's ***A.I.A. Guide to Boston. The Proper Bostonians,*** by Cleveland Amory, and ***The Friends of Eddie Coyle,*** by George V. Higgins, offer looks at wildly different strata of Boston society.

"Paul Revere's Ride," Henry Wadsworth Longfellow's classic but historically inaccurate poem about the events of April 18–19, 1775, is collected in many anthologies. It's a must if you plan to visit Lexington and Concord. If you're venturing to Gloucester (or even if you're not), Sebastian Junger's ***The Perfect Storm*** makes an excellent introduction.

FILMS & TV Television has done more than any movie to make Boston familiar to international audiences, and film is gaining fast. The Boston area isn't the nonstop backdrop that New York and Vancouver have become, but don't be surprised to stumble upon a crew or read about a location shoot in the newspapers.

One of the best Boston movies ever was released in 1997. The extraordinary ***Good Will Hunting*** (starring Matt Damon, Robin Williams, Ben Affleck, and Minnie Driver) not only makes Boston and Cambridge look sensational but also perceptively explores the town-gown divide. Coauthors Affleck and Damon are boyhood friends from Cambridge, and Damon is a couple of semesters short of his Harvard degree. Not to worry—they're a lot easier to get than Academy Awards, and he already has one of those. Damon and Affleck shared the honor for best original screenplay, and Williams was voted best supporting actor.

Eastern Massachusetts was abuzz in 1999 when ***The Perfect Storm*** (George Clooney, Mark Wahlberg) and David Mamet's ***State and Main*** used Cape Ann as a backdrop. Other recent releases filmed in the Boston area include ***A Civil Action*** (John Travolta, Robert Duvall), ***The Spanish Prisoner*** (Steve Martin, Campbell Scott), ***Southie*** (Anne Meara, Donnie Wahlberg), ***Next Stop Wonderland*** (Hope Davis, Alan Gelfant), ***The Love Letter*** (Kate Capshaw, Tom Selleck), and ***The Autumn Heart*** (Tyne Daly, Ally Sheedy).

In ***Blown Away*** (Jeff Bridges, Tommy Lee Jones), the city looks spectacular, especially in the scenes when the action first shifts to Boston. Classic movies that give more than a glimpse of the region include ***The Witches of Eastwick*** (Jack Nicholson, Cher, Susan Sarandon), ***Glory*** (Denzel Washington, Matthew Broderick), ***The Verdict*** (Paul Newman, James Mason), and the sentimental favorite, ***Love Story*** (Ryan O'Neal, Ali MacGraw).

Small-screen favorites like **"Cheers"** (no, the bar isn't anything like the set), Fox's **"Ally McBeal,"** and ABC's **"The Practice"** have all used the city as a backdrop, but most of their filming is done elsewhere. The two legal dramas *do,* however, have a lot of people wondering where in town lawyers look like *that.*

Index

See also Accommodations and Restaurant indexes, below.

General Index

Restaurant Index